ESSAYS IN PRIVATE INTERNATIONAL LAW

ESSAYS IN PRIVATE INTERNATIONAL LAW

PETER NORTH

CLARENDON PRESS · OXFORD
1993

Oxford University Press, Walton Street, Oxford OX2 6DP
Oxford New York Toronto
Delhi Bombay Calcutta Madras Karachi
Kuala Lumpur Singapore Hong Kong Tokyo
Nairobi Dar es Salaam Cape Town
Melbourne Auckland Madrid
and associated companies in
Berlin Ibadan

Oxford is a trade mark of Oxford University Press

Published in the United States
by Oxford University Press Inc., New York

British Library Cataloguing in Publication Data
Data available

Library of Congress Cataloging in Publication Data
North, P. M. (Peter Machin)
Essays in private international law / Peter North.
Includes index.
1. Conflict of laws. 2. Conflict of laws—Great Britain.
I. Title.
K7041.N67 1993 340.9—dc20 92-44802
ISBN 0-19-825826-7

Set by Hope Services (Abingdon) Ltd.
Printed in Great Britain by
Bookcraft (Bath) Ltd
Midsomer Norton, Avon

Preface

THESE nine articles or lectures on private international law were first published over the last fifteen years in various parts of the world. They deal with all three major aspects of the subject: the jurisdiction of the courts, choice of law and the recognition of foreign judgments, but, mirroring my own interests and activities during that period, reform and change is a theme which recurs throughout most of them.

All the pieces in this work, are with one exception, published in essentially the same form as that in which they originally appeared. However, account has been taken of developments in the intervening years by means of an Introduction prefacing each piece. The paper entitled 'Choice in Choice of Law' is the most recent piece and it is published in a substantially amended and expanded form from that which it took when delivered as a lecture in March 1992, with the consequence that no additional Introduction seemed necessary.

P.M.N.

Oxford
August 1992

Contents

Table of Cases

England and Wales

Australia

Canada

Scotland

South Africa

Switzerland

USA

European Court of Justice

Table of Statutes

United Kingdom

AUSTRALIA

BELGIUM

Canada

European Community

France

Germany

Ireland

Japan

The Netherlands

New Zealand

Switzerland

USA

England and Wales Statutory Instruments

I

Is European Harmonization of Private International Law a Myth or a Reality? A British Perspective

INTRODUCTION

THE two main areas of European harmonization of private international law under review here are the Brussels Convention of 1968 on jurisdiction and the enforcement of judgments in civil and commercial matters, as it has been amended over the intervening years, and the 1980 Rome Convention on the law applicable to contractual obligations. The last two or three years have seen important developments in relation to both Conventions, though perhaps more significantly in relation to the Brussels Convention.

The widening scope of the Brussels Convention, first implemented here by the Civil Jurisdiction and Judgments Act 1982, and of the rules contained therein, is underlined in two ways; first by the Convention on the accession of Spain and Portugal to that Convention having been brought into force from December 1991 and, second, by the Civil Jurisdiction and Judgments Act 1991 which came into force at the beginning of May 1992, thus giving effect to the Lugano Convention of 1988 extending a full faith and credit regime from the European Community states to those of the European Free Trade Area. The potential for harmonization throughout Europe is thus, obviously, the greater.

Turning to consider the more detailed operation of the Brussels Convention, it is clear that the English courts have now had to examine and apply its provisions in a wide variety of areas, such as the determination of the principal contractual obligation on which the plaintiff's claim is based,[1] or of the place of harm in a defamation action;[2] the scope of

Reprinted from *Forty Years On: The Evolution of Postwar Private International Law in Europe* (1990), 29–48, published by Kluwer for the Centre of Foreign Law and Private International Law, University of Amsterdam.

[1] Art. 5(1); see the House of Lords' decision in *Union Transport PLC* v. *Continental Lines SA* [1992] 1 WLR 15; and see *Medway Packaging Ltd.* v. *Meurer Maschinen GmbH & Co. KG* [1990] 2 Lloyd's Rep 112.

[2] Art. 5(3); see *Shevill* v. *Presse Alliance SA* [1992] 2 WLR 1.

the exclusive jurisdiction over immoveable property;[3] the effect of a non-exclusive jurisdiction clause;[4] the determination of when an English court is 'first seised' of a matter;[5] whether an *ex parte* injunction obtained elsewhere in the Community may be registered and enforced in England;[6] and the circumstances in which recognition and enforcement may be denied on the ground of fraud.[7]

Two significant English developments should, however, be highlighted. The first is that the European Court of Justice has now ruled on two references made to it by the Court of Appeal.[8] In one case,[9] the European Court took a broad view of the exclusion of 'arbitration' from the Convention;[10] and in the other,[11] the Court gave a broad interpretation to the scope of the provisions on *lis alibi pendens*. The second development concerns the doctrine of *forum non conveniens* where the Court of Appeal in a recent decision[12] has taken a more radical line than was taken in earlier decisions[13] on the extent to which that doctrine could coexist with the Convention. The court concluded that, although the operation of the doctrine was excluded where the courts competing for jurisdiction were both in Contracting States, the doctrine continued to apply where one court was in a Contracting State and the other in a non-Contracting State.[14] This is a step which amounts to a movement away from uniformity of approach to jurisdictional rules within the Community, and indeed EFTA.[15] It is certainly a matter of regret that the views of the European Court of Justice were not sought on this issue.

[3] Art. 16; see *Webb* v. *Webb* [1991] 1 WLR 1410.

[4] Art. 17; see *Kunz* v. *Stella Musical Veranstaltungs GmbH* [1992] Ch 196. This decision provides a good example of reference being made to a decision on the Convention given by another national court, see below p. 19.

[5] Art. 22; see *Dresser UK Ltd.* v. *Falcongate Freight Management Ltd.* [1992] 2 WLR 319, disapproving *Kloeckner & Co. AG* v. *Gatoil Overseas Inc.* [1990] 1 Lloyd's Rep 177; and see *Assurances Generales de France IART* v. *The Chiyoda Fire and Marine Co. (UK) Ltd.* [1992] 1 Lloyd's Rep 325.

[6] Art. 27; see *EMI Records Ltd.* v. *Modern Music Karl-Ulrich Walterbach GmbH* [1992] 1 QB 115.

[7] Arts. 29 and 34; see *Interdesco SA* v. *Nullifire Ltd.* [1992] 1 Lloyd's Rep 180.

[8] There is also now a reported decision of the House of Lords on the Convention: *Union Transport Plc* v. *Continental Lines SA* [1992] 1 WLR 15.

[9] *Marc Rich & Co. AG* v. *Societa Italiana Impianti PA*, Case C–190/89 [1992] 1 Lloyd's Rep 342. The Court of Appeal proceedings are reported as *The Atlantic Emperor* [1989] 1 Lloyd's Rep 348; and see below, p. 20. Later proceedings in the same case are reported as *The Atlantic Emperor (No. 2)* [1992] 1 Lloyd's Rep 624.

[10] Art. 1(4).

[11] *Overseas Union Insurance Ltd.* v. *New Hampshire Insurance Ltd.*, Case C–351/89 [1992] 2 WLR 586.

[12] *Re Harrods (Buenos Aires) Ltd.* [1992] Ch 72; and see *The Po* [1991] 2 Lloyd's Rep 206.

[13] *S & W Berisford Plc* v. *New Hampshire Insurance Co.* [1990] 2 QB 631; *Arkwright Mutual Insurance Co.* v. *Bryanston Insurance Co. Ltd.* [1990] 2 QB 649; and see below, pp. 6–7.

[14] Civil Jurisdiction and Judgments Act 1982, s. 49.

[15] See Cheshire and North, *Private International Law*, 12th edn. (1992), 333.

A number of steps may be taken to develop a harmonized approach to the interpretation of the Convention, not the least being references to the various Official Reports on the Convention and its later amending Conventions.[16] Another step which has been recently emphasized is that of examining the texts of the Convention in languages other than English.[17]

In the case of the Rome Convention on the law applicable to contractual obligations, the most significant recent step[18] is that it was given the force of law in the United Kingdom by the Contracts (Applicable Law) Act 1990 which came into force, bringing the Convention into effect, on 1 April 1991.[19] What is regrettable about this legislation is that it fails to extend the choice of law rules of the Convention to a range of matters excluded from it, such as the determination of the law to govern contractual capacity, or to govern the validity of arbitration agreements or agreements on the choice of court.[20] It is worth noting, however, that the United Kingdom has exercised[21] the power conferred by the Convention[22] to reserve the right not to apply two provisions of the Convention, namely those relating to 'the consequences of nullity of the contract'[23] and to the application of the mandatory rules of third states.[24]

* * *

[16] See below, p. 20; and see *Webb* v. *Webb* [1991] 1 WLR 1410; *Shevill* v. *Presse Alliance SA* [1992] 2 WLR 1; *Interdesco SA* v. *Nullifire Ltd.* [1992] 1 Lloyd's Rep 180.

[17] *Newtherapeutics Ltd.* v. *Katz* [1991] Ch 226, 243–5.

[18] Developments in relation to the Rome Convention are discussed more generally below, pp. 23–27.

[19] The earlier history of the Convention is examined below, pp. 29–34. See Plender, *The European Contracts Convention* (1991).

[20] See below, pp. 25, 35–36; and see North, [1990] I *Hague Recueil* 9, 180–2.

[21] Contracts (Applicable Law) Act 1990, s. 2(2).

[22] Art. 22(1); see below, pp. 26–27, 42–43, 46.

[23] Art. 10(1)(e).

[24] Art. 7(1). One further issue which has arisen is whether the choice of law rules of the Convention are voluntary in that the parties are free to choose whether or not they are to be applied. For the view that they are mandatory, not voluntary, see below, pp. 184–187.

INTRODUCTION

> When we come to matters with a European element, the Treaty [of Rome] is like an incoming tide. It flows into the estuaries and up the rivers. It cannot be held back.[1]

THIS comment was made in 1974 (shortly after the United Kingdom joined the European Community) by Lord Denning, then one of England's leading judges. Whilst there is no doubt that, in the last fifteen years, Community membership has had major influences on political, economic and legal issues in the United Kingdom, the question to be addressed today is whether there has been much private international law in that inflowing tide and—to pursue the metaphor—whether it has mixed with the pure waters of the common law flowing out of the English rivers, or whether like oil and water they coexist together without intermingling. This issue can be examined in two contexts: first, the actual impact of Community rules of private international law on the common approach and, second, the less direct effect on judicial attitudes and the approach to problems. Inevitably, discussion of the first issue will cover material well familiar to private international lawyers from other Member States.

IMPACT OF COMMUNITY PRIVATE INTERNATIONAL LAW

There is a substantial literature in the United Kingdom examining the significance and scope of Community legislation—whether it be actual or draft Conventions or other instruments, such as directives or regulations which contain private international law rules.[2] In particular, major works[3] have been produced on the amended Brussels Convention of 1968 on jurisdiction and the enforcement of judgments in civil and commercial matters and on the consequent United Kingdom legislation, the Civil Jurisdiction and Judgments Act 1982.[4] Whilst detailed analysis of that

[1] *Bulmer Ltd* v. *Bollinger SA* [1974] Ch 401, 418.

[2] See e.g., Fletcher, *Conflict of Laws and European Community Law* (1982) and Lasok and Stone, *Conflict of Laws in the European Community*.

[3] E.g. Collins, *The Civil Jurisdiction and Judgments Act 1982* (1983); Hartley, *Civil Jurisdiction and Judgments* (1984); Anton, *Civil Jurisdiction in Scotland* (1984); Kaye, *Civil Jurisdiction and Enforcement of Foreign Judgments* (1987); Dashwood, Hacon, and White, *A Guide to the Civil Jurisdiction and Judgments Convention* (1987).

[4] This legislation has been amended (as from 1 October 1989) to provide for accession to the Brussels Convention by Greece; see SI 1989, No. 1346. Further legislation will be needed in due course to provide for the Convention on the Accession of Spain and Portugal: [1989] OJ L285/32.

Convention is neither possible nor appropriate here, I shall take the Convention as one of my two examples of the actual impact of Community rules of private international law. My reasons are threefold.

It is undoubtedly, for an English private international lawyer, the most significant piece of Community legislation; it has only recently come into force in the United Kingdom, so that we are now getting, from decided cases, the first impressions of judicial attitudes to it; and the way in which the Convention was implemented reveals something of attitudes in the United Kingdom to Community law in this area—and it will be seen that approaches differ between the various parts of the United Kingdom.

The second example that I shall take is the Rome Convention of 1980 on the law applicable to contractual obligations. This is of interest for a variety of reasons. It seems quite possible that legislation will be introduced in the United Kingdom in the near future to implement it;[5] it appears that Spain has agreed recently to implement it; it is the one completed attempt to harmonize choice of law rules in a major area of law; and, on a more personal note, I am familiar with United Kingdom attitudes during the negotiation as I was a member of the United Kingdom delegation to those negotiations.

THE JUDGMENTS CONVENTION

Accession to this Convention by the United Kingdom posed a variety of problems. Some of the existing case law from the European Court of Justice, especially on Article 17 (choice of jurisdiction clauses), created difficulties particularly with regard to the broad approach of the Commercial Court in London to jurisdictional issues—and these were met by amendments to the Convention. In other respects, the original Convention did not deal, or deal effectively, with legal issues of concern to English lawyers. An obvious example is the need (met in Article 5(6)) to provide jurisdictional rules for litigation involving trusts. A different type of example is provided by Articles 6A and 12A with new rules involving litigation concerning shipping, again a major concern of the English courts in London. Indeed, it is an interesting observation that a majority of the decisions on the Convention so far reported in England concern shipping matters.[6]

[5] See now the Contracts (Applicable Law) Act 1990.

[6] See *The Nordglimt* [1988] QB 183; *The Linda* [1988] 1 Lloyd's Rep 175; *The Sydney Express* [1988] 2 Lloyd's Rep 257; *The Volvox Hollandia* [1988] 2 Lloyd's Rep 361; *The Freccia del Nord* [1989] 1 Lloyd's Rep 388; *The Atlantic Emperor* [1989] 1 Lloyd's Rep 548; *The Deichland* [1990] 1 QB 361; and see the Scottish decision in *Clipper Shipping & Co. Ltd.* v. *S.O. Investment Ltd.* 1989 SLT 204.

On a broader plane, the Convention embodies a quite different approach to matters of jurisdiction from that found in England. The common law has adopted a procedural approach. The court has jurisdiction if the rules for serving a writ on the defendant are satisfied. Basically this means that, if the defendant can be found in England, the court will take jurisdiction, even where that is the limit of his and the litigation's connection with England. So, for example, the court took jurisdiction over a claim against the French art dealer, Daniel Wildenstein, by reason of the fact that a writ was served on him at Ascot race course when he visited England for a few days to go to the horse races.[7] Alternatively, the court can give leave to serve the writ on a defendant who is outside the jurisdiction. This discretionary power[8] requires one of a number of listed connections with England to be shown, such as, in a contractual claim, that the contract was made or broken in England or is governed by English law.[9] The recently developed jurisprudence of the courts has mitigated the effects of what might be regarded as instances of the exercise of exorbitant jurisdiction, by making clear that service out of the jurisdiction is a matter of discretion: but the courts have gone further, and over the past decade the House of Lords has introduced into English law a broad doctrine of *forum non conveniens* governing the circumstances when jurisdiction will be declined, despite satisfaction of the procedural rules,[10] coupled with the further development of rules determining when litigants in England will be ordered not to pursue litigation in another jurisdiction.[11] Nevertheless, the essentially procedural nature of the English jurisdictional rules remains unchanged.

The Convention takes a very different approach. There is a clear code of jurisdictional rules, based on the primacy of the country in which the defendant is domiciled (Article 2), coupled with the additional special bases of jurisdiction (Articles 5–15), a limited number of exclusive grounds (Article 16), and rules on prorogation of jurisdiction (Articles 17 and 18). All of this is based on principle, i.e. selection of the most appropriate link with the parties and the litigation. Procedural rules must be the servant and not the master of jurisdictional decisions. This means that, if the case falls within the Convention rules, service of the writ out of the jurisdiction no longer needs the leave of the court in England.[12] It also means that there is no place for the newly-developed rules on staying of actions and *forum non conveniens*, for section 49 of the Civil Jurisdiction and Judgments Act 1982 only allows such stays to be granted

[7] *Maharanee of Baroda* v. *Wildenstein* [1972] 2 QB 283.

[8] RSC, O 11, r 1.

[9] O 11, r 1(1)(d).

[10] *Spiliada Maritime Corporation* v. *Cansulex Ltd.* [1987] AC 460.

[11] *Société Nationale Industrielle Aérospatiale* v. *Lee Kui Jak* [1987] AC 871.

[12] O 11, r 1(2); *Practice Note* [1987] 1 WLR 86.

'where to do so is not inconsistent with the 1968 Convention'; and English judges have accepted that, under the Convention, 'The question: "which court would be the more convenient or the more appropriate?" does not arise.'[13] Acceptance of that rule by the judges has not, however, inhibited English authors from arguing that a limited or, indeed, a general discretion to stay proceedings falling within the Convention would be desirable.[14]

How far, if at all, has the regime of jurisdictional rules laid down in the Convention more broadly affected attitudes in the United Kingdom to issues of jurisdiction? First of all, there is a willingness (at least at the Governmental level) to see the extension of the full faith and credit regime of the Convention to the EFTA countries, with the United Kingdom's active participation in the discussions leading up to the Lugano Convention of 1988.[15] On the other hand, the final stages in the development in England of a *forum non conveniens* doctrine occurred at the time (1986) when the Convention was just about to come into force in England, but the absence of such a doctrine from the Convention had no influence on English judicial attitudes.[16] This links back to decisions, taken in the United Kingdom prior to the introduction of the Civil Jurisdiction and Judgments Act 1982, as to the effect that the amended Brussels Convention was to have on jurisdictional rules in the United Kingdom dealing with cases which fell outside the scope of the Convention. These were of two kinds: cases involving links with different parts of the United Kingdom, and cases involving connections between one part of the United Kingdom and a country or countries outside the European Community. The United Kingdom was free to have whatever rules of jurisdiction or recognition it chose, for both these kinds of cases. In the first situation, the jurisdictional rules of the Convention have formed the model for an intra-United Kingdom Modified Convention—though with certain adaptations for the fact that the conflict arises within one state. So, for example, there are additional jurisdictional rules to deal with threatened torts (Article 5(3)), and with decisions of companies (Article 5A); whilst, unlike the Brussels Convention, there are no special rules in relation to insurance,[17] nor is there an exclusive head of jurisdiction concerning patents and trademarks.[18] There is also a new regime for

[13] *The Linda* [1988] 1 Lloyd's Rep 175, 179; and see *The Sennar (No. 2)* [1984] 2 Lloyd's Rep 142, 152.

[14] Collins, *The Civil Jurisdiction and Judgments Act 1982*, 85, 97; Hartley, *Civil Jurisdiction and Judgments*, 66, 74–80; cf. Cheshire and North, *Private International Law*, 11th edn. (1987) 328–329.

[15] See [1988] OJ L319/31. Many of the differences between the Lugano Convention and the Brussels Convention are provided for in the amendments to the Brussels Convention contained in the Convention on the Accession of Spain and Portugal.

[16] *Spiliada Maritime Corporation* v. *Cansulex Ltd.* [1987] AC 460.

[17] Cf. Arts. 7–12A.

[18] Cf. Art. 16(4).

the enforcement of intra-United Kingdom judgments[19] which, though separate from the Convention rules, follows its general philosophy of a requirement to recognise and enforce.[20] What has already emerged is that relevant decisions on the operation of the Brussels Convention will be relied on in the United Kingdom in interpreting the Modified Convention.[21]

When we turn to examine the second type of case, jurisdictional rules for claims falling outside the Convention, the influence of the Convention varies quite markedly depending on the part of the United Kingdom being considered. For England and Wales (and Northern Ireland) the Convention has had some, but not much, influence on the jurisdictional rules for such cases. The essential philosophy has been to retain, but also to improve, the traditional rules. There has been no abandonment of the procedural approach to jurisdiction, nor is there any limitation of the broad grounds for allowing a writ to be served on a defendant outside the jurisdiction. If such grounds were exorbitant, they remain so. The existence of the Convention has, however, led to an extension of the powers of the court to grant provisional and protective measures in relation to foreign proceedings,[22] and the Rules of the Supreme Court have been broadened in relation to tort claims,[23] to mirror the ruling of the European Court of Justice[24] that Article 5(3) of the Convention applies to a tort claim where the damage was sustained, or resulted from an act committed, within the jurisdiction. The opportunity has also been taken, in disputes relating to foreign land, to limit the exclusion of the jurisdiction of the English courts by following the approach of the exclusive jurisdiction rule in Article 16(1), with the result that English courts will now entertain proceedings involving foreign land 'unless the proceedings are principally concerned with a question of the title to, or the right to possession of, that property'.[25]

Consideration was given in England to the much broader question of whether the common law's historic approach to jurisdiction should be abandoned and the model of the Convention used for jurisdictional rules involving non-Community linked cases. This idea was rejected essentially because of a desire to retain broad jurisdictional rules in commercial cases. Whilst a rule allowing jurisdiction to be assumed if the defendant

[19] Civil Jurisdiction and Judgments Act 1982, s. 18.

[20] This had, in fact, already been the basic approach within the United Kingdom; see the Judgments Extension Act 1868 and the Inferior Courts Judgments Extension Act 1882.

[21] E.g. *British Steel Corporation* v. *Allivane International Ltd.* [1988] ECC 405.

[22] Civil Jurisdiction and Judgments Act 1982, s. 25, discussed more fully below, pp. 9–11.

[23] RSC, O 11, r 1(1)(f).

[24] *Handelskwekerij GJ Bier NB* v. *Mines de Potasse d'Alsace SA*, Case 21/76 [1976] ECR 1735.

[25] Civil Jurisdiction and Judgments Act 1982, s. 30.

can be found changing planes at Heathrow Airport has little to commend it, its worst excesses were in the process of being mitigated by the developing doctrine of *forum non conveniens*. On the other hand, the perception of London as an international financial, commercial, shipping, insurance, and commodity market centre carried with it a desire to attract to London, and there take jurisdiction over, major commercial litigation as a means of maintaining the development of English commercial law as a part of the modern law merchant. That meant retaining broad jurisdictional rules in commercial matters, including in particular the power to order the service of a writ out of the jurisdiction in the case of a claim relating to a contract which was governed by English law.[26]

By contrast, a very different approach was taken in Scotland where it was recommended[27] that 'the jurisdictional rules in the 1968 Convention should be taken as the norm both where the defender is domiciled in another part of the United Kingdom and where he is domiciled in Scotland or in a non-Contracting State'.[28] Various reasons for this conclusion were given, some of which could have been regarded as of equal force in England, for example that it would be confusing to practitioners to have to cope with two sets of jurisdictional rules depending on whether or not the case fell within the Brussels Convention, and indeed that it might not be easy to answer that question, depending as it normally does on determining the domicile of the defendant. On the other hand, the scheme of the Convention was more like existing Scots law than it was existing English law; so confusion to practitioners from having two similar schemes would be greater in Scotland—and conversely the shock of change in adopting the Convention rules correspondingly less great. Even so, the adoption of the Convention approach in Scotland[29] has not meant the elimination there of what many would regard as exorbitant grounds of jurisdiction, for in addition to the Convention grounds a Scottish court can still, for example, take jurisdiction on the basis of arrestment in Scotland of the defender's moveable property or on the basis of his ownership of Scottish immoveable property.[30] Nevertheless, one must conclude that the Brussels Convention has had greater effect on Scottish than English jurisdictional rules in non-Community cases.

In one area of great practical importance it is possible to see a clear influence from the Brussels Convention on the way in which the law dealing with cases falling outside the Convention should develop. Article 24 of the Convention is short but important, stating that:

[26] RSC, O 11, r 1(1)(d)(iii).
[27] Report of the Scottish Committee on Jurisdiction and Enforcement (1980), 16–9.
[28] Anton, *Civil Jurisdiction in Scotland* (1984), para. 1.35.
[29] Civil Jurisdiction and Judgments Act 1982, Schedule 8.
[30] Ibid., Art. 2(8).

Application may be made to the courts of a Contracting State for such provisional, including protective, measures as may be available under the law of that State, even if, under this Convention, the courts of another Contracting State have jurisdiction as to the substance of the matter.

Since 1975 English courts have had power to issue what have become called Mareva injunctions,[31] restraining a defendant from removing his assets from the jurisdiction pending trial. In the intervening years, the scope of this power has been expanded both by the power to make such orders being placed on a broader statutory basis[32] and by a series of judicial decisions in which, in aid of a Mareva injunction, the defendant has been ordered to disclose information about his assets, including assets outside the jurisdiction.[33] More recently, the English Court of Appeal[34] took a more restrictive approach suggesting that, save in exceptional cases, neither disclosure orders nor injunctions would be granted in relation to foreign assets. The inability to discover the existence and whereabouts of foreign assets would, of course, inhibit a plaintiff from seeking a similar order from a foreign court. The interrelation of all of this with the Brussels Convention may be seen from the fact that, by statute, courts in the United Kingdom may grant interim relief, of which Mareva injunctions provide an example, not only in respect of proceedings within the court's own jurisdiction but also of proceedings in a Contracting State which fall within the Brussels Convention.[35] Thus a Mareva injunction may be issued in England preventing the removal of assets from England even though the proceedings in question are to be brought in France.

There has now been a quartet of English Court of Appeal decisions[36] looking again at the granting of Mareva injunctions and disclosure orders in relation to assets outside the jurisdiction.[37] In all four cases the English courts issued injunctions which covered the defendants' assets worldwide; though the circumstances of the cases differed in that in one case judgment had already been given by the English court;[38] in the second case

[31] Named after one of the early decisions: *Mareva Compania Naviera SA* v. *International Bulk Carriers SA* [1975] 2 Lloyd's Rep 509. Another form of protective measure was developed at much the same time—an Anton Piller order, being an *ex parte* order allowing the plaintiff access to the defendant's premises and documents, again named after a leading case: *Anton Piller KG* v. *Manufacturing Processes Ltd.* [1976] Ch 55.

[32] Supreme Court Act 1981, s. 37.

[33] E.g. *CBS UK Ltd.* v. *Lambert* [1983] Ch 37.

[34] *Ashtiani* v. *Kashi* [1987] QB 888.

[35] Civil Jurisdiction and Judgments Act 1982, s. 25. There is also a power for this to be extended to proceedings in other states, but this has not yet been done.

[36] *Babanaft International Co. SA* v. *Bassatne* [1990] Ch 13; *Republic of Haiti* v. *Duvalier* [1990] 1 QB 202; *Derby & Co. Ltd.* v. *Weldon (No. 1)* [1990] Ch 48; *Derby & Co. Ltd.* v. *Weldon (Nos. 3 and 4)* [1990] Ch 65.

[37] See Collins, (1989) 105 *QR* 262.

[38] *Babanaft International Co. SA* v. *Bassatne*, n. 36 above.

proceedings were pending in France (rather than in England);[39] whilst in the third and fourth cases the pending proceedings were English.[40] What is of interest in the present context is that this broadening of the powers of the court to order protective measures was strongly influenced by Article 24 of the Brussels Convention. Not only had that provision, when implemented in the United Kingdom, emphasized the power to make pre-judgment orders in relation to assets in another Contracting State, it also had a broader impact through the recognition and enforcement provisions of the Convention. This is because extraterritorial prejudgment orders falling within Article 24 can be enforced in the state where the assets are to be found;[41] and it may well be that post-judgments orders can be given similar effect.[42] These arguments led the Court of Appeal to give extraterritorial effect to prejudgment orders in a case where the assets were probably in a range of countries outside the EEC. The confirmation of this practice in the situation where proceedings were pending was again not limited to assets in countries where it was clear that the English order could be enforced. Indeed it was expressly stated that 'it may be appropriate to seek to follow the policy of the Convention even though in the particular case the Convention itself has no direct application'.[43] What has happened, therefore, is that the provisions of the Convention have been influential in the development of rules of wider effect. The making of orders such as Mareva injunctions and disclosure orders is, of course, a matter for the discretion of the court; and absence of reciprocity or of the prospect of recognition of the order may influence the decision in any particular case whether to make the order. Nevertheless, it is clear that the Brussels Convention has here proved to be a significant element in the further general development of the rules relating to a major procedural remedy applicable to circumstances going well beyond those covered by the Convention.

There remains one final aspect of the Brussels Convention to be considered—the concept of domicile. This is, as is well known, a crucial connecting factor in the Convention, determining both whether the Convention is applicable and which court is to have jurisdiction. Crucial though domicile is, there is no definition of it in the Convention; indeed it is left to national law (rather than to some Community-wide concept laid down by the European Court of Justice) to decide where a defendant is domiciled.[44] This has the potential for being the Achilles' heel of the

[39] *Republic of Haiti* v. *Duvalier*, n. 36 above.

[40] The two *Derby & Co. Ltd.* cases, n. 36 above.

[41] See *de Cavel* v. *de Cavel*, Case 143/78, [1979] ECR 1055; *Denilauler* v. *SNC Couchet Freres*, Case 125/79, [1980] ECR 1553.

[42] See the discussion of this issue by Kerr LJ in the *Babanaft Case* [1990] Ch 13, 34–5; and see Collins, *The Civil Jurisdiction and Judgments Act 1982*, 290–4.

[43] [1990] Ch 13, 41.

[44] Art. 52.

desire for jurisdictional uniformity, given the very different concept of domicile in the common law and civil law systems.[45] This problem was avoided by the United Kingdom accepting the desirability of introducing a new concept of domicile for the purposes of jurisdiction under the Brussels Convention and its intra-United Kingdom version. The defects of the traditional common law concept of domicile were identified thus:

> Domicile in the traditional sense would have been too extensive because it would have included persons with a United Kingdom domicile of origin who are not, and possibly have never been, resident there. At the same time the concept would have been too restrictive in the sense that the traditional concept of domicile would have excluded from the jurisdiction of the United Kingdom courts persons habitually resident in the United Kingdom who do not intend to remain there indefinitely. The emphasis on intention, moreover, has always introduced an element of uncertainty into the attribution of a domicile in the traditional sense, an uncertainty inappropriate in a criterion for the determination of jurisdiction in ordinary civil actions.[46]

The outcome was the introduction of a new statutory concept of domicile, formulated on a residence basis such that an individual is domiciled in the United Kingdom if and only if (a) he is resident in the United Kingdom; and (b) the nature and circumstances of his residence indicate that he has a substantial connection with the United Kingdom.[47] This rule is coupled with a rebuttable presumption that the substantial connection test is satisfied by three months residence.[48] So close is this concept to the idea of habitual residence, a connecting factor widely accepted in the United Kingdom as a result of Hague Conventions, especially in the family law field, that serious consideration was given in the United Kingdom simply to defining domicile as habitual residence, but that approach was rejected because of the fact that the Brussels Convention itself uses habitual residence as a connecting factor separate from that of domicile.[49] One might conclude, therefore, that the Brussels Convention has had major influence on a concept, that of domicile, which is often regarded as a hallmark of the common law systems of private international law. Yet this conclusion would only be half true. That influence has indeed been real for the purposes of other changes introduced by the Civil Jurisdiction and Judgments Act 1982, but it has not extended further than that. In 1985 the two Law Commissions published provisional proposals for the reform of the law of domicile but made clear that the

[45] See Anton, *Civil Jurisdiction in Scotland*, para. 4.06.

[46] Ibid., para 4.12.

[47] Civil Jurisdiction and Judgments Act 1982, s. 41(2). It might be noted that Ireland also has introduced a special concept of domicile for the purposes of the Brussels Convention, based there on 'ordinary residence'; see the Jurisdiction of Courts and Enforcement of Judgments (European Communities) Act 1988, .Sch. 5, Part I.

[48] Ibid., s. 42(6).

[49] E.g. Art. 5(2).

rules involved were only the common law rules and not those in the 1982 Act.[50] In their final proposals published in 1987,[51] not only was this line sustained, but there was clear rejection of any idea of substituting habitual residence for domicile as the main common law connecting factor.[52] Indeed their only reference to the domicile concept as laid down in the 1982 Act is to indicate the Law Commissions' resistance to any attempt to amend it to bring it closer into line with the proposed reforms of general domicile law.[53] What is quite clear is that the new statutory domicile rules introduced in the 1982 Act through Community influences have had no effect on general reform of domicile law.

The Contract Convention

The difficulty of unifying choice of law rules within the Community is well illustrated by the history of what became the 1980 Rome Convention on the law applicable to contractual obligations. The first proposal for unification of choice of law rules was made in 1967; a draft convention on contractual and non-contractual obligations was prepared by 1972; the accession of the new Member States in 1973 meant a further series of negotiations; in 1978 the non-contractual obligations aspect of the convention was dropped; a final contractual obligations convention was concluded in 1980.[54] Negotiations then continued at length on the politically sensitive issue as to what jurisdiction (if any) the European Court of Justice should have over this convention. Despite the fact that that issue has now been resolved,[55] the 1980 Convention is not yet in force, although most Member States have ratified it, and there are proposals for its ratification and implementation in the United Kingdom within the next few months.[56] So, twenty years on, and there is still no end to the saga; and one must bear in mind that contract may be one of the easier choice of law areas in which to seek harmonization, as the national laws of the Member States adopt basically similar approaches, allowing freedom of choice of the applicable law and, in the absence of choice, looking for a test of closeness of connection. Indeed the postponement of work on a non-contractual obligations convention—and it looks now more like abandonment than postponement—can be explained by the fact

[50] Law Commission Working Paper No. 88 (1985), para. 1.4.

[51] Law Com. No. 168 (1987).

[52] Ibid., paras. 3.5–3.8.

[53] Ibid., para. 3.14.

[54] To which Greece has since acceded: [1984] OJ L146/27.

[55] See the Protocols on the jurisdiction of the European Court of Justice, to be found in [1989] OJ L48/32.

[56] See now the Contracts (Applicable Law) Act 1990, and see above, p. 3.

that not only was there no uniformity of approach to choice of law in tort or delict within the Community, in some Member States (certainly the common law ones) the law was not only in need of reform but there was real debate as to what shape reform should take.[57] Indeed since then, the Irish Supreme Court seems to have abandoned the old common law rule requiring reference both to the law of the place of the tort and the law of the forum,[58] without indicating what should takes its place.[59]

Considerable achievement though the conclusion of the Contractual Obligations Convention undoubtedly was, it would be wrong to portray it (at least from a common lawyer's standpoint) as involving the abandonment of firmly held views in favour of a grand new European approach. Four aspects of the Convention might be considered. The first is that of change—the introduction of new rules relating to choice of law in contract. Some provisions of the Convention resolve doubts in the present common law. For example, Article 3(1) emphasizes freedom of choice and lays down no fetters on that freedom, apart from the case where the contract is wholly connected with one country but for the choice of law clause (Article 3(3)), and apart from such rules as have to be applied as a matter of the public policy of the forum (Article 16). The common law would seem to require the choice of the applicable law to be 'bona fide and legal',[60] leading to uncertainty as to what that phrase means and as to how strong a connection is needed with the country of the chosen law.[61] The right to vary the choice of the applicable law is undoubtedly permitted and it is made clear that that may be done at any time (Article 3(2)). These are issues on which the common law position is also uncertain.[62] Similarly resolved by the Convention is the question of which law is to govern the validity of a choice of law clause. It has been argued that this should be decided by the putative proper law, but this concept has been alternatively defined as the law which would be applicable in the absence of the choice of law clause or the law which would be applied if the choice of law clause was valid. The Convention adopts, in Article 8(1), the latter approach, being the practically desirable (if logically insecure) solution. Finally, mention might be made of the change of approach for the common law stemming from the Convention in the area of substance and procedure. Included as substantive issues, governed by

[57] This debate continues. The Law Commissions published in 1984 a Working Paper (No. 87) on Private International Law: Choice of Law in Tort and Delict, and a Report, Law Com. No. 193, in 1990.

[58] *Phillips* v. *Eyre* (1870) LR 6 QB1; *Boys* v. *Chaplin* [1971] AC 356.

[59] *Grehan* v. *Medical Incorporated and Pine Valley Associates* [1986] IR 528.

[60] *Vita Food Products Inc.* v. *Unus Shipping Co. Ltd.* [1939] AC 277, 290.

[61] See Cheshire and North, *Private International Law*, 11th edn. (1987), 453–6.

[62] See North, in *Multum non Multa, Festschrift für Kurt Lipstein* (1980), 205, and below, pp. 53–67.

the Convention choice of law rules, are the extinction of obligations, prescription, and limitation of actions (Article 10(1)(d)). Here the Convention was used as a very clear instrument of reform, requiring the abandonment in contract claims of the common law classification of limitation of actions as procedural. This had wider ramifications in the United Kingdom because it led to the general abandonment in 1984 of that procedural classification.[63]

The second and third aspects of the Convention to be examined are those of omissions and reservations. They can be linked together because they are both concerned with the problem of differing approaches to choice of law issues between civil law and common law jurisdictions—differences which had to be evaded in the interests of agreement. Two omissions illustrate this. Article 1 limits the scope of the Convention in a variety of ways but, in particular, it does not apply 'to questions involving the status or legal capacity of natural persons';[64] nor does it apply to arbitration agreements and agreements on the choice of court. Differing classifications are at issue here. Common lawyers regard these excluded matters as raising contractual choice of law issues—though, in the case of capacity, with no very clear view as to what the applicable law should be. Many civil lawyers regard these matters as ones of status and procedure respectively, and out of place in a contractual obligations convention. No resolution of this clash of analyses was possible. Although there was an agreement to return to an examination of arbitration and choice of court clauses once the Convention was concluded, that has never happened. There are a number of reasons for this. Enthusiasm for resolving these issues has waned; the prospects of an agreed solution seem remote; and the common lawyers can, if needs be, get much of what they want in other ways. The problem for the common lawyer is of having a new set of contract choice of law rules in the Convention which cover most, but not all, of the issues he regards as contractual. That would leave him having to refer to the old choice of law rules in a very small number of matters—and it must be remembered that this may in practice mean just one clause in a contract (namely that containing a choice of jurisdiction or arbitration clause) being governed by choice of law rules different from the rest. There is, however, nothing to prevent the Convention rules being applied also to these issues in any United Kingdom legislation implementing the Convention. No reciprocity is involved or any agreement required to achieve this. It will be interesting to see whether this is, in fact, the course which Parliament adopts.[65]

[63] Foreign Limitation Periods Act 1984; and see Law Com. No. 114 (1982).

[64] Subject to a provision of limited effect in Art. 11 dealing with contracts concluded between persons in the same country.

[65] Regrettably it has not in the Contracts (Applicable Law) Act 1990.

There are two provisions in the Convention in respect of which it is possible for a Member State to reserve the right not to apply them,[66] and it is widely expected that the United Kingdom will make reservations in respect of both. The first provision raises classification difficulties similar to the examples just given of matters excluded from the scope of the Convention. Amongst the matters which the law applicable to a contract, as determined by the Convention rules, is to govern is 'The consequences of nullity of the contract' (Article 10(1)(e)). This creates two problems for the common lawyer. The first is that the issue is regarded as quasi-contractual and thus out of place in a convention on contractual obligations. The second is that the result of applying a law chosen by the parties to the consequences of nullity is, to the common lawyer, inappropriate.[67] A power of reservation has proved to be the only solution to this dilemma.

More contentious is the other matter involving a power of reservation. Article 7(1) provides as follows:

> When applying under this Convention the law of a country, effect may be given to the mandatory rules of the law of another country with which the situation has a close connection, if and in so far as, under the law of the latter country, those rules must be applied whatever the law applicable to the contract. In considering whether to give effect to these mandatory rules, regard shall be had to their nature and purpose and to the consequences of their application or non-application.

This provision was vigorously opposed by the United Kingdom, not for reasons of legal theory but rather on pragmatic, practical grounds. The opposition was so determined that, without a power of reservation, there seemed very little likelihood of the United Kingdom Government being prepared to sign the Rome Convention. Whilst there is no doubt that English choice of law rules have allowed reference to be made to the mandatory rules of a country other than that of the forum or of the proper law, namely the law of the place of performance,[68] this is just one identified further legal system and, indeed, most authors explain the reference to illegality under that law as being, not an independent reference, but a reference to part of the substantive contract rules of the proper law of the contract, English law.

Four reasons have been given for the anxieties over Article 7(1):

> It was felt by the United Kingdom that Article 7(1) was a recipe for confusion, in that a judge might feel obliged to steer his way through three possibly mutually inconsistent sets of mandatory rules; for uncertainty, an uncertainty which freedom to choose the applicable law is intended, in the business community, to

[66] Art. 22(1).
[67] See *Contract Conflicts*, ed. North (1982) 16–17 and below, pp. 42–43.
[68] *Ralli Bros.* v. *Compania Naviera Sota y Aznar* [1920] 2 KB 287.

avoid; for expense, in that proof of the mandatory rules of all relevantly connected foreign laws might be called for; and for delay, in that Article 7(1) might provide the means of delaying litigation inordinately, with a fear that it might frighten potential arbitration and litigation away from the United Kingdom.[69]

This last reason is interesting because it links back to the concerns expressed earlier in the context of the Brussels Convention and the retention of broad jurisdictional rules for non-Community cases, and also to the concerns that the United Kingdom had over the role to be played by the European Court of Justice in relation to the Rome Convention. There is no requirement that ultimate courts must refer issues to Luxembourg, simply a power in all appellate courts to do so. Again, a mandatory rule of reference by the House of Lords would have been unacceptable because of the potential for delay in the resolution of international contract claims.

The fourth aspect of the Convention for consideration is one which exposes the common lawyer to charges of cynicism, namely that some of the apparently novel features of the Convention which might be thought to introduce significant new concepts or changes of approach have, in a common law context, less effect than might at first be realized. Three examples can be taken. The first two concern the special rules for consumer contracts (Article 5) and individual employment contracts (Article 6). In both instances, they limit the effect of a choice of law clause so as, in the first case, not to deprive a consumer in certain circumstances of the protection afforded by the mandatory rules of the country of his habitual residence and, in the case of an employee, to provide special rules for determining the applicable law in the absence of choice and to preserve the protection afforded by the mandatory rules of that law, even where there is a choice. Although, occasionally, common law systems provide special protection for a 'weaker' party in the choice of law context through the provision of mandatory rules in the forum,[70] it has not been usual to provide protection through the application of the mandatory rules of some other law, not being the proper law. So these two Articles seem to make a significant change of direction; but that is an illusion. The consumer protection provisions only apply in limited circumstances, requiring an invitation to the consumer or advertising in his country, the use by the defendant of an agent there, or where the seller arranged for the consumer to travel to his country to buy goods. Although all may change with the advent of the Channel Tunnel or with further advances in satellite television advertising, at the moment the prospects of a consumer in the United Kingdom or Ireland falling within those provi-

[69] North, *Contract Conflicts*, 19–20, and below, p. 46.
[70] E.g. Unfair Contract Terms Act 1977, s. 27.

sions are slight. In the case of employment, the chances of a law other than that of the forum being involved are, again, not high, and so Article 6 is of little real effect. It has been said:

> More often than not the law applicable under (Article 6) will be the law of the state where the employee habitually carries out his work. And one suspects that the employee will usually sue in that country. Accordingly, cases where a forum will be called on to apply a law other than its own will be rare.[71]

The third example is the celebrated concept of 'characteristic performance' relied on in Article 4(2) as a presumption to determine the applicable law in the absence of choice. Distinguished Dutch private international lawyers have given careful consideration to this concept and to its place in the Convention.[72] We are told that the concept probably has its origins in Swiss law, so it is undoubtedly a novel feature of the Convention for the common law systems. It provides a compromise between those who seek certainty and predictability in choice of law rules, as are illustrated by the presumptions in Article 4(4) concerning contracts for the carriage of goods, and the common lawyers who see merit in flexibility and have come to abandon presumptions. However, the presumption in favour of the application of the law of the country of the habitual residence (or central administration) of the person (or company) whose performance is characteristic of the contract is only a rebuttable presumption, and it does not apply if the characteristic performance cannot be determined (Article 4(5)). Furthermore, it is to be 'disregarded if it appears from the circumstances as a whole that the contract is more closely connected with another country'. This is where the cynicism comes to the fore. The effect of this proviso is that the underlying choice of law rule is the application of the law of the country of closest connection. 'Characteristic performance' is no more than a means to the end of applying what is, in essence, the common law's current choice of law rule. So very little will have changed except that the route to the current solution may be a little longer. It seems unlikely, therefore, that, in this respect or indeed in many others, the implementation of the Rome Convention will have any fundamental effect on the common law approach to private international law issues.

ATTITUDES

It could not be said that the experience of the two major European Community private international law conventions just discussed evidences

[71] Morse, in: *Contract Conflicts*, ed. North (1982), 143, 172.

[72] d'Oliveira, (1977) 25 *Am J Comp L* 303; Schultsz, in: *Contract Conflicts*, ed. North (1982), 185–201.

a wholesale adoption by the common law systems of new approaches. Indeed, there are many instances where there has been active concern to maintain much of the old and to limit the effect of the new. What has to be stressed is that such attitudes do not stem from dogmatic belief in the principles embodied in the common law—they are influenced far more by pragmatic considerations such as the effect of particular rules on the speed of trials, the opportunities for English commercial law to continue to develop at the forefront of modern mercantile practices, and indeed the linking of legal services with other invisible export services, such as banking and insurance. On the other hand, the adoption of Community measures has not necessarily been grudging, as may be seen with the agreement (implemented in the Civil Jurisdiction and Judgments Act 1982) to use a concept of domicile more like that in other Member States, and from the impact of the Brussels Convention on the broader development of provisional and protective measures. Nor is the intellectual traffic entirely one way; the Brussels Convention in its current form reveals clear evidence of United Kingdom influences in its provisions on shipping, insurance and trusts and in the amended rules on choice of jurisdiction clauses.

Looking ahead, it will be interesting to see how far English judicial attitudes are influenced by the need to apply decisions of the European Court of Justice and by the practical possibility of referring to decisions of other national courts. Of course, English judges have already become accustomed to decision-making in Luxembourg but the experience stemming from the private international law conventions may well be rather different. The conventions are concerned with familiar legal issues and problems, not with ones which might be created simply as a result of membership of the European Community. It is instructive to look at how these matters have been handled by the courts in the few reported English decisions on the Brussels Convention. There has been one instance[73] of examining the way in which the particular problem (the interrelation of Articles 21 and 24) has been considered in another Member State, The Netherlands. This is noteworthy because it is normally rare for English courts to consider decisions from civil law jurisdictions and, although the 1982 Act[74] requires notice to be taken of decisions of the European Court of Justice, it does not say the same of the decisions of national courts. However the means are readily available for this to be done in that at least two series of law reports, European Commercial Cases and International Litigation Procedure, publish, in English, major decisions of national courts on the Brussels Convention. It is also interesting to see the comment[75] that, with regard to a tort

[73] *Republic of Haiti* v. *Duvalier* [1990] 1 QB 202.

[74] S. 3.

[75] *Minster Investments Ltd.* v. *Hyundai Precision and Industry Co. Ltd.* [1988] 2 Lloyd's Rep 621.

claim falling under Article 5(3) of the Brussels Convention, the court must look primarily at the words of the provision itself and that there are limits to the usefulness of a decision of the European Court[76] which must not itself be treated as if it were a statute. A further point to note is that it has not taken long for the English Court of Appeal[77] to make a reference to Luxembourg on the difficult issue of the scope of the provision in Article 1(4) excluding arbitration from the coverage of the Brussels Convention, raising in particular the question whether the Convention rules apply to a dispute over the validity of a contractual term referring matters to arbitration. The attitude of the English court was that this was an important issue as to the scope of the whole Convention and, therefore, a reference was desirable. So, the experience so far does not suggest that English courts will adopt an insular attitude but will adopt a careful but open-minded approach. It is hard, however, to see any evidence as yet that such an attitude will spill over into other private international law areas.

There is one feature of virtually all these recent decisions which evidences the treading of new ground by English judges. In England, the use of *travaux préparatoires* as guides to the interpretation of domestic legislation is not permitted. It is not appropriate for judges to look at Parliamentary debates or the reports of committees or of the Law Commission which preceded the legislation. Indeed, legislative attempts to provide that Law Commission reports may be consulted have failed, though in truth one suspects that some judges, at least, do look at such material as a guide to statutory interpretation. The Civil Jurisdiction and Judgments Act 1982 marks a change, because it expressly permits[78] reference to the Jenard and Schlosser reports (and also now the Evrigenis and Kerameus report on the Greek Accession Convention),[79] and in nearly every reported case on the Brussels Convention the courts have taken the opportunity so to refer. It is right that they should because of the important role that those reports have in the formulation of the Convention as now amended, but it will be interesting to see whether this power leads to greater pressure to examine preliminary material in other contexts.

Looking more broadly at the impact of European law-making on English private international law, there is one very obvious but important point to make. The medium of that law-making in the European Community has been legislation. There is nothing strange in that in systems which have codified rules of private international law, but it was

[76] *Handelskwekerij G.J. Bier NV* v. *Mines de Potasse d'Alsace SA*, Case 21/76, [1976] ECR 1735.

[77] *The Atlantic Emperor* [1989] 1 Lloyd's Rep 548. (And see above, p. 2).

[78] S. 3(3), as amended by SI 1989 No. 1346, para. 8.

[79] No doubt in due course provision will be made for reference to the de Almeida Cruz, Desantes Real, and Jenard Report on the Convention of accession of Spain and Portugal.

said of this area of English law as recently as 1935 that 'it has been only lightly touched by the paralysing hand of the Parliamentary draftsman.'[80] What one needs to notice is that, in the United Kingdom, there has been an enormous change in the last two or three decades and that that has occurred quite independently of the United Kingdom's membership of the European Community. As I said in 1982: 'Private international law is an area where creeping codification has crept so silently that few people other than those directly involved have even noticed that it is happening'.[81] There have been two major influences in this process of providing reformed statutory rules of private international law: the work of the Hague Conference on Private International Law and that of the Law Commissions in the United Kingdom. The former has been instrumental in providing the impetus for the introduction of new statutory private international law rules on adoption, recognition of foreign divorces, trusts and wills. The latter have proposed draft legislation in nearly all other areas of family law, as well as in those of domicile, tort, and limitation of actions. This development will, in one way, limit the potential for European influences because the main structure will have already been created, and English legislation tends to be quite detailed. On the other hand, there is a paradox that international initiatives for reform or change may stand a greater chance of implementation in England than do domestic ones. Private international law legislation has a low priority in the affairs of state, and sometimes it is more effective to be able to say that legislation is needed in order to fulfil our international obligations to ratify a treaty or convention. Whilst I regard the move towards legislative rules as inevitable if reform and development are to be achieved, that is by no means a universally held view in England. For example, Dr. F. A. Mann was fiercely critical of the Rome Contractual Obligations Convention saying,

> The substitution of an allegedly 'clear, firm, statutory basis' for the well-established, yet flexible and largely identical judge-made rules prevailing in England as well as in most other countries means the replacement of a sound and trusted instrument by the hazards of statutory interpretation.[82]

His dislike of legislation was not, however, limited to its intrusions into the common law, for he has been equally robust in his criticism of the Swiss codification of private international law.[83]

[80] Cheshire, *Private International Law*, 1st edn. (1935), preface.
[81] North, (1982) 46 *RabelsZ* 490, 500.
[82] Mann, (1983) 32 *ICLQ* 265, 266.
[83] Mann, (1989) 38 *ICLQ* 715, 716.

CONCLUSIONS

It is hard to draw any positive conclusions or make any clear predictions in relation to the prospects of the drawing together of approaches to private international law issues into a 'European approach'. There is no doubt that the Hague Conference has, for common lawyers, had a major influence in the development, for example, of habitual residence as a connecting factor, bridging the gulf between domicile and nationality, and that, in the recent Convention on the law applicable to trusts and on their recognition,[84] the Conference has provided a medium for civil law countries to cope (if they wish) with the alien concept of the trust. As for European Community initiatives, they have been important in their particular areas but there is a feeling in the United Kingdom that the likelihood of further major private international law initiatives is not great. The two major Conventions to which I have referred will provide a means for a gradual process of influencing the development of European law; indeed, the United Kingdom Government has attempted to do this for a decade or more by its regular practice of making submissions to the European Court of Justice on matters concerning the Brussels Convention even before it was in force in the United Kingdom. The influence will, however, be a very gradual one and it may be a fairly limited one, given the extent of legislative change which has already taken place in the United Kingdom. 1992 will not, I think, be a landmark date for private international law.

[84] Brought into effect in the UK by the Recognition of Trusts Act 1987.

2

The EEC Convention on the Law Applicable to Contractual Obligations (1980): Its History and Main Features

INTRODUCTION

It took ten years from the signing in 1980 of the Rome Convention on the law applicable to contractual obligations for the provisions of the Convention to be given legislative form in the United Kingdom by the Contracts (Applicable Law) Act 1990, and a further year for that legislation to be brought into force on 1 April 1991, a step which brought the whole Convention into force between the Contracting States. There was one major reason for this long delay. When the Convention was concluded in 1980 it was appreciated that there would need to be discussions between the Member States of the European Community over the extent of the jurisdiction over the Convention to be conferred on the European Court of Justice in Luxembourg. What was less than fully appreciated, however, was how difficult it would be to achieve agreement on this issue. Opinion ranged from that of those states which felt the Court should have no jurisdiction over the Convention to those which regarded it as desirable that, as with the (1968) Brussels Convention on jurisdiction and the enforcement of judgments in civil and commercial matters, lower courts should have the power to refer matters to the European Court and final courts of appeal should be required to do so. It was only in late 1988 that two Protocols on the Interpretation of the Rome Convention by the European Court were agreed.[1] What has emerged is essentially a compromise in that all appellate courts may, and none must, refer questions of interpretation of the Convention to the European Court. First instance judges have no power to refer.

Although these Protocols are not yet in force, their agreement broke the log-jam on ratification of the Convention itself and it is now in force in all nine Member States which negotiated it, as well as in Greece. Accession by Spain and Portugal is still awaited. Given that the two

Reprinted from *Contract Conflicts*, ed. North (1982), 3–30, published by North-Holland Publishing Co.

[1] [1989] OJ L48/1–17. For the Tizzano Report thereon, see [1990] OJ C219/1.

Protocols on the jurisdiction of the European Court are not yet in force, no references may be made to that Court. Despite the fact that it was not until 1991 that the Convention cam into force formally, effect had earlier been given to the Convention's choice of law rules in a number of Community states, either by legislation or by judicial decision.[2]

Not surprisingly, the long period of time between completion of the Rome Convention and its implementation has led to a change of perspective on a number of matters, not the least being the question of harmonizing choice of law rules relating to non-contractual obligations. Such rules were included in the original draft Convention and remained under consideration until quite late in the negotiating process.[3] The decision to omit them having been taken in 1978, it was nevertheless suggested in the Report by Giuliano and Lagarde on the Rome Convention that negotiations would begin on a non-contractual obligations convention 'after the first had been worked out'.[4] Not only has this failed to happen, but all prospect of its ever happening would seem, in the United Kingdom at least, to have been abandoned. Certainly, the Law Commissions, which in 1979 had established a Joint Working Party to provide advice to the United Kingdom delegation which would take part in the negotiation of such a convention, have proceeded to produce proposals and draft legislation for the reform, on a national basis, of the tort choice of law rules applicable within the United Kingdom.[5]

Another important topic on which planned future work has not materialized is that of the choice of law rules to govern the validity of arbitration or choice of jurisdiction clauses. There was a difference of view during the negotiations as to whether the validity of such clauses was a matter of substance to be governed by choice of law rules (the United Kingdom view) or a matter of procedure for the law of the forum (which tended to be the civil law view). Reconciliation of these views not having been achieved, it was agreed to exclude such clauses from the scope of the Rome Convention[6] but also to return later to an examination of the matter.[7] No such further examination has been set in hand which has the effect that, for the common lawyer, the coverage of the Convention rules is not as extensive as, it is suggested, would be desirable.[8]

The process of implementing the Convention by legislation had the

[2] See De Boer, (1990) 54 *RabelsZ* 24, 40–1.

[3] Below, pp. 32–33.

[4] [1980] OJ C282/7.

[5] Law Commission Working Paper No. 8 (1984), para. 1.6; Law Com. No. 193 (1990), para. 1.2; and see below, pp. 81–88.

[6] Art. 1(2)(d).

[7] See below, p. 36.

[8] Failure to adopt one means of ameliorating the position is commented on, below, pp. 25, 37.

effect of highlighting a number of matters of concern as to the range and scope of the Convention. One characteristic of the Convention as concluded in Rome in 1980 was that it introduced new choice of law rules in all cases where a choice was required between the laws of different countries.[9] This also meant that the rules applied irrespective of whether the case was connected with, or the law to be applied was that of, a Member State of the European Community.[10] Nevertheless attempts were made in the House of Lords during the passage of the Contracts (Applicable Law) Act 1990 to limit its scope, suggesting for example that the legislation should only apply between contracting parties resident in, or with their central administration in, a Contracting State.[11] Such amendments were rightly rejected. First of all, they were inconsistent with the specific terms of the Convention and would, therefore, have required the Convention to be renegotiated. Second, they were undesirable in that businessmen and lawyers would have had to apply two different sets of choice of law rules, choice between which would depend on the territorial connections of the parties, which in many instances were unlikely to be directly relevant to the territorial connections of the contract.

Some of the matters excluded from the scope of the Convention continue to give cause for concern. It has been noted already[12] that the choice of law rules in the Convention do not apply to the validity of arbitration and choice of court clauses; nor does the Convention apply, except in a very limited degree,[13] to matters of capacity.[14] This raises the prospect of having two sets of choice of law rules applicable to terms or issues arising within the same contract. One way in which it was proposed[15] to avoid this was for Parliament to extend the choice of law provisions of the Convention, though not of course the Convention itself, to such excluded matters. The 1990 Act does not, however, adopt that approach or indeed provide any special choice of law rules for such matters.[16] Resort must still be had to the common law, which means not only the continuation of two choice of law regimes in contract, but also that uncertainties remain as to what should be the law to govern capacity to contract.[17]

The exclusion from the scope of the Convention of contracts of insurance covering risks situated within the territories of the Member States of the Community[18] was justified on the ground that separate directives

[9] Art. 1(1).

[10] Below, pp. 34–35. Indeed Art. 2 states that 'Any law specified by this Convention shall be applied whether or not it is the law of a Contracting State'.

[11] *Hansard*, HL 515, 1537–41.

[12] Above, p. 24.

[13] Art. 11.

[14] Below, pp. 35–37.

[15] Below, p. 37.

[16] Regret over that outcome is expressed, above, p. 24.

[17] Cheshire and North, *Private International Law*, 12th edn. (1992), 510–12.

[18] Art. 1(3).

would deal with such matters. In fact, when the Rome Convention was concluded there were no such insurance directives, containing special choice of law rules, in force, and anxiety was expressed over such exclusion.[19] There are now two recent directives on insurance matters both of which contain special choice of law rules.[20] Thus, the criticism of the exclusion of insurance matters from the Convention is to a degree met, but at a high price. Not only is there now a quite separate choice of law regime for such insurance contracts, but the choice of law rules in the directives are complex and unwieldy,[21] and contain limits on party autonomy whose justification is hard to perceive.

When one turns to the matter of the scope of the applicable law under the Convention,[22] there were two matters particularly worthy of comment at the time the Convention was concluded. The first was that the choice of law rules of the Convention applied to 'prescription and limitation of actions'.[23] In other words, such issues were given a substantive, rather than a procedural, classification. This was contrary to the then position in English private international law.[24] However, the approach of the Convention to this matter was undoubtedly influential[25] in leading to wider reforms contained in the Foreign Limitation Periods Act 1984 which introduced a more general substantive classification. The second matter to be commented on is that the scope of the applicable law extends, under the Convention, to 'the consequences of nullity of the contract'.[26] This caused difficulty to some Member States, including the United Kingdom, which did not regard such a matter as contractual.[27] Such difficulty was met by including in the Convention a power of reservation[28] which the United Kingdom exercised on ratifying the Convention,[29] thus excluding that matter from the scope of the choice of law rules in operation in the United Kingdom.

A further area where the Convention allows a power of reservation is in relation to whether effect can be given to the mandatory rules of a third State, i.e. one which is neither the forum nor that of the applicable law.[30] The Convention provision[31] which allows effect to be given to such rules attracted opposition during the negotiations, particularly from the

[19] See below, pp. 36–37. Indeed Denmark applied the Convention rules on choice of law, until such time as directives with special choice of laws rules were introduced; see Philip, *Festskrift till Kurt Gronfors* (1991) 347, 350.

[20] Directive 88/357, [1988] OJ L172, Art. 7; Directive 90/619, [1990] OJ L330/30, Art. 4.

[21] See Plender, *The European Contracts Convention* (1991), 80–3.

[22] Art. 10.

[23] Art. 10(1)(d).

[24] See below, p. 42.

[25] Law Com. No. 114 (1982), para. 3.9.

[26] Art. 10(1)(e).

[27] See below, pp. 42–43.

[28] Under Art. 22(1)(b).

[29] Rather than on signing the Convention as suggested below, pp. 42, 50. See now the Contracts (Applicable Law) Act 1990, s. 2(2).

[30] See below, pp. 45–46.

[31] Art. 7(1).

United Kingdom, and the power of reservation[32] to exclude that provision was exercised by the United Kingdom[33] on ratifying[34] the Convention.[35]

Because the delay between completion and implementation of the Convention was so long, it is not yet possible to assess, in the light of judicial decisions, the impact which the Convention will have on the common law choice of law rules.[36] Views have certainly differed in England as to the merits and desirability of the Convention.[37] Amongst the varied criteria which might be applied to determine the longer term effects of the Convention[38] is whether it will have any impact on choice of law rules in countries outside the European Community. Whilst no provision is made for such countries to become parties to the Convention, the prospect of agreement on a parallel convention whereby the European Community states agree with the EFTA states the extension of the Rome Convention rules to those states seems significantly to have increased in the light of the Lugano Convention of 1988 which, in essence, extends to the EFTA states the jurisdictional and recognition rules of the 1968 Brussels Convention.[39]

* * *

[32] Under Art. 22(1)(a).

[33] And also by Germany, Ireland, and Luxembourg.

[34] Rather than on signing the Convention as suggested, below, pp. 46, 50.

[35] See the Contracts (Applicable Law) Act 1990, s. 2(2).

[36] The Convention only applies in the United Kingdom to contracts made after the date on which it entered into force there: Art. 17. It has been argued that the parties ought to be free to choose whether the common law choice of law rules should continue to apply, in place of the rules in the Convention; see Mann, (1991) 107 *LQR* 353. For reasons for rejecting such an argument, see below, pp. 184–187.

[37] Contrast Mann, (1983) 32 *ICLQ* 265 with Williams (1986), 35 *ICLQ* 1, 31.

[38] See North, [1990] I *Hague Recueil* 9, 194–204.

[39] See the Civil Jurisdiction and Judgments Act 1991.

INTRODUCTION

INTERNATIONAL efforts to harmonize rules of private international law relating to obligations are not new. Sometimes the harmonization may be incidental to the main purpose—as when the inclusion of some rules of private international law is thought necessary as an adjunct to the main task of the unification of parts of the substantive law of obligations. This peripheral interest in private international law can be seen in aspects of the work of Unidroit[1] and of UNCITRAL.[2] More central concern with the private international law rules relating to obligations is to be found, quite naturally, in the activities of the Hague Conference on Private International Law. Although in the early days of the Hague Conference there was little activity in the realm of obligations,[3] things had changed by the 1928 Session when the Fourth Commission at that session turned its attention to the international sale of goods; but the deliberations did not lead to a concluded convention.[4] With the renaissance of the Hague Conference in 1951, the pace quickened and since then there has been a whole series of Conventions dealing with aspects of the private international law of obligations, for example, international sales of goods (1955); choice of court in international sales contracts (1958); traffic accidents (1971); and products liability (1973); and further work was done at the 1980 session on international sale of goods, especially in relation to consumer contracts.

One characteristic of this work, and probably a proper and inevitable one given the wide range of countries and legal systems now represented in the Hague Conference, is its specific and detailed nature. The Conventions relate to specific aspects of obligations, rather than to whole areas such as contract or tort/delict. In this respect the original objectives of the work on the private international law of obligations, undertaken within the framework of the EEC, were much more grandiose in range of subject matter—though far more limited, at that time at least, in terms of countries and legal systems. The original objective was to harmonize all private international law rules relating to obligations, both contractual and non-contractual, throughout the EEC. Although, as we shall see, only part of this objective has been achieved in the 1980 Rome Convention on the law applicable to contractual obligations[5] which, from

[1] E.g., the draft convention providing a uniform law on agency of an international character in the sale and purchase of goods.

[2] E.g., the 1980 Vienna Convention on Contracts for the International Sale of Goods, (1980) Cmnd. 8074, Arts. 1 and 7.

[3] See van Hoogstraten, (1963) 12 *ICLQ* 148.

[4] *Actes de la sixième session*, 1928, 364–85.

[5] The text of the Convention is published in [1980] OJ L266 and in Cmnd. 8489 (1972).

its title, indicates the exclusion of non-contractual obligations, this Convention does provide a much broader degree of harmonization than those put forward by other international bodies.

THE BACKGROUND TO AND NEGOTIATION OF THE ROME CONVENTION

In 1967 Belgium proposed to the EEC Commission, on behalf of all three Benelux countries, that the Member States of the EEC might attempt the unification of private international law rules throughout the Community, taking as a basis the draft Benelux uniform law. Four areas of law were selected for detailed study, one of which was the law applicable to contractual and non-contractual obligations, the only topic on which work has, so far, led to a concluded Convention. It is clear that, from the very outset, it was thought that this work would further the general aims and objectives of the EEC. This is seen from the address by Mr T. Vogelaar, the Director-General for the Internal Market and Approximation of Legislation, at the opening meeting of government experts in 1969:

> There are three main considerations guiding our proposal for harmonising the rules of conflict for a few well-defined types of legal relations. The first is detailed by the history of private international law: to try to unify everything is to attempt too much and would take too long. The second is the urgent necessity for greater legal certainty in some sectors of major economic importance. The third is the wish to forestall any aggravation of the difference between the rules of private international law of the various Member States.[6]

There seems little doubt that the general economic integration of the Community carries the case for, at least, some legal harmonization—namely in those areas of commerce most closely affecting the economy. Company law provides an obvious example; products liability and insurance law might be regarded as others. The rules for the regulation of international contracts, especially choice of law rules, seem clearly to fall within this category.

A further major influence on those responsible for deciding to proceed with the work, and in particular with the work on obligations, was that it was seen as a natural sequel to the decision to turn the EEC into one large law-district for the purpose of the rules for the jurisdiction of the courts in EEC connected cases, and for the purpose of the recognition of foreign judgments, a decision which culminated in the 1968 Brussels Convention on jurisdiction and enforcement of judgments in civil and

[6] Giuliano/Lagarde Report on the Convention on the law applicable to contractual obligations, [1980] OJ C282/4.

commercial matters. If recognition of the judgments of the courts of one Member State is mandatory in the courts of the other Member States, then there is an argument that they should all apply the same substantive law, in order to avoid such forum shopping as the 1968 Brussels Convention permits. However, the harmonization within the EEC of major areas of substantive law is unlikely to be achieved for many years, if ever; so the obvious answer is to harmonize the choice of law rules in order to lead to the result that, no matter where in the EEC an action is brought, harmonized choice of law rules will ensure that the law of the same country is always applied. A sceptic might say, however, that rules of evidence and procedure may be as significant in deciding the outcome of a case as the determination of the applicable law.[7]

There was, however, a fundamental difference between the 1968 Convention and the work on the private international law of obligations culminating in the 1980 Rome Convention. The legal basis for the former Convention is to be found clearly established in Article 220 of the Treaty of Rome. This had the important consequences that new Member States acceding to the EEC undertook to accede to the conventions provided for in Article 220, and undertook to enter into negotiations with the original Member States in order to make the necessary adjustments thereto.[8] One outcome of the enlargement of the EEC with the accession of Denmark, Ireland and the United Kingdom was the 1978 Convention[9] amending the Brussels Convention. There is no similar legal basis for the work on contractual obligations. Whilst the original Member States regarded such work as a natural sequel to the 1968 Brussels Convention, it was in no way formally linked to that Convention; indeed some at least of the new Member States were, and still are, highly sceptical of the link between the two fields of endeavour.

The differing legal status of the work on the private international law of obligations has had three important consequences. There being no legal basis in the Treaty of Rome, for the 1980 Rome Convention, it ought to be regarded, not strictly speaking as an EEC Convention, but rather as a Convention between nine sovereign States who happened to be the Member States of the EEC. This leads to the two further differences: first, that the European Court of Justice does not have jurisdiction over the interpretation of the Convention unless and until such jurisdiction is specifically conferred upon it by the states parties to the Convention, and then only to the extent that any Protocol so doing

[7] Collins, (1976) 25 *ICLQ* 35–6.

[8] Act of Accession 1972, Art. 3.2.

[9] The Convention on the Accession to the 1968 Convention and the 1971 Protocol of Denmark, Ireland and the United Kingdom. Legislation implementing the 1968 and 1978 Conventions is to be found in the Civil Jurisdiction and Judgments Act 1982.

might provide. As yet, there has been no agreement to confer any such jurisdiction on the European Court of Justice.[10] The difference of opinion within the EEC on this issue is wide, ranging from the view that the Rome Convention falls outside the law-making powers of the EEC so that the Luxembourg Court should have no jurisdiction at all, to the view that the links between the EEC and the Rome Convention are so close that the Court of Justice should have the extensive grounds of jurisdiction provided for in Article 177 of the Treaty of Rome.

The third difference concerns the accession of new Member States. There is no binding obligation on them to accede to the Convention. A draft convention on the law applicable to contractual and non-contractual obligations had been concluded by the end of 1972, but there was no obligation on the three new Member States to accede to it and, as we shall see, there was a period of prolonged negotiations before agreement was reached between the nine Member States in 1980 on a Convention limited to contractual obligations. Similarly, when Greece joined the EEC in 1981 no obligation was imposed in the Act of Accession to accede to the Rome Convention—only to those Conventions falling under Article 220 of the Treaty of Rome.[11] It ought, however, to be mentioned that, in a Joint Declaration appended to the Rome Convention, it is provided that the then nine Member States

> having regard to the contribution of the Convention on the law applicable to contractual obligations to the unification of choice of law rules within the European Communities, express the view that any State which becomes a member of the European Communities should accede to this Convention.[12]

No doubt the accession of Greece would be much welcomed throughout the EEC.

It would be wrong, however, to convey the impression, whatever may be the formal legal position, that the Rome Convention does not have extremely close EEC links. A brief glance at the history of the negotiations from 1968 to 1980 will serve to confirm this. Indeed, all the negotiations leading up to the submission in 1979 of a draft convention to the governments of the Member States were conducted under the aegis of the EEC Commission and with the assistance of its officials and staff. Progress in the early stages of the preparation of a draft convention was speedy. In February 1970, M. P. Jenard, Director of Administration in the Belgian Ministry of Foreign Affairs and External Trade was appointed as Chairman of the working group of experts from the six

[10] Though see above, pp. 23–24. It ought, however, to be mentioned that Art. 18 of the Rome Convention requires that regard shall be had to the international character of the rules in the Convention and to the desirability of achieving uniformity in their interpretation and application.

[11] Act of Accession 1979, Art. 3.2.

[12] [1980] OJ L266/14.

Member States. This was an excellent appointment and M. Jenard remained as Chairman of the Group until the final stages of the negotiation of the Convention in the Council of Ministers in 1980. The successful conclusion of the negotiations owed much to his patient and resourceful chairmanship. By the summer of 1972, the Working Group had completed a preliminary draft convention on the law applicable to contractual and non-contractual obligations which was then submitted to the Governments of the Member States for comments.

However, 1973 brought the accession of three new Member States to the EEC, states all of whose legal systems differed in material respects from those of the original six. In the event, the momentum of the work slackened. The new states needed time for consultations, which in the United Kingdom were undertaken primarily by the two Law Commissions.[13] There was uncertainty over the United Kingdom's continued membership of the EEC (which was not settled until the 1975 referendum) and the views of governments had to be examined, as well as comments made by other experts, for example, at colloquia held in Copenhagen in 1974[14] and in London in 1976.[15] Once the working group resumed full activities again, now with representatives from the expanded nine Member States of the EEC, it became clear that quite a few of the decisions already taken in preparing the 1972 preliminary draft convention would have to be reopened. This was partly because of the need to accommodate the different approaches of the common law and Scandinavian legal systems now represented in the Community; and partly because, with second thoughts, the Group as a whole found major improvements could be made.

Whilst progress was steady, it was slow, even though the basic approach to choice of law in contract was similar throughout most of the EEC, namely, wide freedom to choose the applicable law coupled with the application of the most closely connected law in the absence of choice. Tort or delict presented much greater problems. There was no uniformity of approach. Although support for the *lex loci delicti* was strong (though its definition was difficult), that was not the common law rule. Whilst many might think that the double-barrelled common law rule, based on *Phillips* v. *Eyre*[16] and *Boys* v. *Chaplin*,[17] was in need of reform, there was no certainty that the preferred reformed rule would be

[13] See the Law Commission and Scottish Law Commission Consultative Document on the draft Convention, August 1974.

[14] The proceedings are published in *European Private International Law of Obligations*, (eds. Lando, von Hoffman, and Siehr) (1975).

[15] These proceedings are published in *Harmonisation of Private International Law by the EEC*, (ed. Lipstein) (1978).

[16] (1870) LR 6 QB 1.

[17] [1971] AC 356.

that of application of the *lex loci delicti*. So, for some countries at least, harmonization of choice of law rules in tort involved major reform as well as restatement—a much longer process. Even greater difficulty was posed by other non-contractual obligations. Here the problems involved fundamental issues of classification or characterization. Was the law of trusts to be included? To what extent did problems of restitution relate to the law of obligations or to the law of property? How far was the regulation of anti-competitive activity to be regarded as a specialized area of law outside the field of obligations? Counsels of prudence prevailed. It was thought better to complete that which could undoubtedly be achieved. So, in 1978, the decision was taken to limit the draft convention then under discussion to the law applicable to contractual obligations. Only when that was completed might attention then be turned to non-contractual obligations, and probably even then only to tort/delict. The Report on the Rome Convention,[18] prepared by Professor Giuliano of the University of Milan and Professor Lagarde of the University of Paris I, records that 'the Group decided to limit the present convention to contracts alone and to begin negotiations for a second Convention, on non-contractual obligations, after the first had been worked out'.[19] It seems unlikely that there will be a second Convention, at least in the foreseeable future. No further work has been done on it. There seems to be little enthusiasm in the Commission of the EEC for such work and, so far as the United Kingdom is concerned, the two Law Commissions are going ahead with the formulation of proposals for the reform of the choice of law rules in tort/delict on a United Kingdom-, not an EEC-wide, basis.[20]

Once the draft convention was confined to contractual obligations in 1978, the task of completing the negotiations was not great. A final draft was finished by the Working Group early in 1979 and by the end of that year the comments of the governments of the Member States were submitted to the Council Secretariat. Final examination of the draft Convention was undertaken by a Council Working Party during the spring of 1980 and the Convention was opened for signature at a Council of Ministers Meeting of Ministers of Justice in Rome on 19 June 1980, and was immediately signed by seven of the then nine Member States. It

[18] [1980] OJ C282. The inclusion of this Report in the Official Journal is of considerable importance in the UK because the Report contains a great many significant glosses on the Convention of which it is essential that the courts take account in interpreting the Convention. It is interesting to note that, in the legislation which implements the 1968 and 1978 Conventions on jurisdiction and the enforcement of judgments, specific reference is made to the equivalent Reports on those two Conventions: see the Civil Jurisdiction and Judgements Act 1982, s. 3(3).

[19] [1980] OJ C282/7.

[20] Law Commission Sixteenth Annual Report, 1980–81, Law Com. No. 113, para. 2.68, and see below, pp. 81–88.

has since been signed by Denmark and the United Kingdom,[21] though not yet by Greece. No Member States has, however, yet ratified it, and the Convention requires ratification by seven states before it comes into force. In many of the Member States national legislation will be required to implement the Convention. Even when implemented, the Convention is not retrospective in effect.[22] However, any Member State is, of course, free to implement the rules in the Convention as embodying its private international law rules in relation to contractual obligations whether or not the Convention has come into force. Furthermore, there is nothing to prevent a Member State from applying the rules of the Convention to matters which are excluded from the scope of the Convention which, as will be seen below, may be significant for the United Kingdom in relation to arbitration clauses and choice of court clauses.

THE ROME CONVENTION: ITS MAIN FEATURES

What is attempted here is not a detailed analysis, Article by Article of the Rome Convention, but rather an overview of the convention and its main characteristics.

The Scope of the Rome Convention

The scope of the Convention is laid down in Articles 1 and 2, which comprise Title I of the Convention—Titles II and III covering respectively the Uniform Rules provided in the Convention and the Final Provisions relating to such matters as ratification, revision and denunciation. There are three issues to be examined with regard to the scope of the Convention. The first is that the rules of the Convention 'apply to contractual obligations in any situation involving a choice between the laws of different countries.'[23] This means that the Convention is not limited to international cases. An earlier draft referred to 'situations of an international character', but this was dropped when it was seen to be far from clear in meaning; and its inclusion would have meant that cases falling outside that description, but requiring the determination of the applicable law, would fall outside the Convention and remain governed by residual national rules of private international law. The fact that the Convention is not limited to international cases means that it applies, for example, to

[21] The UK signed on 7 December 1981, see Cmnd. 8489 (1972) 16.
[22] Art. 17.
[23] Art. 1(1).

Anglo-Scottish conflicts[24] or to intra-USA conflicts,[25] should they come before the courts of a Member State in which the Convention is in force. It is important to note that, once a contract contains a choice of law clause even in what is otherwise a purely domestic case,[26] then that choice of a foreign law brings the Convention into operation because the issue has arisen as to whether the *lex fori* or the chosen law applies.

The second matter related to scope is that the Convention is worldwide in effect. What this means is that it will replace the contract choice of law rules in the Member States in which it is implemented not just for cases with an EEC connection, as for instance the domicile of the defendant,[27] but whenever a choice of law issue arises. Article 2 provides that 'Any law specified by this Convention shall be applied whether or not it is the law of a Contracting State'. This has the effect that, the choice of law rules therein will be applied by an English court whether or not the contract has any connection with England or any other part of the EEC.

Third, the Convention starts from the basic proposition that it applies uniformly to all types of contract. This generality is then cut down in three ways. First, special rules are provided for some particular types of contract. Sometimes these are no more than special rebuttable presumptions as in the case of contracts concerning immoveable property[28] or carriage of goods.[29] In other cases, namely consumer[30] and employment contracts,[31] special choice of law rules are provided, particularly in relation to the law applicable in the absence of choice. The second limitation is that certain types of contract or contractual issue are excluded from the Convention. As the Convention is limited to contractual obligations, there is no need, as there was in earlier drafts, to make special provision to exclude non-contractual obligations such as property rights and rights arising from intellectual property.

One or two of the matters specifically excluded by Article 1 are worthy of comment.[32] Article 1(2)(a) excludes 'questions involving the status or

[24] There is, in fact, a power under Art. 19(2) for a Member State, such as the UK, in which different territorial units have their own rules of law, not to apply the Convention to conflicts solely between the laws of such units. It seems unlikely, however, that the UK would wish to preserve its existing common law rules solely for intra-UK conflicts. (See now the Contracts (Applicable Law) Act 1990, s. 2(3) applying the convention to conflicts within the UK).

[25] Under Art. 19(1), where a state comprises several territorial units, each with its own law, such as the three law districts within the UK, the separate states of the USA, or Australia, or the separate Canadian provinces, each shall constitute a separate country for the purposes of the Convention.

[26] Some limitation on this freedom is, however, provided by Art. 3(3), discussed below, p. 39.

[27] This being the primary connecting factor under the 1968 Convention on jurisdiction and enforcement of judgments, Art. 2.

[28] Art. 4(3).

[29] Art. 4(4).

[30] Art. 5, see North (ed.), *Contract Conflicts*, (1982) ch 6.

[31] Art. 6, see *Contract Conflicts*, ch 7.

[32] For the complete list, see Art. 1(2), (3), (4).

legal capacity of natural persons, without prejudice to Article 11'. Article 11 in fact makes only very restricted provision for choice of law in relation to capacity to contract, being limited to contracts concluded between persons in the same country, one of whom is a natural person. The reason for the very limited treatment of capacity in the Convention lies in a difficulty of classification. Put very simply, to the common lawyer capacity to contract is a contractual issue; to the civil lawyer it is an issue relating to status and should find no place in the Convention.

Two other areas which caused difficulty and led to their eventual exclusion from the Convention were arbitration and choice of court clauses, and choice of law in insurance contracts. So far as arbitration and choice of court clauses are concerned, there were two schools of thought. One was that, first, such topics are more procedural than contractual in nature and, second, adequate regulation of arbitration agreements is to be found in the various international Conventions on arbitration, such as the 1927 Geneva Convention, the 1958 New York Convention, and the 1961 European Convention to which most, though not all, Member States were parties; and in any event few problems seemed to arise in practice over the law applicable to the validity of arbitration, or choice of court, agreements. The other school of thought, whose main proponent was the United Kingdom delegation, was that the various international conventions did not in fact deal adequately, or at all, with the question of the applicable law to govern the validity of the agreement to arbitrate; and, furthermore, there was no uniformity of accession to these conventions within the EEC and so if those topics were excluded from the Rome Convention there would be no harmonization of an important matter in international commerce. Moreover, the practical result of exclusion would be that, where an arbitration or choice of court clause was included in a contract, the whole of the contract but for that clause would be governed by the rules in the Rome Convention, but the law to be applied to that one clause would remain to be determined by national unharmonized rules of private international law. This conflict was resolved by an agreement to exclude arbitration and choice of court clauses from the Convention but to return to an examination of these problems once the Convention had been finally drawn up. No such steps to prepare a Protocol to the Convention to deal with this matter have been taken and it now seems unlikely that they ever will.

The third excluded matter to which reference will be made here is that of insurance contracts. Although contracts of reinsurance are within the Convention,[33] it does not apply 'to contracts of insurance which cover risks situated in the territories of the Member States of the European Economic Community. In order to determine whether a risk is situated in

[33] Art. 1(4).

these territories the court shall apply its internal law.'[34] So, if the risk is situated in Denmark the Convention does not apply, but if the risk is in Sweden it does. At first sight, such an exclusion seems bizarre in the extreme. The reason for it is to be found in the work continuing within the EEC in the field of insurance—in particular the negotiation of a draft directive on the provision of insurance services in the non-life field. The intention was that such a directive should contain choice of law rules for insurance risks within the EEC, leaving the Convention to provide the rules for risks outside the Community. Such a solution seems admirable in theory, but is breaking down in practice. Despite years of negotiation, agreement on choice of law rules for the draft Directive seems no nearer. There is a basic difference of view between those Member States who would be content to apply the rules of the Convention, including freedom to choose the applicable law, to such insurance contracts,[35] and those who will accept no, or only very limited, freedom of choice. Indeed the problem is worse compounded because it is not even clear that the draft Directive would cover all non-life risks (let alone life risks) situated within the EEC.

However, the practical difficulties created by the exclusion from the Convention of issues of capacity, arbitration and choice of court agreements and insurance contracts covering EEC risks are not as great as might at first sight appear. Although there is no harmonization of choice of law rules on these matters, the spectre of dual sets of choice of law rules coexisting in each Member State can be avoided, if desired, when the Convention is implemented. For example, there is nothing to prevent Parliament from deciding to apply the Convention rules to matters excluded from the Convention. In that way, the current common law choice of law rules could be completely replaced by the new rules of the Convention. What cannot be done, however, is for the legislature to derogate from the special rules in the Convention on such matters as consumer[36] and employment contracts.[37] Furthermore, if agreement is eventually reached on choice of law rules for EEC insurance contracts, those special rules would have to be applied throughout the EEC.[38]

Choice of Law Rules of the Convention

The Convention contains three basic rules for determining the applicable law. The first is that the parties are free to choose the law applicable to

[34] Art. 1(3).

[35] See Law Commission and Scottish Law Commission Report on choice of law rules in the Draft Non-Life Insurance Services Directive, Apr. 1979.

[36] Art. 5. [37] Art. 6.

[38] Indeed, the Convention provides that choice of law rules in other Community instruments are to take precedence over the rules in the Convention: Art. 20.

their contract.[39] The second is that, in the absence of choice, the contract is to be governed by the law of the country with which it is most closely connected.[40] Third, a contract is to be formally valid if it satisfies the formal requirements either of the law applicable under the appropriate one of the two previous propositions or of the country where it was concluded.[41] All three of these propositions are, of course, over-simplified and aspects of all three are discussed far more fully elsewhere.[42] It may, however, be convenient to elaborate here just a little on these three basic rules.

Express choice of the applicable law

Party autonomy in choice of law is permitted in all the Member States, in most other countries and in many international conventions. It is hardly surprising, therefore, that it is the starting point in the Rome Convention. Furthermore, here as elsewhere in the Convention, *renvoi* is excluded.[43] Determination of the applicable law means the internal contract law of the country identified, to the exclusion of its rules of private international law. The choice of the applicable law need not be express, so long as it is a real choice. It can be determined, for example, from the use of a standard form contract in the international commodity market, from a previous course of dealing, or from the choice of a forum or place of arbitration. Furthermore, *depeçage* is permitted. The chosen law can be applied to part only of the contract. The parties are also free to vary the applicable law[44] in that a law once chosen, or otherwise applicable, may be replaced by a later choice of a new governing law; though not so as to prejudice the formal validity of the contract nor adversely to affect the rights of third parties.[45]

The freedom to choose the applicable law is unlimited. It is possible to choose a law which is quite unconnected with the contract. Indeed, as we have seen, in the case of a purely domestic contract, it may only be the

[39] Art. 3. [40] Art. 4. [41] Art. 9. [42] See *Contract Conflicts*, chs 2–3.

[43] Art. 15.

[44] North, 'Varying the Proper Law', in *Multum non Multa: Festschrift für Kurt Lipstein* (1980), 205, and below, pp. 53–67.

[45] Art. 3(2). A further issue in relation to choice of law is that of the law to determine the validity of the choice. Art. 8(1) (which is applied to choice of the applicable law by Art. 3(4)) settles for the 'bootstraps' approach whereby the validity of the choice is determined by the law chosen: see Lipstein (ed.) in *Harmonisation of Private International Law by the EEC* (1978), 1, 5–6 and North, in *Multum non Multa* (1980), 205, 212–13, and below, pp. 59–60. In fact. Art. 8 governs not only the validity of a choice of law clause, but provides generally that the existence and validity of a contract, or any term thereof, shall be governed by the law that would be applicable if the contract or term were valid. Art. 8(2) deals with the problems that are likely to arise, for example, from rules implying agreement from silence, especially where there is a choice of law clause. Although the existence of consent is referred, by Art. 8(1), to the chosen law, Art. 8(2) permits a party to rely on the law of his habitual residence to establish that he did not consent if it appears that, in the circumstances, it would not be reasonable to determine this issue according to the law specified under Art. 8(1)—a form of judicial discretion as to the determination of the applicable law.

choice of a foreign law which brings the Convention into operation. If, however, the parties do choose a foreign law when the contract is otherwise entirely connected with one country, then Article 3(3) provides that such choice shall not prejudice the application of mandatory rules of the law of that country. 'Mandatory rules' are defined as rules 'which cannot be derogated from by contract'. This provision is of particular significance where the otherwise applicable law is not that of the forum, as the forum's mandatory rules may be applied by reason of Article 7(2).[46] Take the following example: an action is brought in France, because of an agreement to submit to the jurisdiction of the French courts,[47] but the contract, which relates to the consumer sale of goods, is wholly connected with England, both parties being resident there. Any exemption clause in the contract is regulated by the Unfair Contract Terms Act 1977, but the parties choose German law as applicable to the contract. The French court, whilst accepting the choice of German law in general, must apply the controls on exemption clauses contained in the 1977 Act because they cannot be evaded by choice of a foreign law,[48] i.e., they are mandatory in that they cannot be derogated from by contract.

Applicable law in the absence of choice

The applicable law in the absence of choice is, under Article 4, that of the country[49] with which the contract is most closely connected. Again, *depeçage* is permitted but only by way of exception in the case of severable parts of the contract, for example, as in joint ventures. Indeed the Giuliano/Lagarde Report states that 'the court must have recourse to severance as seldom as possible'.[50] The Report also indicates[51] that, in determining the country of closest connection, 'it is also possible to take account of factors which supervened after the conclusion of the contract'. This differs from the current English position under which the courts may not use the subsequent conduct of the parties as an aid in the interpretation of the contract, save as evidence of a variation of the contract or of the creation of a new contract.[52]

[46] Discussed below, p. 45.
[47] Under Art. 17 of the 1968 Convention on jurisdiction and enforcement of judgments.
[48] Unfair Contract Terms Act 1977, s. 27(2).
[49] There is no reference in the Convention, as there is in the more recent English cases, to a 'system of law' rather than to a 'country'; see, e.g. *James Miller & Partners Ltd.* v. *Whitworth Street Estates (Manchester) Ltd.* [1970] AC 583, 603–6, 614–16; *Compagnie d'Armement Maritime SA* v. *Compagnie Tunisienne de Navigation SA* [1971] AC 572, 583, 603; *Coast Lines Ltd.* v. *Hudig and Veder Chartering NV* [1972] QB 34, 44, 46, 50.
[50] [1980] OJ C282/23.
[51] Ibid., 282/20.
[52] *James Miller & Partners Ltd.* v. *Whitworth Street Estates (Manchester) Ltd.* [1970] AC 583, 603, 611, 614–15; *Compagnie d'Armement Maritime SA* v. *Compagnie Tunisienne de Navigation SA* [1971] AC 572, 602–8.

The general rule laid down in Article 4(1) is qualified by a number of rebuttable presumptions which apply unless it appears from the circumstances that the contract is more closely connected with another country.[53] For instance, where the subject matter of the contract is a right in immoveable property or a right to use immoveable property, there is a presumption under Article 4(3) that the contract is most closely connected with the country where the immoveable property is situated. While this presumption applies to contracts for the sale or leasing of immoveable property, it does not apply to contracts for the construction or repair of such property.[54] The latter contracts are governed by the general rule of Article 4(1).

Under Article 4(4), contracts for the carriage of goods and single voyage charter-parties and other contracts whose main purpose is the carriage of goods are presumed to be most closely connected with a country which is both that of the principal place of business of the carrier and also either the place of loading, or of discharge, or the principal place of business of the consignor. The whole question of contracts for the carriage of goods is examined more fully elsewhere.[55] There are just two points that might be made here. The first is that, whatever may be the provisions of Article 4 in relation to carriage of goods, choice of law rules in other international conventions on transport take precedence over the rules in the Rome Convention, by reason of Article 21. Secondly, it should be emphasized that the special presumption in Article 4(4) applies only to contracts for the carriage of goods; it does not apply to contracts for the carriage of passengers. The latter fall under the general rules of Article 4. Although there may be mixed contracts for the carriage of goods and passengers, it was thought to be impracticable to apply the presumption in Article 4(4) to the case of different passengers on the same journey, with the result that the contract with each passenger might well be governed by a different law.

The most important presumption is that found in Article 4(2) and this presumption is of general application. Indeed, this presumption, which embodies the concept of 'characteristic performance', provides one of the main novel features of the Convention when compared with common law choice of law rules. Under Article 4(2), in all contracts other than those relating to immoveables or carriage of goods, there is a rebuttable presumption that the contract is most closely connected with the country where the party who is to effect the 'characteristic performance' of the contract has his habitual residence or, in the case of a body corporate or incorporate, has its central administration. If, however, the contract is entered into in the course of the trade or profession of the party who is

[53] Art. 4(5). [54] Giuliano/Lagarde Report, [1980] OJ C282/21.
[55] See *Contract Conflicts*, ch 8.

to effect the characteristic performance, then the applicable law is presumed to be that of the country of that party's principal place of business or of the place of business through which, under the terms of the contract, performance is to be effected.

A general critique of characteristic performance is provided elsewhere,[56] but the main purpose of this presumption is to provide a compromise—a compromise between those who seek certainty and predictability in the determination of the applicable law under Article 4(4) and those who, like English lawyers, see merit in the flexibility of the general rule and see little virtue in presumptions, and believe that if there are to be presumptions, they must be rebuttable, and that that fact greatly diminishes the prospect of achieving the certainty for the attainment of which they were introduced. Indeed, there is uncertainty in the very concept of characteristic performance. There is no real experience in the legal system of any of the Member States of the EEC in the application of this concept, which is probably Swiss in origin.[57] The Giuliano/Lagarde Report does provide some assistance with the identification of the characteristic performance of a contract. Unilateral contracts present no problem; but in the case of bilateral contracts it is suggested[58] that the payment of money is not the characteristic performance of the contract; rather is it the performance of the obligation for which the payment is due, i.e., the provision of goods or services, transport, banking operations and the like. If the courts follow such interpretation, then in the commonest of all international contracts, sale of goods, there will be a presumption under Article 4(2) in favour of the law of the seller's place of business.

Formal validity

Article 9, which deals with formal validity, follows the general outline of the law in many countries with a validating rule of dual reference. A contract is formally valid if it satisfies the formal requirements of either the proper law or the law of the place where it was concluded. The first part of the rule causes no difficulty. One looks to the law which governs the contract under the rules laid down by the Convention, which depend on whether or not there has been a choice by the parties of the applicable law. In the case, however, of the alternative law to be applied, it is not satisfactory to refer without more to the law of the place of contracting, because of the logical difficulty that the determination of that place may

[56] Ibid.

[57] Vischer, *Internationales Vertragsrecht* (1962), 89–144; d'Oliveira, (1977) 25 *Am Jo Comp L* 303.

[58] Giuliano/Lagarde Report, [1980] OJ C282/20.

depend on the validity of the contract, which is the very matter at issue. In order to avoid this problem, the place where the contract is concluded is only applied where the contract is concluded between persons who are in the same country. If they are in different countries, then satisfaction of the formal requirements of the law of either of those countries will suffice.[59]

Scope of the applicable law

Article 10 lists some of the matters which are to be governed by the chosen law or the law which, in the absence of choice, is determined according to the rules laid down in Article 4. It is a non-exclusive list and includes such matters as interpretation, performance, and the consequences of breach. There are, however, two matters of particular significance, at least from a United Kingdom viewpoint. The first is that the proper law is to apply to 'the various ways of extinguishing obligations, *and prescription and limitation of actions*'.[60] Under present English law, limitation of actions (though not prescription) is characterized as a procedural issue to be governed, in English proceedings, by English law as the *lex fori*.[61] The rule has been criticized and proposals for its abandonment in favour of a substantive classification have been put forward by the Law Commission.[62]

The second matter concerns Article 10(1)(e) which provides that the proper law shall govern 'the consequences of nullity of the contract'. This heading was added to Article 10 at a very late stage of the negotiations and proved to be the source of some controversy. The purpose of this addition was to make it quite clear that, for example, the right to claim the refund of money paid under a void contract should be governed by the law applicable to the (void) contract. This caused such difficulty to some Member States that the Convention provides[63] that a State may reserve the right not to apply the provisions of Article 10(1)(e); and the United Kingdom exercised such a power of reservation on signing the Convention. The difficulties with Article 10(1)(e) are of two kinds. The first is theoretical. It is that the right to recover money paid under, for

[59] There are also special rules in Art. 9(3)–(6) dealing with contracts entered into by agents, the formal validity of acts as opposed to contracts, and the formal validity of consumer contracts and contracts concerning immoveables.

[60] Art. 10(1)(d), emphasis added.

[61] *British Linen Co.* v. *Drummond* (1830) 10 B & C 903; *Huber* v. *Steiner* (1835) 2 Bing NC 202; *Don* v. *Lippmann* (1837) 5 Cl & Fin 1; *Harris* v. *Quine* (1869) LR 4 QB 653.

[62] Law Commission Working Paper No. 75 (1980): Classification of Limitation in Private International Law. See now the Foreign Limitation Periods Act 1984.

[63] Art. 22(1)(b).

example, a void contract is not classified in the common law world as a contractual obligation, but relates rather to quasi-contract or the law of restitution. That being so, it can properly find no place in a Convention whose choice of law rules are specifically confined to contractual obligations. Second, it is far from clear that Article 10(1)(e) achieves a desirable result. It might be argued that, even if the obligation is quasi-contractual, it is, under English rules of private international law,[64] governed by the proper law of that obligation and that this will almost inevitably be the same as the proper law of the contract which has been held to be void; so one reaches the same result by a more indirect and tortuous route than that provided in Article 10(1)(e). The position is not, however, as simple as that. Such English authority as there is on the law to govern restitutionary or quasi-contractual claims is all limited to cases where there is no choice of the applicable law.[65] It is quite reasonable in such a case to conclude that the proper law of the contract should govern. Where, however, the proper law is determined by the express choice of the parties, it is very doubtful whether that result should follow. Suppose, for example, that two Englishmen enter into a contract for the sale of a car. All the elements of the contract are English except for the fact that the car is to be delivered in France; and there is an express choice of French law as the applicable law. But for that choice, the proper law would be English law. The buyer pays the price; the contract is for some reason void; the car is never delivered and the buyer seeks the return of his money. There has been no factual connection with France as the money was paid in England and credited to the seller's English account. French law is only relevant because, notwithstanding the voidness of the contract, the choice of law clause is good by reason of the 'bootstraps rule' of Article 8.[66] It seems quite inappropriate for French law now to determine the extent to which the buyer is able to recover the money that he has paid under the void contract.

Mandatory rules

Finally,[67] we must turn to the treatment in the Convention of 'mandatory rules', an aspect of the Convention which caused considerable anxieties in

[64] Dicey and Morris, *The Conflict of Laws*, 10th edn. (1980), ch 30.

[65] See e.g. *Fibrosa Spolka Akcyjna* v. *Fairbairn Lawson Combe Barbour Ltd.* [1943] AC 32; *Arab Bank* v. *Barclays Bank* [1953] 2 QB 527, 572; *BP Exploration Co. (Libya) Ltd.* v. *Hunt (No 2)* [1979] 1 WLR 783, affd [1983] 2 AC 352; *Etler* v. *Kertesz* (1960) 26 DLR (2d) 209.

[66] Discussed at n. 45 above.

[67] Other significant matters with which the Convention deals and which are not discussed here are: voluntary assignment (Art. 12), subrogation (Art. 13), and burden of proof (Art. 14).

the United Kingdom during its negotiation and which may prove to be its most controversial feature. Extended treatment of mandatory rules and their relationship with public policy (*ordre public*) is found elsewhere.[68] It will suffice here merely to give an indication of the major difficulties. There are four main areas in which the matter of mandatory rules arises: limitation on freedom of choice of the applicable law where all the elements of the contract are otherwise connected with a different country (Article 3(2)); limitation on freedom of choice in certain consumer contracts (Article 5); in employment contracts (Article 6); and the general provisions on mandatory rules contained in Article 7, which not only allows the court to continue to apply the mandatory rules of the forum, but also empowers it to apply, in appropriate circumstances, the mandatory rules of a third country which is neither the forum nor that of the proper law. Finally, it should not be forgotten that the Convention, in Article 16, preserves the widely accepted rule of private international law that the application of a rule of the law of any country specified by the choice of law rules of the Convention may be refused, but only if such application is manifestly incompatible with the public policy (*ordre public*) of the forum.

There are two major issues which arise with respect to the treatment in the Convention of mandatory rules. The first is one of definition; the second is one of substance. The definition issue may be posed simply: what are 'mandatory rules'? They are defined in Article 3(3) as 'rules of law of a country which cannot be derogated from by contract'. That Article then goes on to suggest that such definition is to be used consistently throughout the Convention because it continued thus: 'hereinafter called "mandatory rules"'. There would seem to be little difficulty with the definition in the context in which it was given. Article 3(3) allows the parties to choose the law of any country but, if all the elements of the contract are connected with one country, the choice of the law of a second country is not to prejudice the application of the mandatory rules of the first country. The objective is clear: the parties cannot evade the application of any of the mandatory rules of their domestic law by a choice of law clause. 'Mandatory rules' has, and rightly has, a broad meaning extending to all domestic law which cannot be derogated from by contract.

A similarly broad meaning may be justified in the second and third contexts in which the concept is encountered: consumer and employment contracts. In both contexts, the purpose of the reference to mandatory rules is to limit the freedom to choose the applicable law. Under Article 5(2) a choice of the applicable law, in the restricted class of consumer

[68] *Contract Conflicts*, chs 4–5.

contracts covered by Article 5, is not to have the result of depriving the consumer of protection afforded to him by mandatory rules of the law of the country of his habitual residence. Similarly, under Article 6, choice of law in a contract of employment is not to deprive the employee of the protection of mandatory rules of the law of the country which would have been applicable (under the rules laid down in Article 6) had there been no choice. Once again, 'mandatory rules' seem to have their broad meaning—all relevant rules of law of consumer and employment protection are to be applied notwithstanding the freedom of choice. The only limit on, for example, the application of consumer protection rules of the country of the consumer's residence could, presumably, be any spatial limitation contained in such rules. It would be quixotic to apply such a rule under the Convention even though, under the law of the country in question, it did not extend to contracts of an international character.[69]

The picture changes when Article 7 is considered. Article 7(2) preserves a generally accepted private international law rule, namely that, whatever may be the proper law and whether it is determined by choice of the parties or under the rules contained in Article 4, the judge may apply rules of the law of the forum 'in a situation where they are mandatory irrespective of the law applicable to the contract'. This must contemplate a narrower range of mandatory rules than those defined in Article 3(3). Indeed, the Giuliano/Lagarde Report, not only refers[70] to such mandatory rules as 'lois d'application immédiate', but also exemplifies them as 'notably rules on cartels, competition and restrictive practices, consumer protection and certain rules concerning carriage'. The common lawyer would probably regard this class as rules which, notwithstanding a foreign applicable law, the forum's public policy requires to be applied. This is a very limited class of 'internationally mandatory rules'. By allowing freedom of choice, you accept that many of the requirements of your own law will not be applied, but there is a residue which must be applied in your courts, irrespective, as Article 7(2) says, of the law applicable to the contract. The purist can reconcile this narrower concept of 'mandatory rules' with the much broader definition in Article 3(3) by pointing out that the phrase 'mandatory rules' which is defined in Article 3(3) is not in fact used in Article 7(2). It is, however, used in Article 7(1) to which we now turn.

Under Article 7(1), a judge may give effect to the mandatory rules of a country, other than that of the proper law or the forum, if 'the situation has a close connection' with that other country and if, under the law of that country, those mandatory rules must be applied whatever the law

[69] See, for example, the English law on unfair dismissal, discussed in *Contract Conflicts*, ch 7.

[70] [1980] OJ C282/28.

applicable to the contract. What this means, combining Article 3(3) and Article 7(1), is that if in such a third country there are rules which cannot be derogated from by contract, they may be applied by the judge, provided that those rules must, under the law of that third country, be applied whatever the law applicable to the contract. So, a judge in England concerned with a contract whose proper law is French, but which is closely connected with Denmark, may apply Danish mandatory rules, i.e., rules which cannot be contracted out of, provided that, under Danish law, those rules are internationally mandatory, that is applicable in Denmark notwithstanding a foreign (here French) applicable law.

It seems clear that two different kinds of mandatory rules are referred to in the Convention and both are in issue in Article 7(1). That complexity in Article 7(1) takes us on to the second major issue concerning mandatory rules: the issue of substance. The idea of reference to the mandatory rules of not only the proper law and the forum (France and England in the example in the previous paragraph) but also the law of a third state was greeted with great scepticism by some delegations, most noticeably the United Kingdom, notwithstanding a similar approach in, for example, the 1978 Hague Convention on the law applicable to agency, and some Dutch authority[71] in its support. It was felt by the United Kingdom that Article 7(1) was a recipe for confusion, in that a judge might feel obliged to steer his way through three possibly mutually inconsistent sets of mandatory rules; for uncertainty, an uncertainty which the freedom to choose the applicable law is intended, in the business community, to avoid; for expense, in that proof of the mandatory rules of all relevantly connected foreign laws might be called for; and for delay, in that Article 7(1) might provide the means of delaying litigation inordinately, with a fear that it might frighten potential arbitration and litigation away from the United Kingdom. The only way in which this concern could be met was to provide a power of reservation, so that a Member State could reserve the right not to apply Article 7(1),[72] a power which the United Kingdom exercised on signing the Convention.

CONCLUSIONS

What general assessment of the Convention can one provide, given that it has now been signed by all the Member States that negotiated it, and that the next few years are likely to see its implementation in some at

[71] The *Alnati* case, Dutch Supreme Court (Hoge Raad), 13 May 1966; *Rev crit dr int pr*, 1967, 522; *Kharajtsingh* v. *Sewrajsingh*, Dutch Supreme Court (Hoge Raad), 12 January 1979; *Rev crit dr int pr* 1980, 68; and see Van Rooij, ibid., 69–79.

[72] Art. 22(1)(a).

least of those states, and possibly its adoption elsewhere as a model for reform of national choice of law rules and, perhaps, as the basis for further discussion and negotiation in the wider forum of the Hague Conference on Private International Law? It would be wrong not to point out that the very existence of the Convention has its critics, one of the most fervent of whom is Nadelmann. His prime concern has been that the harmonization and reform of choice of law rules by the Member States tends to supplant the work of the Hague Conference on Private International Law. His criticism is forceful:

> The Common Market has apparently chosen to pre-empt for itself codification of the rules of conflict of laws, thus blocking the Hague Conference from doing the job for which it was created. This is a heavy responsibility. Having the Conference operate at the Market's pleasure, to pick up crumbs here and there is not likely to appeal to the other Member States.[73]

Indeed, it appears that the existence of the draft EEC Convention and the continuing negotiations upon it contributed significantly to the decision of the Hague Conference in 1976[74] not to take up the suggestion, made in 1972 by the USA,[75] that the Conference should work on contract and torts. Part of the complaint is that, if the work of the Hague Conference is ousted by that of the EEC, then the chances of broader unification of private international law are lost, there being some three times as many members of the Hague Conference as of the EEC—and, of course, non-European countries like the USA, are excluded from the process.

Whilst there is no doubt that the harmonization achieved by the Rome Convention is on a more limited geographical scale, this does not necessarily mean that such regional codification risks, in Nadelmann's words, 'freezing the law'.[76] It must not be forgotten that the existing Hague Conventions in the field of obligations are essentially European in geographical scope. The only non-European state that is a party to the 1955 sale of goods convention is Niger; and neither of the traffic accidents or products liability Conventions has even been signed by a non-European state. Furthermore, the Rome Convention constitutes a major contribution to the codification and harmonization of the private international law of contract and, as such, will not only provide a model for, or assistance in, similar activity in other jurisdictions, as with the drafting of the new Swiss Law on private international law,[77] but may also provide a

73 Nadelmann, (1977) 41 *Law and Contemporary Problems: Contemporary Perspectives in Conflict of Laws*, 54, 71.

74 *Actes et documents de la Treizième session* (1976), I, 159–164; Nadelmann (1977) 41 *Law and Contemporary Problems*, 65–9.

75 *Actes et documents de la Douzième session* (1972), I, 86.

76 Op cit, 65.

77 See *Contract Conflicts*, ch 12.

basis for future examination by the Hague Conference[78] of choice of law in contract. There is one further effect that adoption by the United Kingdom of the Rome Convention may have. The private international law rules relating to contract are similar, if not identical, throughout the common law world outside the United States.[79] The decisions of the English courts in international commercial matters have a significant influence in other common law jurisdictions. The implementation by the United Kingdom of the Rome Convention may lead to a divergence of approach between English rules of private international law on the one hand and rules as developed in countries like Australia and Canada on the other.[80] The more the English courts heed the exhortation in Article 18 to achieve uniformity in the interpretation and application of the rules in the Convention, the more likely is there to be a further growing closer together of the common law and civil law in Europe and the likelihood of differing common law approaches developing. One should not, however, exaggerate this possibility as many of the uniform rules in the Convention are rules which are to be found in the private international law of most, if not all, common law countries.

Consideration of the work of the Hague Conference in the field of obligations leads on to a further potential source of difficulty or conflict in the Rome Convention. The Convention not only gives precedence to other EEC instruments laying down choice of law rules,[81] but also states that the Convention is not to prejudice the application of any other international convention to which a Member State is a party, or wishes to become a party.[82] Conventions which obviously fall into this category are the various multilateral transport conventions. Also included, however, are all the Hague Conventions, the most significant of which in the present context is the 1955 Convention on the law applicable to international sales of goods.[83] The 1955 Convention is in force in four Member States of the EEC: Belgium, Denmark, France and Italy. Unless those countries denounce that Convention, it will remain in force there even when the

[78] See the Final Act of the Fourteenth Session of the Hague Conference (1980), Section E, para. 5.

[79] For an American view of the Rome Convention, see *Contract Conflicts*, ch 13.

[80] For an Australian view of the Rome Convention, see *Contract Conflicts*, ch 14; for Canada, see Blom, (1980) 18 *Can YB Int Law* 161, 200.

[81] Art. 20. An obviously relevant instrument would be the draft non-life insurance services Directive, discussed above, p. 37 (and see pp. 25–26). There have also been discussions on a draft regulation on choice of law in employment contracts (now withdrawn): see *Contract Conflicts*, ch 7.

[82] Art. 21. A special procedure of consultation is laid down in Art. 24 for a Member State wishing to become a party to a multilateral convention, one of whose principal aims is to lay down choice of law rules in contract. Such consultation is not necessary in the case of a Member State who is already a party to such a convention: Art. 24(2).

[83] Revision of this Convention is presently under consideration by the Hague Conference; see the Final Act of the Fourteenth Session (1980), Section B, and Section E, para. 1.

Rome Convention is implemented and, in those countries, it will take precedence over the Rome Convention. There is, therefore, a real danger that the harmonization objectives of the Rome Convention will be frustrated.[84] International sale of goods contracts provide the paradigm case of contracts involving the determination of the applicable law. Yet, in such a contract, with an English seller and a French buyer, the English courts would determine the applicable law by reference to the Rome Convention and the French courts by reference to the 1955 Hague Convention.

There is one final matter as to the scope of the Rome Convention which ought to be raised, namely accession to the Convention by third states. We have seen that it is hoped that new Member States of the EEC will accede to the Convention; but what of other non-EEC states such as Switzerland, Norway and Sweden? No provision is made in the Convention for such accession, because the various delegations could not agree on the desirability of so providing. If a third state sought to accede to the Convention, then there would need to be consultations on this issue between the Member States[85] and there might well be difficulties. Many of the provisions in the Rome Convention, especially those in Part III: 'Final Provisions', are drafted on the basis of the parties to the Convention being Member States of the EEC. Obvious problems would be created for a non-Member State by the precedence given in Article 20 to Community law. Similar problems would arise from jurisdiction over the interpretation of the Convention being conferred on the European Court of Justice. Perhaps the best way out of these difficulties might be for a third state which wished to adopt the rules of the Convention to do so by implementing the uniform rules of the Convention as part of its national law, though without formally acceding to the Convention.

So much for the opposition to or difficulties posed by the Rome Convention. The practical effects of the Convention for the English practitioner are discussed in detail elsewhere,[86] but suffice it to say here that implementation of the Convention in England involves little major change. Freedom to choose the applicable law is preserved. The law applicable in the absence of choice is that of the country with which the contract is most closely connected—the proper law approach. It is true that presumptions, recently ousted from the English choice of law rules, will re-appear but they are not likely significantly to affect the determination of the law applicable in any particular case—not even as regards the presumption relating to 'characteristic performance'. Special choice of law

[84] A further danger to the harmonized approach of the Convention is seen in Art. 23 which, with due consultation, permits a Member State to adopt a new choice of law rule with respect to any particular category of contract within the scope of the Convention.

[85] See Giuliano/Lagarde Report, [1980] OJ C282/41.

[86] *Contract Conflicts*, ch 9.

rules for consumer contracts are not going to have a great deal of effect in England because the rules deal with very limited classes of consumer contracts, few of which occur in England. Special rules for employment contracts may be of more practical significance. The decision by the United Kingdom Government to exercise its powers of reservation in regard to Article 7(1) and Article 10(1)(e) has the effect in the United Kingdom of removing from the Convention its most criticized aspect—the widespread application of foreign mandatory rules.

At the end of the day, the result of implementation of the Rome Convention in England will be that the choice of law rules in contract are put on a clear, firm, statutory basis. There will be no great substantial change in the rules which have worked well for a long period; but there will be the benefit of substantial harmonization throughout the EEC in an area of law of real significance for the free provision of goods and service within the Community.

3

Varying the Proper Law

INTRODUCTION

THERE is extensive discussion in this piece of the rules on variation of the applicable law to be found in a draft version of the European Community Convention on the law applicable to contractual obligations.[1] The Convention was finally concluded in Rome in 1980, implemented in this country by the Contracts (Applicable Law) Act 1990 and came into force on 1 April 1991.[2] The form in which it came into force was unchanged from the draft here discussed.[3]

The point is discussed, below,[4] that at common law it was not permitted to take into account conduct of the parties subsequent to the time of contracting in order to determine the proper law, in cases where no choice had been made by the parties;[5] though such conduct was relevant to the determination of whether there had been an agreement to vary the original contract. Under the Rome Convention the position would appear to be different. If there has been no choice of the governing law, that law is to be determined by reference to the closest connection test under Article 4(1). Assuming that the varied presumptions listed in Article 4[6] do not resolve the matter, reference may be made to an unrestricted range of factors in order to determine the country of closest connection. Furthermore, we are told that 'in order to determine the country with which the contract is most closely connected, it is also possible to take account of factors which supervened after the conclusion of the contract.'[7]

Reprinted from *Multum non Multa: Festschrift für Kurt Lipstein* (1980), 205–20, with the permission of C. F. Müller Juristischer Verlag GmbH.

[1] For further discussion of this issue, see Fletcher, *Conflict of Laws and European Community Law* (1982) 159–61; Diamond [1986] IV *Hague Recueil* 236, 262–4; and Plender, *The European Contracts Convention* (1991), paras. 5.15–5.20.

[2] Above, pp. 23–50.

[3] It should be noted, however, that in relation to Art. 7(1) (discussed below pp. 60–61) the United Kingdom exercised a power of reservation (in Art. 22(1)(a)) in relation to it: Contracts (Applicable Law) Act 1990, s. 2(2).

[4] p. 55.

[5] On which see also *Amin Rasheed Shipping Corporation* v. *Kuwait Insurance Co.* [1984] AC 50.

[6] Above, pp. 39–41.

[7] Giuliano and Lagarde Report on the Convention, [1980] OJ C282/20.

This development has, quite rightly, been criticized.[8] As a choice of law provision, its effect has been described as 'both inconvenient and unjust'.[9] Its defects are twofold. If later events are retrospectively to determine the law of the place of closest connection then this either means that the contract existed for a period with no governing law, which would undoubtedly be contrary to English common law analysis, or the original law of closest connection is varied by the introduction of later factors which may be the result of unilateral action by one of the parties. Neither situation if defensible.

A suggested alternative approach[10] is to characterize the issue of the admissibility of evidence of post-contractual conduct as one of interpretation, to be governed by the applicable law.[11] A number of problems arise, however, with this approach. Admissability of evidence is a matter of procedure, not of interpretation, and should, therefore, be governed by the law of the forum. Even if it is to be regarded as a matter of interpretation, the problem remains of deciding what is the applicable law whose rules are to govern the effect of post-contracting factors. We are told[12] that the issue is to be submitted to both or all 'the putative applicable laws', provided they agree on the admissability of such factors, but no effective solution is suggested where they do not so agree. A further underlying problem here is that, though admissability of evidence is not a choice of law issue governed by the Convention, the comment in the Giuliano and Lagarde Report is clearly directed at the interpretation of the choice of law provision in Article 4(1). The solution to the problem ought to be the direct one that, notwithstanding the official nature and force of the Report, it should not on this issue be followed.

* * *

[8] Lasok and Stone, *Conflict of Laws in the European Community* (1987), 363; Plender, *The European Contracts Convention* (1991), para. 6.04.

[9] Lasok and Stone, *Conflict of Laws*, 363.

[10] Plender, *The European Contracts Convention*, para. 6.04.

[11] Under Art. 10(1)(a).

[12] Plender, *The European Contracts Convention*, para. 6.04.

INTRODUCTION

In a paper delivered to the Ford 'Legal Workshop' in July 1976, the major theme of which was the draft EEC convention on the law applicable to contractual and non-contractual obligations,[1] Kurt Lipstein provided an illuminating analysis of the main characteristics of that convention.[2] In the course of his discussion of the contract choice of law rules in the draft convention, Lipstein adverted to the question whether a choice of the proper law may be made after the time of conclusion of the contract.[3] This is an issue discussion of which is beginning to appear in the common law world,[4] but which has figured in continental literature[5] and judgments[6] for a considerable time, and it is with this issue that this essay is primarily concerned.

There seems little doubt that recent interest in the question of the variation of the applicable law has been generated by the fact that this issue is dealt with specifically in the draft obligations convention.[7] There are two different problems to be addressed when considering variation of the proper law. The first is whether it is, or ought to be, possible to alter the law applicable to a contract once that contract has been concluded. The second is to decide by what law the validity of any later choice of the applicable law should be governed, whether for example it falls to be determined by the law which already governs the contract or by the newly chosen applicable law. A related issue is whether this whole problem is to be classified as a matter of substantive contract law, and thus, presumably, to be governed by the appropriate contract law rules of one of the proper laws, or as a matter of private international law governed by the appropriate rules of the *lex fori*.

[1] The draft convention has since been limited to contractual obligations.

[2] *Harmonization of Private International Law by the EEC*, ed. Lipstein (1978), 1–14; and see Lipstein, in *European Private International Law of Obligations*, ed. Lando, von Hoffman, and Siehr (1975), 155–164 (hereafter cited as *EPILO*).

[3] Ibid., at 7; and in *EPILO* at 158.

[4] Perhaps it would be more accurate to say 'in the literature written in English'; see Dicey and Morris, *The Conflict of Laws*, 9th edn. (1975), 726–7; Lando (1974) 38 *RabelsZ* 6, 25–6; Kahn-Freund [1974] III *Hague Recueil* 147, 402–3; Diamond [1979] *Current Legal Problems* 155, 162–5; Lew, *Applicable Law in International Commercial Arbitration* (1978), 159–63.

[5] E.g. Tomaszewski, [1972] *Rev crit dr int pr* 567; Skapski, [1972] *Hague Recueil* 499, 539–41.

[6] E.g. Cass. Civ. 18 Nov. 1959, *Rev crit dr int pr* 1960, 83; Corte Suprema Cass. 28 June 1966, No. 1680, *Riv dir int priv proc* 1967, 126.

[7] Art. 3(2).

IS THERE FREEDOM TO CHOOSE A NEW APPLICABLE LAW?

The answer to this question as far as the law of the different parts of the United Kingdom and of the other Member States of the EEC is concerned will be easy to find when the draft obligations convention comes into force. The convention provides that 'a contract shall be governed by the law chosen by the parties',[8] but Article 3(2) goes on to stipulate that:

> The parties may at any time agree to subject the contract to a law other than that which previously governed it, whether as a result of an earlier choice under this Article or of other provisions of this Convention. Any variation by the parties of the law to be applied made after the conclusion of the contract shall not . . . adversely affect the rights of third parties.

So, once the United Kingdom has accepted and implemented the draft obligations convention, Article 3(2) will become a rule of English private international law and it would permit the parties to change the applicable law, whether the law already applicable had been chosen or had been determined under the rules of Article 4 of the draft convention for deciding the applicable law in the absence of choice. However, a later variation of the applicable law must be by choice of the parties under Article 3; it cannot be achieved by a post-contractual variation of the factors which lead to the determination of the 'proper law' under Article 4.

A brief examination of Article 3 raises a further series of questions, at least for an English lawyer. How far does it represent existing English common law rules of private international law? Is it desirable to admit of a power to vary the proper law such as is contained in Article 3? Should the question of the freedom to vary the applicable law be submitted to the private international law rules of the forum or should this power to vary be determined by the law already applicable to the contract? If the applicable law is later varied, does the new proper law apply retrospectively to the date of the creation of the contract? If so, then how should the rights of third parties be treated? All these questions will be considered in turn.

Present English law on varying the proper law

The fundamental propositions from which any analysis of the present English common law rules on varying the proper law must begin are that

1. the proper law of a contract, whether chosen or not, is determined as at the date of making the contract;[9]

[8] Art. 3(1). [9] *Rossano* v. *Manufacturers' Life Insurance Co.* [1963] 2 QB 352, 362.

2. the courts will give effect to any changes in the proper law occurring between the date of contracting and the date of performance;[10]
3. the conduct of the parties subsequent to the time of contracting may not be taken into account in determining the proper law;[11]
4. the conduct of the parties subsequent to the time of contracting may be taken into account in order to determine whether the parties have agreed to vary their original contract by a subsequent agreement,[12] whether they have entered into a collateral contract[13] or whether their later conduct amounts to an estoppel;[14]
5. the parties may, at any time during the running of a contract, agree that the contract should be discharged and replaced by a new contract governed by a new proper law.[15]

What seems to emerge from the case law, though this is mainly dicta, is that there is no reason why the parties to a contract should not agree that the law governing the contract whether or not expressly chosen should not be varied by what amounts, in effect, to the discharge of one contract and its replacement by a new contract governed by the new proper law. This situation can best be illustrated by *Kremezi* v. *Ridgway*[16] where there appears to have been a discharge of the first contract and its replacement by a later contract. A British naval officer entered into an agreement in Greece to marry a Greek girl resident in Athens. This contract was later made again in England 'with the intention that the new contract should be a solemn substitution for any previous contract between the parties'.[17] In an action by the girl for breach of promise of marriage, the court accepted that the first contract had been replaced by the later contract in England and sought merely to determine the proper law of the later contract. There was no decision as to the proper law of

[10] *Re Chesterman's Trust* [1923] 2 Ch 466, 478; *Re Helbert Wagg & Co. Ltd.'s Claim* [1956] Ch 323, 341–2; *Rossano* v. *Manufacturers' Life Insurance Co.*, above, 362; and see Dicey and Morris, *The Conflict of Laws*, 9th edn. (1973), 46–7.

[11] *James Miller & Partners Ltd.* v. *Whitworth Street Estates (Manchester) Ltd.* [1970] AC 583, 603, 606, 611; *Compagnie d'Armement Maritime SA* v. *Compagnie Tunisienne de Navigation SA* [1971] AC 572, 593, 602–3; *Wickman Machine Tool Sales Ltd.* v. *Schuler AG* [1974] AC 235, 252, 265–70, 272.

[12] *James Miller & Partners Ltd.* v. *Whitworth Street Estates (Manchester) Ltd.*, above, 603, 614–15; *Compagnie d'Armement Maritime SA* v. *Compagnie Tunisienne de Navigation SA*, above, 602–3.

[13] *Compagnie d'Armement Maritime SA* v. *Compagnie Tunisienne de Navigation SA*, above, 602–3.

[14] *James Miller & Partners Ltd.* v. *Whitworth Street Estates (Manchester) Ltd.*, above, 611, 614–15.

[15] *Duke of Marlborough* v. *Attorney-General* [1945] Ch 78, 85; *Iveagh* v. *Inland Revenue Commissioners* [1954] Ch 364, 370; and see *Kremezi* v. *Ridgway* [1949] 1 All ER 662.

[16] [1949] 1 All ER 662.

[17] Ibid., 663.

the first contract or as to whether by that law a new contract, subject perhaps to a new proper law, could be substituted.[18]

There appears to be no direct authority on whether the parties may vary the proper law, not by discharging the old contract and creating a new one, but by allowing the original contract to continue in force governed by a new proper law. The clearest statement in favour of allowing the parties to vary the proper law in such a way is to be found in the words of Lord Reid when considering the extent to which the court may have regard to the conduct of the parties after the making of the contract as a means of determining the proper law.

> It has been assumed in the course of this case that it is proper, in determining what was the proper law, to have regard to actings of the parties after their contract had been made. Of course the actings of the parties (including any words which they used) may be sufficient to show that they made a new contract. *If they made no agreement originally as to the proper law, such actions may show that they made an agreement about that at a later stage. Or if they did make an agreement originally such actings may show that they later agreed to alter it.*[19]

Whilst the dictum gives a clear indication that parties may choose a proper law for the first time after the date of the contract or may vary an earlier chosen proper law,[20] no positive indication is given as to what law determines whether the parties have this freedom so to vary the proper law. Nevertheless it seems to be implicit in Lord Reid's statement that he was referring to a rule of English law as being the private international law of the forum.[21] Indeed, it is a truism to state that English courts always apply their own rules of private international law even in a case of *renvoi*, for such a reference to the private international law of another country is, itself, made under a rule of English private international law.

An alternative approach to the question of varying the proper law which may be found in English legal writing, though apparently unsupported by legal decisions, is that propounded by Wolff[22] and supported by Mann.[23] On this approach, it is suggested, first of all, that English law does permit the parties to vary the proper law but the authority cited in support of that proposition (which may well be correct) is *Kremezi* v. *Ridgway* which, as we have seen,[24] is a case concerned with the discharge of one contract and the substitution of a new one, rather than a true variation of the proper law. Second, and more important, Wolff and

[18] In this case there was no choice by the parties of the proper law to govern either contract.

[19] *James Miller & Partners Ltd.* v. *Whitworth Street Estates (Manchester) Ltd.* [1970[AC 583, 603 (italics added).

[20] See also *Fattorini* v. *Johannesburg Board of Executors & Trust Co. Ltd.* 1948 (4) SA 806, 812–13.

[21] This approach is supported by Kahn-Freund, [1974] III *Hague Recueil* 147, 402.

[22] *Private International Law*, 2nd edn. (1950), para. 408.

[23] (1954) 31 *BYBIL* 222, n. 2.

[24] Above, p. 55.

Mann agree that the question whether the parties are to be regarded as free to vary the proper law is to be determined, not by the private international law rules of the forum, but 'by the law . . . which first governed the contract.'[25] However, no justification for this conclusion is provided.

Variation of the proper law in other jurisdictions.[26]

Not only do other countries permit the courts to take post-contractual conduct into account in interpreting the contract, including the determination of the applicable law,[27] but many countries permit a variation of the proper law during the currency of the contract. There seems little doubt that, in practice, the parties can always choose the *lex fori* as the applicable law by ignoring any foreign elements at the time of the proceedings. The court will apply the *lex fori* if no other law is pleaded. Indeed, even if there is an express choice in the contract, this will in practice be ignored if the parties proceed on the basis of forum law being applied.[28] Furthermore, and perhaps inevitably, a number of civil law countries permit an express choice of forum law to be made at any time after contracting, right up to and including the time of the proceedings.[29]

There would appear to be a problem in those jurisdictions, such as Germany, where the judge is under an obligation to act, of his own motion, to determine the applicable foreign law,[30] especially where there is a choice of law clause. Nevertheless, even here, there is an acceptance of freedom tacitly to choose the applicable law at the time of the proceedings merely by ignoring the foreign law and referring only to the *lex fori*.[31] However, courts in Germany are prepared to go further than this and permit an express choice of the applicable law at any time after contracting, notwithstanding that the applicable law may already be

[25] Wolff, *Private International Law*, para. 408; and see Diamond, [1979] *Current Legal Problems* 155, 165.

[26] For a full discussion see Tomaszewski, [1972] *Rev crit dr int pr* 567, especially 570–88; Lando, *International Encyclopedia of Comparative Law*, Vol. III: Private International Law, ch 24 – Contracts, 51–2 (hereafter cited as *Encyclopedia*); Giuliano, *Rapport concernant l'avant-project de convention sur la loi applicable aux obligations contractuelles et noncontractuelles*, EEC Document Nos. xiv/408/72 and xiv/579/71, 40–1 (reproduced in *EPILO* 241 *et seq*; *Riv dir int priv proc* 1973, 198 *et seq*) (hereafter cited as Giuliano, *Report*); see also Kahn-Freund [1974] III *Hague Recueil* 147, 403.

[27] See Mann, (1973) 89 *LQR* 464.

[28] Lando, *Encyclopedia*, 51.

[29] See e.g. Cass. Civ. 18 Nov. 1959, Rev. 1960, 83; for France, see further Batiffol, *Droit International Privé*, 6th edn. (1976), ii, paras. 573, 592; for Germany, see Drobnig, *American-German Private International Law*, 2nd edn. (1972), 228.

[30] Kahn-Freund [1974] III *Hague Recueil* 147, 261.

[31] Melchior, *Grundlagen*, (1932) para. 283, p. 240; Drobnig, *American-German Private International Law*, 229–30; Lando, *Encyclopedia*, 51–2.

determined by an express choice of the parties.[32] A similar approach is to be seen in the Scandinavian countries, namely, that the parties may choose a new applicable law subsequent to the time of contracting.[33] Again, under Swiss law, it is possible for the applicable law to be varied after the completion of the contract.[34]

A major exception to the general rule allowing variation of the applicable law is found in the decision of the Italian Court of Cassation in the case of *Assael Nissim* v. *Crespi*[35] where it was held that choice of the applicable law by the parties was not permitted once the contract had been concluded. The choice of the proper law could only be made at the time of contracting.[36]

The desirability of freedom to vary the proper law

Leaving aside the issue by what law freedom to vary the proper law should be determined, there is a preliminary fundamental issue of policy to be faced, namely whether freedom to vary the proper law ought to be accepted. If one starts from a basic principle of freedom of contract, including party autonomy in the sense of freedom to choose the proper law, then freedom to vary, as well as initially to choose, the proper law appears equally acceptable from a theoretical point of view. It may be subject to the same limitations as condition a freedom to choose the applicable law at the time of contracting but, subject to that, freedom to vary the proper law is but another aspect of freedom to contract. If parties are free to terminate a contract by agreement, they should also be free to continue the contract though subject to a different legal system. There is, indeed, a further practical argument in favour of such freedom. Initial choice of the applicable law is often made in the interests of commercial certainty. The reason for a later choice, especially where there has been no initial choice, may well be for just the same reasons.

Kahn-Freund has suggested[37] that, logically, there should be no freedom to vary the proper law though logic and even practical arguments must yield to the 'overwhelming requirements of procedure'. What are the practical and procedural arguments to be weighed in the balance? In favour of the immutability of the original proper law is the conceptual argument, rejected by Kahn-Freund[38] as being unfashionable, that a con-

[32] Nussbaum, *Deutsches Internationales Privatrecht*, (1932) 250; Drobnig, *American-German Private International Law*, 230.
[33] Lando, *Encyclopedia*, 52.
[34] Ibid.; and see Kahn-Freund [1974] III *Hague Recueil* 147, 403.
[35] 28 June 1966, *Riv dir int priv proc* 1967, 126.
[36] For criticism of this rule, see Treves, [1967] *Riv dir int priv proc* 315.
[37] [1974] III *Hague Recueil* 147, 402–3.
[38] Ibid., 402.

tractual obligation cannot exist in more than one legal system either simultaneously or consecutively. However, even this conceptual argument depends for its force on the effect of a later choice. If this amounts to the discharge of the old contract and the creation of a new one, there is no conceptual difficulty. The problem only arises if one assumes a continuing contractual obligation with a content which varies with the law applicable to it and only if the change of proper law does not have retrospective effect under the relevant legal systems.[39]

A practical argument against variation is that the applicable law determines validity.[40] If a contract is invalid under its original applicable law, can it be validated by a later choice or vice versa? Again, this poses no problem where there are in reality two contracts, the change in the proper law involving a form of novation.[41] Even in the case where the contract remains in existence but only the applicable law is varied, it should be emphasized that the problem of change from validity to invalidity or vice versa may well be more apparent than real. If the original contract is invalid under its proper law, there is in law no contract. The choice of a new proper law creates a contract for the first time leaving the parties free to extend its operation, as a term of the new contract, to the time when the old 'contract' was in operation. In the converse case of a valid contract apparently invalidated by the choice of a new proper law, the old contract may never be altered. If the efficacy of the choice of the new applicable law is to be determined by that newly chosen law itself, there has been no valid choice and so no change in the law applicable to the original contract whose validity is unaffected.

Whether the validity of a choice of law is to be determined by the law chosen is a controversial matter. A variety of alternative solutions have been offered[42] ranging from the law of the forum,[43] the most appropriate law in the discretion of the court,[44] and the law which would be applied in the absence of choice.[45] Nevertheless, although the 'bootstrap' rule of

[39] Retrospectively is discussed below, pp. 64–66.

[40] Kahn-Freund [1974] III *Hague Recueil* 147, 402–3.

[41] Undoubtedly, a significant practical problem relating to a change from validity to invalidity concerns acquired rights and the position of third parties but this is considered separately, see below, pp. 66–67.

[42] Lando, *Encyclopedia*, 44–6; Lipstein (ed.) *Harmonisation of Private International Law in the EEC*, (1978) 56; Lando (1974) 38 *RabelsZ* 6, 22–4; Collins (1976) 25 *ICLQ* 35, 52–3.

[43] This is the view adopted in Italy: Giuliano, *Report* 26, and which has been applied in Germany: RG 20 Feb. 1929, and in France: Cass civ 7 July 1954, *Rev crit dr int pr* 1955, 129. See also Jaffey, (1975) 24 *ICLQ* 603, 604–6.

[44] German courts have taken this view: RG 3 Feb. 1933; BGH 29 Nov. 1961; and it can also be supported by *Fricke* v. *Isbrandtsen Co.*, 152 F Supp 465 (1957).

[45] Cheshire and North *Private International Law*, 10th edn. (1979), 216. Whether it is correct to describe this approach as involving the 'putative proper law' or whether that term should be reserved for the application of the 'law which would be the proper law of the contract if the contract was validly concluded' (Dicey and Morris, *The Conflict of Laws*, 9th

applying the law chosen by the parties to determine the validity of that choice can be attacked on the ground of logic and of impracticability if each party purports to choose a different law[46] and has been much criticized,[47] it is the rule which is now to be found in the draft EEC obligations convention[48] and can be justified on the grounds of simplicity and certainty.[49]

A further argument which has been put forward against permitting a variation of the applicable law is that to do so may allow limitations on the freedom to choose the applicable law to be avoided and, indeed, it has been suggested[50] that the limitations on freedom of choice in employment contracts laid down in the draft EEC obligations convention[51] are such that freedom to vary the proper law ought not to apply to employment contracts. This argument seems to be misconceived. A rule limiting initial freedom of choice is part of the private international law of the forum; a rule permitting variation of the applicable law is, it is submitted, a private international law rule of the forum. There is no reason why the limitations on an initial choice of the applicable law should not apply equally to a later choice.[52]

It has also been suggested[53] that the variation of the proper law as permitted by Article 3(2) of the draft EEC obligations convention may allow evasion of the mandatory rules of the already applicable law. It is not easy to identify any real problem here. Let us assume that, in the absence of choice, a contract will be governed by the law of State A as the proper law. That law may contain mandatory rules applicable to the contract in question. If the parties, at the time of contracting, choose the law of State B to govern their contract, the mandatory rules of State A will not apply unless, where England is the forum, the English court strikes down the choice of law clause as not being 'bona fide and legal'[54] or as evasive.[55] Similarly, under the draft EEC obligations convention, Article

edn. (1973), 763) including the chosen law is probably no more than a matter of semantics. However, the criticism of the approach in Cheshire and North, (10th edn.) made by Libling, (1979) 42 *MLR* 169, 170 is far wide of the mark for it ignores the considerable controversy over the law to be applied to determine the validity of a choice of law clause. See also Siesby, *EPILO* 206, 208.

46 See RG 10 Feb. 1929, discussed by Lando, (1974) 38 *RabelsZ* 6, 23–4.

47 Cavers, (1975) 48 *So Cal LR* 603, 609–11; Nadelmann, (1976) 24 *Am Jo Comp L* 1, 8–9; and see Jaffey, (1975) 24 *ICLQ* 603, 604–5.

48 Arts. 3(4), 8(1), 9(3).

49 Vischer, [1974] II *Hague Recueil* 1, 46; and see Lando, (1974) 38 *RabelsZ* 6, 23.

50 Hoyer, *EPILO* 114, 116.

51 Art. 6.

52 See von Hoffman, *EPILO* 1, 6; and see Lando, (1974) 38 *RabelsZ* 6, 26; Vischer, [1974] II *Hague Recueil* 1, 48–9.

53 Collins, (1976) 25 *ICLQ* 35, 43–4; but cf. Tomaszewski, [1972] *Rev crit dr int pr* 567, 593–4.

54 *Vita Food Products Inc.* v. *Unus Shipping Co. Ltd.* [1939] AC 277, 290.

55 See, e.g., Unfair Contract Terms Act 1977, s. 27(2)(a).

7(1) would render it possible for the mandatory rules of State A to be applied by the English court. If the choice of the applicable law is made after the time of contracting, the same controls on such a choice will apply as if it were an initial choice, and that must be correct. But surely no further controls are necessary. What merit can there be in allowing parties, with foresight, to avoid the application of the law of State A by an initial choice of law clause, but to prevent them from doing so by a later post-contracting clause, bearing in mind that the parties could always agree to discharge the contract governed by the law of State A and enter a new one governed by the law of State B? If the parties are free to renegotiate their whole agreement, including the choice of law clause, they should equally be free to renegotiate the latter alone.[56]

In favour of freedom to vary the applicable law are not only the arguments based on the general desirability of party autonomy and commercial convenience, already mentioned,[57] but the further argument that in practice, in many legal systems, it is possible to achieve a variation as a matter of procedure.[58] In English law, notwithstanding the international aspects of a case, the court will apply English law, as the *lex fori*, to any dispute unless one party refers to another law.[59] Even if there is an express choice of law clause, that chosen foreign law will be assumed to be the same as English law unless there is some proof of the foreign rule. By such a conspiracy of silence the parties can, at the stage of litigation, effectively vary the applicable law notwithstanding any legal prohibition. Not only is this device possible under common law systems of private international law where foreign law is a matter of evidence and proof by the parties but also even in those civil law systems under which the judge is obliged, of his own motion, to consider the applicability of foreign law. This certainly seems to be the position in Germany,[60] provided the parties have pleaded the rules of the *lex fori*. If there is no allegation by the parties as to the applicable law, then it appears that the court must investigate the applicability of foreign law unless the court can deduce that the parties have agreed, even at the late stage of actual litigation, to refer the issue to the *lex fori*.[61]

[56] See Lipstein (ed.) *Harmonisation of Private International Law by the E.E.C.* (1978) 1, 7.
[57] Above, p. 58.
[58] See Kahn-Freund, [1974] III *Hague Recueil* 147, 403; Lando, *Encyclopedia*, 52–3; and see above, p. 57.
[59] Cheshire and North, *Private International Law*, 10th edn. (1979), ch v.
[60] See above, p. 57.
[61] See Lando, *Encyclopedia*, 53; Giuliano, *Report*, 30.

THE LAW TO GOVERN VARIATION OF THE APPLICABLE LAW

If one assume that the argument in principle has been made out for permitting the parties to vary the applicable law by the choice of a new proper law subsequent to the time of contracting, a further important question with two subsidiary issues remains for consideration. The main question is that of determining by which law the power to vary the applicable law should be governed. The subsidiary issues concern the retrospectivity of any variation and its effect on third parties. All three questions will be examined in turn.

What law should govern the variation of the applicable law?

There seem to be two, or perhaps three, possible answers to this question.[62] One could say that whether the parties are free to vary the proper law is itself a matter of choice of law and thus an issue for the private international law rules of the forum; or one could classify the issue as relating to a variation of the terms and effect of a contract already in existence and thus to be governed by the substantive contractual rules of the already applicable proper law or, possibly, of the proper law to be applied if the choice of a new law is to be permitted.[63]

These different solutions can all muster arguments in their support. The law already applicable to the contract prior to the purported variation of the proper law may well have rules of substantive contract law regulating the rights of the parties to vary, or even to discharge, their contractual obligations. It cannot be doubted that the choice of a new proper law may well have the effect of varying the existing rights and duties of the parties and might, in an extreme case, have the effect of rendering the contract void and thus, in effect, of discharging the contractual obligations. These are matters of substantive law governing rights which already exist under the contract and their variation should be a matter for the law already governing such substantive rights, so the argument runs. One might ask, however, whether there is any real danger or difficulty in ignoring the controls on variation under the already applicable law. Undoubtedly, the issues of retrospectivity and the need to protect the rights of third parties merit examination.[64] Apart from that, the parties are being permitted to agree that another law is to be applied. They

[62] See Tomaszewski, [1972] *Rev crit dr int pr*, 567, 595–6.
[63] On the analogy of the 'bootstrap' rule applicable to the validity of a choice of the proper law, see above, pp. 59–60.
[64] See below, pp. 64–67.

can, thereby, avoid the substantive law of the existing proper law. However, their agreement must itself be valid—though this then raises the question: by what law is the validity to be determined?[65] The main choice is between the existing proper law and its rules as to agreement or the 'bootstrap' approach of the draft obligations convention[66] which refers the validity of choice to the chosen law. If this requirement is satisfied, there would appear to be no more of a policy objection to choice of a law to vary the contract than to an initial choice of the applicable law, thereby ousting the proper law which would have been applicable in the absence of choice.

The other main approach is to say that choice of the applicable law after the date of contracting is not to be characterized as an issue of substantive law governing the variation of contractual rights but is rather an issue of private international law concerning party autonomy in choice of law.[67] On that basis, the issue falls to be determined as a private international law issue governed by the private international law of the forum. It might be argued that that leads to uncertainty—whether the parties are free to vary the applicable law, and thus their contractual rights and duties, will depend on the forum in which the issue is litigated. On reflection, this argument has no greater force in the context of variation of the applicable law than it has in considering the availability of an initial choice or even the determination of the law to be applied in the absence of choice. If the parties have not expressed a choice as to the governing law, their rights and duties under the contract will, at the end of the day, depend on the identification of the proper law by the private international law rules of whichever country becomes the forum for the litigation.

An overwhelming argument in favour of characterizing the issue of varying the proper law as an issue of private international law governed by the *lex fori* is to be found in a pragmatic consideration: namely, the reason why the parties may have sought variation. This may well be because the original applicable law is either uncertain in operation or difficult even to identify. The reason for the agreed choice by commercial men of a new applicable law is frequently to avoid these uncertainties. It would wholly defeat this laudable objective if the parties were to be told that whether they may choose a new applicable law is to be governed by the original governing law when the whole purpose of the exercise is to avoid the problem of deciding what law did originally govern.

There is a further practical consideration which operates even where

[65] Discussed above, pp. 59–60.

[66] Arts. 3(4), 8(1), 9(3).

[67] Kahn-Freund, in [1974] II *Hague Recueil* 147, 402, regards it as obvious that the issue is one of choice of law for the *lex fori*.

the original governing law has been determined by an express choice of the parties. The parties may discover that the substantive rules of this governing law have an effect different from that originally contemplated by them. For example, that law may prohibit, or require, the creation of various obligations under the contract. In order to avoid these consequences the parties can always agree to discharge their obligations, terminate the contract, and then enter into a new contract governed by what they regard as a 'more suitable' proper law. If they can do that by way of discharge it would seem to be merely obstructive to prevent them from achieving the same result by way of agreement to vary the proper law. We have also seen[68] that the parties may well be able to achieve the practical result of varying the applicable law in favour of the *lex fori* by failing to plead the proper law. If they can, indirectly, achieve this end by a procedural subterfuge, there is much to be said for accepting that they have done so directly by means of the choice of law rules of the forum.

A further advantage of applying the private international law rules of the *lex fori* to the question of variation is that such an approach avoids difficulties of classification if the already applicable law, or even the newly chosen law, is applied. It has been assumed so far that if the applicable law is to govern variation this is because variation is a matter relating to the substance of the contract. It cannot be denied that substantive contract law may well contain specific rules as to how and when a contract may be varied.[69] However, this substantive law is most unlikely to have rules to deal with variation by choice of a new applicable law, for choice of the applicable law is generally regarded as an issue of private international law. So the effect of variation being regarded as a substantive issue may well, in practice, result in the forum being required to apply the rules of private international law of the country of the applicable law. This seems to amount almost to a form of *renvoi* and English law,[70] along with that of other legal systems,[71] has denied *renvoi* any place in the field of contract.

Retrospectivity[72]

The question whether a variation of the applicable law should have retrospective effect is one on which views are divided, though rarely are reasons given for the views expressed. Where the effect of variation of the

[68] Above, p. 57.
[69] See, e.g., Chitty, *Contracts*, 24th edn. (1977), i: 1376–80.
[70] *Re United Railways of the Havana and Regla Warehouses, Ltd.* [1960] Ch 52, 96–7, 115.
[71] See the draft obligations convention, Art. 15.
[72] See Tomaszewski, [1972] *Rev crit dr int pr* 567, 596–8.

proper law is that the contract governed by the original proper law is discharged and replaced by a new contract with a new proper law, there can be little doubt that the new contract is not automatically retrospective in effect. It may, however, be the case that the parties agree that the new contract should apply to events occurring before the novation. Where there is no discharge, but the original contract continues in force though subject to a new proper law, the German courts seem prepared only to give the change prospective effect,[73] a view shared by some writers.[74] However, Article 3(2) of the draft EEC obligations convention, which allows the parties to vary the proper law, contains no ban on retrospectivity and commentators seem generally to accept the correctness of such an approach.[75]

The major problem with retrospectivity is the position of third parties;[76] but subject to that, it seems desirable in many ways that change of the applicable law should relate back to the creation of the contract. An obvious reason is that the new proper law might invalidate the contract by, for example, rendering one party incapable or the transaction illegal. It would be unfortunate if such invalidity were to take effect only from the date of variation because the contract would be valid up to that date but at an end thereafter without any means of regulating the respective positions of the parties as at the time of variation. Such a position would then evidence all the disadvantages of the effects of the English doctrine of frustration of contracts prior to their amelioration in 1943.[77]

In many cases the effect of varying the proper law will have a less dramatic effect on the rights and duties of the parties. Nevertheless, it could be the case that one party acted prior to variation in a way which, under the law then applicable, amounted to complete performance but which under the new applicable law was not sufficient. However, variation of the proper law requires agreement and in such a case there is no reason why at the same time as agreeing to vary the proper law, the parties should not also reach agreement on the effects that such variation is to have on earlier contractual acts.

The most powerful argument in favour of the change of proper law having retrospective effect is, once again, a pragmatic argument. If the parties have, at some time after the commencement of the contract, decided to make a choice of the applicable law, the reason for their

[73] Nussbaum, *Deutsches Internationales Privatrecht*, (1932), 250; and see Kahn-Freund, [1974] III *Hague Recueil* 147, 403.

[74] Wolff, *Private International Law*, 2nd edn. (1950), para. 408.

[75] See Lando, (1974) 38 *RabelsZ* 6, 26; and in *Encyclopedia*, 52; and see the analysis of views in Tomaszewski, [1972] *Rev crit dr int pr* 567, 597–8; see also Mann, (1954) 31 *BYBIL* 217, 222, n. 2.

[76] Discussed, below pp. 66–67.

[77] Law Reform (Frustrated Contracts) Act 1943.

choice is likely to lie in their desire to avoid uncertainty as to what law governs their contract. This desire for certainty evidenced by their choice of the applicable law is frustrated if the parties are to be told that their choice is only to have prospective effect, for they will then have to determine the original proper law which would govern all matters relating to the creation of the contract and contractual conduct up to the moment of variation. Businessmen might well then take the view that the freedom to vary the applicable law is of little value.[78]

Position of third parties

There seems little doubt that, if variation of the proper law is to be permitted with retrospective effect, then special provision must be made for the rights of third parties such as is to be found in Article 3(2) of the draft EEC obligations convention: 'Any variation by the parties of the law to be applied made after the conclusion of the contract shall not adversely affect the rights of third parties.'

This provision has been described as 'novel but acceptable',[79] and has met with general approval.[80] Various examples have been given of situations when a third party might have acquired rights under the contract prior to the variation of the proper law,[81] such as where the original law governing an insurance contract conferred a right on a third party beneficiary irrevocable under that law but not under the new proper law[82] or where a third party has garnished or has a charge over a claim valid under the original, but not the new, proper law.[83]

It has been pointed out by Tomaszewski[84] that the theoretical justification for the view that third parties should be unaffected by a change in the applicable law is not particularly easy to find. It cannot be based on any theory of acquired rights except in a most forced way. This is because the variation of the proper law ought to leave unaffected both

[78] One argument that has been advanced is that, in those jurisdictions which reject dépeçage, retrospectivity is a logical and perhaps necessary consequence: see Tomaszewski, [1972] *Rev crit dr int pr* 567, 596–7; Vischer, *Internationales Vertragsrecht* (1962), 84. This does not seem necessarily to follow. Rejection of the idea that different aspects of a contract may from the outset be governed by different laws does not inevitably lead to the conclusion that a single element of the contract cannot be governed by different laws at different times.

[79] Lipstein, *EPILO*, 155, 158; and see von Hoffman, *EPILO* 1, 6.

[80] E.g., Lando, (1974) 38 *RabelsZ* 6, 26, and in *Encyclopedia*, 52; and see the authorities cited by Tomaszewski, [1972] *Rev crit dr int pr* 567, 599 n. 1; cf. Collins, (1976) 25 *ICLQ* 35, 44.

[81] See Tomaszewski, [1972] *Rev crit dr int pr* 567, 598–9.

[82] Lando, (1974) 38 *RabelsZ* 6, 26, citing Vischer, *Internationales Vertragsrecht* (1962), 84.

[83] Lipstein, *EPILO* 155, 158.

[84] Tomaszewski, [1972] *Rev crit dr int pr* 567, 599–600.

the rights and obligations of third parties.[85] Tomaszewski's argument, that the interests of a third party fall to be regulated by the law governing his relationship with the party, or parties, to the main contract, irrespective of any change in the law governing the main contract, must be right. This is undoubtedly the view accepted by English law in the analogous case of the assignment of a debt where the assignment by the creditor to a third party is governed by the proper law of the assignment but the obligations of the debtor to the third party remain subject to the proper law of the original debt;[86] and this general approach has found acceptance in the draft EEC obligations convention.[87]

[85] Can one say that a third party can acquire a right not to have his obligations increased? If not, then Art. 3(2) of the draft EEC obligations convention may be a little limited in scope, in that it does not refer to third party obligations.

[86] Cheshire and North, *Private International Law*, 10th edn. (1979), 536–48.

[87] Art. 12.

4

Torts in the Dismal Swamp: Choice of Law Revisited

INTRODUCTION

RECENT developments,[1] of which two are worthy of comment, in the field of choice of law in tort have been concentrated in the judicial field. Law reform agencies' proposals for reform have not progressed further than outlined below. A final report on choice of law is still awaited from the Australian Law Reform Commission,[2] and there has been no public indication of whether the government intends to implement, with or without modifications, the Report of the Law Commissions on Choice of Law in Tort and Delict.[3] One, however, of the recent judicial developments is English, the other Australian.

The existence of a flexible exception to the double-barrelled tort choice of law requiring actionability both by the law of the place of the tort and of the forum[4] has been confirmed in *Johnson* v. *Coventry Churchill International Ltd.*[5] The plaintiff was an English carpenter employed (in answer to an English newspaper advertisement) by an English employment agency to work in Germany under what was held to be a contract of service. The plaintiff was injured whilst working on a German building site. The defendants' conduct was in breach of their English law obligation to provide a safe system of work but was not in breach of German law as their conduct was not wilful. Under the double actionability rule, the plaintiff's claim would fail unless one head of the rule was to be ignored. The court decided that the absence of actionability under German law could be ignored with the result that English law, that of the forum, was to be applied, enabling the plaintiff to recover. Although this decision provides a further example of a homeward trend to the law of

Reprinted with the permission of the Northern Ireland Legal Quarterly from (1991) 42 *N Ireland LQ* 183–98, the 1991 MacDermott Lecture, delivered on 25 April 1991 at the Queen's University of Belfast.

[1] For a recent wide-ranging review of tort choice of law rules, see Pryles, [1991] II *Hague Recueil* 9. At 108 he supports the criticisms made, below pp. 85–88, of the Law Commissions' proposals for torts committed in the United Kingdom.

[2] Below, p. 81. [3] Law Com. No. 193 (1990), below, pp. 83–88.

[4] See *Boys* v. *Chaplin* [1971] AC 356. [5] [1992] 3 All ER 14.

the forum,[6] it does so in circumstances where the result seems quite acceptable. Indeed, had the claim been formulated in contract, rather than in tort, the outcome would, in the absence of an express choice of law clause, appear to have been the same; furthermore, the case seems so clear cut as to fall easily within the exception proposed by the Law Commisions to the rule that the law of the place of injury should govern.[7]

The second major judicial development consists of an attempt by the High Court of Australia to bring some order to the choice of law confusion stemming from its own decision in *Breavington* v. *Godleman*,[8] where the Court reached the result of applying the law of the place of the tort by no fewer than five different routes.[9] In the more recent decision in *McKain* v. *R. W. Miller & Co. (South Australia) Pty. Ltd.*[10] a claim in New South Wales for injuries suffered in South Australia, which claim was time-barred in South Australia but not in New South Wales, was held to fail. In rejecting this claim, a majority also rejected the idea (acceptable to the other three judges) that reference should solely be made to the law of the place where the tort was committed. Instead, for torts committed in Australia, the double actionability rule was confirmed, without the possibility of any flexible exception. No further clear guidance was given by the Court in the case of torts committed outside Australia. The outcome is an unreasonably rigid rule for Australian torts and an undesirable uncertainty as to the law to govern foreign torts. This can but strength the need for legislative solutions.

*　*　*

> The realm of the conflict of laws is a dismal swamp, filled with quaking quagmires, and inhabited by learned but eccentric professors who theorize about mysterious matters in strange and incomprehensible jargon. The ordinary court, or lawyer, is quite lost when engulfed and entangled in it.[1]

INTRODUCTION

IT might seem to be quite unreasonable to invite the reader to trudge through the swamp with an eccentric guide. All the more does this appear to be true when one considers Lord MacDermott's own views as to the scope of the lectures established in his honour. He believed that 'these Lectures should deal, not so much with the law in its technical or academic aspects, as with its impact on the prosperity and influence of our nation as a community, and on the progress and happiness of its citizens'.[2] It is, however, the case that some areas of the law which, at first sight, appear highly technical may, when stripped to their essentials, be perceived to be of considerable practical significance to the average citizen. I have long held the view, influenced no doubt by the experience of a substantial period as a law reformer, that the conflict of laws, or private international law as most Europeans describe the subject, is one whose direct impact is under-estimated by lawyers, let alone by lay men and women.

The profile of the subject has been raised a little higher by reason of our membership of, and activities within, the European Community. Indeed, that body's influence is of current topical significance with the passage by Parliament of the Contracts (Applicable Law) Act 1990, giving effect to a Convention negotiated by the Member States of the Community and concluded in Rome in 1980, on the law applicable to contractual obligations. This is topical because the United Kingdom has ratified this Convention, a step which has now brought it into force.[3] One might think that, of all areas of the conflict of laws, contract would be the one most likely to impinge on the consciousness of the citizen. After all, entering into contracts is probably the most common legal act that any of us performs. However, contracts with a truly international element are not often entered into by private citizens in this country. More

[1] Prosser, (1953) 51 *Mich L Rev* 959, 971.
[2] Lord MacDermott, (1972) 23 *NILQ* 475.
[3] As from 1 April 1991.

common may be ones, as by mail order, with another contracting party from another part of the United Kingdom; but problems as to the law to be applied are unlikely to be real, given that the substantive contract rules will be the same or very similar. Much the same may be said of mail order contracts between Belfast and Dublin. Even for the international businessman, his potential anxieties in knowing whether a dispute will be heard in one country or another, or in knowing which country's law will be applied, are much diminished by the widespread use of contractual clauses, often of a standard form, providing for the place where any dispute is to be litigated or arbitrated, and for the law which is to be applied. Our legislation, based on European Community Conventions, preserves both of these freedoms to include choice of jurisdiction[4] and choice of law of law clauses.[5]

It is to the other main area of the law of obligations, torts, that more attention might be paid as being one where the average citizen could well encounter conflict of laws problems, albeit without realizing it. As good a means as any of exemplifying this is our reliance on the motor-car. This is the most complex product that most people possess. It is also the case that many of those which are privately owned have been imported. If one of those imported cars has been negligently manufactured in Japan or Germany, France or Italy, there is the prospect of an international product liability claim with all its attendant range of jurisdictional and choice of law issues.[6] The reason why such international tort claims are not regularly pursued is because the buyer of the imported car will, for practical reasons, pursue his claim in contract against the local supplier. It is obviously easier to do so.

Escape into contract is not an option which is usually available where, however, the tort issue arises from a traffic accident. So the private citizen taking his car abroad as a tourist, or even going on a fly/drive visit, is more clearly exposed to the risks of being bogged down in the conflict of laws swamp than ever he or she imagined when setting out carefree on holiday: though it is the case that, for some, insurance may prove to be a means of fencing off the swamp. Nevertheless, a real potential for problems to arise still remains, and one might have assumed that, when problems did arise, the means of resolving them would be clearly established. This is far from being the case. There has been at least one international initiative[7] to provide harmonized choice of law rules to be applied to international traffic accidents, but it has proved to be of very limited success and has not been implemented in any common law country.[8]

[4] Civil Jurisdiction and Judgments Act 1982, Sch. 1, Art. 17.
[5] Contracts (Applicable Law) Act 1990, Sch. 1, Art. 3.
[6] Morse, [1989] *Current Legal Problems* 167.
[7] The 1968 Hague Convention on the Law Applicable to Traffic Accidents.
[8] North, [1990] I *Hague Recueil* 9, 247–8.

The problem with which I am concerned can readily be exemplified. Let us assume that two students from Queen's University, Belfast, decide to go to Dublin for the weekend in a car belonging to and driven by one of them. Assume further that in Dublin the driver crashes the car, injuring his passenger and a pedestrian, a Dublin resident. That incident could give rise to an action by the pedestrian against the driver which would be likely to be brought in Dublin, and an action against the driver by the passenger, likely to be brought in Belfast. Can we confidently state what law the courts in each jurisdiction would apply to the case before them and why? The answer has to be 'No'—thought on these facts the position is probably less clear in Dublin than in Belfast. In simple terms, the courts in Belfast would start by asking whether the conduct of the driver was actionable both in Northern Ireland and in the Republic of Ireland, followed by asking whether in the circumstances of this case, with both parties from Northern Ireland, Irish tort law might be ignored.[9] The courts in Dublin would, on the basis of a recent decision of the Irish Supreme Court,[10] conclude that they should not apply rules similar to those just outlined for Northern Ireland, but there is no clear indication from the Court of what rules they should apply. On the particular facts given, it is highly likely that the courts in Dublin would apply Irish tort law. Were, however, the facts to be reversed so that what was in issue was litigation in Dublin over an accident in Belfast involving two law students from University College, Dublin, the choice of law problem for the Irish courts would be far more real. The dispassionate observer might well conclude that the conflict of laws swamp is indeed dismal, and deep, if there are no clear choice of law rules to resolve such a common occurrence as a cross-border traffic accident. We need, therefore, to look at the present state of the law in a little more detail.

THE LAW IN OUTLINE

The basic structure of our choice of law rules stems from the decision in *Phillips* v. *Eyre*.[11] The defendant in this case had been Governor of Jamaica at the time of a rebellion on the island. The plaintiff alleged assault and false imprisonment on the part of the defendant in putting down the rebellion. The local legislature passed an Act of Indemnity retrospectively justifying the defendant's conduct, but this legislation was ineffective in England, the forum. In dismissing the plaintiff's claim on the basis that the defendant's conduct was justified in Jamaica, Willes J

[9] See *Phillips* v. *Eyre* (1870) LR 6 QB 1; *Boys* v. *Chaplin* [1971] AC 356.
[10] *Greehan* v. *Medical Incorporated and Pine Valley Associates* [1986] IR 528.
[11] (1870) LR 6 QB 1.

enshrined the tort choice of law rule in language which has since been given almost statutory effect: 'as a general rule, in order to found a suit in England for a wrong alleged to have been committed abroad, two conditions must be fulfilled. First, the wrong must be of such a character that it would have been actionable if committed in England . . . Secondly, the act must not have been justifiable by the law of the place where it was done.'[12]

This dictum confirms an earlier view as to the importance to be attached to the law of the forum,[13] and for the following hundred years or so it was accepted that it was not necessary that there be civil liability in the country where the tort was committed. It was enough that the conduct was regarded there as criminal.[14] The one major development came with the decision of the House of Lords in *Boys* v. *Chaplin*,[15] interestingly a simple traffic accident case. The accident occurred in Malta. The defendant was serving there in the Royal Navy and he admitted driving his car so negligently that it ran into a motorcycle whose driver and pillion passenger, the plaintiff, were both serving in Malta in the Royal Air Force. The pillion passenger claimed damages for his injuries in an action brought in England. Under English law, he was entitled to some £2,000, but, under the law of Malta, he would be restricted to some £50. This relatively minor traffic accident claim had eventually to be resolved by the House of Lords, despite the defendant's admission of liability. It was the unanimous view of the House that the plaintiff should recover the English level of damages, though it is far from easy to find a majority in support of any proposition of law to be extracted from the decision. Indeed it has been argued, rather despairingly, that no binding ratio can be found in the case at all.[16] However, with some ingenuity and relying to a degree on what courts in later cases have thought the House of Lords decided, it is possible to extract certain propositions from the decision. First, the general tort choice of law rule remains a double-barrelled rule, requiring reference both to the law of the forum and to that of the place of the tort. Second, the conduct must be civilly actionable under both laws, rather than merely not justifiable under the law of the place of the tort, though civil actionability under that law does not seem to require actionability as a tort.[17] Third, there is some type of flexible exception to the

[12] (1870) LR 6 QB 1, 28–9. [13] *The Halley* (1868) LR 2 PC 193.

[14] *Machado* v. *Fontes* [1897] 2 QB 1. In its most extreme form, this requirement has been satisfied in relation to an innocent defendant where his co-defendant was criminally liable: *Donald* v. *Huntley Service Centre Ltd.* (1988) 42 DLR (4th) 501; or in relation to a defendant actually acquitted in the place of the accident but whose conduct there was still regarded as criminal by a civil court in the forum: *McLean* v. *Pettigrew* [1945] 2 DLR 65.

[15] [1971] AC 356. [16] McGregor, (1970) 33 *MLR* 1, 14–15.

[17] See e.g. *Borg-Warner (Australia) Ltd.* v. *Zupan* [1982] VR 437, 454; *Def Lepp Music* v. *Stuart Brown* [1986] RPC 273, 277; *James Burrough Distilleries Plc* v. *Speymalt Whisky*

general rule which, indeed, in *Boys* v. *Chaplin* itself justified in the eyes of a majority the decision to exclude the application of the law of Malta. One might also add a fourth proposition to be extracted from, or confirmed by, a more recent decision of the Court of Appeal,[18] namely that, where the tort is committed in the forum, that law alone is to be applied and there is no place for any flexible exception.

THE PROBLEMS

It might appear from what has just been said that there are four sign-posts through the torts choice of law swamp, allowing us, therefore, to determine with some confidence how torts choice of law issues should be resolved. The weakness of that view is that it assumes that the signposts are both clear and pointing in a desirable direction. Some consideration needs now to be given to the problems to which the present state of the law gives rise. An immediate criticism is that of uncertainty as to what really are the current choice of law rules, how they are to be applied in varying circumstances, and what the scope of any flexible exception is to be. Perhaps the clearest criticism of the law is, however, that of unfair-ness to the plaintiff. He will lose if there is a good defence available under the law either of the forum or of the place of the tort, as is clearly illustrated by an intra-United Kingdom traffic accident case, *McElroy* v. *McAllister*.[19] The defendant and the deceased were both Scots and the lorry being driven by the defendant, and in which the deceased was a passenger, was involved in a collision in the north of England with another lorry. The lorries tried to pass on a narrow road; the lorry driven by the defendant fell down an embankment and the passenger was killed. His widow was the plaintiff in an action in Scotland seeking damages on three bases: (1) that her husband's right of action for negligence survived his death; (2) that she was entitled to *solatium* for the loss of support and the grief that she had suffered as his widow; and (3) that she should recover funeral expenses. However, her first claim, though good under English law, failed under Scots law; her second claim succeeded under Scots law but failed under English. It was only the claim for £40 funeral expenses which gave rise to liability under both and for which she could recover—a manifest example of getting the worst of both worlds.

A further criticism is of the dominance, under the present rules, of the

Distributors Ltd. 1989 SLT 561, 565–6; contrast *Adams* v. *Cape Industries Plc* [1990] 2 Ch 433, 509.

[18] *Metall und Rohstoff AG* v. *Donaldson Lufkin & Jenrette Inc.* [1990] 1 QB 391, 446–7, overruled on other grounds by *Lonhro Plc* v. *Fayed* [1991] 3 W.R 188.

[19] 1949 SC 110.

law of the forum. Choice of law rules are generally designed to select the most appropriate law to be applied to cases with connections with more than one country. They should be designed to serve a world where trade, travel and communications are international. They should not be xenophobic. On the other hand, they should not exclude the application of the law of the country where the issue is being litigated if it is the most appropriately connected law, nor should the overriding public policy interests of the forum be ignored, though public policy is a horse to be ridden rarely and with caution. Furthermore, the application of forum law is particularly inappropriate where the choice of law issue is viewed prospectively, that is, to try to determine what law will be applied if a problem arises, rather than retrospectively, that is, trying to determine what law is to be applied given that the dispute has now arisen. Aside from tort, the one area where forum law is generally applied is divorce and its related areas of disputes over child custody and financial relief. This might be justified (though any real justification is hard to find) on the ground that these are issues where resolution of the matter by a judge is, in form at least, actually required and so, given that, the ease, cheapness and simplicity of applying forum law prevail. Tort issues are not quite the same. Admittedly they do not involve the forward planning that contract often does. Indeed in the field of traffic accidents, all responsible motorists hope and intend not to have such accidents. Nevertheless, motorists do, and are required to, take steps prospectively to address the risk of accidents, through the medium of insurance. Indeed it might be asked why we should not go further and be able to choose the law to govern torts which we may commit, or which we have committed, just as we can agree the law to govern our contractual relationships.

Reliance on the law of the forum has another defect. It pushes the choice of law issue back into the realm of making jurisdictional decisions. There is little doubt that, as a consequence of the recent acceptance that our courts should have broad powers to order the staying of proceedings which nevertheless satisfy our jurisdictional rules, on the basis of *forum non conveniens*,[20] and that the courts should have (more limited) powers to enjoin the pursuit of foreign proceedings,[21] there is a likelihood that more disputes will be contested at the jurisdictional stage.[22] Of course, if jurisdiction is denied by the court, then that will be the end of the matter and no choice of law issue could arise. Where, however, jurisdiction is accepted, there is a real problem with a forum-based choice of law rule. Paradoxically, as the courts have extended their discretion to decline jurisdiction, the bases for assuming jurisdiction have, if anything, been

[20] *Spiliada Maritime Corpn.* v. *Cansulex Ltd.* [1987] AC 460.
[21] *Société Nationale Industrielle Aerospatiale* v. *Lee Kui Jak* [1989] AC 871.
[22] Briggs, (1989) 9 *OJLS* 251, 252–4.

expanding, evidenced not least by the Civil Jurisdiction and Judgments Act 1982, giving effect in the United Kingdom to the Brussels Convention on jurisdiction and the enforcement of judgments in civil and commercial matters. Expansion of the grounds of jurisdiction in tort can clearly be exemplified. Influenced by a decision of the European Court of Justice in 1976,[23] jurisdiction will now, for example, be taken over a tort claim, whether or not the matter fails within the European Community provisions,[24] if either the damage was sustained, or it resulted from an act committed, within the jurisdiction.[25] So if my car is negligently repaired in Belfast and the wheel comes off causing me to crash in Oxford, both the English and the Northern Ireland courts could exercise jurisdiction over the claim. The forum law to be applied will depend on where I choose to sue. The only saving grace is that, in this particular example, the applicable tort law in both countries is likely to be the same. Furthermore, the broader the range of internationally acceptable bases of jurisdiction in tort cases, the greater the likelihood (if forum law is to be applied) that the plaintiff will go 'forum-shopping'—manipulating the law to be applied, and thus the outcome of the case, by his choice of forum.

If one turns to the other head of the double-barrelled rule, reference to the law of the place where the tort was committed, problems are to be found there also. In deciding where a tort is committed, one cannot really rely, for choice of law purposes, on the double reference rule just mentioned and recently introduced for jurisdictional purposes. If actionability by the law both of the place of acting and of the place of harm was required that would simply exacerbate the problem of the law being unduly defendant-oriented. On the other hand, a rule which simply allowed a claim to succeed if there was actionability by one of these laws but not by the other would no doubt solve the problem, though by providing a solution that merited no more justification than that, i.e. it solved a problem created by another solution. Furthermore, the currently most acceptable test for determining where a tort is committed, certainly for negligence and fraud cases, is by reference to the country where the substance of the cause of action arose—but that is unsatisfactory for choice of law purposes because of its inherent uncertainty which can only effectively be removed by judicial intervention and, indeed, because it does not necessarily point to one single jurisdiction.

[23] *Handelskwerkerij G J Bier* v. *Mines de Potasse d'Alsace*, Case 21/76, [1976] ECR 1735; [1978] QB 708.

[24] Civil Jurisdiction and Judgments Act 1982, Sch. 1, Art. 5(3).

[25] RSC, and RSC(NI), O 11, r 1(1)(f).

THE COURTS' SOLUTIONS

Courts have not been unaware of some of these difficulties and criticisms, though it is striking that the House of Lords, for example, when given the opportunity in *Boys* v. *Chaplin* to review the law, chose not only to confirm the double-barrelled rule but also gave particular prominence to the application of the law of the forum. Judicial intervention has, at best, provided only limited improvement. For example, the Irish Supreme Court in 1986 concluded[26] that determination of the law to be applied to a tort claim for products liability, involving injury to the plaintiff in Ireland resulting from negligent manufacture of a heart valve in California, was relevant to the logically anterior issue of whether the Irish courts should assume jurisdiction over such a claim. Examination of the tort choice of law rules led Walsh J to reject the double-barrelled rule in the following terms:

> The rule in *Phillips* v. *Eyre* . . . has nothing to recommend it because it is capable of producing quite arbitrary decisions and it is a mixture of parochialism and a vehicle for being, in some cases, unduly generous to the plaintiff and, in others, unduly harsh. In my view, so far as choice of law in torts is concerned, the Irish courts should be sufficiently flexible to be capable of responding to the individual issues presented in each case and to the social and economic dimensions of applying any particular choice of law rule in the proceedings in question.[27]

This reads rather like an exhortation to a law reform agency to propose new rules. It provides, however, minimal guidance as to what those rules might be. In proposing that the courts should respond to individual issues, it increases the likelihood of litigation and ignores the broad range of disputes which should be resolved outside the courts.

The majority in the House of Lords in *Boys* v. *Chaplin* undoubtedly improved the law, by ensuring that there had to be civil actionability by the law of the place of the tort, rather than it sufficing that the conduct was not justifiable under that law, and by the introduction of a flexible exception. Nevertheless, the price paid for such limited improvements was high. By retaining the pre-eminence of the law of the forum, the apparently constructive step of giving the law of the place of the tort more significance paradoxically exacerbates a major problem, by making it harder for the plaintiff to satisfy that head of the double-barrelled rule. Furthermore, the flexibility exception is, itself, flawed. It is, by its very nature, conducive of uncertainty and it requires a judicial decision to make it work. However, when that happens, the way in which it is used reinforces the role of the law of the forum. It has consistently been used

[26] *Grehan* v. *Medical Incorporated and Pine Valley Associates* [1986] IR 528.
[27] Ibid., 541.

to exclude any reference to the law of the place of the tort when that law would have denied recovery. Herein lies another paradox, for the use of the exception relieves the plaintiff of one of his burdens, but by concentrating exclusively on the less obviously relevant law. It is hardly surprising, given the forum emphasis of the exception in operation, that the English Court of Appeal[28] has simply ruled the exception inapplicable where the forum and the place of the tort are the same country.

Seven judges sitting in the High Court of Australia have, however, achieved little more than the five judges in the House of Lords or the three in the Irish Supreme Court. In 1988, the High Court was faced in *Breavington* v. *Godleman*[29] with another motor accident case. The plaintiff lived in the Northern Territory where, travelling as a passenger in a car, he was hurt in a collision between it and another car. He sued both drivers, and his claim against the driver of the car in which he had been travelling was brought in Victoria where that driver had become resident. Under the law of Victoria, the forum, the claim would be governed by ordinary common law tort rules; but under the law of the Northern Territory, the place of the tort, there was a statutory 'no fault' compensation scheme in force. This excluded recovery in a tort claim for loss of earnings, and imposed a ceiling on the level of damages recoverable for pain and suffering. The crucial issue before the High Court was whether the Northern Territory rule excluding recovery for loss of earnings applied to a tort claim brought in Victoria.

It was the unanimous view of the seven judges that the plaintiff was excluded from such recovery. Whilst, however, there was unanimity of view as to the result, it was reached by no fewer than five different routes. Three judges regarded inter-state tort claims within a federal country as requiring special rules; but two of them found the solution in an inflexible application of the law of the place of the tort,[30] whilst the third put his faith in complete flexibility, seeking to identify from all the circumstances 'the predominant territorial nexus'.[31] The four other judges sought the solution through general rules of private international law, rather than through constitutional law. Three of them accepted the double-barrelled rule which emerged from *Boys* v. *Chaplin*, requiring actionability under both the law of the place of the tort and the law of the forum. However, two of the three rejected any possibility of a flexible exception to this rule,[32] whilst the third was prepared to envisage an exception of limited effect.[33] The seventh judge, Mason CJ, started from

[28] *Metall und Rohstoff AG* v. *Donaldson Lufkin & Jenrette Inc.* [1990] 1 QB 391, overruled on other grounds by *Lonrho Plc* v. *Fayed* [1991] 3 WLR 188.

[29] (1988) 80 ALR 362.

[30] Ibid., 387, per Wilson and Gaudron JJ.

[31] Ibid., 409–10 and 415, per Deane J.

[32] Ibid., 398 and 423, per Brennan and Dawson JJ.

[33] Ibid., 434, per Toohey J.

the proposition that there was a double-barrelled actionability rule, but, ingeniously, he interpreted this to mean that the court should normally apply the law of the place of the tort, subject to a flexible exception in favour of the law of the forum.[34] Whilst this approach goes quite some way to rid this area of law of forum-dominance, it failed to command any wider support with his colleagues in the High Court.

Where does all this leave us? It has been said that 'the variety of inconsistent views in *Breavington* might be thought to have consigned choice of law in Australia to a black hole'.[35] That might merely appear to be a technologically superior variant of the dismal swamp with which I began. On at least three occasions since 1988 Australian courts have attempted to determine for what principles of law *Breavington* is authority. The first of these cases[36] was decided by the same High Court judges on the same day as *Breavington* and adds little apart from confirmation of the diversity of view. Early in 1990 the New South Wales Court of Appeal[37] extracted a ratio from *Breavington* that, where a tort was committed in Australia, the court should apply the law of the State where the tort was committed. Late in 1990 the High Court of Australia returned to the problems raised by torts in the international sphere, though this time primarily in the jurisdictional context. In this latest decision, *Voth* v. *Manildra Flour Mills Pty. Ltd.*,[38] the Court was faced with a claim for damages for professional negligence, the tort being committed (if at all) in Missouri. It was decided that New South Wales was clearly an inappropriate forum and that proceedings there should be stayed.[39] A significant factor in reaching this decision was the conclusion, of a majority, that under the second head of the rule in *Phillips* v. *Eyre* there had to be civil liability under the law of Missouri, the place of the tort. Indeed it was said that that law was 'fundamental'[40] in determining the dispute between the parties. Analysis of the law to be applied in an international, rather than inter-State, tort claim went no deeper than that—but, reading

[34] (1988) 80 ALR 362, 371–3.

[35] Morse, [1989] *Current Legal Problems* 167, 195. Even an Australian judge has had to admit that 'it is not easy to derive the holding in *Breavington* which is binding on this, as on other Australian courts' and that 'this is no small misfortune'; *Byrnes* v. *Groote Eylandt Mining Co. Pty. Ltd.* (1990) 93 ALR 131, 135 and 139, per Kirby P; and see O'Brien, (1990) 12 *Adelaide L Rev* 449, 462–3.

[36] *Perrett* v. *Robinson* (1988) 80 ALR 441.

[37] *Byrnes* v. *Groote Eylandt Mining Co. Pty. Ltd.* (1990) 93 ALR 131.

[38] (1990) 97 ALR 124.

[39] The broad importance of the decision lies in the fact that the High Court affirmed (and explained) its earlier decision on *forum non conveniens* in *Oceanic Sun Line Special Shipping Co. Inc.* v. *Fay* (1988) 165 CLR 197, and declined to follow the decision of the House of Lords in *Spiliada Maritime Corpn.* v. *Cansulex Ltd.* [1987] AC 460. It is, however, striking in the present case (when compared with *Breavington* and *Oceanic Sun*) to see how the judges strove to produce an agreed approach: (1990) 97 ALR 124, 132 and 146–7.

[40] (1990) 97 ALR 124, 145.

the judgments, one is left with an impression that the balance of significance has been, again, tipped in favour of the law of the place of the tort and away from the law of the forum.

LAW REFORM PROPOSALS

Australia

There seems little doubt that the judicial process in the United Kingdom, Ireland and Australia has failed to produce coherent, clear and just rules for the identification of the law to be applied in a cross-border tort claim. That being so, the law reform baton has to be passed to the legislature, and to those who may be called upon to advise on private international law matters as part of that process, namely the law reform agencies. In Australia, within four months of the decision in *Breavington*, the Attorney-General had referred a wide range of choice of law issues to the Australian Law Reform Commission, stating that the Commission was to report on them not later than 31 June 1991. This reference goes wider than choice of law in tort, but the Commission acted with commendable speed, producing an Issues Paper in 1989[41] and a Discussion Paper in 1990.[42] It is apparent from the latter document that, in relation to choice of law in tort, a significant influence on its analysis was provided by the earlier provisional views of the English and Scottish Law Commissions on this issue.[43] These have led to the publication of a final Report[44] with draft legislation, and it is to the solutions there proposed by the Law Commissions that I shall now turn.

The United Kingdom

It has to be said that the Law Commissions have acted with less urgency than their Australian counterparts. The initiative for the Commissions' activity in this field came not from dissatisfaction with the confirmation in 1971 of forum predominance, as a result of *Boys* v. *Chaplin*, nor from the inability clearly to determine the ratio of that decision, but rather from activity within the European Community. The work which culminated in 1980 in the Rome Convention on the law applicable to

41 Federal and Territory Choice of Law Rules, Issues Paper No. 8 (1989).

42 Choice of Law Rules, Discussion Paper No. 44 (1990).

43 Law Commission Working Paper No. 87 (1984).

44 Private International Law: Choice of Law in Tort and Delict (Law Com. No. 193, 1990). The proposals are intended to apply to Northern Ireland; see para. 3.59.

contractual obligations[45] had started life in 1967 as a proposal for a convention on both contractual and non-contractual obligations. Although the latter aspect was dropped from the Brussels negotiations in 1978,[46] it was then expected that work would be resumed on preparing a convention on non-contractual obligations once a contract convention was successfully concluded. Despite the fact that this resumption of work never occurred, work continued in the two Commissions with the objective of making proposals for reform of our own tort choice of law rules.

The Law Commissions' Provisional Views

The Commissions' Working Paper, published in 1984, was a very substantial document containing analyses of a whole range of general tort issues which might arise in a choice of law context, as well as analyses of problems relevant to individual torts. The essential elements of the provisional proposals can, however, be simply stated. Fundamental reform was needed and the double-barrelled rule in *Phillips* v. *Eyre* should be swept away. In its place, first, party autonomy should be permitted. Where parties thought ahead and contemplated potential tort liability arising from their relationship, they should be allowed to agree by contract what law should govern their liability—subject to an overriding power in the courts to disallow a choice on public policy grounds. Furthermore, when the reality of a traffic accident or other tort was upon them, they would be free after the event to agree what law should govern their liability. This is always possible now, as a consequence of a failure to plead the foreign law, with the result that the law of the forum is applied; but choice after the event should not be limited to the law of the forum. Freedom to choose brings certainty and clarity into the law and reduces expense. It is far from clear whether the current rules permit such a choice. Certainly is it not possible to point to reported cases in support.

In the absence of choice of the applicable law, the Commissions put forward for consultation two Models of choice of law rules. Model 1 applied the law of the place of the tort, coupled with definitions of where the main torts were committed. Thus a personal injury tort was committed in the country where a person was when the injury occurred; death where the victim was when fatally injured; and defamation was committed in the country of publication. Other torts were held to be committed in 'the country in which the most significant elements in the train of events occurred'. The general rule that the law of the place of the tort should be applied was subject to an exception in favour of the law of the country with which the occurrence and the parties had the closest and most real connection, provided that a 'threshold test' was satisfied. This

[45] See above, pp. 23–50, 71.

[46] See North, [1990] 1 *Hague Recueil* 9, 250–1.

required the parties and the occurrence to have an insignificant connection with the country of the place of the tort and a substantial connection with the other country.

Model 2 was almost the converse of Model 1. It adopted a 'proper law' approach, so that the general rule was the application of the law of the country with which the parties and the occurrence had the closest and most real connection. This was coupled with rebuttable presumptions as to closest connection in the case of the main torts, mirroring the definitions of the place of a tort under Model 1. So, in the case of defamation, the country of closest connection was presumed to be that of publication. The presumptions could only be rebutted, however, if a similar 'threshold test' to that in Model 1 was satisfied, i.e. insignificant connection with the country of the presumption and substantial connection with another country.

The Law Commissions' Report: an outline and an assessment

The response of commentators was generally to welcome the proposals for substantial reform, and the Law Commissions make clear in their Report that Model 1 was favoured by a significant majority. The Commissions are right, in my view, to have concluded that the rule in that Model 'is clear and simple, combining the certainty of a general rule that the *lex loci delicti* should apply, with the flexibility of a proper law exception'.[47] I support and welcome their decision to construct new legislative choice of law rules on that basis.

Turning now to examine the proposed new rules in a little more detail, the first point to note is that they are to replace fully the existing common law rules, it being made clear also that a claim may be classified as tortious for the purpose of the new choice of law rules notwithstanding the fact that it gives rise to no such cause of action here. A good example, and one given by the Commissions, is a claim for an invasion of a right of privacy, to which the new rules should apply even though there is no such right of action under our law. It is surely right that the new choice of law rules should provide a fully coherent system in themselves; and here there is a sharp contrast to be drawn with the new statutory contract choice of law rules,[48] where the opportunity has been lost to apply those rules to all contractual issues.[49] Also to be welcomed is the

[47] Law Com. No. 193, 1990, para. 1.8. Cf. Carter, (1991) 107 *LQR* 405.

[48] Contracts (Applicable Law) Act 1990, above, pp. 23–50, 71.

[49] This is because the possibility of applying the rules of the 1980 Rome Convention to issues excluded from it (as the United Kingdom was entitled to do), such as contractual choice of court or arbitration clauses or issues of capacity, was not accepted. Nor even does the legislation provide other rules for such matters, leaving everyone to hark back to the old, in all other respects replaced, common law rules. See above pp. 25, 35–37.

fact that the proposed new legislation not only adopts the Model I approach, but improves upon it in its presentation. Instead of applying the law of the place of the tort as the general rule, coupled with definitions of what that place is in cases involving death, personal injury or damage to property, the formulation is more direct. For example, in the case of a tort claim in respect of a death, the draft legislation states:

> The applicable law . . . shall in so far as [proceedings] are brought in respect of . . .
>
> (b) the death of an individual resulting from personal injury, be the law of the country or territory where that individual was when he sustained the injury.[50]

This approach of stating directly what law is to be applied has been carried through to the formulation of the rule to govern other torts, such as those concerned with damage to economic interests. Instead of stating, as Model I did, that the law of the place of the tort is to be applied and that that place is to be defined as the country 'in which the most significant elements in the train of events occurred', it is acknowledged, rightly again I suggest, that it is no more than a fiction to call that place the 'place of the tort'. Especially is this true of a tort which has substantial connections with several countries. It is more direct to do as is proposed, and state that the applicable law is to be the law of the country 'where the most significant elements of the events constituting the subject matter of the proceedings took place'.[51] Furthermore it seems wise to propose, as the Commissions have done, that, if that country cannot be identified, the applicable law is to be that of the country 'with which the subject-matter of the proceedings has the most real and substantial connection'.[52]

Model I was subject to an exception in favour of the country of closest connection, and this broad approach is carried through by the Commissions into their final recommendations, though with a number of modifications. The first is that, in assessing the closeness of connection, all factors may be weighed in the balance, not just connection with the occurrence and the parties—including, for example, the consequences of events which constitute the subject matter of the proceedings. A second modification is to lower the threshold for the operation of the exception, by abandoning reference to insignificance of connection with the country of the otherwise applicable law and instead seeking a comparison of the factors which connect the case with that country and any other. If that comparison leads to a conclusion that 'it would be substantially more

[50] Draft Tort and Delict (Applicable Law) Bill, cl 2(1); Law Com. No. 193 (1990), 36.

[51] This general formulation is also to be applied to defamation, subject to cl 3(2) of the Draft Bill.

[52] Draft Bill, cl 2(3).

appropriate' for the law of that other country to be applied, then the general rule is to be displaced.[53]

At this point, the first twinges of anxiety arise over the Law Commissions' proposals. There is no doubt that the ability to displace the general rule is desirable; the problem is to determine how easy that displacement is to be. This poses the classic conflict between certainty and flexibility. A rule which demands the inflexible application of the law of the place of the tort will create serious injustice, and it was reaction against just such a rule which has led to over half a century of turmoil in the United States in determining choice of law rules, particularly for tort claims. A rule which simply requires identification of the most closely connected law, a 'proper law of the tort' or a 'real and substantial connection' approach, is a recipe for uncertainty and inconsistency, as the American experience bears witness. Furthermore, such a rule is to a large degree unworkable without the intervention of lawyers and judges. It is, therefore, an expensive and inefficient rule. The justice which it provides, if it does, is at too high a price. Ideally we want the best of both worlds—the certainty and ease of a clear signpost through the swamp, coupled with the ability to digress from the signposted route when it is evident that firmer ground lies elsewhere.

The new balance struck by the Law Commissions between flexibility and certainty puts a higher value on the former than did their earlier provisional proposals, and marks, it is suggested, a retrograde step. The easier it is to move into the exceptional regime, the harder it is for parties to regulate their affairs without judicial intervention.[54] That will deter people from pursuing claims—especially, for example, a pedestrian injured in a traffic accident. That provides a greater injustice than does a less flexible rule leading to the application, occasionally, of a less closely connected law. It is hard to dissent from the view of the Australian Law Reform Commission that 'infrequent individual injustices from a relatively inflexible choice of law rule may be preferable to the increased expense and uncertainty resulting from more flexible rules.'[55]

When looking beyond the general choice of law rules proposed by the Commissions, anxiety over their recommendations becomes more marked. This concern is centred on a significant exclusion from their proposals and on one particular specific recommendation. The sin of omission, if it may be so described, is the failure to make any mention of party autonomy, despite discussion of it in the earlier Working Paper. Taking as the law reform objective the creation of new choice of law rules which can be applied justly and with a minimum of difficulty, there is a strong case for allowing the parties, by contract, before or after the event, to choose the

[53] Ibid., cl 2(4).

[54] See Anton, *Private International Law*, 2nd edn. (1990), 416.

[55] Discussion Paper No. 44 (1990), para. 8.8.

law to govern tort liability. Indeed, the introduction of such a rule has been described as 'long overdue'.[56] It might be argued that, if such a power to choose the applicable law existed at common law, there is nothing in the Law Commissions' draft Bill to exclude that possibility in the future. That is true, but the failure of the Commissions to recommend such a development may well count against its judicial introduction and, if it is desirable to introduce it into the law, as I have no doubt it is, then the legislation to give effect to the Commissions' draft Bill provides the obvious opportunity to do so, an opportunity which should be taken. To continue the earlier metaphor, the parties should be allowed to lay their own track through the swamp.

Turning now to the sin of commission, the proposed new choice of law rules are subject to a major exception in the case of torts committed in any part of the United Kingdom—an exception which was not foreshadowed in the earlier Working Paper. Indeed, it was there accepted that any new choice of law rules should apply to torts committed within the United Kingdom, with the consequence that the law of the part of the United Kingdom where the tort was committed could be displaced in favour of the application of the law of another country, being that of closest connection, where that connection was substantial—an uncommon, but not improbable, situation.[57] What is now proposed is a separate rule to govern torts committed within the United Kingdom. This would be to the effect that, where the most significant elements of allegedly tortious conduct took place in a part of the United Kingdom, the law of that part had to be applied; there would be no exceptions to this rule.[58] Furthermore, in relation to defamation published both abroad and in the United Kingdom, it is specifically proposed that the law of the forum in the part of the United Kingdom in which proceedings are brought should alone be applicable.

Just as we thought we saw the prospect of abandoning the narrow, territorialist, homeward trend first branch of the rule in *Phillips* v. *Eyre*, i.e. the application of the law of the forum, we see that branch apparently resuscitated in a new guise in this exceptional regime for torts committed in the United Kingdom. The reasons given by the Law Commissions for their change of mind are not convincing. We are told that the application of the law of a part of the United Kingdom to a claim against a defendant who lives there upholds two principles of the conflict of laws: 'that justice is done to a person if his own law is applied, and that a person should not be liable to a greater or lesser extent than he is liable by the law of the place where he acted'.[59] We are also told that the special rule

[56] Castel, *Canadian Conflict of Laws*, 2nd edn. (1986), 621, and see below pp. 187–191.
[57] Law Commission Working Paper No. 87 (1984), para. 5.92.
[58] Draft Bill, cl 3(1).
[59] Law Com. No. 193 (1990), para. 3.17.

for United Kingdom torts will avoid difficult problems. It is said, in relation to defamation, that 'it seems unfair that someone who lives permanently in this country and who makes a statement in this country which is truthful, fair comment or privileged under our domestic law should be liable according to the terms of an otherwise applicable foreign law, simply because the statement was also published abroad'.[60]

This approach simply does not stand up to detailed analysis in terms of fairness and justice.[61] It has to be assumed that there can arise a case where, for example, a person suffers personal injury in a part of the United Kingdom, say Northern Ireland, but that under the closest connection exception the law of Northern Ireland would not be applied, the exception pointing, say, to the law of the Republic. A specific example might be the one given earlier where two law students from University College, Dublin, came to Belfast for the weekend and one negligently injured the other in a driving accident. We are told by the Law Commissions that, because the tort is committed in a part of the United Kingdom, the closer connection with the Republic is to be ignored and the law of Northern Ireland is to be applied. Assume, however, that the law–fact pattern is reversed, and that the case concerns two law students from Queen's University, Belfast, involved in an accident in Dublin. Here, though the general rule points to the application of the law of the Republic of Ireland, the closest connection exception indicates that the law of Northern Ireland is to be applied; a conclusion which the Commissions' general proposals uphold. The forum domination of the proposed special rule for United Kingdom torts is thus obvious. The justifications for preferring the application of the law of the place of closest connection are in no way altered if the tort is committed in Belfast rather than in Dublin.

Anxiety is just as great in relation to the special forum-oriented rule for defamation. We are told that it is unfair to hold a publisher liable in English proceedings for a defamatory statement published outside the United Kingdom if the same statement was lawfully published in England. It is, however, no less unfair to prevent a person from recovering damages in England from an English publisher for a statement published in Ireland, and which is defamatory of him under the law of that country, simply because the publisher makes the same statement in England, protected by an English law defence to defamation. The foreign tort is no less serious an invasion of the plaintiff's foreign rights even though no English tort has also been committed.

The exceptional rule requiring the application of the law of a part of the United Kingdom to a tort committed there is unnecessary under the

[60] Ibid., para. 3.18. [61] Contrast Briggs, (1989) 105 *LQR* 359, 362.

general rule unless the law of another jurisdiction ought, exceptionally, to be applied. In that case, however, refusal to apply the foreign law amounts to an abandonment of the internationalism on which modern choice of law rules should be founded. The exceptional rule is fundamentally flawed, even with regard to the reasons given for its introduction. To retain this exception in legislation would be to preserve an element of the discredited common law rules which the law reform process is designed to eradicate. Parliament should reject this special rule for torts committed within the United Kingdom.

CONCLUSION

Where then does this all leave the torts choice of law process? It seems clear, I fear, that the judges have led us right into the middle of the swamp. It is now for Parliament, relying on some (though not all) of the signposts provided by the Law Commissions, to be our guide to firmer ground. I hope that such legislative guidance will soon be provided.

5

Contract as a Tort Defence in the Conflict of Laws

INTRODUCTION

WHERE, for example, an employee is injured abroad as the result of his employer's negligence, a variety of issues may arise as to the interrelation of the contractual relationship between the parties with a possible claim in tort. It has been clear for some time that, for jurisdictional purposes, the plaintiff is free to decide whether to frame his claim in contract or in tort.[1] The same may now confidently be said for choice of law purposes,[2] with the result that if the claim is framed in contract it will be governed by the choice of law rules contained in the Rome Convention on the law applicable to contractual obligations, implemented by the Contracts (Applicable Law) Act 1990[3] and, if in tort, by the double-barrelled rule requiring actionability both by the law of the forum and the law of the place of the tort.[4]

A more complex issue is that of determining the law or laws which govern the effect of a contractual exemption as a defence to a tort claim. Of the three matters discussed below,[5] this is the one[6] which merits some introductory comment. The leading English authority is *Sayers* v. *International Drilling Co. NV*,[7] where an English plaintiff who was injured abroad was employed under a contract containing an exemption clause, which, though void under English domestic law, was held by the Court of Appeal to be valid under Dutch law, the proper law of the contract.

This article is reproduced from (1977) 26 *ICLQ* 914–31 with permission from the publishers, The British Institute of International and Comparative Law, 17 Russell Square, London WC1B 5DR.

1 *Matthews* v. *Kuwait Bechtel Corporation* [1959] 2 QB 57.

2 *Coupland* v. *Arabian Gulf Oil Co* [1983] 1 WLR 1136 and 1151; *Johnson* v. *Coventry Churchill International Ltd.* [1992] 3 All ER 14.

3 Above, pp. 23–50.

4 See *Phillips* v. *Eyre* (1870) LR 6 QB 1 and *Boys* v. *Chaplin* [1971] AC 356, above, pp. 73–75.

5 The other two are: the effect of the existence of a contract as a defence to a tort claim; and the extent to which a contract may constitute a waiver or release from tortious liability.

6 See below, pp. 97–104.

7 [1971] 1 WLR 1176. There was no evidence in *Coupland* v. *Arabian Gulf Oil Co.* [1983] 1 WLR 1136, 1151; 1151, 1153–4 of a contractual defence.

Were the facts of this case to arise now, the determination of the applicable law would have to be made by reference to Article 6(2) of the Rome Convention, though it has been argued[8] that a court might well still conclude that Dutch law was the law applicable to the contract. There is, however, some evidence[9] that the Court of Appeal erred in its conclusion that the exemption clause was in the circumstances valid under Dutch law. Were the contract to contain an express choice of law clause in favour of Dutch law, then the facts would appear to be such that an English court would disregard the exemption clause under section 27(2) of the Unfair Contract Terms Act 1977.[10]

The decision of the majority in *Sayers* was simply to examine the issue as one of contract, concluding that, as the exemption clause was valid, the plaintiff's claim in tort failed. This unthinking analysis is criticized below[11] and has been criticized by others[12] but a similar approach would appear to have been adopted by the High Court of Australia,[13] though with little express consideration of the interrelation of tort and contract issues.[14] Such matters have, however, attracted the attention of the Law Commissions in their consideration of reform of the tort choice of law rules. In their Working Paper[15] the Commissions concluded that, as argued below, the present state of English law probably was, and indeed should be, that the validity of a contractual term containing an exemption clause is to be governed by the law applicable to the contract, but that the effect of the term, if valid, as a defence to a tort claim is to be decided by the law (or laws) governing the tort. Their final Report reveals a less confident approach as the members of the Commisions were divided on the issue, some supporting the Working Paper approach which should, in their view, be cast in legislative form,[16] while others favoured

[8] Morse, in *Contract Conflicts*, ed. North (1982), 143, 160–2.

[9] De Boer, *Beyond Lex Loci Delicti* (1987), 186.

[10] Dicey and Morris, *The Conflict of Laws*, 11th edn. (1987), 1404.

[11] P. 101.

[12] Morse, *Torts in Private International Law* (1978), 187–94; (1984) 33 *ICLQ* 437, 459; Pryles, [1991] II *Hague Recueil* 9, 184–5; though cf. Carter, (1983) 54 *BYBIL* 301, 305–6.

[13] *Oceanic Sun Line Special Shipping Co. Inc.* v. *Fay* (1988) 165 CLR 197; North, [1990] I *Hague Recueil* 9, 228–9.

[14] Though see Gaudron J, (1988) 165 CLR 197, 266.

[15] Working Paper No. 87 (1984), paras. 2.89–2.101, 6.51.

[16] The operation of this approach, thought by the Commissions to be that of the present law, would be affected by their general proposals for reform of tort choice of law rules contained in Law Com. No. 193 (1990). There they recommend that the double-barrelled choice of law rule be abolished and replaced by a series of rules which, broadly speaking, amount to the application of the law of the place of the tort, except where that is within the UK, in which case the law of the forum is to be applied. For further discussion, see above, pp. 83–88. The effect of these changes on the rules governing a contractual defence would be that, where an employee was injured abroad through the negligence of his employer, there being no other country more closely connected with the tort, for any contractual exemption clause to be effective it would need to be valid under the law applicable by reason of the Contracts (Applicable Law) Act 1990 and also to constitute an effective defence under the law of the country where the plaintiff was injured.

the application of the proper law of the contract, rather than the law applicable to the tort, to govern the effect of a contractual defence. As a result the Commissions chose not to resolve this difference of approach by deciding not to recommend legislation on this point.[17] This means that final determination of English law on this issue[18] is to be at the expense of the parties in private litigation.

* * *

[17] Law Com. No. 193 (1990), paras. 3.49–3.50.

[18] Also unresolved is the subsidiary issue, discussed below, pp. 102–104, as to whether the contractual validity of the exemption clause is to be governed by the contract law identified by the choice of law rules of the forum or of the law governing liability in tort. Both approaches have attracted more recent support. The former is supported by: Law Commission Working Paper No. 87 (1984), paras. 6.52–6.53 and Morse, *Torts in Private International Law* (1978), 191; the latter by Pryles, [1991] II *Hague Recueil* 9, 191.

FOR about a decade John Morris and I conducted seminars together in the conflict of laws at Oxford. It seemed to me to be appropriate that my contribution to this issue should concentrate on a problem that we had cause to consider in our seminars on a number of occasions.

Common lawyers find themselves having to deal with an increasing number of problems concerned with the interrelation of contract and tort.[1] Recent years have seen consideration given to such problems as the difference between the rules of remoteness in the two areas of law, differences as to the running of limitation periods, and the question whether claims based on misrepresentation will lie alternatively in contract and tort. The conflict of laws has not been excluded from this debate,[2] the significance of which depends upon the fact that the choice-of-law rules differ markedly as between the two bases of liability. Contractual liability is governed by the proper law of the country, or legal system, with which the contract has the most real and substantial connection.[3] Tort claims, on the other hand, must be actionable both by English law as the *lex fori* and by the *lex loci delicti*,[4] subject to such amelioration of this rule as was provided by the House of Lords in 1969.[5] This is not the place to examine either the tort or contract rules at length. Suffice it to say that they reveal marked differences from one another.

These differences create a variety of problems. The most obvious is one of classification, i.e. can the issue be classed as contract rather than tort in order to avoid the antiquated choice-of-law rules in tort?[6] This has been described most pithily as 'escape into contract.'[7] This escape encompasses such issues as concurrence of actions[8] or the effect of a direct action claim against the insurer of a tortfeasor.[9] There is, however, a further series of issues arising from the interrelation of contract and tort law, namely the extent to which an apparently good tort claim is nullified or defeated by what might generally be described as a contractual defence. It is these issues with which this essay is concerned and they

[1] E.g. Guest, (1961) 3 *U Malaya L Rev* 191; Poulton, (1966) 82 *LQR* 346; Millner, *Negligence in Modern Law* (1967), ch 4.

[2] Collins, (1967) 16 *ICLQ* 103; (1972) 21 *ICLQ* 320; Kahn-Freund, [1968] II *Hague Recueil* 1, 129–57; Stromholm, *Torts in the Conflict of Laws* (1961), ch 5.

[3] *Bonython* v. *Commonwealth of Australia* [1951] AC 201, 219.

[4] *Phillips* v. *Eyre* (1870) LR 6 QB 1.

[5] *Boys* v. *Chaplin* [1971] AC 356.

[6] Morris, *The Conflict of Laws* (1971), 274–6; Cheshire, *Private International Law*, 9th edn. (1974), 284–5; Kahn-Freund, [1968] II *Hague Recueil* 1, 146.

[7] Kahn-Freund, [1968] II *Hague Recueil* 1, 129.

[8] Ibid., 130–41; and see Collins, (1967) 16 *ICLQ* 103, 108–12.

[9] Ibid., 149–57.

appear to be three in number. What is the effect of the existence of a contract as a defence to a tort claim? What is the effect of a contractual exemption clause on a tort claim? How far may a contract constitute a waiver or release from tortious liability?

CONTRACT AS DEFENCE TO TORT CLAIM

The situation envisaged here is that the conduct of the defendant would appear to constitute a tort, but for the fact that there is a contract between the parties, the existence or terms of which deprive the defendant's conduct of its tortious character. This is different from the orthodox concept of a clause exempting from tortious liability which envisages the commission of a tort but relief from liability. The most straightforward example is provided by *Galaxias SS Co.* v. *Panagos Christofis.*[10] There, the defendants were members of the crew of a Greek merchant ship who were sued by the owners of the ship for damages for trespass and for breach of contract. The crew had gone on strike in Norway but eventually agreed to work the ship to England. When the ship docked at Newcastle, there was an enquiry by Greek officials, the result of which was that the crew were paid off but refused to leave the ship. It is this refusal to leave which formed the basis of the shipowners' claim in trespass. The members of the crew claimed that under the terms of their contract of employment they were still entitled to remain on board.

The problem before Sellers J in this case was essentially whether the terms of the contract of employment permitted the crew to remain on board the ship. If so, they had committed no trespass because the contract would render their presence there lawful. It was held that 'the issues which arise are governed by Greek law,'[11] which is taken in the judgment to mean that all contractual issues were governed by Greek law, i.e. the proper law of the employment contract was Greek. Under the relevant rules and provisions of Greek law, the members of the crew were in breach of their contract of employment; their discharge was lawful; they were not entitled to remain on board and they were liable in trespass.[12]

This case illustrates in a relatively simple fashion the issue whether a contract between the parties can eliminate liability in tort. The case is, on orthodox analysis, a conflicts case so far as contract is concerned but not so far as tort law is involved. The place of the alleged trespass and the forum were both England. In that case it would seem that there is no possibility of applying any law but English law to the issue of liability in

[10] (1948) 81 LlLR 449; and see *Leask* v. *French* 1949 SA (4) 887.
[11] Ibid., 503. [12] Cf. Collins, (1967) 16 *ICLQ* 103, 113.

tort.[13] So the issue then becomes one of asking whether, under English tort law, trespass is committed by one who has a contractual right to be present. It is clear that it is not, provided there is a valid subsisting contract, or other genuine consent to the presence. The one remaining issue then becomes whether the contract still subsisted. At this point a choice of law issue arises and it is for Greek law, as the proper law of the contract, to determine whether the contract subsisted. It was no concern of Greek law whether a contract prevented the tort of trespass from being committed.

Two later cases support a similar approach, this time in the context of the tort of detinue.[14] The first of these is *Zivnostenska Banka National Corporation* v. *Frankman*.[15] In 1935, a Czech subject resident in Czechoslovakia bought bonds in London which were deposited with the defendant bank in London. Eventually, the plaintiff, nephew of the original purchaser, became entitled to the bonds and sought their deliver from the defendant bank. This was refused on the ground that it was prohibited under Czech law; whereupon the plaintiff brought an action of detinue for the bonds or their value.

Once again, there is no conflicts tort issue as the bonds are being detained in England which is the forum. The essential issue is whether there is some further factor which renders the detention lawful. Under English domestic law, no tort is committed if the detention is in pursuance of a contractual right. Did the defendant bank have a contractual right to retain the bonds? The House of Lords had no doubt that 'first and last the law of the contract was Czechoslovakian law.'[16] Under that law the contract was valid and it was unlawful to hand the bonds over to the plaintiff. Therefore the detention was lawful and not tortious.

The second case concerned with detinue, *Kahler* v. *Midland Bank*,[17] is very similar in many, but not all, respects. The facts were that the plaintiff, resident in and a national of Czechoslovakia, bought securities in London. His Czech bank deposited these securities with the Midland Bank in England. At the beginning of the war, the plaintiff, a Jew, wished to leave Czechoslovakia and in order to get permission so to do, he was compelled to transfer his account to another Czech bank acting under German control. The original bank informed the Midland Bank that the securities were now to be held for the account of the second bank acting under German instructions. After the war, the plaintiff claimed the securities from the Midland Bank and, when they refused to surrender them, brought an action in detinue. The Midland Bank refused delivery on the ground that the securities were held to the account of the

[13] E.g. *Szalatnay-Stacho* v. *Fink* [1947] KB 1; Cheshire, n. 6 above, 287–8.

[14] See also *The Sindh* [1975] 1 Lloyd's Rep 372.

[15] [1950] AC 57.

[16] Ibid., 69.

[17] [1950] AC 24.

second bank and it was illegal under Czech law for that bank to deliver the securities to the plaintiff.

Yet again, the tort claim is exclusively English. It is only the contractual defence which raises a conflicts issue. The House of Lords held that the proper law of the contract between the plaintiff and the second Czech bank was Czech law, by which law delivery of the securities was illegal. However, as has been pointed out by Kahn-Freund,[18] rather more careful analysis is required in this case; analysis of English domestic law rather than the conflict of laws. The question of whether the Midland Bank's detention of securities, which it is admitted are owned by the plaintiff, is lawful is a matter of English tort law. If the plaintiff, or his agent, has contractually agreed with the Midland Bank to the deposit, then clearly if the detention is lawful under the proper law of that contract, there is no tort of detinue committed in England. However, the plaintiff's agreement was with his Czech bank. There was no contract between the plaintiff and the defendant bank. This raises an issue of English tort law as to whether the plaintiff can show a right to immediate possession of the securities. The stumbling block is his contract with the Czech bank under which he is not entitled to delivery. Kahn-Freund argues that, so far as the Midland Bank is concerned, this is *res inter alios acta* and that

> the admissibility of defences derived from this Czechoslovak contract in an action based on an English law tort was (or should have been) governed by English law and by nothing else, and in accordance with English law those defences should have been held to be inadmissible.[19]

I am sure that the major part of this statement is correct and was acted upon by the House of Lords. It is the final conclusion that is contentious. If it is a good defence to a detinue claim, under English tort law, that the plaintiff is not entitled to immediate possession of the chattels, this is an English defence, not a foreign defence. As a matter of English tort law there is no doubt that an action of detinue will fail if the plaintiff is unable to prove a right to immediate possession.[20] What this case decided is that it is a good defence to plead an interest in a third party which denies the plaintiff's right to possession. This is made clear by Lord MacDermott:

> Can such a defendant, though claiming no adverse right or interest in himself, plead that some third party has such a right or interest and that, by reason thereof, the plaintiff is not entitled to immediate possession? There seems to be no clear authority on the point but, on principle, I do not see why a defence of this nature should be denied, at any rate where the relationship between the third party and the defendant is that of bailor and bailee.[21]

[18] [1968] II *Hague Recueil* 1, 147.

[19] Ibid.

[20] *Gordon* v. *Harper* (1796) 7 TR 9; *Bradley* v. *Copley* (1845) 1 CB 685.

[21] [1950] AC 24, 38.

This makes it clear that any criticism of the decision ought to be directed at this conclusion as to English tort law, and not to any misapplication of the appropriate conflict rules. It was held to be a good English defence that the plaintiff had no right to immediate possession by reason of a contract valid under Czech law, its proper law.

It was said earlier that these cases are all relatively simple because no tort conflict issue was raised. More substantial problems arise if the rule in *Phillips* v. *Eyre*[22] has also to be brought into play. This envisages the forum and the place of the tort being different countries and is best illustrated by a hypothetical example, as no Commonwealth authority seems directly to raise this issue.

X, an English company, enters into a contract to supply Y in British Columbia with a burglar alarm system. The proper law of this contract is the law of British Columbia by which law the contract is valid. When a similar system fails to prevent a burglary, Y becomes agitated and questions the efficiency of the system which X has installed. X represents to Y that the system is foolproof. This statement is negligently made; Y is burgled and suffers substantial economic loss. Y brings an action in England against X claiming damages, in tort, for negligent misrepresentation.[23] The action is brought in England because that is where X resides and has his assets and it is phrased as a claim in tort because the contract, but not the tort, limitation period has expired in England.[24] The tort of negligent misrepresentation was committed in British Columbia[25] and England is the forum. As a matter of domestic tort law, the conduct of X may be regarded as actionable as a tort in England notwithstanding the contractual nexus with Y.[26] However, it may well be the case that no claim in tort will lie under the law of British Columbia because the misconduct of X is insufficiently independent of the contract.[27] It can also be assumed that the contract limitation period in British Columbia has expired.[28]

In this case the contractual nexus between the parties would prevent there being tort liability under the *lex loci delicti* but would not have this effect under English law, the *lex fori*. How then is the case to be resolved? Applying the first head of the tort rule in *Phillips* v. *Eyre*, it must be

[22] It is not intended here to discuss the difficulties of determining what law governs liability in tort, whether it be the rigid rule in *Phillips* v. *Eyre*, that rule subject to some generalised exception, or the proper law of the tort. On these issues, see Morris, n. 6 above, pp. 271–74; Cheshire, n. 6 above, 267–88.

[23] Based on *Hedley Byrne & Co. Ltd.* v. *Heller & Partners Ltd.* [1964] AC 405.

[24] See, e.g. *Bagot* v. *Stevens Scanlan & Co.* [1966] 1 QB 197 as interpreted in *Sparham-Souter* v. *Town and Country Developments (Essex) Ltd.* [1976] QB 858.

[25] *Original Blouse Co. Ltd.* v. *Bruck Mills Ltd.* (1963) 42 DLR (2d) 174: cf. *Cordova Land Co.* v. *Victor Brothers Inc.* [1966] 1 WLR 793.

[26] *Esso Petroleum Co. Ltd.* v. *Marden* [1976] QB 801.

[27] *J Nunes Diamonds Ltd.* v. *Dominion Electric Protection Co.* [1972] SCR 769.

[28] Limitations Act 1975, s. 3(4).

asked whether the conduct of the defendant is actionable as a tort in England. It is clear that it is, whether or not the contract is valid under its proper law, the law of British Columbia. Under the second head of *Phillips* v. *Eyre*, it must be asked whether there is actionability in British Columbia.[29] So far as tortious liability is concerned, the answer is in the negative if the representation falls within the terms of the contract. That is a matter for the proper law of the contract and, by the law of British Columbia, the contract is valid and the representation constitutes a term thereof. So tortious liability is excluded. However, the second head of *Phillips* v. *Eyre* requires, not tortious actionability by the *lex loci delicti*, but 'civil actionability' thereby.[30] Contractual liability under the law of British Columbia is undoubtedly civil liability. The one remaining issue, therefore, is whether a contractual claim which is time barred under the *lex loci delicti* still satisfies the requirement of actionability. If one can say that limitation periods are merely procedural then procedure is a matter for the *lex fori* only and the British Columbia limitation period can be ignored. In fact, the British Columbia legislation states that the expiration of the limitation period 'extinguishes' the cause of action,[31] thereby lending some support to a characterization of the rule as substantive, with the conclusion that the defendant's conduct has ceased to be civilly actionable. Even if that be the case, one might well argue that *Boys* v. *Chaplin* requires no more than initial civil actionability by the *lex loci* and the fact that the limitation period has elapsed might be ignored.

The major significance of this type of case is that it is for the law, or laws, governing liability in tort to determine whether a valid contract has any effect on tort liability and it is then for the law governing the validity of the contract so to determine. This analysis is equally relevant to the second category of case, the effect of a contractual exemption clause on a claim in tort.

CONTRACTUAL EXEMPTION CLAUSE AS A DEFENCE TO TORT CLAIM

This second contractual problem concerns the effect of exemption clauses on liability in tort. What is at issue is the question as to how one determines the effect of an exemption clause when the law governing contractual liability is different from that governing liability in tort.

[29] One effect of *Boys* v. *Chaplin* [1971] AC 356 is to require 'actionability' in the *locus delicti* rather than non-justifiability under the now overruled decision in *Machado* v. *Fontes* [1897] 2 QB 231. In an English forum it is this English rule which is to be applied, notwithstanding the fact that *Machado* v. *Fontes* might still be good law under the conflict rules of British Columbia: *La Van* v. *Danyluk* (1970) 75 WWR 505.

[30] *Boys* v. *Chaplin* [1976] AC 356, 389.

[31] Limitations Act 1975, s. 9.

Within the purely contractual context, there seems little doubt that questions as to the validity of an exemption clause are issues of substance to be governed by the proper law of the contract[32] and, again, it is not proposed to examine here the principles upon which the proper law is determined. Assuming that it can be established what law governs the contractual validity of the clause in question and that it can be established what law or laws determine liability in tort, how does one determine the effect of a contractual exemption clause on liability in tort?

There is a variety of possible approaches. One can say that the matter is wholly contractual and ignore all issues of tortious liability;[33] one can say that this is a special issue, separate from either that of contractual or tortious liability, subject to its own choice of law rules;[34] one can treat the matter exclusively as an issue in tort or, finally, one can take the view that choice of law rules in contract and tort have roles to play, though different ones. This last view is that which has the greatest conceptual appeal and the implications of which it is intended to examine here.

The best exposition of this analysis is given by Kahn-Freund in his 1968 Hague Lectures.[35] The analysis is essentially the same as was applied to the problem of the effect of a contract on tortious liability. One must distinguish two problems. Is an exemption clause available or, as Kahn-Freund says, admissible as a defence to liability in tort? This is characterized as an issue of tort law to be governed by the appropriate choice of law rule which, for the sake of this discussion, we shall again assume to be the double actionability rule in *Phillips* v. *Eyre*. The second question is whether the exemption clause is valid. This is characterized as a contractual issue to be governed by the proper law of the contract. It is assumed that these two questions, availability/admissibility of the clause and validity thereof, are separate issues governed by different choice of law rules, for:

> There is all the difference in the world between inadmissibility and invalidity. Inadmissibility in our context is a rule designed to safeguard the application of the principles of delictual liability . . . invalidity, however, has to do with some defect of the exceptions clause itself, not with its specific relation to the law of delict.[36]

It is proposed to consider the application of this analysis by examining a number of leading cases concerned with the effect of clauses exempting or limiting liability in tort. It should be borne in mind that here we are concerned with the effect on tortious liability of a particular clause in the contract relieving from such future liability, rather than the exclusion of

[32] See *Coast Lines Ltd.* v. *Hudig and Veder Chartering NV* [1972] 2 QB 34.

[33] This seems to have been the approach of Salmon and Stamp LJJ in *Sayers* v. *International Drilling Co. NV* [1971] 1 WLR 1176.

[34] The approach of Lord Denning MR in *Sayers*.

[35] [1968] II *Hague Recueil* 1, 142–5.

[36] Ibid., 144.

tortious liability by the fact of a contractual relationship or a later contractual agreement not to sue.

The most straightforward case to deal with is one that raises conflicts problems only in the contractual sphere, that is, where the forum and the place of the tort are the same. A good illustration of this is the Scottish decision in *Brodin* v. *A/R Seljan*.[37] The deceased was a Norwegian employed as a seaman on an oil tanker owned by the defenders, a Norwegian company. He was injured in an accident on board the tanker as it was docking in a Scottish port. He died before his claim for damages came to trial. The proper law of his contract of employment was the law of Norway, and it was argued by the defenders that any claim to damages was excluded by the terms of the contract limiting his rights to compensation to those available under Norwegian law. Such a limitation of liability or exemption clause was void under Scottish law by reason of the Law Reform (Personal Injuries) Act 1948.[38]

Here we have a case where the *locus* of the tort and the forum are both Scotland, thus giving rise, on an orthodox interpretation of *Phillips* v. *Eyre*, to no tort conflict issue. Lord Kissen in the Court of Session held that a claim in delict could not, under Scots law, be met by an exemption clause which contravened the 1948 Act. The contractual defence was not available or admissible under the law governing tort liability. For 'whatever the law chosen by the parties to govern the contract or whatever the law of a contract may be, that law must, I think, yield to an Act of Parliament which has provided otherwise. The provision is, in other words, unenforceable in Scotland, whatever its effect elsewhere.'[39] So, if the contractual defence is not available, there is no need to examine its efficacy under the proper law of the contract.

The problem becomes more complex when the tort conflict rules are called into play because then it is necessary to examine the availability of the contract defence under the tort law of two legal systems. Nevertheless, it is suggested that the basic analysis should be the same. Let us see how far this is borne out by the cases, the first of which is *Canadian Pacific Railway Co.* v. *Parent*.[40] The deceased, domiciled in Quebec, was employed as a stockman by a firm in Manitoba to bring cattle from Winnipeg to Montreal. The cattle were consigned to the defendant railway by the deceased's employer under a contractual provision that, if a man was allowed to travel with the cattle at less than full fare, the defendant railway should be exempt from liability for 'death, injury or damage' whether or not due to their fault. The deceased signed a personal pass, which did not exempt the defendants from liability for his death, but did exclude their liability in respect of 'accident or damage to

[37] 1973 SLT 198. [38] S. 1(3). [39] 1973 SLT 198, 202. [40] [1917] AC 195.

person or property.' The deceased was killed through the negligence of the defendants when the train was passing through Ontario. His widow brought an action for damages in Quebec.

Under the law of Quebec, the widow had an independent right of action for her loss.[41] Under the law of Manitoba and of Ontario, the right of action of the widow depended upon the right of action of the deceased and would be lost if he had validly contracted away such right of action. The Privy Council held that the deceased assented to the agreement in the pass. Essentially this meant that the defendant railway had contractually excluded their liability to the deceased by means of a contract entered into on his behalf by his employers.[42] Under the law of Ontario, the *lex loci delicti*, there was no right of action in tort at the suit of the dependants because the deceased himself could not have sued. The Privy Council also concluded that, under the law of Quebec, there was no right of action because Article 1056 applied only to acts committed within Quebec. This really amounts to an application of the analysis relied on above. First, the delict was not actionable by the *lex fori*, Quebec, because the accident occurred in Ontario. Second, the contract provided a good defence under the law of Ontario. What is of significance is that the Privy Council never expressly determined what law governed the validity of the contract, though they had no doubt of its validity.[43] Of course, there was no need to determine the validity of the contract or even of its effect under the law of Ontario, given the fact that no action would lie under the law of Quebec, the *lex fori*.[44]

The second case involving an exemption clause as a defence to a tort action where the forum and the *locus delicti* are different is *Sayers* v. *International Drilling Co. NV*.[45] The plaintiff was an Englishman who entered into a contract of employment with the defendants, a Dutch oil drilling company. The plaintiff worked for the defendants on an oil rig in Nigerian territorial waters where he was injured by the alleged negligence of his fellow employees. The employment contract contained an exemption clause under which the employee agreed to accept benefits under the

[41] Art. 1056 of the Quebec Civil Code.

[42] E.g. *Grand Trunk Railway Co.* v. *Robinson* [1915] AC 740.

[43] It was certainly held to be subject to the federal provisions contained in s. 340 of the Railway Act, RSC 1906, c. 37. In the Supreme Court of Canada (1915) 51 SCR 234, the majority had taken the view that the contract was void because the deceased had had insufficient notice and therefore the defendants were liable. It was not considered necessary to decide whether the contract was governed by the law of Quebec, Ontario or Manitoba. However Anglin J held, at 279–82, that the contract was valid and was, therefore, a good defence in Ontario. Nevertheless he concluded that the defendant's conduct was actionable in Quebec and, despite the contract, was not justifiable in Ontario and, therefore, the defendants were still liable.

[44] The rule in *Phillips* v. *Eyre* forms part of the law of Quebec: *O'Connor* v. *Wray* [1930] SCR 231.

[45] [1971] 1 WLR 1176; Collins, (1972) 21 *ICLQ* 320; and see Smith, (1972) 21 *ICLQ* 164.

defendants' compensation scheme but was precluded from any compensation under English law. This exemption clause was held to be valid under Dutch law in the case of international contracts but was void under English law as it contravened the provisions of the Law Reform (Personal Injuries) Act 1948.[46] The plaintiff claimed damages for his injuries.

It was ordered that the issues raised in relation to the contract should be tried as a preliminary issue and Bean J held that the proper law of the contract was Dutch law, by which the exemption clause was valid and the claim failed. On appeal to the Court of Appeal, Salmon and Stamp LJJ restricted their examination of the case to the question of determining the proper law of the contract and they agreed with the trial judge that Dutch law applied and the appeal was dismissed. This approach is unfortunate because, as we have seen, the effect of an exemption clause on tortious liability raises issues of tort law as well as the question of the validity of the contractual exemption clause.

Lord Denning MR adopted a wider, and more satisfactory, analysis of the issues before the court, though one may question his resolution of them. He started from the premise that the claim was one in tort raising a contractual defence. He concluded that a tort claim is governed by the proper law of the tort.[47] Whilst I have suggested elsewhere that this is not the ratio of *Boys* v. *Chaplin*,[48] there seems little doubt that the facts of *Sayers* do raise an issue of choice of law in torts. Lord Denning MR concluded that the proper law of this tort was Dutch law, despite the fact it was an accident to an Englishman on an oil rig in Nigerian territorial waters. So far as the contract was concerned, he disagreed with his brethren and concluded that the proper law thereof was English law. But he considered that:

> We cannot apply two systems of law, one for the claim in tort, and the other for the defence in contract. We must apply one system of law by which to decide both claim and defence. To decide it I would ask this question: What is the proper law by which to determine the issues in this case? And I would answer it by saying: it is the system of law with which the issues have the closest connection.[49]

At the end of the day, his Lordship decided that the proper law of this issue was Dutch law and, again, the claim failed.

Various criticisms have been made of this conclusion on the facts of the case,[50] but it is open to two further and major objections. It assumes that the test for determining the proper law of a tort and of a contract

[46] S. 1(3); the same subsection as was considered in *Brodin* v. *A/R Seljan* 1973 SLT 198, see n. 37 above.

[47] [1971] 1 WLR 1176, 1180.

[48] Cheshire, n. 6 above, 268–9.

[49] [1971] 1 WLR 1176, 1181.

[50] Collins, (1972) 21 *ICLQ* 320, 328–9.

are the same—some form of 'grouping of contacts' test. This test may be true of contract but would not appear to fulfil the requirements of those who advocate a proper law approach to torts where there is far more of a weighing of interests and policies involved—more of a rule-selecting, than a jurisdiction-selecting, approach. Secondly, Lord Denning MR's analysis takes no account of the problem examined in the first part of this essay, namely the effect of a contract as such on tortious liability. Is this also to be decided according to a proper law of the issue approach? If so, it must surely mean that the contract choice of law rule will be subjugated to the tort rule.

How might *Sayers* have been decided, applying the analysis suggested earlier, i.e. that the availability or admissibility of an exemption clause as a defence is a matter of tort law and the validity of the clause is a matter of contract law? On this analysis, the first question would be whether the defendants' conduct was actionable under English law, the *lex fori*. Could an exemption clause relieve the employer from liability in tort? At first sight, section 1(3) of the 1948 Act indicates that it cannot; that the exemption clause is void and that the conduct is actionable in England. A more careful approach might suggest inquiry as to the extra-territorial effect of the 1948 Act.[51] Even if one then concludes that the conduct was actionable in England, resort must be had to the law of Nigeria as the *locus delicti* to determine whether the conduct was civilly actionable there. One cannot agree with Lord Denning MR that 'The Nigerians had nothing to do with the rig. So Nigeria is out.'[52] The only way that Nigeria could be 'out' is if the facts were such as to invoke the flexibility approach from *Boys* v. *Chaplin* justifying, as in that case, ignoring the *lex loci delicti*. It is only if an exemption clause provides a defence under the applicable tort laws (or law) that the question arises as to the validity of the exemption clause. Dutch law, regarded as the proper law of the contract by the majority, is only relevant to decide the validity of the contract, provided the 1948 Act does not apply under English law, and provided there is no similar applicable provision under Nigerian law.

It might be argued that a simpler approach to this problem is to start with the contract and ask whether the exemption clause is valid under the proper law of the contract. If it is not, then the matter appears to be at an end because there is no contractual defence even if such were permitted as a matter of tort law. Such an approach conceals a potential problem. It assumes that the proper law of the contract is determined by the

[51] Even on the analysis actually adopted in the Court of Appeal, the court should have considered whether the 1948 Act embodied a mandatory rule of English public policy applicable to all claims before English courts: cf. *Brodin* v. *A/R Seljan* 1973 SLT 198, n. 37 above, and see Collins, (1972) 21 *ICLQ* 320, 329–33.

[52] [1971] 1 WLR 1176, 1181.

conflict rules of the forum and that the law chosen thereunder determines the validity of the contract both for the law of the forum and for the *lex loci delicti*. An alternative approach, which involves looking to the tort issue before the contract one, is to ask the *lex loci delicti* whether an exemption clause can provide a defence to a tort claim. If the answer is 'yes' provided, obviously, it is a valid exemption clause, then it can be argued that it is for the conflict rules of the *lex loci delicti* to determine the validity of the contract and of the exemption clause. The outcome of a case could be very different depending upon which of these two approaches is adopted, as a variant of the facts of *Sayers* may illustrate.

On the first approach, let us assume that both English and Nigerian law admit the availability of a contractual defence, i.e. the 1948 Act does not have extraterritorial effect and there is no Nigerian equivalent of the 1948 Act. Applying the conflict contract choice of law rules of the *lex fori*, English law, it is assumed that the validity of the contract in this hypothetical example is governed by English law.[53] By English law, the exemption clause is void; the defence fails and the claim succeeds.

A different answer may be reached on the second approach. Both English and Nigerian law admit the availability of the contractual defence. Under English conflict rules, it is assumed that the proper law of the contract is English; the exemption clause is void and the defendants' conduct is actionable in England. We must now turn to Nigerian law and apply Nigerian contract choice of law rules to decide whether the defendants' conduct is actionable in Nigeria. Let us assume that the proper law of the contract, under Nigerian conflict rules, is Dutch law. Under that law, the contract is valid; the exemption clause is good; the conduct is not actionable in Nigeria and the claim fails.

So, a choice between the two approaches may be important. Which approach is preferable? Collins would seem to prefer the first view, that is, the exclusive application of the conflicts rule of the forum, for he says:

> If the plaintiff sues on a foreign tort, he is met by a defence that liability is excluded under the *lex loci delicti*. It may depend on the scope and form of the rule of the *lex loci* regarding exculpatory clauses. If its rule is that one *may* exclude liability, then it could be argued that there is no exemption because the contractual term is invalid by its law. It must be for the *lex fori* to determine the validity of the contractual exemption according to its proper law. It would be an unnecessary extension of the *renvoi* principle to delegate this function to the *lex loci delicti*. But if the defence is framed in the nature of *volenti non fit iniuria* it would appear that, if the *lex loci delicti* admits such a defence irrespective of the validity of the contract, the act would be 'justifiable' by the *lex loci delicti*.[54]

This rejection of *renvoi* may be at the price of conflicting results depending upon classification. There is no doubt that problems of

[53] The view of Lord Denning MR in *Sayers*.

[54] (1967) 16 *ICLQ* 103, 115.

classification may arise in the context of defences to tort actions. It is assumed, in the above quotation, that *volenti* is a tort defence whose operation and effect is wholly within the ambit of the *lex loci delicti*. Yet, the validity of a contractual term as a defence is a matter for the conflict laws of the forum. This means that, though we are spared the complexities of *renvoi*, the outcome of the case will depend on how the forum classifies the defences of the *lex loci delicti*. In some situations this may be unavoidable, as in the Canadian decisions on the availability of the defence of common employment,[55] and in such a case the characterization is made according to the legal categories of the *lex fori*.[56] Nevertheless, where possible these problems are to be avoided and so they would be if the availability of a contractual defence under the *lex loci delicti* was a matter for the tort law and the conflict choice of law rules of that jurisdiction. It is suggested, therefore, that it is for the *lex loci delicti* to determine the validity of a contractual exemption clause under its own conflicts rules.[57] Any other answer would mean an English court purporting to decide whether conduct was actionable under the *lex loci delicti*, applying English choice of law rules in contract and ignoring the different conclusion which would have been reached in the foreign court. This would be all the more unacceptable if the effect of an exemption clause in the *lex loci delicti* was not to bar an action in tort but to prevent a tort ever having been committed.[58] In that event, the *lex loci delicti* should determine that no tort had been committed by reason of the exemption clause, valid under its own, but not the forum's, conflict rules.

CONTRACTUAL RELEASE FROM TORTIOUS LIABILITY

The third and final problem area to be considered is as to how far a contract may constitute a waiver or release from tortious liability. We are here concerned with what American writers describe as post-tort releases;[59] a pre-tort release is the problem discussed in the previous section, namely the operation of such provisions as exemption and limitation of liability clauses.[60] The post-tort release poses two problems—what law

[55] *Dupont* v. *Quebec Steamship Co.* (1896) QR 11 SC 188; *Story* v. *Stratford Mill Building Co.* (1913) 18 DLR 309, 315; and see *Logan* v. *Lee* (1907) 39 SCR 311; *Maclean* v. *Grand Trunk Railway Co.* (1911) 21 KB 269; Dicey and Morris, *The Conflict of Laws*, 9th edn. (1973), 963–4; Collins, (1967) 16 *ICLQ* 103, 115–16; Kahn-Freund, [1968] II *Hague Recueil* 1, 146.

[56] Dicey and Morris, n. 55 above, 963.

[57] Kahn-Freund, [1968] II *Hague Recueil* 1, 145 poses, but does not answer, a similar problem.

[58] Coote, *Exception Clauses* (1964), esp. 34–6.

[59] Note, (1960) 60 *Col L Rev* 522.

[60] For the US law, see (1960) 60 *Col L Rev* 522, 530–3.

governs the validity of the agreement to release the tortfeasor from his liability? and, what is the effect of such a release on the liability of other joint tortfeasors? There is little Commonwealth authority on either issue and, indeed, relatively little American authority.

The first problem, as to what law governs the validity of the agreement to release the tortfeasor from liability, is very similar to the tort/contract issues already discussed. The appropriate analysis would appear to be that the question whether a post-tort agreement is available/admissible to release from tort liability is a matter of tort law. On an orthodox view, this will involve examination of such availability under both the *lex fori* and the *lex loci delicti*. It is, however, a matter for the contractual *lex causae*[61] to determine the validity of the contractual agreement containing the release.

If we look briefly at the American cases, it will be seen that there is no uniformity of view as to whether the effect of a release is characterized as a contractual or a delictual issue. In *Snashall* v. *Metropolitan Railroad*[62] the court applied the *lex fori*, which was also the *lex loci delicti*, to determine whether a married woman had capacity to contract and thus grant a release, rather than the law of her domicile and the place of contracting. This indicates that not only the availability of the release as a defence to a tort claim, but also the contractual validity thereof, are matters for the *lex causae* of the tort.[63] A different approach is seen in *Leach* v. *Mason Valley Mines*[64] where a Nevada court allowed a release, executed in California, to relieve from liability for a tort committed in Nevada, despite a Nevadan statute stipulating that a release could not be relied on in such a case. Here the essential characterization of the issue appears to be contractual.

A much more recent decision, *Nelson* v. *Browning*,[65] appears to support the earlier view, that the *lex causae* of the tort issue prevails. In this case an action for damages for personal injuries was brought in Missouri, where the accident occurred, by a plaintiff who had executed a release in Arkansas. The plaintiff was a minor and the release was valid under the law of Arkansas but voidable, at the plaintiff's option, under the law of Missouri. It was held that the effect of the release was a matter for Missouri law:

> While generally matters bearing upon the execution and validity of a contract are determined by the law of the place where the contract is made . . . the validity of

[61] The determination of the law governing the contract is subject to the same possibilities of the application of the *renvoi* doctrine as was suggested earlier in the discussion of exemption clauses.

[62] 19 DC 399 (1890).

[63] A similar approach seems to be exemplified by *Justis* v. *Atchison, Topeka and Santa Fe Railway* 108 P 328 (1910).

[64] 161 P 513 (1916).

[65] 391 SW 2d 873 (1965).

a contract of release as a defence to an action of tort is governed by the law of the State that created or gave rise to the right released.[66]

The one Commonwealth case of interest in this context is *Scott* v. *American Airlines Inc.*[67] The plaintiff and her deceased husband were both United States citizens from Michigan. The defendant was an American company. The husband was killed when the defendant's plane crashed in Ontario. After the crash, the plaintiff entered an agreement with her husband's employers' insurance company, for compensation. This compensation was paid under the Michigan workmen's compensation legislation. When the plaintiff claimed damages in Ontario under the Fatal Accidents Act, the defendant argued that, by electing to take compensation, she had forfeited the right to bring an action for damages. Any rights she might have had were now subrogated to the insurance company. This is not a straightforward case of a release; but in effect the defendant's argument is that the agreement between the plaintiff and the insurance company relieves the defendant from liability. The court has no doubts that under the law of Michigan, where the compensation agreement was entered into, it did have the effect of preventing a further claim in tort. The contract was valid under the law of Michigan, which was not only the place of contracting, but Michigan law would today have been regarded as the proper law of the contract. That being so, the plaintiff:

> waived her common law remedy to sue in tort either in Michigan or Ontario. . . . Her right of action was extinguished by the agreement under the law of the country in which the agreement was made and of which she is a citizen. There is no right to bring action in another country. She cannot sue in both places, because there is only one cause of action. She could not have sued in Michigan after electing to accept the compensation offered, and therefore she cannot sue in Ontario.[68]

This seems clearly to embody a contractual approach, very similar to that of the majority in *Sayers*. There is little doubt that the applicable tort law in *Scott* was the law of Ontario, both the *lex fori* and the *lex loci delicti*. Yet there is no discussion of whether the compensation agreement relieves from tortious liability under Ontario law. Again, as was suggested earlier, the better approach is to ask whether the *lex causae* of the tort issue makes a contractual release or agreement available as a defence, i.e. a problem for Ontario law. If so, it is then for the contractual *lex causae* to determine the validity of the agreement.

[66] 391 SW 2d 873, 879 (1965). The authorities relied on for this conclusion are all cases concerned with the effect of the release of one tortfeasor on the liability of a joint tortfeasor. In such a case there is wider agreement that this is a tort issue. The *Restatement* 2d s. 170, Comment b. adopts the contractual classification as between the parties to the release.

[67] [1944] 3 DLR 27.

[68] Ibid., 29.

This type of analysis can be adopted not only in the case of the effect of a release between the actual parties thereto, but also when one has to consider the effect of a release on other joint tortfeasors.[69] In this field, the only relevant authorities are American and they tend to support a tort classification.[70] An oft cited authority is *Bittner* v. *Little,*[71] where the plaintiff was injured in Virginia as the result of the negligence of D_1 and D_2. In New York, he executed a release to D_1 but reserved his rights against D_2. That reservation was effective under New York law, but, under the law of Virginia, the release of one tortfeasor released all. The plaintiff then sued D_2 before a federal court in Pennsylvania where it was held that the law of Virginia, the place of the tort, governed the effect of the release and the claim failed. A New York court had come to a similar conclusion the previous year[72] on the ground that 'this is a matter of substance and must therefore be governed by the law of the *situs* of the tort.'[73] Confusion has crept into the American cases since the abandonment of the *lex situs* choice of law rule in tort in favour of Fuld J's approach in *Babcock* v. *Jackson.*[74] In the New York decision in *Root* v. *Kaufman*[75] it seems to be assumed that the necessity to distinguish between a contract or tort classification has disappeared because all that was done in *Babcock* was to extend to tort law the 'grouping of contact' test already accepted as the choice of law rule in contract.[76] This fails to take into account both that the tort test is based as much on a weighing as a counting of contacts and that express choice of the applicable law is possible in contract but is not generally accepted in tort.

What conclusions can be drawn from this brief consideration of the American authorities on the effect of the release of one joint tortfeasor on the liability of another? It seems quite illogical to characterize the issue as other than primarily a tort issue. There is no contractual nexus between the plaintiff and the second tortfeasor. Their relationship is essentially one governed by tort law. So, for English law, the problem is really whether, under the *lex fori* and the *lex loci delicti*, the release of the first tortfeasor provides a defence to the second; i.e. how far does this constitute a tort

[69] Wade, (1953) 6 *Vanderbilt L Rev* 464, 469–72; Ehrenzweig, (1960) 46 *Va L Rev* 712; Note, (1960) 60 *Col L Rev* 523, 527–530; Annotation, 69 *ALR* (2d) 1034.

[70] There are some older cases which applied the law of the place of execution of the release; e.g. *Richardson* v. *Pacific Power & Light Co.*, 118 P 2d 985 (1941); *Western Spring Service Co.* v. *Andrew* 229 F 2d 413 (1956). In this latter case, as in most cases of a contractual classification, the *lex situs* of the tort was the same as the law governing the contract.

[71] 270 F 2d 286 (1959); and see, e.g. *Hayden* v. *Ford Motor Co.* 278 F Supp. 267 (1967).

[72] *De Bono* v. *Bittner* 178 NYS 2d 419 (1958). [73] Ibid., 420.

[74] 240 NYS 2d 743 (1963).

[75] 265 NYS 2d 201 (1965). There is a somewhat more sophisticated approach in *Manos* v. *Trans World Airlines Inc.* 295 F Supp 1166 (1968).

[76] *Auten* v. *Auten* 124 NE 2d 99 (1954).

defence. Whether the agreement between the plaintiff and the first tortfeasor is a valid agreement is, as with all these contractual issues, a matter for the contractual *lex causae*, but that is the only matter for that law.

The conclusion to be drawn from this examination of a variety of problems concerned with the interrelation of tort and contract issues in the conflict of laws is that they may all be solved in the same basic manner. The availability of the contractual defence is a matter of tort law but the validity of the contract in which it is to be found is a matter of contract law. It may convincingly be argued that it is high time English law abandoned the double-barrelled tort rule of *Phillips* v. *Eyre*; but until it is abandoned, these problems necessitate a determination of whether the relevant contractual defence is available under both the *lex fori* and the *lex loci delicti*.

6

Development of Rules of Private International Law in the Field of Family Law

INTRODUCTION

It is suggested here that the development of interest analysis and other 'rule-selecting' approaches to choice of law has had very little direct impact on the development of private international law rules applicable to marriage and divorce. It remains rare to find detailed examination of the impact of such approaches on choice of law rules in the field of family law.[1] What has become more common, however, is to find general criticisms of interest analysis as providing a choice of law methodology;[2] though it is certainly not without its recent defenders.[3]

In terms of the development of English choice of law rules relating to marriage, three matters deserve highlighting. The first is that it remains unclear whether, in the context of essential validity, primacy is to be given to the application of the domiciliary law or that of the intended matrimonial home. Indeed, the Law Commission has stated that 'there is no decision which prevents the Court of Appeal or the House of Lords from adopting either test'.[4] Second, greater attention has been paid to whether there are alternative choice of law approaches which might be developed in the context of essential validity of marriage.[5] One approach

Reprinted by permission of the Curatorium of the Hague Academy of International Law from (1980 I) 166 *Recueil des Cours* 9, 31–88.

[1] Notable exceptions are Fine, (1980) 26 *Loyola L Rev* 31 and 295, and Davie, 'An Examination of Policy-orientated Choice of Law Theory with Particular Reference to Family Law Matters', *D Phil Thesis*, (Oxford, 1991); see also Smart, (1985) 14 *Anglo-American LR* 225 and Clarkson, (1990) 10 *Legal Studies* 80 where there is some analysis of marriage choice of law rules in terms of conflicting interests.

[2] Juenger, (1984) 32 *Am Jo Comp L* 1; (1985) 46 *Ohio State LJ* 509; [1985] IV *Hague Recueil* 123, 227–52; (1988) 21 *UC Davis LR* 515; Rosenberg, (1981) 81 *Col LR* 772; Ely, (1981) 23 *William and Mary L Rev* 173; Brilmayer, (1980) 78 *Mich LR* 392; (1984) 35 *Mercer LR* 555; (1985) 46 *Ohio State LJ* 459; (1989) 98 *Yale LJ* 1277; Kozyris, (1985) 46 *Ohio State LJ* 569; Dane, (1987) 96 *Yale LJ* 1191.

[3] Kay, (1983) 34 *Mercer LR* 521; [1989] III *Hague Recueil* 9; Weintraub, (1985) 46 *Ohio State LJ* 493; Posnak, (1988) 36 *Am Jo Comp L* 681; Sedler, (1983) 34 *Mercer LR* 593; (1985) 46 *Ohio State LJ* 483.

[4] Law Com. Working Paper No. 89 (1985), 60.

[5] Ibid., 94–6; North, [1990] I *Hague Recueil* 9, 59 *et seq.*

which has attracted both judicial[6] and academic[7] support is the application of some form of proper law of the marriage; though this is a development which I believe to be seriously flawed.[8]

The third matter concerns reform of the marriage choice of law rules which has been examined by the Law Commission.[9] Interest in the present context lies not so much in their unfortunate conclusion that, though the rules were unclear, they were still developing and so should not be reformed,[10] but rather in their examination of the various routes to reform open to them. There was, unusually,[11] direct consideration of whether conventional jurisdiction-selecting choice of law rules should be abandoned in favour of rules developed on an American rule-selecting approach. In their Working Paper, the Law Commission rejected[12] rule-selection for a variety of reasons, most notably the difficulty in determining the policies underlying conflicting substantive rules of marriage law, and the risks to certainty and predictability, both of real importance in marriage, which rule-selection involves.

* * *

[6] *Vervaeke* v. *Smith* [1983] 1 AC 145, 165–6; *Lawrence* v. *Lawrence* [1985] Fam 106; *Entry Clearance Officer, Dhaka* v. *Ranu Begum* [1986] Imm AR 460; *R* v. *Immigration Appeal Tribunal, ex p Rafika Bibi* [1989] Imm AR 1.

[7] Fentiman, [1985] *CLJ* 256; (1986) 6 *OJLS* 353, 354–60; Smart, (1985) 14 *Anglo-American LR* 225.

[8] North, [1990] I *Hague Recueil* 9, 65–8.

[9] Law Com. Working Paper No. 89 (1985); Law Com. No. 165 (1987).

[10] Law Com. No. 165 (1987), para. 2.14, criticized in Cheshire and North, *Private International Law*, 12th edn. (1992), 606–7.

[11] There is, however, detailed analysis by the Law Commission of rule-selection approaches in the context of reform of the tort choice of law rules: see Law Com. Working Paper No. 87 (1984), paras. 4.35–4.54. Nevertheless such approaches were clearly rejected: Law Com. No. 193 (1990), paras. 1.7–1.8.

[12] Law Com. Working Paper No. 89 (1985), paras. 2.31–2.34.

FAMILY LAW AND THE AMERICAN REVOLUTION

Introduction

Rule selection or jurisdiction selection?

THERE are a number of general propositions that may be made concerning the law to be applied to family law issues—such as that the essential validity of a marriage is to be governed by the law of the domicile or the law of the nationality, as a matter of status; that, on the basis of *locus regit actum*, the formal validity of a marriage is governed by the law of the place of celebration; that a divorce will be granted according to the law of the forum, or alternatively, according to the law applicable to matters of status. Support for all these different rules may be found in one legal system or another but, different though they are, they have one thing in common. They are, in the terminology of the American 'revolution'[1] in the conflict of laws, jurisdiction-selecting rules.[2] They require the court to apply the law of the country chosen by the private international law rule irrespective of the content of the substantive rule of law thereby selected. They are, in that respect, different from the rule-selection techniques of the more recent American writings and decisions with their emphasis on a balancing of the respective interests involved in the application of a particular substantive rule of one legal system rather than a different substantive rule of another legal system.

This is not the place to provide a detailed analysis of the various approaches to such interest analysis which have become well known in the USA over the past decades.[3] Our prime concern here is with the application of such interest analysis to the particular field of family law and to consider what the future holds for such a general approach in this field.

The question of choosing between a rule-selection or a jurisdiction-selection approach has been expressed most clearly by Cavers: 'should a court in dealing with a claim that a foreign law is applicable to the case before it or to an issue in that case choose between its own and the foreign legal system or, instead, choose between its own rule and the foreign rule?'[4] The American answer is to prefer rule-selection, but this can, both in academic theory and in judicial decisions,[5] take a variety of forms.

[1] Cf. Kegel, [1964] II *Hague Recueil* 95.
[2] Or as Cavers has described them, state-selecting, [1970] III *Hague Recueil* 75, 103.
[3] See, e.g. Kegel, [1964] II *Hague Recueil* 95; Cavers, [1970] III *Hague Recueil* 75, 103.
[4] Cavers, [1970] III *Hague Recueil* 75, 122.
[5] Virtually none of which concern family law.

However, before one even attempts to select between these variations on a revolutionary theme, it is necessary to examine a further preliminary issue which may eradicate the need for any choice at all, namely the question whether there is a true or false conflict.

True and false conflicts

A jurisdiction-selecting approach to choice of law leads to the application of the rules of law of the chosen jurisdiction irrespective of which of the rules of substantive law of two or more apparently involved legal systems is to be applied. There is a basic premise here that rules from two or more legal systems do have a claim to be applied. If they do not, and on analysis only one has such a claim, there is no choice to be made. This latter situation has been described as a 'false conflict';[6] the former case where more than one set of rules has a legitimate claim to application, thereby necessitating the development of rules for choosing between them, is a 'true conflict'. There is a third possibility,[7] which has been described as a 'no-interest' case,[8] where a conflict of decision may result from the application of the laws of the different states, but where neither state has an interest in its law being applied.[9]

> The classic 'no interest' case is one in which the plaintiff's state has a law favorable to the defendant and the defendant's state has a law favorable to the plaintiff . . . The plaintiff's state has no interest in protecting the defendant who comes from another state and the defendant's state has no reason to give the plaintiff more compensation than he would get under the law of his own state.[10]

It will be apparent that in this whole area a two-stage analysis is involved. First, does the case involve a true or a false conflict? We are told that that question is to be answered by a proper interpretation of the rules in issue in the light of their respective purposes and the facts of the case.[11] Indeed, we are told that if, after such a test has been applied, a

[6] This phrase can cover both the case where the laws of the two states are identical or would produce the same result; e.g., *Scheer* v. *Rockne Motors Corp.* 68 F 2d 942 (1934), and that where the laws are different, but only one has an interest in being applied: e.g., *Babcock* v. *Jackson* 12 NY 2d 473; 191 NE 2d 279 (1963).

[7] Altogether seven possible 'false conflict' situations have been identified: see Westen, (1967) 55 *Cal L Rev* 74, 76–8.

[8] For an early analysis of this situation, see Currie, *Selected Essays on the Conflict of Laws* (1963), 152–6. A further variant, that of 'the disinterested third state' is discussed below, see pp. 116–117.

[9] It might be illustrated by *Hurtado* v. *Superior Court* 11 Cal 3d 574; 522 P 2d 666 (1974), where the problem was resolved by reliance on a presumption in favour of applying forum law unless an interest could be shown for the application of the foreign law.

[10] Weintraub, (1977) 41 *Law and Contemporary Problems*, 2: 146, 153; cf. Cavers, [1970] III *Hague Recueil* 75, 130–1.

[11] Cavers, [1970] III *Hague Recueil* 75, 129.

true conflict is seen to exist, we are to apply the test more carefully again in the hopes that on truer analysis the conflict will prove to be false and the need for choice of law rules that much the less.[12] A cynic might suggest that there are never really false conflicts; merely cases where the arguments in favour of applying one law rather than the other are much more powerful. If you can exaggerate this into a false conflict then, so the argument goes, the choice of law problem disappears.

If, despite those efforts to get the problem of choice of law to go away, it stubbornly remains in the form of a 'true' conflict, the second stage of analysis is reached, namely the selection between the various rules which have a legitimate claim to application. There is no agreement amongst the American 'revolutionaries' as to how this selection is to be made. Let us, however, consider some of the different rule-selection techniques that have been put forward.

The Revolutionaries

Governmental interest analysis and the lex fori

The father of this approach[13] is Brainerd Currie, though he has many disciples. I cannot improve on this succinct analysis of Currie's views given by David Cavers in his General Course of lectures at the Hague Academy in 1970:

> A court 'asked to apply the law of a foreign State different from the law of the forum' should—
> (1) Inquire into 'the policies expressed in the respective laws' and the circumstances that may render reasonable the application of those policies, employing 'the ordinary processes of construction and interpretation'.
> (2) If only one State has an interest in the application of its policy, apply the law of that State.
> (3) If the two States' interests appear in conflict, consider whether 'a moderate and restrained interpretation of one policy or interest of one state or the other may avoid conflict'.
> (4) If a conflict between the States' 'legitimate interests' persists, apply the forum's law.[14]

It will be apparent that the first three stages involve the determination of whether the conflict is true or false. It is only the fourth and final stage which provides a test for resolving a true conflict and that test is really

[12] (1963) 63 *Col L Rev* 1233, 1421–2 and he there suggests that this is what the court did in *Bernkrant* v. *Fowler* 55 Cal 2d 588; 360 P 2d 906 (1961).

[13] *Bernhard* v. *Harrah's Club* 16 Cal 3d 313, 319; 546 P 2d 719, 722 (1976).

[14] Cavers, [1970] *Hague Recueil* 75, 146–7.

rather unsophisticated and hardly consonant with the 'internationalism' of private international law. Moreover the whole scheme suffers from major defects in an international, rather than an inter-state (i.e., within the USA), context.[15] The emphasis on conflict resolution is placed on the initial analysis into true or false conflicts; the rule for the resolution of true conflicts amounts to an abandonment of any attempt to balance the state, or governmental, interests which have played such a significant role in the earlier stages. Indeed, the weighing of the respective interests of the forum state and the other interested state is categorically rejected by Currie. This is so even when the non-forum state may clearly be seen to have the greater interest. His reason, in the context of the evolution of choice of law rules, is not convincing. He says that 'courts should not attempt the weighing operation; that they are not equipped to marshal the facts necessary to inform their decisions in such a process; and that the choice between conflicting interests should be left to Congress'.[16] Courts are regarded as able to identify the policies and state interests in issue in conflicting rules and to identify whether there is a true conflict, but they are regarded as incapable of resolving such conflict. This is the more surprising in a country where, at least since the days of Cardozo and Brandeis, appellate courts have acknowledged, perhaps more clearly than in any other jurisdiction, that they are involved in a policy making role, that every decision involving a choice between different legal policies is judicial law making. It appears that Currie rejects a choice between the policies behind the rules of different states (perhaps for constitutional reasons) whilst all around him policy decisions are made both in the context of the interpretation of the Constitution and in deciding the future development of rules of private law both at state and federal level. It should not be forgotten that adoption by the courts of Currie's own approach involved a major judicial policy decision.[17]

Two other major disadvantages of his approach can be identified. The balancing of interests implied in the analysis assumes a judicial ability both to identify and to evaluate the policies expressed in the respective laws. The difficulties are legion.[18] For example, if the laws are statutory, and the vast majority of American interest-analysis cases have concerned statutory rules, does the judge look at the policies underlying them at the time the statute was passed, or at the time of the action before him? It may be that the statute was passed to achieve one social purpose, but is now used, say a hundred years later, to achieve another. It may even be

[15] See Shapira, *The Interest Approach to Choice of Law* (1970), 34–44.

[16] Currie, *Selected Essays on the Conflict of Laws* (1963), 602, and see ibid., 182.

[17] E.g., *Babcock* v. *Jackson* 12 NY 2d 473; 191 NE 2d 279 (1963). Cardozo would not have adopted the approach of Chief Judge Fuld in this case: see Cardozo, *The Paradoxes of Legal Science* (1928), 67.

[18] Cf. Shapira, *The Interest Approach to Choice of Law* (1970), ch. v.

regarded by some to be out-moded and undesirable, but legislative inertia is such that its repeal is unlikely. What policy does it now embody? If the temporal problem is overcome, how is the policy underlying the rule to be determined? Is the court to consider evidence of the debates in the legislature during the passage of the legislation, or of reports of bodies which led to the introduction of the legislation, coupled perhaps with argument, from the other side, as to why those policies are now outdated and why the statute is justified on other policy grounds, or none at all? The problem is worse confounded for those jurisdictions, such as England, where the courts will not consider the legislative history as an aid to the interpretation of statutes. Again, there may be a statute imposing liability in one state, but not in another. The reason for the absence of legislation in the latter state may be conscious decision, lack of legislative time, or a feeling that such development (if any) ought to be left to judicial, and not legislative, decision. Similar problems exist with the identification of the policy underlying rules of law based on decisions of the courts, rather than found in statutes. There is the problem of the age of the decision and in England, for example, cases decided in the seventeenth century, and certainly those of the nineteenth century, laid down major rules of law which are still applied. The judge may never have articulated his policy reasons at the time of judgment; the policy underlying retention of the rule may have changed; and the state's interest in the application of that rule to the present case is likely to be no more than pure conjecture.

It might be argued in reply to such criticisms that courts in the USA have in recent years been willing and able to resolve issues of choice of law very much on the lines of Currie's analysis without appearing to be worried by the alleged difficulties just outlined. It is true that judges have been untroubled by many of these difficulties. Indeed, they have ignored them. They have assumed that they can identify the policy underlying the rule of another state without further enquiry. They tend to say 'If we had such a rule in our jurisdiction, the reason for it would have been so and so. That must be the reason for, and policy behind, that rule in the other state.' The perspective is that of the forum state. This may, in fact, often lead to as correct a result as can be expected when the court in one state in the USA is considering the rule in another sister state or even in a neighbouring Canadian province. It has been said, for example, that 'the conditions are totally different [from an international case] in the sister states of this country. The law of another state is in our language; its principles are substantially the same and their tenor is readily ascertained by reference to the reporter systems.'[19] One could conclude that it is

[19] *Prudential Insurance Company of America* v. *O'Grady* 396 P 2d 246, 248 (1964). Indeed this distinction between inter-state and international conflicts may be seen from the fact that many American states authorize their courts to take judicial notice of the law of

likely that judges and legislators in the jurisdictions involved think alike. Even so, the process of identification of policies is somewhat haphazard. For example, in one case,[20] a court in New Jersey had to determine the purpose behind a statutory provision in Iowa denying recovery to a guest passenger in a car in an action by him against the driver unless the latter was drunk or reckless. This was done by looking at three Iowa decisions, one of which was nearly 40 years old, and extracting from them three dicta as to the purposes behind the statute. These were then taken as the purposes and shown to be irrelevant to the facts of the case so that Iowa was held to have no interest in the application of its statute. A further purpose behind the statute was suggested which would have indicated an Iowa interest. This was rejected because 'Iowa has never expressed such a purpose behind its guest statute, and it is not appropriate for us to impute inarticulated purposes to the legislature of another state'.[21] All seems to depend on the chance possibility of dicta!

The position is likely to be very different in international, rather than inter-state (or intra-North American), conflicts. The task for an American judge in seeking the policy, original or present, underlying for example Article 1382 of the French Civil Code and the present interest of France in its application to a claim before the particular American state court is immeasurably more difficult. This is one of the reasons why great scepticism has been voiced as to whether this type of interest analysis and selection between rules has a role to play outside the USA.[22] Whilst it may be argued that 'the exaggerated pursuit of self-interest by individual states which [Currie's] theory might seem to encourage'[23] can be curbed in an inter-state conflict by constraints of the United States Constitution,[24] such a restraining influence is absent in an international case with a non-American forum. English courts, at least, are suspicious of adopting American developments of the law which have been limited primarily to relations between different states within the USA.[25]

The second major disadvantage of Currie's approach concerns what he has described as 'the disinterested third State'.[26] If we assume a true

other American states but not of foreign countries: see Leflar, *American Conflicts Law*, 3rd edn. (1977), 259–62; and see the Uniform Judicial Notice of Foreign Law Act.

[20] *Pfau* v. *Trent Aluminum Co* 55 NJ 511; 263 A 2d 129 (1970).

[21] 263 A 2d 129, 134.

[22] e.g., Kegel, (1979) 27 *Am Jo Comp L* 615; also published in *Festschrift für Gunther Beitzke* (1979), 551; cf. Cavers, [1970] III *Hague Recueil* 75, 120–1.

[23] Morris, *The Conflict of Laws*, 2nd edn. (1979), 515.

[24] Currie devoted much of his *Selected Essays on the Conflict of Laws* (1963) to these constitutional safeguards, see chs. 5, 6, 10, 11; and see Kegel, [1964] II *Hague Recueil* 95, 165–76, 195–8.

[25] *Government of India* v. *Taylor* [1955] AC 491, 507; *Boys* v. *Chaplin* [1968] 2 QB 1, 32.

[26] *Selected Essays on the Conflict of Laws*, 62–4, 120–1, 606–9; (1963) 28 *Law and Contemporary Problems* 754.

conflict, but one in which the law of the forum has no interest, then his scheme appears to break down. To apply the law of the forum to resolve the deadlock between the laws of the two other interested states has little merit if the forum is avowedly a disinterested third state: and no rule is provided for choosing between the laws of those states which do have an interest. Currie's answer is either to go ahead and apply the law of the forum despite its lack of interest or to imagine what particular choice of law rules might have been laid down by the legislature of the forum and apply those.[27] If the court believes that the legislature would have adopted Currie's views, the *circulus inextricabilis* is complete.

Other criticisms of Currie's views can be put forward—such as the uncertainty, as well as the difficulty, involved in the determination of the various governmental interests and of the balance between them.[28] It may be no coincidence that the development of interest analysis has been primarily in the field of tort law in general, and traffic and aircraft accidents in particular. Here the function of the law is substantially pathological. There has been an accident. The central issue is now to determine which law is to decide how the pieces are to be swept up. The view of the court is essentially retrospective.[29] Whilst insurance companies and their legal advisers have an interest in certainty in order to facilitate the settlement of claims, it is a far less significant interest than is involved when the perspective of the issue is prospective, as in the property field or in some areas of family law. Certainty is far more important if the question is 'what legal requirements must I satisfy in order to marry, or to transfer property?' It may be no coincidence that the application of interest analysis in the property field has tended to lead to the same law, or rules of law, being applied as would have been applicable under a jurisdiction-selecting approach.[30] Indeed, Willis Reese has indicated that interest analysis may have no role at all to play in the determination of the law applicable to issues concerning land:

'The rule that transfers of interests in land are governed by the law that would be applied by the courts of the situs is both broad and jurisdiction-selecting. Yet is is supported by substantial considerations, and to date the courts have evinced little

[27] For criticism of this, and other aspects of Currie's approach, see Shapira, *The Interest Approach to Choice of Law* (1970), 175–85.

[28] Cavers, [1970] III *Hague Recueil* 75, 147–8.

[29] It might also be borne in mind that there are pressures in the USA, which do not exist in other jurisdictions, for the litigation of tort claims in any event. Lawyers have an interest through the contingent fee system; plaintiffs hope those lawyers will be able to convince juries to make very high damage awards. The plaintiff may have little to lose, so he sues; and this type of claim for damages for death or personal injuries arising from a traffic accident, a plane crash, or a defective product has a high potential for raising choice of law issues.

[30] See e.g., *Re Crichton's Estate* 20 NY 2d 124; 228 NE 2d 799 (1967).

tendency to depart from it . . . The rule has merit and should not be abandoned without good cause shown.'[31]

A further criticism of Currie's approach is that the determination, and indeed weighing, of governmental interests may be appropriate in the field of public international law, but has no place in the field of private international law.[32] What has to be resolved is a conflict between the private interests of individual parties to a dispute or litigation; what Kegel described as 'conflicts justice'.[33] It has been argued in Currie's defence that 'one can still . . . attribute to a State an interest in seeing the purposes of its substantive private laws effectuated in situations where those purposes will be advanced by the laws' application'.[34] Undoubtedly, a state retains a residual interest in the application of its own laws when it is also the forum, as is seen in the internationally accepted application of the forum's rules of public policy, or '*ordre public*'. One may even go further and give the forum a discretion to apply the 'mandatory rules' of some state other than that whose law is held generally to be applicable.[35] There is often also a natural tendency in courts to think that its rule is 'better' than some competing rule;[36] but whether these State interests should be raised to the higher purpose of determining the applicable law seems debatable.[37]

Comparative impairment

There is a body of opinion in the USA which, though prepared to go much of the way with Currie's interest analysis and the identification and

[31] [1976] II *Hague Recueil* 1, 157.

[32] An additional criticism is that a forum-oriented rule for true conflicts is conducive to 'forum-shopping'. Control is then dependent on constitutional restraints or on a developed (but vague) doctrine of *forum non conveniens*. This is discussed further below, pp. 124, 128–129. Another alternative would be to extend interest analysis to include jurisdictional criteria: see Jackson, *The 'Conflicts' Process* (1975).

[33] [1964] II *Hague Recueil* 95, 180–9, and see the criticisms in Morris, *The Conflict of Laws*, 2nd edn. (1975), 514–16; see also Shapira, *The Interest Approach to Choice of Law* (1970), chs. 3, 4.

[34] Cavers, [1970] III *Hague Recueil* 75, 148.

[35] EEC Convention on the law applicable to contractual obligations, Art. 7(1); and see also Art. 16 of the Hague Convention on the law applicable to agency (1977); Art. 18 of the draft Swiss Federal Law on Private International Law, on which see Vischer, (1977) 41 *Law and Contemporary Problems* 2, 131, 142–2; McCaffrey, (1980) 28 *Am Jo Comp L* 235, 255–6.

[36] The potentiality of the interest analysis approach to increase this tendency has been criticized: see Morris, *Conflict of Laws*, 2nd edn. (1979), 509–10; but others regard it as a positive virtue, a factor to be relied on in rule selection: see Leflar, *American Conflicts Law*, 3rd edn. (1979), 212–15.

[37] There is an ultimate power to preserve the interests of the forum state through the medium of its rules of private international law. It could simply declare that its law was always to be applied, as in effect is the rule applied in common law jurisdictions to choice of law in divorce, discussed below pp. 158–162.

thus elimination, of false conflicts, is not willing to accept the *lex fori* solution of true conflicts. Courts are able to and ought to weigh the conflicting interests. The criterion for such evaluation ought to be that of 'comparative impairment'. This approach, first propounded in 1963 by Baxter,[38] requires the court to determine which of the conflicting states' interests would be more impaired if its policy were subordinated to the policy of the other state. Though this approach is open to all the objections that may be made against any rule-selection approach, with its underlying premise that the identification of governmental interests or state policies implicit in the conflicting rules is easy to accomplish, it does meet some of the criticisms of Currie's mechanistic *lex fori* approach and of his failure to solve the problem of the disinterested third state.

The comparative impairment approach has been specifically adopted by the Supreme Court of California on more than one occasion[39] and might be illustrated by *Offshore Rental Co. Inc.* v. *Continental Oil Co.*[40] The plaintiff was a Californian corporation with its main place of business in California. One of its main activities was leasing oil drilling equipment for use in Louisiana and one of its employees was injured in Louisiana as the result of the negligence of the defendant company. This employee was a vice-president of the plaintiff company, a 'key' employee. Though the employee was presumably compensated for his injuries, the plaintiff, his employer, claimed $5 million as damages for the loss of his services. Such an action could be maintained under the law of California, but not of Louisiana. A choice of law problem was thus involved.

The court accepted, as it had in the past,[41] that choice of law in torts was governed by 'governmental interest analysis' and it had first of all to determine, on examination of the governmental policies underlying the laws of the two interested states, whether there was a true conflict.[42] The policy of denial of recovery in Louisiana was 'to protect negligent resident tortfeasors acting within Louisiana's borders from the financial hardships caused by the assessment of excessive legal liability or exaggerated claims resulting from the loss of services of a key employee'.[43] The defendant was a Louisiana resident and so the interest in the application

[38] Baxter, (1963) 16 *Stan L Rev* 1; and see Horowitz, (1974) 21 *UCLA L Rev.* 719, 748–58. The approach stems from an earlier Supreme Court of California decision: *People* v. *One 1953 Ford Victoria* (1957) 48 Cal 2d 595; 311 P 2d 480.

[39] *Bernhard* v. *Harrah's Club* 16 Cal 3d 313; 546 P 2d 719 (1976); *Offshore Rental Co. Inc.* v. *Continental Oil Co.* 22 Cal 3d 157; 583 P 2d 721 (1978); and see *Hall* v. *University of Nevada* 74 Cal App 3d 280 (1977); *Cutler* v. *Bank of America National Trust and Savings Association* 441 F Supp 863 (1977); *Cable* v. *Sahara Tahoe Corporation* 93 Cal App 3d 384; 155 Cal Rep 770 (1979).

[40] 22 Cal 3d 157; 583 P 2d 721 (1978).

[41] E.g., *Reich* v. *Purcell* 67 Cal 2d 551; 432 P 2d 727 (1967).

[42] See *Hurtado* v. *Superior Court* (1974) 11 Cal 3d 574; 522 P 2d 666.

[43] 583 P 2d 721, 725.

of the law of that state was made out. Turning to California, an interest in the application of the law was also made out, the plaintiff being a California employer, because California

> expresses an interest in protecting Californian employers from economic harm because of negligent injury to a key employee inflicted by a third party. Moreover, California's policy of protection extends beyond such an injury inflicted within California, since California's economy and tax revenues are affected regardless of the situs of physical injury.[44]

There was a true conflict between the laws of the two states, but the court rejected the Currie approach of automatic application of forum law. Instead, the comparative impairment analysis was adopted. The court described it thus:

> In sum, the comparative impairment approach to the resolution of true conflicts attempts to determine the relative commitment of the respective states to the laws involved. The approach incorporates several factors for consideration: the history and current status of the states' laws: the function and purpose of those laws.[45]

In its application, the court favoured the application of Louisiana law—not the forum law. What influenced the court was that the rule in Louisiana accorded with the main stream of thought in other American jurisdictions and this 'prevalent and progressive' law had recently been judicially affirmed in Louisiana;[46] whilst the Californian rule was contained in an 'antique' and 'obsolescent' statute which had not recently been considered by the Californian courts. A further factor which weighed with the court was that the burden of obtaining insurance against the loss in question ought to be borne by the plaintiff.[47]

One immediate criticism which may be made of this evaluation is that there is a distinct impression given that the court clearly preferred the rule of Louisiana law; it was the 'better rule of law'.[48] We are told, however, that in applying the comparative impairment test 'the quality of the conflicting laws as a matter of social policy is not an issue'.[49] It might equally be asked how the desirability of one party or the other taking out insurance affects the comparative impairment of the governmental interests of the two states whose laws are in conflict.

In the earlier decision in *Bernhard* v. *Harrah's Club*,[50] the Supreme Court of California was faced with a true conflict between the laws of

[44] 583 P 2d 721, 725. [45] Ibid., 727.

[46] *Bonfanti Industries Inc.* v. *Teke Inc.* 224 So 2d 15 (La) (1969).

[47] This factor also weighed with the California Court of Appeal in *Hall* v. *University of Nevada* 74 Cal App 3d 280, 286 (1977).

[48] Cf Leflar, *American Conflicts Law*, 3rd edn. (1977), 212–15.

[49] *Cutler* v. *Bank of America National Trust and Savings Association* 441 F Supp 863, 866 (1977); and see *Bernhard* v. *Harrah's Club* 546 P 2d 719, 723–4 (1976).

[50] 16 Cal 3d 313; 546 P 2d 719 (1976).

California and Nevada. In favouring the application of Californian law, the court concluded that cases of road accidents in California caused by drivers who got drunk in Nevada would occur so rarely that to apply Californian law would not seriously impair Nevada's interests. This suggests that a further criterion is, again, not the evaluation of the policies in conflict, but 'the statistical rarity of the fact situation'.[51] This criterion assumes judicial willingness to discover and examine such statistical evidence as there may be on the type of international incident involved. This might be plausible inter-state, but hardly internationally. Furthermore, it is a two-edged, forum-oriented argument. It can be said of either law that, if the cases are rare, it will not impair the interests of either state for the other law to be applied.[52] I suspect that whenever the comparative impairment can, objectively, be found to be equally balanced, as has been argued was the position here,[53] the case will be resolved by the application of forum law. Weintraub's verdict on comparative impairment is that 'unless supplemented by specific objective criteria, [it] is unlikely to be a method that is cogent, feasible to administer, and predictable'.[54]

Principles of preference

As long ago as 1933, Cavers advocated the abandonment of a jurisdiction-selection approach in favour of rule-selection as the criterion for the development of choice of law rules. His was a voice crying out in a wilderness dominated by the jurisdiction-selecting approach of the first American Restatement on the Conflict of Laws. By the time of the publication in 1965 of his major work *The Choice-of-law Process* and of his General Course of Lectures at the Hague Academy of International Law,[55] the wilderness had become the promised land.

Cavers and Currie have much in common.[56] They are both supporters of rule-selection; both would utilise this analysis to identify cases of true and false conflict. Resolution of false conflicts is easy—there is no conflict. The parting of the ways comes with true conflicts. Cavers would not accept 'Currie's stern rejection of all choice-of-law rules.[57] Instead, he would seek to develop choice of law rules for the resolution of true conflicts. Accepting that the detailed development of rule-selection rules

[51] Bradley, (1976) 29 *Stan L Rev* 127, 146.

[52] Leflar, (1977) 41 *Law and Contemporary Problems* 2: 10, 22; Weintraub, (1977) 41 *Law and Contemporary Problems* 2: 146, 158.

[53] Bradley, (1976) 29 *Stan L Rev* 127, 146.

[54] Weintraub, (1977) 41 *Law and Contemporary Problems* 2: 146, 158.

[55] [1970] III *Hague Recueil* 75. Cavers' work in 1933 took a long time to come to judicial fruition; but, as David Currie has observed: 'Revolutions cannot always be completed overnight, especially when judges are asked to make them': (1968) 15 *UCLA L Rev* 595, 596.

[56] See Cavers, *The Choice-of-Law Process* (1965), 89–96.

[57] Ibid., 94.

may be a long process, he suggests that the courts should develop broad principles of preference:

> The court is to seek a rule for choice of law or a principle of preference which would either reflect relevant multistate policies or provide the basis for a reasonable accommodation of the laws' conflicting purposes. A principle of preference would be applicable to all cases having the same general pattern of law and fact and would identify a preferred result on choice-of-law grounds. If the case could not thus be generalised, the court should state the reasons leading it to prefer one result to the other on choice-of-law grounds. In either case it should apply the law leading to the preferred result.[58]

This is the gradualist approach. It involves the introduction of broad principles of preference, worked out by Cavers in some fields namely, torts,[59] contracts, and conveyances, but not developed at all in others including family law, our main concern here. The primary objective is to do justice between the parties and, from these just principles, it is envisaged that more specific detailed rules will emerge as a result of judicial development.[60]

The main appeal of this rule-selection approach is that it attempts a solution to the true conflict, rather than Currie-like throwing up one's hands in despair. However, major difficulties remain. The problems of identifying policies remain, the Achilles' heel[61] of all rule-selection. The problems of uncertainty and unpredictability remain, especially in areas where the law's function is essentially prospective, i.e., a yardstick for future planning. It might be argued that, even in these fields of law, little litigated but much relied on, certainty will come with the gradual evolution of settled, more principled, specific choice of law rules. However, 50 years is too long for me, at least, to wait for the establishment of rules to determine, for example, whether my marriage is valid. Again, one is left with the impression that courts in one political state comprising several law districts may be able to identify the conflicting interests underlying different rules of law and, indeed, may be able to devise principles for preferring one rather than another. But, as Morris has asked,

[58] *The Choice-of-Law Process* (1965), 64.

[59] The particular principles formulated for torts have been criticized by Shapira, *The Interest Approach to Choice of Law* (1970), 221–4 for ignoring the role played by forum law, failure to account for the factor of private interests, revealing a marked territorialist bias, failure to accommodate all tort standards of conduct or financial protection, and for manifesting an unmistakable preference for the rule imposing liability.

[60] The working out of such detailed rules may be seen in New York in *Neumeier* v. *Kuehner* 31 NY 2d 121; 286 NE 2d 454 (1972) where Fuld CJ laid down three rules (the first two being very specific) to deal with conflicts involving the liability of a host driver to his guest passenger.

[61] Morris, *The Conflict of Laws*, 2nd edn. (1979), 515.

in an international case, how could a judge express a preference for the rules adopted by one country or another when those countries are not component parts of a federal system but are linked only by diplomatic relations or (perhaps) by a common cultural heritage?[62]

Cavers himself would answer this by admitting that 'discretion is a safe tool only in the hands of the disinterested. Such disinterestedness may more readily be credited to courts within the bounds of a federal union.[63]

Interpretation of forum policy

This title, already used by others,[64] is intended to encapsulate the approach of Ehrenzweig. He was a persistent critic of all of the new approaches to choice of law put forward in the USA in the two decades before his death in 1974. He rejected both governmental interest analysis and conventional jurisdiction-selecting choice of law techniques. He maintained that courts have, in fact, applied the *lex fori* as the general rule, with only exceptional application of foreign law.[65] Indeed, he would not consider that foreign law was 'applicable' or could 'govern' a case, merely that it was 'tolerated'.[66] The best succinct statement of his views appears in his General Course of Lectures given at the Hague Academy of International Law in 1968:

1. The substantive rules of the forum are often interpreted spatially, as a matter of non-choice, as applicable to cases with foreign elements.
2. Forum law also applies as a matter of non-choice to questions of procedure and factual interpretation, to moral data, and by virtue of the ordre public international or party agreement.
3. In the absence of a superlaw, such as a treaty or a constitutional command, choice of law is a function of the law of the forum.
4. Choice of a foreign rule must be distinguished from the application of such a rule as a datum of the forum's rule of decision.
5. Choice of law is frequently determined by formulated or inchoate legislative or judicial rules of choice which are independent of any de-lege-lata theory of conflicts law and thus unconcerned with such current tests as interests, concerns, or relationships.
6. In the absence of a formulated or inchoate rule of choice, the application of

[62] Morris, *The Conflict of Laws*, 2nd edn. (1979), 518. A similar view was adopted by Ehrenzweig, (1957) 41 *Minn L Rev* 717, and see Scoles, (1966) 54 *Cal L Rev* 1599; Hay, (1971) 35 *RabelsZ* 429; Shapira, *The Interest Approach to Choice of Law* (1970), 34–44.

[63] Cavers, (1933) 47 *Harv L Rev* 173, 203. On the development of special rules of private international law for truly international cases, for those arising within federal or similar multi-law district states, and for cases connected with closely related but independent states, see Graveson, [1974] I *Hague Recueil* 187; Fawcett, (1978) 7 *Anglo-Am L Rev* 230.

[64] E.g., Cavers, [1970] III *Hague Recueil* 75, 150.

[65] Ehrenzweig, (1960) 58 *Mich L Rev* 637, 643–5.

[66] Ehrenzweig, *Conflict of Laws* (1962), 311.

a foreign rule can and must be derived from the interpretation of the substantive rule of the forum in the light of its policy.
7. If this interpretation does not lead to the application of a foreign rule, the substantive rule of the forum applies as residuary.[67]

It is difficult to identify, with any precision, exactly what Ehrenzweig advocates. For 'while Currie paints with the precision of a Holbein (or Bruegel), Ehrenzweig's canvas shimmers and changes'.[68] However, the major plank of Ehrenzweig's approach is the presumption of the application of forum law and this is what can be most criticized.[69] It is a recipe for forum shopping save in those exceptional cases, such as issues of status or property law, where foreign law may be applied. There may be constitutional constraints on forum shopping in the USA, but they do not necessarily exist elsewhere. Restraint might be found in the doctrine of *forum non conveniens*, but it is hardly a convincing choice of law approach which requires extension of that jurisdictional doctrine to make it work. It is an approach without guidelines to the solution of specific problems: for 'he often offers no guides to the courts whom he directs to derive by interpretation from domestic rules and policies the solutions to problems which, *ex hypothesi*, are not domestic'.[70]

The most significant relationship

The American Law Institute's Restatement of the Conflict of Laws, Second, adopts as its basic criterion for choice of law the application of the law of the state which has the most significant relationship to the particular issue under principles laid down in section 6 of the Restatement. This requires the court to follow a statutory directive of its own state on choice of law but, in the absence of such a directive, the factors relevant to the choice of the applicable law include:

1. the needs of the interstate and international systems,
2. the relevant policies of the forum,
3. the relevant policies of other interested states and the relative interests of those states in the determination of the particular issue,
4. the protection of justified expectations,
5. the basic policies underlying the particular field of law,
6. certainty, predictability and uniformity of result, and
7. ease in the determination and application of the law to be applied.[71]

[67] Ehrenzweig, [1968] II *Hague Recueil* 178, 214–15 (slightly shortened).
[68] Kegel, [1964] II *Hague Recueil* 95, 224.
[69] Fuller criticism is to be found in Kegel, [1964] II *Hague Recueil* 95, 224–6; and see Shapira, *The Interest Approach to Choice of Law* (1970), 205–8.
[70] Cavers, [1970] III *Hague Recueil* 75, 151.
[71] Leflar would add a further factor—a preference for the better rule of law; see

The most significant relationship test, with these choice influencing factors, is applied to a whole variety of conflicts issues, ranging from contract[72] and tort[73] to marriage[74] and property.[75] This test is closely associated with Willis Reese, the Reporter of the Second Restatement and, indeed, a similar test was first put forward by him as long ago as 1952.[76]

Reese would describe the test provided in the Restatement as an 'approach' to choice of law, not as providing rules for the solution of specific choice of law problems.[77] Nevertheless, he regards this as but the means to the end of clear, firm, precise rules for the resolution of choice of law issues:

> I believe that one ultimate goal, be it ever so distant, should be the development of hard-and-fast rules of choice of law. I believe that in many instances these rules should be directed, at least initially, at a particular issue. And I believe that in the development of these rules consideration should be given to the basic objectives of choice of law, to the relevant local law rules of the potentially interested states and, of course, to the contacts of the parties and of the occurrence with these states.[78]

There is much in this statement of objectives with which I and, I suspect, many other private international lawyers would agree. It is appealing because, in truth, it attempts to have the best of all worlds. It provides specific choice of law rules, rather than the forum-oriented approaches of Currie and Ehrenzweig. It does not require an analysis into true and false conflicts with its difficulties of determining in detail the interests of the states whose laws are competing, or the policies underlying the creation or retention of such rules; yet it provides some consolation, in the reference in section 6 to 'the relevant policies of other interested states and the relative interests of those states in the determination of the particular issue', to those who are supporters of interest analysis. It acknowledges the desirability of certainty and ease of application of the law, surely very necessary elements in the formulation of new rules of law. It requires a new look at the old choice of law rules, and encourages that new look to be issue-oriented rather than aimed at whole areas of the law such as

American Conflicts Law, 3rd edn. (1977), 195, 212–14 and this view is supported by Ehrenzweig in (1967) 53 *Va L Rev* 847. This factor has received some judicial support, as in *Clark* v. *Clark* 107 NH 351; 222 A 2d 205 (1966); *Heath* v. *Zellmer* 35 Wis 2d 578; 151 NW 2d 664 (1967); *Brown* v. *Church of the Holy Name of Jesus* 105 RI 322; 252 A 2d 176 (1969); *Milkovich* v. *Saari* 295 Minn 155; 203 NW 2d 408 (1973); *Schwartz* v. *Consolidated Freightways of Delaware* 221 NW 2d 665 (Minn 1974). However, it is generally criticized; see Cavers, *The Choice-of-Law Process*, 85–6; [1970] III *Hague Recueil* 75, 175; Morris, *The Conflict of Laws*, 2nd edn. (1979), 520–1; *Bernhard* v. *Harrah's Club* 16 Cal 3d 313; 546 P 2d 719 (1976).

[72] S. 188. [73] S. 145. [74] S. 283. [75] S. 222.

[76] Cheetham and Reese, (1952) 52 *Col L Rev* 959.

[77] [1976] II *Hague Recueil* 1, 44–65. [78] Ibid., 180.

'contract', 'tort', or 'marriage'. Indeed, it is both jurisdiction-selecting and rule-selecting at the same time.[79] The purpose of indicating that regard should be had to the policies of the interested states and their relative interests in the determination of the particular issue must be in order to aid the selection of the more appropriately applicable rule—a form of interest analysis or rule-selection. In giving consideration, as Reese does in the passage just quoted, to the contacts of the parties and of the occurrence with the interested states, Reese relies on a 'grouping of contacts' approach which is predominantly jurisdiction-selecting.

Two kinds of criticism may be made of this approach. The general criticism may be made, as I have just suggested, that 'the factors often point in different directions and carry in themselves no measures of their significance'.[80] The other type of criticism relates to the part that the approach of the Restatement Second, or even of any element of the American conflicts revolution, is intended to play in the development of choice of law rules. The list of choice-influencing factors in section 6 reads like an exhortation to a law reformer—listing the criteria he might take into account in propounding new, probably more detailed, choice of law rules. The various Restatements of the law in the United States have had a major influence on the reform of the law—but they have done so against a background of judicial creativity, the willingness of judges to abandon the old in favour of reform, without over much concern for the uncertainty that may come in the wake of the first reforming steps. The development of the choice of law rules in tort in New York provides a good example[81]—from the pioneering decision in 1963 in *Babcock* v. *Jackson*[82] to abandon the old *lex loci delicti* rule to the laying down in 1972 in *Neumeier* v. *Kuehner*[83] of specific rules to govern choice of law in cases involving the liability of a driver to his guest passenger. Without a judicial willingness to abandon the basic jurisdiction-selecting philosophy of the old rules in favour of the gradual, but uncertain evolution of narrower, but arguably more appropriate, choice of law rules, the Restatement Second cannot provide the stimulus for judicial law-making outside the USA.[84] It may, however, have a larger part to play in the reform of choice of law through the medium of international law reform agencies such as the Hague Conference on Private International Law, or

[79] It has been described as 'schizophrenic', 'an endeavour to erect an essentially jurisdiction-selective structure while, at the same time, to pay lip service to the relevance of interests based on rule-supporting purposes': Shapira, *The Interest Approach to Choice of Law* (1970), 214. The author regards this as a vice; ibid., 217; other might see it as a virtue.

[80] Cavers, [1970] III *Hague Recueil* 75, 145. This criticism was foreseen in the Restatement 2d, see comment (*c*) to section 6.

[81] See Weintraub, (1977) 41 *Law and Contemporary Problems* 2: 146, 148–53.

[82] 12 NY 2d 473; 191 NE 2d 279 (1963).

[83] 31 NY 2d 121; 286 NE 2d 454 (1972).

[84] Cf. *Boys* v. *Chaplin* [1971] AC 356, 389–91.

indeed national law reform bodies such as the various law reform commissions established in various parts of the world, mainly in the Commonwealth, in recent years.

The Impact of the Revolution on Choice of Rules for Family Law

The overwhelming impression is that the upheaval in conflicts thinking and analysis in the USA over the past two decades has had little impact in the field of family law. There would appear to have been no major judicial developments influenced by any of the 'revolutionaries' and, with notable exceptions,[85] there has been little American academic writing in this area.

Can one find reasons for this lack of judicial activity in choice of law in marriage and divorce? It does not seem to be because all the present jurisdiction-selecting rules, such as the rule that the validity of a marriage is determined either by the law of the place of celebration or of the parties' ante-nuptial domiciles, are patently beyond reproach. Indeed, Reese has singled out marriage, along with contract and tort, as areas 'which are not currently regulated satisfactorily by rules of choice of law. It is in such areas that attempts at rule-making should be made'.[86]

One reason may be that those who have advocated the new approaches to choice of law have been primarily interested in fields of law other than family law, in particular in torts and contracts. Cavers virtually ignores family law issues in his seminal work *The Choice-of-Law Process*;[87] in his General Course of lectures delivered at the Hague Academy of International Law in 1970 four pages only are devoted to choice of law[88] in marriage and, whilst fuller discussion is given to divorce jurisdiction and recognition,[89] it is essentially an account of the present law; little or no interest analysis is applied to it; no principles of preference are preferred. Similar lack of interest in family law matters is to be deduced from Currie's writings. It has been pointed out[90] that none of Currie's many publications deals directly with family law, though occasionally he touches on family law issues in other contexts.[91] Furthermore, when

[85] Engdahl, (1969) 55 *Iowa L Rev* 56; Baade, (1972) 72 *Col L Rev* 329.
[86] [1976] II *Hague Recueil* 1, 190; and see Cavers, *The Choice-of-Law Process* (1965), 116.
[87] It is referred to only once, 116–17, apart from reference to international conventions in the field, 254–6.
[88] [1970] III *Hague Recueil* 75, 241–5.
[89] Ibid., 245–76.
[90] Baade, (1972) 72 *Col L Rev* 328, 329.
[91] E.g., *Selected Essays on the Conflict of Laws* (1963), 70–2, 659–72, 675–81.

Currie does consider matters referring to status, he takes the view that only very rarely do they raise choice of law issues properly so-called:

Except in suits for declaratory judgments, the determination of status is almost never the ultimate object of an action. The question is seldom presented in the abstract, but almost always in the context of a primary question, such as the right to inherit or the right to letters of administration. In these cases it is often perfectly clear that the law of the forum supplies the rule of decision for determining the litigation between the parties; the 'choice-of-law' rule, which seems inaptly named in this role, performs a different function.[92]

The same criticism that family law matters are ignored cannot be made, or be made to the same extent, of Reese and the Restatement Second. All the major family law issues in private international law are covered in the Restatement Second.[93] Nevertheless choice of law in all matters affecting status is accommodated in eight sections, whereas choice of law in tort requires thirty-six sections, and contract requires twenty-eight. The impression is given that family law issues are, in the choice of law context, not thought to be very significant. As one commentator on the family law aspects of the Restatement Second has put it: 'I could not help feeling that I was dealing with a stepchild. Professor Reese does not seem to have either an easy familiarity with, or a particularly keen interest in, the law of divorce and, especially the law of marriage.'[94] Perhaps in reaction to that criticism, Reese devoted a chapter of his General Course of Lectures at the Hague Academy of International Law in 1976 to choice of law issues relating to marriage[95] and does there re-examine some of the leading authorities in the light of the choice influencing factors of the Restatement Second.

One is left with an overall impression that family law matters have largely been ignored by the American 'revolutionary' writers, but does this wholly account for the lack of judicial activity in applying their new approaches to status issues? I think not. There are surprisingly few conflicts decisions this century in the United States on matters of family law, and of marriage in particular. Writers all tend to cite the same few leading authorities,[96] and the authorities relied on in the Restatement Second on the law relating to validity of marriage[97] are drawn almost as

[92] *Selected Essays on the Conflict of Laws* (1963), 69–70.

[93] Ss. 69–79 (Jurisdiction); ss. 92–8 (Recognition of Judgments generally); ss. 283–90 (Choice of Law). Choice of Law is also provided for in the Uniform Marriage and Divorce Act 1971, amended in 1973, s. 210.

[94] Baade, (1972) 72 *Col L Rev* 329, 380.

[95] [1976] II *Hague Recueil* 1, 160–79.

[96] E.g., *Meisenhelder* v. *Chicago and NW Rly*. 170 Minn 317; 213 NW 32 (1927); *Re Ommang's Estate* 183 Minn 92; 23 NW 529 (1931); *Vergnani* v. *Guidetti* 308 Mass 450; 32 NE 2d 272 (1941); *Re Dalip Singh Bir's Estate* 83 Cal App 2d 256; 188 P 2d 499 (1948); *Re May's Estate* 305 NY 486; 114 NE 2d 4 (1953); *Wilkins* v. *Zelichowski* 26 NJ 370; 140 A 2d 65 (1958); *Catalano* v. *Catalano* 148 Conn 288; 170 A 2d 726 (1961).

[97] See Comment to s. 283.

much from academic writing as from decided cases. Divorce recognition is an obvious exception but there the predominant interest in the cases has been in the constitutional field[98] with concern, for example, over the giving of full faith and credit to sister state judgments; the overruling of *Haddock* v. *Haddock*[99] (where recognition was denied in New York to a decree of the courts of Connecticut where the husband was domiciled) by the later Supreme Court decision in *Williams* v. *North Carolina*[100] which upheld the jurisdictional supremacy of the courts of the domicile;[101] followed by the resolution of the problem whether inter-state recognition depends on the divorce being bilateral or whether recognition would be given to an *ex parte* decree.[102] This significance of constitutional issues in some fields of family law has been given as one of the reasons for Currie's lack of interest in, or attention to, choice of law problems in family law: 'Currie sensed a basic incompatibility between governmental-interest analysis and full faith and credit.[103]

If one excludes family law issues with constitutional connotations, those that remain are concerned primarily with foreign (i.e. non-American) divorces and with marriage. Inter-state marriage conflicts unconnected with divorce or ancillary relief are rare because the substantive marriage laws of the states are very similar.[104] Furthermore, the adoption in a number of states of statutory choice of law rules[105] relating to marriage means that there is less judicial freedom to apply interest-analysis in this field. A striking illustration of this is provided by a Californian decision[106] where the Court of Appeal rejected an interest analysis approach[107] to determine the choice of law rules applicable to marriage, regarding the matter as precluded by the Californian Civil Code.[108]

That leaves foreign divorces and foreign marriages. One would have

[98] *Rosenstiel* v. *Rosenstiel* 16 NY 2d 64; 209 NE 2d 709 (1965) is a significant exception.

[99] 201 US 562 (1906). [100] 317 US 287 (1942).

[101] And see *Alton* v. *Alton* 207 F 2d 667 (1953); *Granville-Smith* v. *Granville-Smith* 349 US 1 (1955).

[102] See *Sherrer* v. *Sherrer* 334 US 343 (1948); *Estin* v. *Estin* 334 US 541 (1948).

[103] Baade, (1972) 72 *Col L Rev* 329, 330.

[104] There will be still fewer differences if there is widespread adoption of the Uniform Marriage and Divorce Act 1971, amended in 1973. By 1978 this Act had substantially been adopted in seven States: Arizona, Colorado, Georgia, Kentucky, Minnesota, Montana, Washington.

[105] For example, the Uniform Marriage and Divorce Act contains, in s. 210, the following provision: 'All marriages contracted within this State prior to the effective date of this Act, or outside this State, that were valid at the time of the contract or subsequently validated by the laws of the place in which they were contracted or by the domicil of the parties, are valid in this State.'

[106] *In Re Estate of Levie* 50 Cal App 3d 572; 123 Cal Rep 445 (1975).

[107] Based on *Hurtado* v. *Superior Court* 11 Cal 3d 574; 522 P 2d 666 (1974).

[108] S. 4104 provides: 'All marriages contracted without this state, which would be valid by the laws of the jurisdiction in which the same were contracted, are valid in this state.'

expected both to have given rise to important decisions and significant debate in a country with a continuous history of immigration. That has not, however, been the case—perhaps because for many years it has been easier to obtain a divorce in the USA than in many of the countries from which the immigrants have come.[109] Cavers' answer to the criticism of lack of interest in choice of law in family law issues would be similar to that advanced already—the main problems arise not in choice of law, but in fields of jurisdiction over, and recognition of, matrimonial causes. Even in the case of marriage law he believes that 'the crucial issue . . . is often whether a prior divorce decree or annulment is invalid and open to attack'.[110]

One final reason for the lack of enthusiasm in applying interest analysis to family law matters may be because of a suspicion that, in some areas at least, the game is not worth the candle; the whole elaborate exercise might lead you back to the rules with which you began. Morris has given a striking illustration of this[111] when discussing the admission by Cavers that he does not object to a jurisdiction-selecting rule if it is 'the product of two decisions choosing, on policy ground, between competing rules in cases in which the law-fact patterns are reversed'.[112] Morris suggests that this is the process of synthesis by which many existing jurisdiction-selecting rules were reached and he exemplifies this by the rule that, subject to certain exceptions, the formal validity of a marriage is governed by the law of the place of celebration. Why bother with interest-analysis if it leads, as Morris argues it does in this case, to the same result?

It is proposed in the next section to take one or two well-established rules of choice of law in family matters and to re-examine them in the light of the conflicting interests and policies which might be held to be at issue.

A RE-EXAMINATION OF SOME BASIC CHOICE OF LAW RULES

Introduction

In the previous section an attempt was made to provide a brief account of the revolutionary theoretical developments in the choice of law process which have been propounded over the last few decades in the USA. I have attempted to indicate my unease with much of what has been pro-

[109] There are, of course, some decisions involving international marriage conflicts; see, e.g., *Vergnani* v. *Guidetti* 308 Mass 450; 32 NE 2d 272 (1941); *Toth* v. *Toth* 50 Mich App 150; 212 NW 2d 812 (1973).

[110] Cavers, *The Choice-of-Law Process* (1965), 117.

[111] Morris, *The Conflict of Laws*, 2nd edn. (1979), 510–11.

[112] *The Choice-of-Law Process*, 9, n. 24.

posed, at least in an international, rather than inter-state, context, and to indicate that, even in the USA, there has been no obvious readiness, for a variety of reasons, to apply the new order in the field of family law. One might stop there and say that that indicates that there is nothing wrong with choice of law rules in marriage and divorce. Mechanical and jurisdiction-selecting they may be, but there is no great need or desire to change them. That would be an unfortunate reaction. It may be that, at the end of the day, some of the rules will be found to have well stood the test of time but there are commentators, not predominantly in the USA, who have advocated a new look at choice of law rules in family law, a new look which seeks to identify the policies at issue in the formulation of such rules in order to determine how well they are accommodated by the present rules.[113] Enquiry might be regarded as unnecessary if there was in fact unanimity of approach on the law to be applied but that is far from the case. Take the laws governing capacity to marry, or more broadly put, the essential validity of a marriage. In the USA, this is normally governed by the law of the place of celebration;[114] in England[115] by the law of the ante-nuptial domiciles of the parties[116] or, perhaps, by the law of the intended matrimonial home;[117] in much of Europe the governing law is the *lex patriae*, the law of the nationality.[118] It is undoubtedly an over-simplification to leave the analysis there, with a tripartite division of choice of law rules to govern essential validity. Each rule has exceptions. For example, in the USA the Uniform Marriage Evasion Act, adopted in a small number of states,[119] provided[120] that a marriage, valid by the law of the place of celebration, would not be recognized as valid if void by the law of the domicile, particularly if there was an intent to evade that law. Likewise the English rule has exceptions in favour of the place of celebration. A marriage in England is almost certainly void, though valid under the law of the domicile, if the requirements of English law as to essential validity are not complied with;[121] the authorities

[113] E.g., Hartley, (1972) 34 *MLR* 571; Maddaugh, (1973) 23 *U Tor LJ* 117; Swan, (1974) 24 *U Tor LJ* 17; Jaffey, (1978) 41 *MLR* 38.

[114] *Re May's Estate* 305 NY 486; 114 NE 2d 4 (1953); Weintraub, *Commentary on the Conflict of Laws* (1971), 168–75. This is also the rule in parts of Latin America and Scandinavia: Palsson, *International Encyclopedia of Comparative Law*, iii, ch. 16; *Marriage and Divorce Comparative Conflict of Laws* (1974), para. 58.

[115] And in much of the Commonwealth.

[116] *Padolecchia* v. *Padolecchia* [1968] P 314.

[117] *Radwan* v. *Radwan (No. 2)* [1973] Fam 35.

[118] See Palsson, *International Encyclopedia of Comparative Law*, iii; ch. 16; *Marriage and Divorce in Comparative Conflict of Laws* (1974), para. 66.

[119] E.g., Revised Statutes of Illinois, c. 89, ss. 19–24. It was adopted in five states: Illinois, Louisiana, Massachusetts, Vermont and Wisconsin.

[120] The National Conference of Commissioners on Uniform State Laws withdrew the Uniform Marriage Evasion Act in 1943 because it was obsolete.

[121] Cheshire and North, *Private International Law*, 10th edn. (1979), 343.

conflict as to whether a foreign *lex loci celebrationis* must be complied with.[122] Whilst it may be the case that all the different choice of law rules are so qualified by exceptions that the ultimate effect of the rule is less far removed from another than might at first sight appear, they certainly start from quite different standpoints. Is this because different countries place much stronger emphasis on different aspects of marriage law? I shall attempt here to isolate three major choice of law rules in family law—those governing the essential and formal validity of marriages, and the choice of law rule in divorce—and to re-examine them bearing in mind the new approaches to choice of law in the USA, in order to try to identify the policies at issue and the extent to which they are met in the various jurisdiction-selecting rules presently found in different legal systems.

One further preliminary point must be made. A reconsideration of 'orthodox' choice of law rules, especially in the light of the ideas from the USA, must involve a willingness to accept issue-oriented rules in place of the present very broad and general rules.[123] It may be that the rules which might be evolved for a variety of different issues turn out to be the same, thus permitting their coalescence into one broad rule, but one must be prepared to look critically at the universality of present rules as to status.[124] It might be asked, for example, whether a marriage has to be valid or invalid for all purposes. It is, in fact, clear from the present state of English family law choice of law rules that, jurisdiction-selecting though they may be, universality is not a rigid criterion and is not as fully entrenched as some have suggested.[125] Let me take three examples. Until 1972,[126] English courts would not grant matrimonial relief to actually or potentially polygamous marriages. This meant that they would refuse to decide, in the context of a nullity petition[127] or a petition for a declaration of status,[128] whether or not a polygamous marriage was valid. On the other hand, they had no hesitation in recognizing the validity of a polygamous marriage as a bar to a later monogamous (but bigamous)[129] one or in accepting that the widow of a polygamous marriage had a right of intestate succession to her late husband's estate.[130] The second example is provided by the problem of the 'incidental question' in the family

[122] *Breen* v. *Breen* [1964] P 144 (compliance required); *Reed* v. *Reed* (1969) 6 DLR (3d) 617 (no compliance necessary).

[123] This is clearly the case under the Restatement 2d, s. 283.

[124] See Engdahl, (1969) 55 *Iowa L Rev* 56, 72 *et seq.*; Reese, [1976] II *Hague Recueil* 1, 160–78; Restatement 2d, s. 283, Comment (*d*); cf. Cavers, [1970] III *Hague Recueil* 75, 244–5.

[125] Engdahl, (1969) 55 *Iowa L Rev* 56, 77–99.

[126] See the Matrimonial Proceedings (Polygamous Marriages) Act 1972; now see the Matrimonial Causes Act 1973, s. 47.

[127] *Risk* v. *Risk* [1951] P 50.

[128] *Brinkley* v. *AG* (1890) 15 PD 76, 79–80.

[129] *Baindail* v. *Baindail* [1946] P 122.

[130] *Coleman* v. *Shang* [1961] AC 481 (a Privy Council decision); see also *Re Dalup Singh Bir's Estate* 83 Cal App 2d 256; 188 P 2d 499 (1948).

law field. The most likely case to arise is that where there is a clash between the rules relating to validity of marriage and those for the recognition of foreign divorces. Until 1972, English law maintained the universality of marriage rule with strange consequences which may be illustrated by a decision from 1968: *R* v. *Brentwood Superintendent Registrar of Marriages, Ex parte Arias*.[131] The husband was an Italian national, the wife a Swiss national; both were domiciled in Switzerland where the wife obtained a divorce. That divorce would be recognized in England at common law, being a decree of the courts of the common domicile. Under Swiss law, capacity to marry depended on the law of the nationality. The wife, being Swiss and validly divorced under Swiss law, remarried in Switzerland. The husband wished to remarry in England. English law referred his capacity to marry to Swiss law, as the law of the domicile, which in turn referred it to Italian law as the law of the nationality. Italian law did not recognize the Swiss divorce, so the husband was incapable of remarriage under Italian law and therefore incapable under Swiss and English law. England would recognize the husband's divorce but not allow him to remarry.

A completed reversal of this position came by statute in 1971,[132] a reversal which carries with it abandonment of universality. It is now the case that, if a foreign divorce is recognized in England, the parties are capable of remarrying in England, notwithstanding the fact that the divorce is not recognized in the country of their domicile, or in any other country.[133] Remarriage outside the United Kingdom is not covered by the provision and there the universality rule still reigns.[134]

Finally, an English judge[135] has also been prepared to acknowledge that choice of law rules as to the essential validity of marriage do not have to be of universal application. He was prepared to regard capacity to enter a polygamous marriage as being governed by the law of the intended matrimonial home,[136] whereas other issues of essential validity might well fall under the dual domicile test.[137]

This does not, of course, go as far in its undermining of universality as a rule which accepts that a marriage may be valid for one purpose, but not for another.[138] A good American illustration of this kind of abandonment of universality is provided by *Estate of Borax* v. *Commissioner of*

[131] [1968] 2 QB 956.

[132] Recognition of Divorces and Legal Separations Act 1972, s. 7, implementing Art. 11 of the 1970 Hague Convention on the Recognition of Divorces and Legal Separations.

[133] The English courts seem to have adopted a similar rule in the case of recognition of foreign nullity decrees: *Perrini* v. *Perrini* [1979] Fam 84.

[134] See North, *Private International Law of Matrimonial Causes* (1977), 193–4. (But see now the Family Law Act 1986, s. 50).

[135] Cumming-Bruce J. in *Radwan* v. *Radwan (No. 2)* [1973] Fam 35.

[136] Riding roughshod in the process over the Matrimonial Causes Act 1973, s. 11 (d).

[137] [1973] Fam 35, 54.

[138] See Swan, (1974) 24 *U Tor LJ* 17.

Internal Revenue[139] A husband obtained a divorce in Mexico from his first wife and soon afterwards remarried. The first wife obtained a declaration from the New York courts that the divorce would not be recognized, that the second marriage was invalid and that she was still regarded as married to the husband. Nevertheless the husband and the second 'wife' lived together and claimed tax deductions on the basis that they were validly married. When the Commissioner of Internal Revenue claimed payment of tax underpaid in consequence of the husband and second 'wife' not in fact being married, the United States Court of Appeals (Second Circuit) decided that they were prepared, notwithstanding the earlier New York decision, to regard the Mexican divorce as valid and the second marriage, therefore, as also valid for tax purposes. A different view of the divorce and remarriage was reached depending on whether the issue in question was seen as one of tax law or marital status.

Essential Validity of Marriage

General issues

We have seen earlier that the three major alternative choice of law rules to govern the essential validity of a marriage are the law of the placed of celebration, the law of the domicile or the law of the nationality. What are the policies that these rules may be trying to implement? Here, as elsewhere, we must identify two sets of policy issues. The first set consists of those issues which underlie domestic substantive rules as to marriage law. If one adopts a choice of law analysis concentrating, in the first instance, on individual issues such as what should be the choice of law rule in cases of non-age or of consanguinity or affinity rather than looking for more sweeping rules, such as a single rule governing all issues of essential validity, it is necessary to identify the policy interests in issue in the particular context. Only when these have been identified can one go on to look at the second set of policies, namely those relevant to the formulation of choice of law rules, e.g., the weight to be given to predictability and certainty, to upholding the validity of marriage and the like. We cannot do as the American Restatement Second suggests and weigh as a choice-influencing factor 'the relevant policies of the forum' unless and until they have been identified. We must embark, therefore, on a two-stage policy analysis.

[139] 349 F 2d 666 (1965), cert denied 383 US 935 (1966). See Currie, (1966) 34 *U Chi L Rev* 26, 64–75.

Policy bases of substantive marriage law

Before seeking to identify some of the relevant policies, it must be pointed out that such identification depends very much on the social and cultural background of the seeker, for marriage law is intricately bound up with the moral and religious attitudes of society. Policies which can be identified by someone with an English background might be as follows:

1. Validation of marriage in order to provide and preserve a family unit, this being regarded as the desirable environment for the bringing up of children.

2. Prevention of the obligations, sexual and financial, of marriage being undertaken at too young an age (i.e., the non-age rule). In some societies, physical maturity provides a rough guide, as where the age is set at 12 for girls and 14 for boys. This cannot be the criterion in England where the age is 16,[140] greater weight being placed on emotional maturity.

3. Desire to restrict too close inter-breeding. This may be a reason underlying some rules on consanguinity. The eugenic or genetic arguments[141] against incestuous marriages or, more remotely, first cousin marriages are strongest in a small isolated community where there may be some genetic danger from continuous inbreeding. In most of Western Europe, these dangers are likely to be much less because the risk of a repetitive pattern is less great. Furthermore, there can be no such risk in the case of affinity, so further justification must be sought.

4. Religion. Until the twentieth century, in England one of the main foundations for the law of affinity was the doctrine of the Church of England and indeed Blackstone said that the canonical disabilities, including both consanguinity and affinity, 'are either grounded upon the express words of the divine law, or are consequences plainly deducible from thence'.[142]

5. Maintenance of family stability. Rules of affinity, preventing intermarriage between those who are themselves related by marriage, can be supported on this ground. The possibility of marriage between stepfather and stepdaughter is likely to prove highly disruptive of the stepfather's first marriage. Marriage between adoptive siblings might equally be opposed as disruptive of the family unit. Relaxation of the rules of affinity to permit marriage with a deceased spouse's sister or brother is not nearly as disruptive of the family stability as marriages with a

140 Marriage Act 1949, s. 2.

141 See Cretney, *Principles of Family Law*, 3rd edn. (1979), 38–9; Bailey and McCabe, [1979] *Crim L Rev* 749, 757–8. Genetic counselling is increasingly common, and may give rise to civil liability; see Capron, (1979) 79 *Col L Rev* 618.

142 *Commentaries*, ii: ch. 15, 434.

divorced spouse's sister or brother. The former was permitted[143] in England long before the latter.[144]

6. Moral and cultural structure of society. This is an element hard to separate from religion, but undoubtedly, in combination, they can be called in aid as justification for a ban on marriages between parties of the same sex, or a ban on bigamy and polygamy. Conversely, polygamy itself can, in other societies, be supported on religious grounds. This general interest of the State in the regulation of the institution of marriage was put clearly by a nineteenth-century English judge:

> Marriage is the very foundation of civil society, and no part of the laws and institutions of a country can be of more vital importance to its subjects than those which regulate the manner and conditions of forming, and if necessary, of dissolving, the marriage contract.[145]

7. Propagation of children. If spouses cannot have children then this may be a ground for the annulment of the marriage—whether it be because of impotence or wilful refusal to consummate the marriage, or because the parties are of the same sex.

8. Voluntary nature of marriage. Marriages entered into as a result of duress, fear, fraud or various kinds of mistake offend against this policy.

9. Health factors. This might be exemplified by the ground of annulment that the other spouse was suffering at the time of the marriage from venereal disease in a communicable form. The policy here is, at least in part, to protect the health of the other spouse.

These policies, which are far from exhaustive, are drawn from the English law of marriage and no doubt other marriage regimes will and do give greater weight to other policies. What is clear is that the policies underlying marriage law are usually pre-eminently connected with the moral and often religious structure of the particular society in question.

Policy bases of choice of law rules

Let us now consider the various factors which might be taken into account in devising choice of law rules to determine the law applicable to matters of essential validity.[146]

1. Presumption in favour of validity of marriage. As Jaffey has said: 'choice of law rules as to the validity of marriage should, so far as possi-

[143] Deceased Wife's Sister's Marriage Act 1907; Deceased Brother's Widow's Marriage Act 1921; Marriage (Prohibited Degrees of Relationship) Act 1931.

[144] Under the Marriage (Enabling) Act 1960.

[145] *Shaw* v. *Gould* (1868) LR 3 HL 55, 82 per Lord Westbury.

[146] I have here drawn on the analysis provided by Hartley, (1972) 35 *MLR* 571 and on the list of factors in the Restatement 2d, s. 6.

ble, be such that a marriage, duly celebrated between willing parties, will not be held invalid without good reason'.[147]

2. The policies underlying the substantive family law of the forum. All policy identification is subject to dangers and difficulties as I tried to indicate in the previous section when discussing the Achilles' heel of interest analysis. Nevertheless, it is likely to be easier for a court to identify the policies of the forum than of any other legal system. One element of the forum policy always to be borne in mind is whether the rule in question is intended or, as there is likely to be no direct evidence of intention, can be thought to be intended to have international effect. It must be remembered that the international elements may be of varied kinds, such as the foreign place of celebration, or the foreign domicile or nationality of one or both parties.

3. The policies underlying the substantive rules of family law of potentially 'interested' foreign states. I need not reiterate the difficulties in determining foreign domestic policies. The difficulty is exacerbated in family law and especially in the field of essential validity of marriage because the identification of the policies may necessitate sophisticated examination of the social, cultural and religious framework in which they operate. There is the added difficulty that, though a marriage may not produce as many potentially 'interested' legal systems as an accident involving an international airliner, it may produce more interested States than the average tort claim. Imagine a student who is an Iranian national, living permanently in Paris, wishing to get married to a fellow student who is a New Zealand national with a permanent home in Australia. They are students in Oxford where they wish to marry; or perhaps, more sadly, a petition is presented to the English court seeking annulment of the marriage. A claim might be made for the interests of Iranian, French, New Zealand, Australian and English law in being applied either exclusively or jointly with another law.

4. Protection of the justified expectations of the parties. This is a regularly cited factor to be taken into account in devising choice of law rules,[148] but is none the less relevant for its obviousness. Indeed, it has been suggested that, because 'parties enter into marriage with forethought',[149] this is a far more important factor in the law of marriage, than, say, in tort law. This must surely be correct because people are entitled to assume when they get married that, in the eyes of the law at least, they are likely to stay married.

5. Need for certainty and stability. The interrelation of this factor with

[147] (1978) 41 *MLR* 38. This factor seems to be regarded by Swan as strong enough presumptively to outweigh all others: see Swan, (1974) 24 *U Tor LJ* 16, 27, 39–41.

[148] Restatement 2d, s. 6(2)(d); Hartley, (1972) 35 *MLR* 571.

[149] Restatement 2d, s. 283, Comment (b).

the previous one is, I hope, immediately apparent. The parties to a marriage have a real concern that not only will their legitimate expectations as to the validity of their marriage be realized, but also that such validity will not be in issue if they change their home, or even their nationality, nor will the validity depend, in the event of marital breakdown, on the forum where any issue is litigated. This last aspect of predictability is particularly difficult to satisfy in the absence of international agreement and it will be interesting to see to what extent the agreement reached in the 1976 Hague Convention on celebration and recognition of the validity of marriages is generally adopted. I am not hopeful that it will be.[150]

6. The intrinsic merit of the legal rule. This has been put forward by an English writer as an appropriate factor to be considered[151] and it will be seen to involve very much the same approach as Leflar's introduction of the idea of the 'better rule of law'.[152] I would suggest that to invite a court to weigh its substantive rule against those of other interested States in order to determine which was the 'better' rule is inappropriate at any time, and especially so in the context of marriage law. Whether it is better for a man to be allowed one wife or four is a question which cannot be answered save in the context of the cultural and religious backgrounds of the spouses. It cannot be said that the one rule has greater merit than the other unless you make that assessment solely within the perspective of the forum's attitudes to marriage and that is a role that ought to be denied to the *lex fori* save in the case of issues of overriding public policy.

We must now put these various policies, relating both to substantive law and to choice of law, to the test in the context of the essential validity of marriage. I propose to take, as a prime example of essential validity, the rule relating to non-age, and to re-examine in that context and in the light of interest analysis three leading cases drawn from the common law systems.[153]

Re-examination of three choice of law decisions on non-age

Pugh v. *Pugh*

The main English authority on choice of law in the case of non-age is *Pugh* v. *Pugh*.[154] The husband and wife were married in Austria in 1946.

[150] The Hague Conventions in family law matters concluded before the First World War have not been conspicuously successful; see Palsson, *Marriage and Divorce in Comparative Conflict of Laws* (1974), 29–30. For other family law conventions see ibid., 33–6.

[151] Hartley, (1972) 35 *MLR* 571.

[152] Leflar, *American Conflicts Law*, 3rd edn. (1977), 212–15.

[153] *Pugh* v. *Pugh* [1951] P 482; *Wilkins* v. *Zelichowski* 26 NJ 370; 140 A 2d 65 (1958); *State of Arkansas* v. *Graves* 228 Ark 378; 307 SW 2d 545 (1957).

[154] [1951] P 482.

At the time of the marriage, the wife was domiciled in Hungary, though she and her parents were refugees, having left Hungary in 1945. The husband was a British army officer, domiciled in England but serving in Austria. At the time of the marriage, the wife was only 15 years old. After living together in various places where the husband was stationed, the spouses went to England in 1950 to live permanently and the wife petitioned the English courts for a decree of nullity on the ground of non-age.

Three different legal systems may be relevant in order to determine the validity of the marriage: Hungarian, Austrian and English. Under Hungarian law the marriage was voidable if the wife was under 16 but, as she had not avoided it before she was 17, it became valid; the marriage was valid under Austrian law. The rule of English law was contained in section 1 of the Age of Marriage Act 1929[155] which provided that 'A marriage between two persons either of whom is under the age of 16 shall be void'. Two questions arose for decision.[156] What law, or laws, applied to the capacity of the spouses to marry? Second, if English law was applicable, did the 1929 Act have extra-territorial effect and, if so, what effect on the issue of capacity in this case? The judge considered that matters of formal validity were for Austrian law, as the law of the place of celebration, but that non-age was a matter of essential validity to be governed by the law of the spouses' domiciles.[157] Whether the wife was domiciled at the time of the marriage in Hungary or Austria, she had capacity under both laws; so all that needed to be considered further was English law, the law of the husband's domicile.

At first sight, the husband would appear also to have capacity because he was well over the age of 16 at the time of the marriage. However, it was not quite as simple as that. First, it was held that the 1929 Act had extraterritorial effect in that it applied to all marriages of English domiciliaries whether in England or abroad. Second, the statute was interpreted as preventing an English domiciliary from entering into a valid marriage if either spouse, not just the English domiciled spouse, was under the age of 16. Although the husband was of age, he was incapable of marrying a wife under age according to English law (even though she was not domiciled in England).[158] The marriage was therefore void and a nullity decree was granted to the wife.

[155] See now the Marriage Act 1949, s. 2.

[156] The answers to these questions had already been the subject of some academic speculation; see Beckett, (1934) 15 *BYBIL*, 46, 64–5; Morris, (1946) 62 *LQR* 170–3.

[157] [1951] P 482, 493–4.

[158] It might be argued that the case could be read as authority for the general proposition that each spouse must have capacity under both his own and the other spouse's domiciliary law (so that in fact it was the wife here who lacked capacity); see *Szechter* v. *Szechter* [1971] P 286; but such a double-barrelled choice of law rule is generally disapproved of; see, e.g.,

How far does this decision accord with the policies which might be thought to underlie both the substantive and choice of law rules relating to non-age? Clearly it does not accord with the policies behind the substantive law of Austria or Hungary. Austria regarded 15-year-old girls as sufficiently mature to enter into marriage; Hungary accepted that marriage so young might be impetuous and gave a year for reflection which had long elapsed. Neither of these domestic policies was upheld by annulling the marriage. What of English marriage law policy? This was considered by the judge in *Pugh* v. *Pugh* and expounded thus:

> According to modern thought it is considered socially and morally wrong that persons of an age, at which we now believe them to be immature and provide for their education, should have the stresses, responsibilities and sexual freedom of marriage and the physical strain of childbirth. Child marriages are by common consent believed to be bad for the participants and bad for the institution of marriage. Acts making carnal knowledge of young girls an offence are an indication of modern views on this subject. The remedy that 'the Parliament has resolved' for this mischief and defect is to make marriages void where either of the parties is under sixteen years of age.[159]

Undoubtedly there is here an articulated statement of policies underlying the English rule and it is relevant to the extent that the wife was only 15 and therefore deprived, under Austrian and Hungarian law, of the protection that English law feels should be afforded to 15-year-old girls. We have to go further than this, however, and attempt to determine whether the policy of the English rule extends to all marriages of 15-year-old girls anywhere in the world, irrespective of the domicile or nationality of themselves or their husbands. Two extreme cases can be put where the limits of the policy are, I believe, obvious. A marriage in England between two English domiciliaries, who intended to live in England, would be a nullity, because it fell within the policy of the 1929 Act, if the wife (or indeed the husband) was under 16. On the other hand, a marriage in Nigeria between spouses who were both domiciled in, and nationals, of Nigeria, intending to make their home there, would be outside the policy of the Act. Even if one spouse was under 16 and the English court had jurisdiction over a nullity petition, the validity of the marriage should be upheld.[160]

The problem must then be to determine the scope of the policy interests underlying the English rule within these outer limits. The rule could

North, *Private International Law of Matrimonial Causes* (1977), 120. In any event the judge took the view that it was the husband who lacked capacity: see [1951] P 482, 494.

[159] [1951] P 482, 492.

[160] Cf. *Mohamed* v. *Knott* [1969] 1 QB 1, discussed below pp. 143–144, which concerned such a Nigerian marriage, but one where the parties later came to England.

readily be considered to apply to all 15-year-olds domiciled in England at the time of their marriage, whether they marry in England or abroad, especially if they marry abroad in order to evade the age rule;[161] and to all 15-year-olds who marry in England wherever they are domiciled. The facts of *Pugh* v. *Pugh* lie beyond these policy limits. The marriage was not in England and there is no evidence that it took place in Austria for reasons other than those of convenience; Austria being the home of the bride and her parents. An English domiciliary was involved, but the policy behind the English rule does not extending to protecting adult English army officers from the rigours of marriage. There is, however, one basis on which the policy behind the English rule might be considered to extend to the facts of *Pugh* v. *Pugh*. The English rule could be taken to apply even to the marriages abroad of foreign domiciliaries if they intend to (and do) reside in England, on the ground that the interest of the State in the social welfare of the community would be infringed if the parties to an under-age marriage are to be regarded in England as husband and wife. It could further be argued that this policy interest may be identified in *Pugh* v. *Pugh* in that the husband intended, at the time of the marriage, to return to England when his army duties permitted, and the spouses did in fact come to England four years after they were married. The most one can say in conclusion is that it is arguable that the policy of the English rule as to age might be thought to extend to the case where the only connection with England was an intention to reside in England: though in this case the connection did not materialize until some time after the wife had reached the English age of marriage.

So much for the policies underlying the substantive rule of law which compete for application in this case. We must now consider the criteria on which a choice of the applicable law might be made. If we adopted a governmental-interest analysis, the first question to be answered would be whether the case revealed a true or a false conflict. This involves attempting to identify the interests of Austria, Hungary and England in the application of their rules as to age of marriage. A case can be made for all three laws having an interest and thus for there being a true conflict, though the analysis which follows is inevitably superficial. Thorough analysis would require greater knowledge of the policies of Austrian and Hungarian law in 1945, and earlier, than I could ever hope to possess. My only consolation is that my analysis is no more superficial than that attempted by other writers.[162] If England has no interest, but the other countries do, then although there are two interested States there is no real conflict as both uphold the validity of the marriage. Austria's interest

[161] [1951] P 482, 492.

[162] Hartley, (1972) 35 *MLR* 571, 577–8; Swan, (1974) 24 *U Tor LJ* 17, 33–4; Jaffey, (1978) 41 *MLR* 38, 45–6.

might lie in the fact that the marriage was celebrated there and it appears that the marriage would be valid under Austrian law.[163] Austria was not chosen in order to evade the application of some foreign law and it can be argued that, as marriage laws are so integral a part of the fabric of society, the place of celebration would require its laws to be complied with in their entirety. Hungarian interest can be found in the fact that the girl was domiciled there and so the limits of the protection afforded to a 15-year-old should be determined by that law. Both laws have a further interest in upholding of the validity of marriages freely entered into and the marriage in question was valid under their laws.

What interest was there in the application of English law? The interest of English law, in the view of Pearce J, was that 'child marriages are . . . believed to be bad for the participants and bad for the institution of marriage'.[164] Whilst it can be argued that it is no function of English law to protect foreign domiciled 15-year-old girls, and that English adult males need no protection, there is an arguable English interest in the protection of the institution of marriage if the parties to an under-age marriage are going to live in England, as they were eventually to do in this case.

A case can therefore be made out for all three countries having an interest in the application of their marriage rule and, thus, for there being a true conflict. Faced with that result, Currie would invite us to re-examine the issue more rigorously and perhaps carefully[165] and, if we do that, we can find powerful arguments against the application of the laws of any of the three allegedly interested states. Hungary's interest is that of the law of the domicile in matters of status. However, the wife and her family had left Hungary to avoid the Russian advance in 1945. Their prospects of return were slight indeed; they never did return. Hungary's interest survives merely because a domicile in English law cannot be abandoned until another is acquired; but there seems little doubt that the wife, a refugee, had only a tenuous connection with Hungary. Was there really much interest left in Hungarian law such that it should determine the degree of protection to be afforded to a 15-year-old refugee who had fled from the country never to return and who married a foreigner in yet another foreign country? On more penetrating analysis the interest of Austrian law is also rather slight. It can be based on little more than the celebration of the marriage there, but it was a marriage between a foreign refugee and a member of the occupying forces, neither of them intending to remain in Austria. Nor indeed did they remain there permanently because, from 1946–50, they lived in various places in Austria and Germany depending on where the husband was stationed and in 1950 they went permanently to live in England. It is not immediately obvious

163 [1951] P 482, 483.
164 Ibid., 492.
165 Currie, (1963) 63 *Col L Rev* 1233, 1241–2.

that Austria has an interest in determining the degree of protection to be afforded to a foreign national and domiciliary, marrying another foreign national and domiciliary, neither intending to remain in Austria, just because the marriage was celebrated there.

How strong then really is the claim of English law to be applied? One purpose of the English rule is to protect an immature person from 'the stresses, responsibilities and sexual freedom of marriage and the physical strain of childbirth'.[166] There must be some limits to this. It cannot apply to all marriages everywhere. It can arguably be said to be intended to protect young people resident in England, or domiciled in England, or even British nationals, if they marry in England or even if they marry abroad. Some prior connection with England seems intended, as Pearce J recognized.[167] It cannot have been intended to extend the general protection of English law to a foreign national and domiciliary marrying in a foreign country especially when she was not regarded as in need of protection under either the law of her domicile or of the place of celebration. The idea that English law was intended to protect a male Army officer from the 'stresses and responsibilities of marriage' in marrying a 15-year-old Hungarian refugee in Austria seems laughable.

What then of the other possible interest in the application of English law—the prevention of marriages which are likely to be unstable?[168] There is no indication that the residence or intended residence of either or both spouses was an underlying element of the English rule. If it was, the argument that the spouses in *Pugh* v. *Pugh* ultimately intended to live in England loses some of its force as providing an interest in the application of English law when it is borne in mind that to apply the English rule in order to maintain the institution of marriage would have had the result of invalidating a marriage which had lasted four years and of bastardizing the one child of the marriage, the wife being 19 when she came to live in England. This argument must proceed on the basis that it is damaging to the English institution of marriage for spouses to live in England and to be regarded as validly married if either of them is under the age of 16, or was at the time of the marriage under that age even though above it when they first came to England, as in *Pugh* v. *Pugh* itself. That this argument is untenable may be seen from the later English decision of *Mohamed* v. *Knott*.[169] Both spouses were Nigerian and domiciled in Nigeria where they married. The husband was 26 and the wife 13. The marriage was valid under the law of Nigeria. The couple came to England shortly after the marriage and it was held that the marriage was to be recognized in England as a valid marriage. Indeed the only

[166] [1951] P 482, 492. [167] Ibid., 492–3.
[168] Ibid., 492; and see Hartley, (1972) 35 *MLR* 571, 577; Jaffey, (1978) 41 *MLR* 38, 45–6.
[169] [1969] 1 QB 1.

argument advanced against the validity of the marriage was that it was potentially polygamous in nature, not the fact that the wife was below the English age of marriage even though she came to live in England only three months after the marriage took place.

The conclusion which may now be reached after a more careful examination of the interests of Hungary, Austria and England in having their marriage laws applied to *Pugh* v. *Pugh* is that the interest of each legal system is slight. There seems little merit in reaching the conclusion that English law must be applied either just because England has some slight interest in its application or because it is the law of the forum. Whether, to adopt Leflar's criterion,[170] English law is to be applied as 'the better rule of law' involves the making of the well-nigh impossible value judgment as to whether the English 16-years-of-age rule is 'better' when applied to the marriage of a Hungarian in Austria than the relevant Hungarian or Austrian rule. In applying the American ideas canvassed so far to the facts of *Pugh* v. *Pugh*, what has been achieved is, perhaps, a heightened awareness of the issues or factors involved in the choice of law process, but little in the way of clarity, of real identification of the choice to be made between conflicting policies, or anything like the 'right' answer or even the better choice of law rule. Even the development of 'principles of preference' as advocated by Cavers[171] seems to founder on the difficulty of forming any clear view as to whether *Pugh* v. *Pugh* involves a 'true' or a 'false' conflict.

How would the American Restatement Second resolve the question of the law to be applied on the facts of *Pugh* v. *Pugh*? Section 283 of the Restatement Second provides that:

(1) The validity of a marriage will be determined by the local law of the state which, with respect to the particular issue, has the most significant relationship to the spouses and the marriage under the principles stated in s. 6.[172]
(2) A marriage which satisfies the requirements of the state where the marriage was contracted will everywhere be recognised as valid unless it violates the strong public policy of another state which had the most significant relationship to the spouses and the marriage at the time of the marriage.[173]

Section 283(2) seems applicable to the marriage in *Pugh* v. *Pugh* because the marriage was valid by the law of Austria. The answer is clear, and easy to determine, unless some other country has 'the most significant relationship' and recognition of the validity of the marriage would violate its 'strong public policy'. It is not easy to make a case for either England or Hungary having a very significant relationship with both parties and

[170] *American Conflicts Law*, 3rd edn. (1977), 212–15.
[171] See above, pp. 121–123.
[172] See above, pp. 124–127.
[173] Contrast s. 210 of the Uniform Marriage and Divorce Act 1971, as amended in 1973.

the marriage at the time of the marriage. Probably the relationship with Austria was the closest at that time. In any event, it is hard to see that recognition of the validity of the marriage would, in the light of *Mohamed* v. *Knott*, violate England's strong public policy.[174] The conclusion one might draw is that the Restatement provides a rule which is simple to apply, and thus much less costly in terms of legal advice, the necessity of litigation, the use of expert witnesses, etc., and reaches a result which upholds the validity of the marriage and produces greater 'conflicts justice' than the actual decision in *Pugh* v. *Pugh*.

However, the cynic's reaction to that conclusion is that section 283(2) has these desirable effects simply because it amounts to an application of the old 'pre-revolutionary' jurisdiction-selecting choice of law rule of American conflict of laws, but restricted to cases where the marriage is valid by the law of the place of celebration. Indeed one criticism launched by Baade against section 283(2) is its very orthodoxy. He describes it as 'Bad Restatement',[175] and the reasons he gives are:

> First, the law of one jurisdiction is chosen in deliberate disregard of the governmental interests of the state that concededly has the most significant contacts. Second, the incidence of this mechanical choice-of-law rule is to be mitigated not by resort to interest analysis (as it cannot be on its own premises), but by resort to a shopworn concept of demonstrable ambiguity [i.e., public policy].[176]

If we turn to section 283(1), this is regarded by Baade as having obvious merits—it adopts an issue by issue approach, and abandons reliance on the rigid application of the *lex loci celebrationis* where the marriage is invalid by that law.[177] However, reliance on the 'most significant relationship' formula is criticized because that formula 'has turned out to be question-begging, of little use in all but the simplest cases, and of no use at all in what prove to be intractable true-conflict cases'.[178] This is because the principles listed in section 6 on which the determination of the most significant relationship depends are given no comparative weight and may point in different directions at once. In effect, they are criticized as a compromise between rule-selection and jurisdiction-selection, whereas Baade prefers the purer interest analysis of concentrating on 'the "purposes, policies, aims and objectives of each of the competing local law rules"; everything else is material only because it is reflected in these rules as teleologically interpreted'.[179]

The fallacy of this approach is seen in Baade's suggestion that, if a law professor can provide the appropriate analysis of foreign-country governmental interests with 'a few idle hours' work with foreign law books and

[174] See Lawson, 'Governmental Interest Analysis and Other Policy-oriented Choice-of-Law Theories Applied in International Cases', *D.Phil. Thesis* (Oxford, 1973), 467–8.

[175] (1972) 72 *Col L Rev*, 329, 358; and see Cavers, [1970] III *Hague Recueil* 75, 242.

[176] Ibid., 358–9. [177] Ibid., 379. [178] Ibid., 380. [179] Ibid., 378.

pocket dictionaries',[180] there is no reason why judges and counsel should not do likewise. All that a few idle hours work with foreign law books is likely to do is to give a spurious patina of intellectual respectability to any analysis of the policies underlying the laws of the different 'interested' states. Furthermore, it assumes that the validity of every foreign marriage or even marriage-to-be will have to be subjected to this research and courtroom process. No doubt this would be welcomed by lawyers, but not by their clients.

Wilkins v. *Zelichowski*

One of the more recent American decisions on non-age in the conflict of laws is *Wilkins* v. *Zelichowski*.[181] The husband and wife married in Indiana at a time when they were both domiciled in New Jersey. The wife was aged 16 at the time of the marriage. The spouses had run away to marry in Indiana because 'it was the quickest place' and they returned to New Jersey immediately after the marriage ceremony to live and set up home there. A child was born to them in the following year. The wife later sought an annulment of the marriage.

Under the law of Indiana, girls over the age of 16 had capacity to marry, though the consent of their parents was required until they were 18. However a marriage entered into without such consent was nonetheless valid.[182] Under the law of New Jersey a decree of nullity could be granted to a girl who was under the age of 18 when she married, provided that she had not confirmed the marriage on reaching 18, which the wife in this case had not done. However, if there was a child of the marriage, as here, the marriage could only be annulled if such decision 'will not be against the best interests of the child'.

The lower courts found that annulment would be in the best interests of the child, but refused relief on the grounds that the marriage was valid in Indiana and ought, therefore, to be regarded as valid in New Jersey. The Supreme Court of New Jersey took a very different view and granted the relief sought. The essence of their reasoning is to be found in the following passage:

> It is undisputed that if the marriage between the plaintiff and the defendant had taken place here, the public policy of New Jersey would be applicable and the plaintiff would be entitled to the annullment; and it seems clear to us that if New Jersey's public policy is to remain at all meaningful it must be considered equally applicable though their marriage took place in Indiana. While that State was interested in the formal ceremonial requirements of the marriage it had no interest whatever in the marital status of the parties. Indeed, New Jersey was the only

[180] (1972) 72 *Col L Rev* 329, 378. [181] 26 NJ 370; 140 A 2d 65 (1958).
[182] See Baade (1972) 72 *Col L Rev* 329, 359.

State having any interest in that status, for both parties were domiciled in New Jersey before and after their marriage and their matrimonial domicile was established here. The purpose in having the ceremony take place in Indiana was to evade New Jersey's marriage policy and we see no just or compelling reason for permitting it to succeed.[183]

Whilst this decision denying recognition to a marriage valid by the law of the place of celebration antedates at least the judicial development of the 'American revolution', it has been relied upon as exemplifying the merits of some of the new approaches. Baade regards it as 'the classic example of a false-conflict case correctly so identified and decided'.[184] He places reliance on the first sentence of the passage just quoted as indicating 'the policy behind the statute law of New Jersey, as ascertained by inquiry into the purposes sought to be served by it'.[185] It is undoubtedly true that the Supreme Court of New Jersey did examine the reasons given in 1907 for the introduction of the New Jersey rule on non-age and they pointed to 'the vigor of New Jersey's policy against marriages by persons under the prescribed age'.[186] There is no evidence, however, that this policy applies to parties who are not domiciled in New Jersey. There is no suggestion that a marriage anywhere in the world will be annulled in New Jersey if one spouse was under 18 at the time of the marriage. The decision in *Wilkins* v. *Zeichowski* can be regarded by a conservative conflicts lawyer as doing no more than drawing the distinction, drawn in England a hundred years earlier,[187] between matters of essential validity to be governed by the personal law and matters of formal validity to be governed by the law of the place of celebration and, indeed, probably for the same reason, namely to combat evasion.

Supporters of the Restatement Second would also welcome the result in *Wilkins* v. *Zelichowski*, as does Reese himself,[188] as an example of the proviso to section 283(2) in operation. The marriage was valid under the law of the place of celebration, Indiana, and so should be recognized in New Jersey 'unless it violates the strong public policy' of New Jersey. Reese finds ample evidence of the strength of New Jersey public policy justifying non-recognition. By way of an aside, an orthodox English conflicts lawyer would also agree with the result because the court applied the law of the domicile, and of the intended matrimonial home, to determine the essential validity of the marriage.

183 140 A 2d 65, 67–8.
184 (1972) 72 *Col L Rev* 329, 360.
185 Ibid.
186 140 A 2d 65, 67.
187 *Brook* v. *Brook* (1861) 9 HL Cas 193.
188 [1976] II *Hague Recueil* 1, 166–71.

State of Arkansas v. *Graves*

The question of non-age in the conflict of laws came before the Supreme Court of Arkansas in the case of *State of Arkansas* v. *Graves*,[189] just a few months before the decision of the Supreme Court of New Jersey in *Wilkins* v. *Zelichowski*, but with a very different outcome. The parents of a 13-year-old girl were prosecuted for the offence of contributing to the delinquency of a minor on the ground that the marriage she had entered into was void and that her parents had consented to her marriage. All depended on the validity of the marriage. The girl was 13, her husband was 17; they and their parents were all resident and domiciled in Arkansas. They married, with the consent of their parents, in Mississippi and immediately returned to Arkansas to live. The marriage was valid under the law of Mississippi but both parties were under age according to the law of Arkansas.

The Supreme Court of Arkansas started from the proposition that a marriage valid where celebrated is recognized as being valid everywhere, subject to a number of exceptions, the only relevant ones being the existence of a statutory provision declaring void a marriage validly entered into in another state, or that recognition of the marriage would be contrary to the strong public policy of Arkansas. There was no relevant statutory provision and a majority held that 'it can hardly be said that the public policy of this State against under-age marriages is so strong that such a marriage, valid in the state where it was contracted, is void in this State'.[190] The validity of the marriage was upheld.

Many would be dissatisfied with such a conclusion. That children domiciled and resident in Arkansas who visited Mississippi merely long enough to marry and then returned to live together in Arkansas should be allowed to evade the Arkansas laws as to age of marriage, albeit with the consent of their parents, seems absurd. The supporter of orthodox jurisdiction-selecting would say that the fault lies in the choice of law rule referring all matters of essential and formal validity to the law of the place of celebration. All would have been well under the English rule which applies the law of the domicile to matters of essential validity.

What result would the 'revolutionaries' have reached on the facts of this case? The Restatement Second would, prima facie, have upheld the validity of the marriage because it fell within the rule in section 283(2) that a marriage valid according to the law of the place of celebration should be regarded as valid. It is hard to argue that one should here apply the proviso of non-recognition if the marriage violates the strong public policy of the most significantly connected state. That state was undoubtedly Arkansas but the court held that the public policy of

[189] 228 Ark 378; 307 SW 2d 545 (1957). [190] 307 SW 2d 545, 550 (1957).

Arkansas was not violated by recognition. Indeed, this case provides a good example of the conflict between section 283(1) and section 283(2) of the Restatement. The former would have led to the application of the law of Arkansas—clearly the more appropriate law; but this application was excluded by section 283(2).

Reese has suggested that section 283 reflects three underlying interests: namely, state interest, protection of the expectations of the parties, and the general policy favouring validation of marriage, and that the last two are implemented by section 283(2) because the parties 'must have intended to enter into a valid marriage and, if they thought about the matter at all, they would in all probability have expected that the law of the state of celebration would be applied'.[191] However, in the case of evasion the parties can do no more than hope that their marriage is valid in circumstances where they have clearly considered the matter carefully. Though the conflicts lawyer may conclude that there is a far greater interest in the application of Arkansas law rather than Missouri law, the application of Arkansas law is unlikely to be achieved unless there is a marriage evasion statute, or a similar judicial development, in the country of most significant relationship.

Consideration of interest analysis necessitates an initial decision as to whether there was a true or false conflict. One might assume that the conflict was false because the law of Mississippi had no interest in the application of its law as to the age of marriage when the only connection with that state was that the marriage was celebrated there. On the other hand, it might be thought that the Arkansas rule was intended to protect Arkansas residents and domiciliaries who intended to live in that State, even though they married elsewhere. However, the Arkansas Supreme Court tended to deny any such interest, saying 'there is no strong public policy in this State requiring the courts to declare that marriages such as the one involved here are void *ab initio*'.[192] Indeed, the Arkansas courts had held under-age marriages celebrated in Arkansas to be merely voidable, despite the statutory provision that they were 'absolutely void'. Had it been the policy of Arkansas law to strike down out-of-state marriages by Arkansas domiciliaries, then it has been suggested[193] that Arkansas would have enacted a marriage evasion statute. If interest analysis is to be based on what the courts conceive as the policies behind the rules,[194] it has let us down again here because the Arkansas Supreme Court indi-

[191] [1976] II *Hague Recueil* 1, 176. [192] 307 SW 2d 545, 549 (1957).

[193] Bare, (1959) 16 *Washington and Lee L Rev* 87, 90.

[194] As Baade certainly indicates in his analysis of *Wilkins* v. *Zelichowski* in (1972) 72 *Col L Rev* 329, 360. It is undoubtedly the case that in determining the 'strong' public policy of a state, reference is to be made to the decisions of the courts of that state: Restatement 2d, s. 283, Comment (*k*). Life becomes insufferably complicated if reference is to be made to those

cated that Arkansas had no interest in the application of its law. The case seems to be a false conflict with the result that the 'wrong' result is reached, namely the application of Mississippi law—or even the conclusion that neither state has an interest in the application of its own law. The only way that a different result can be reached is by doing what a majority of the Supreme Court of Arkansas was unprepared to do and find an interest in the application of the law of that state. Once that is done then it readily follows that Arkansas law should be applied.

Formal Validity of Marriages[195]

In the common law world, it has been long established that the law to govern the formal validity of a marriage is the law of the country of celebration.[196] This rule is subject to a number of limited exceptions primarily concerned with the situation where it is impossible or manifestly unreasonable to comply with the local law.[197] It is also subject to the problem of characterization in that it may have to be decided whether the issue relates to essential or formal validity, a problem which has proved particularly tiresome for the English courts in the context of the characterization of lack of parental consent.[198]

We must here, as in the context of essential validity,[199] attempt to identify two sets of policies, those which may be taken to justify domestic substantive rules as to formal validity and those which may be taken into account in devising appropriate choice of law rules. There is a wide variety of matters which concern formal validity, but they include such issues as the nature of any ceremony required, whether there must be a religious or civil ceremony, whether a licence to marry must be obtained, the notice that must be given of intention to marry, the premises on which, and the times at which, marriages may be celebrated, whether witnesses are required, and whether proxy marriages are permitted.

General issues

Policy bases of substantive rules as to formalities

As with policies underlying essential validity, the identification of policies relevant to formal validity is closely bound up with the cultural and reli-

decisions to determine the 'strong' public policy, but not to determine any 'weaker' interest such as may determine whether the conflict is 'true' or 'false'.

195 Mendes da Costa, (1958) 7 *ICLQ* 217.

196 Dicey and Morris, *The Conflict of Laws*, 9th edn., 234–41.

197 Ibid., 241–4.

198 *Simonin* v. *Mallac* (1860) 2 Sw and Tr 67; *Ogden* v. *Ogden* [1908] P 46.

199 See above, pp. 134–138.

gious background of the society whose rules are under review. Some relevant policies, viewed through the eyes of a western commentator, are these:

1. Certainty. It is desirable that the spouses and other interested parties should be aware that a marriage has been entered into.

2. Proof. Not only should it be certain that a marriage has been entered into but this should be easy to prove. This underlies the need for marriages to be solemnized before witnesses and the need for registration, so that access to public records makes proof all the easier, especially when the spouses are dead.

3. Publicity. There has long been opposition to clandestine marriages and the requirements of publication of banns, or the giving of notice of marriage, or the prohibition of marriages at night all evidence this requirement of publicity.

4. Avoidance of over-hasty marriages. Marry in haste (or in drink) and repent at leisure, so the saying goes. A requirement of notice of intention to marry being publicly given provides a minimal 'cooling-off' period.

5. Religion. In some countries, the religious element in marriage is reinforced by the fact that only a religious marriage ceremony is possible; in others a choice of civil or religious ceremony is provided; in some the nature of the ceremony available depends on the spouses' religion.

6. Constitutional factors. In other countries, the constitutional separation of Church and State is maintained by accepting only a civil ceremony as conferring legal marital status.

7. Health factors. Medical examination as a necessary formal preliminary to marriage will tend to reduce the incidence of venereal disease and could play a part in the avoidance of genetic problems.

8. Prevention of marriage obligations being undertaken at too young an age. This is exemplified by the requirement of parental or other consent to marry below a certain age.

Policy bases of choice of law rules

The various factors which might be taken into account in devising choice of law rules to determine the formal validity of a marriage do not really differ from those already discussed in the context of essential validity.[200] These are the validation of marriages, consideration of the domestic family law policies of the forum and of 'interested' foreign states, the protection of the justified expectations of the parties, the need for certainty and stability, and the intrinsic merit of the legal rule. Other factors have been put forward, in the context of attempts to justify the application of the

[200] See above, pp. 136–138.

law of the country of celebration of the marriage, such as hoped-for reciprocity, i.e., if courts in state A apply the law of State B to marriages celebrated there, then courts of State B might apply the law of State A if the marriage is celebrated in the latter state.[201]

We will now, as with essential validity, attempt to put these policies, relating both to substantive law and to choice of law, to the test in the context of formal validity, considering two leading cases in the light of both the orthodox jurisdiction-selecting approach and the recent American developments in rule-selection.

Two leading cases re-examined

Berthiaume v. *Dastous*

The leading Commonwealth authority on choice of law to govern the formal validity of a marriage is *Berthiaume* v. *Dastous*,[202] a decision of the Judicial Committee of the Privy Council on appeal from Quebec. The facts are quite simple. The husband and wife were both domiciled in Quebec. The wife was aged 17 and in 1913 visited Paris with her father just after leaving school. There she met the husband who had been living in Paris for several years. They were married in Paris by a Roman Catholic priest, the husband having obtained a certificate from the British consulate prior to the marriage. In 1926, the wife petitioned the French courts for divorce and she then discovered 'that the certificate which her fiancé had procured at the British consulate was only a notice of intended marriage, and that the officiating curé had carelessly omitted to notice that it was not a certificate of marriage'.[203] The French divorce petition was dismissed in the absence of a certificate of marriage and eventually the wife petitioned in Quebec for, *inter alia*, a declaration as to the validity of her marriage. Under French law the marriage was void; under the law of Quebec a marriage there celebrated by a priest or other officer 'authorised by law to keep registers of acts of civil status'[204] was valid. The Privy Council had no doubt that French law, as the law of the place of celebration, determined the validity of this marriage which was, therefore, held to be void.

In a passage which has been often cited since, Viscount Dunedin said:

> If there is one question better settled than any other in international law, it is that as regards marriage—putting aside the question of capacity—locus regit actum. If a marriage is good by the laws of the country where it is effected, it is good all the world over, no matter whether the proceeding or ceremony which constituted

[201] Fine, (1976) 7 *Fed L Rev* 49, 51. [202] [1930] AC 79. [203] Ibid., 82.
[204] Quebec Civil Code, Art. 129.

marriage according to the law of the place would or would not constitute marriage in the country of the domicil of one or other of the spouses. If the so-called marriage is no marriage in the place where it is celebrated, there is no marriage anywhere, although the ceremony or proceeding if conducted in the place of the parties' domicil would be considered a good marriage.[205]

This embodies a rule which as we have seen is generally accepted internationally. Compliance with the formal requirements of the *lex loci celebrationis* is normally both sufficient and necessary.[206]

Critics of jurisdiction-selecting rules would attack this rule as formalistic and for taking no account of the policies underlying the rules as to formalities in different interested jurisdictions. Let us turn once again, therefore, to consider the various modern American approaches to choice of law and to examine their possible impact on what is one of the most settled jurisdiction-selecting choice of law rules. In doing so, we must not forget that the rule may well itself be the product of a balancing of conflicting choice of law policies.[207] Our first enquiry must be as to whether *Berthiaume* v. *Dastous* reveals a true or false conflict. There are two different sets of interests to consider—Quebec and France. The interest in the application of French law is obvious. If a French court is later to be asked to grant matrimonial relief to the parties to a marriage celebrated in France, as happened in the present case, France has a clear interest in the method of proof of the validity of the marriage. France draws a clear distinction between Church and State in matters of marriage law. 'The law of France is peremptory. There must be a civil ceremony of marriage, and if that has not taken place any religious ceremony is an idle performance so far as the law is concerned.'[208]

Does Quebec, the law of the forum, have an interest? At least one commentator[209] has seen an apparent interest in the application of Quebec law. It is argued that Quebec law embodies a policy that a religious ceremony is adequate to bring home the civil as well as the religious nature of the marital obligations being assumed by the spouses, and that this is relevant here because both parties were Quebec domiciliaries. On further analysis,[210] the interest of Quebec was found to be more apparent than real because the freedom to choose between a civil or religious ceremony should be restricted to marriages in Quebec. This is all the stronger in the present case where the spouses appear to have lived most, if not all, of

[205] [1930] AC 79, 83.
[206] Palsson, *International Encyclopedia of Comparative Law*, iii: ch. 16; *Marriage and Divorce in Comparative Conflict of Laws* (1974), 26–8.
[207] Morris, *The Conflict of Laws*, 2nd edn. (1980), 510–11.
[208] [1930] AC 79, 84.
[209] Lawson, 'Governmental Interest Analysis and Other Policy-Oriented Choice-of-Law Theories Applied in International Cases', *D Phil Thesis*, (Oxford, 1973), 474–5.
[210] Ibid., 475–6.

their married life in France.[211] There is a powerful Quebec interest in certainty of proof, but it is one which only compliance with French law can satisfy. Indeed, the Quebec Civil Code only permits a marriage to be celebrated by 'priests, rectors, ministers and other officers authorised by law to keep registers of acts of civil status'.[212] There is no evidence that the French curé was so qualified under Quebec law, which suggests that the marriage ought to have been regarded as void even if Quebec law had been applied.[213] At the end of the day, our analysis, which has inevitably somewhat cavalierly determined the potential interests of the 'interested' states, indicates a false conflict. Currie and Cavers would approve of the decision to apply French law. The simple jurisdiction-selecting approach has, on these facts, reached the same 'correct' result as the rather more laborious, or sophisticated (depending on your point of view) rule-selecting approach.

Consideration of the Restatement Second provides a more interesting problem. It will be recalled that, under section 283(2), there is a strong presumption of validity if the marriage is valid according to the law of the place of performance, whether the issue in question relates to formalities or essential validity. That provision is of no assistance here because the marriage was invalid under French law and we are thrown back on to the general proposition in section 283(1) that reference must be made to the law of the state which, with respect to the particular issue, has the most significant relationship to the spouses and the marriage under the principles in section 6. The particular issue is whether a religious ceremony will suffice or whether there must also be a civil marriage certificate. Some policies point towards the application of Quebec law, especially if, as the lower courts in Quebec believed, the validity of the marriage could be upheld. Such a result would, on that basis, accord with the policies of the forum[214] and validation would certainly protect the justified expectations of the parties. They thought for well over a decade that they were married; neither had any realization of the mistake made at the time of the ceremony. However, other factors point strongly towards the application of French law. The policies underlying the French requirements of form indicate that they should be applied to marriages in France, particularly where the parties continue to live in France.[215] Certainly, predictability, and uniformity of result are achieved

[211] (1928) 45 KB 391, 394 (Report of the proceedings in the Quebec Court of King's Bench).

[212] Art. 129.

[213] As it was in the lower courts which upheld the validity of the marriage: (1928) 66 SC 241; (1928) 45 KB 391.

[214] Though, as has been indicated earlier, it is hard to see how this could be the policy of Quebec law.

[215] Cf. Maddaugh, (1973) 23 *U Tor LJ* 117, 139.

by the application of the law of the place of celebration, as are 'the basic policies underlying the particular field of law', namely the requirement of a civil ceremony.

At the end of the day, all analyses point towards the correctness of the decision in *Berthiaume* v. *Dastous*. It is just more cumbersome to reach it by a 'revolutionary' approach—one which may require judicial decision before reliable advice can be given to the parties, either before or after they go through a marriage ceremony.

Vergnani v. *Guidetti*

The generally accepted rule in the USA has been that a marriage which satisfied the formal requirements of the place of celebration should be regarded as valid and that, conversely, formal invalidity under the *lex loci celebrationis* generally meant that the marriage would be regarded as void.[216] This latter conclusion is illustrated by one of the few cases on formal validity referred to in the American literature on interest analysis,[217] namely *Vergnani* v. *Guidetti*.[218] The husband and wife went through a religious ceremony of marriage in Italy in 1901, but did not go through any civil ceremony. It would appear that both were, at that time, Italian nationals and domiciliaries. The day after the ceremony, the husband left for the USA; the wife stayed in Italy and they never met again. Their son was born some three months after they had gone through the marriage ceremony. When the husband died intestate in 1936, the son who seems always to have remained in Italy claimed to be the only heir of his father. The Massachusetts court held that the question of the son's legitimacy depended on whether his parents were lawfully married according to the civil law of Italy. Expert evidence on Italian law indicated that in 1901 a purely religious ceremony was not recognized and that the issue of such a marriage would not be regarded as legitimate.[219] That being so, the marriage was regarded as invalid and the son as illegitimate.

This decision provides as clear an example of the application of the orthodox choice of law rule referring to the *lex loci celebrationis* as one could wish to find. Indeed the connection with Italy at the time of the marriage was overwhelming. The only foreign connection was that the

[216] Sometimes this conclusion could be avoided by the foreign law's use of *renvoi*; see *In Re Lando's Estate* 112 Minn 257; 127 NW 1125 (1910); or the fact that the *lex loci celebrationis* did not insist on compliance with its own rules: *Smith* v. *Smith* 52 NJL 207; 19 A 255 (1890).

[217] Currie, [1964] *Duke LJ* 424, 425–6 (and also *Selected Essays on the Conflict of Laws* (1963), 72); Baade, (1972) 72 *Col L Rev* 329.

[218] 308 Mass 450; 32 NE 2d 272 (1941).

[219] 32 NE 2d 272, 276.

next day the husband was to leave for the USA to find work[220] with no indication whether he would be successful and stay (as he did), nor of the state in which he would ultimately settle. What then would interest analysis make of this decision? Currie has criticized the decision as a mischievous result of the application of 'formulated rules of choice of law',[221] saying: 'thus Massachusetts bastardised and disinherited the son of an American because his parents had been married in church instead of in the town hall across the street—in Italy at a time when the Italian Code recognised only civil ceremonies.[222]

Baade is a little less contemptuous of the decision, admitting that it is not an easy case,[223] but concluding nevertheless that the son should have been regarded by the Massachusetts court as legitimate.

So far as children and collaterals are concerned, the purpose of the Massachusetts intestacy laws is, presumably, to give effect to the typical presumptive intent of the decedent. It seems reasonable enough to assume that this decedent should be protected in his likely belief that by going through a marriage ceremony that would have been perfectly valid in Massachusetts, he had conferred some expectancy status on his son . . . which obviated the need to consult a lawyer and draw up a will.[224]

The assumptions in the passage just quoted are so speculative and, it is suggested, unrealistic that dislike of the decision in this case might be thought to centre more on the law relating to illegitimacy than on choice of law relating to marriage. It seems unlikely in the extreme that the father, in Italy out of work and having decided to emigrate, when faced with the fact that the mother was several months pregnant, took the decision to go through a religious rather than civil ceremony 'in the likely belief' as to the legal effect of such an act on the validity of his marriage or the legitimacy of his child-to-be in relation to some American state. If one wishes to continue the speculation, it seems just as likely that the decision was taken just before his departure; there was time for nothing but a religious ceremony; the spouses would at least be married in the eyes of their faith and when both mother and child arrived in the USA, as was the original intention, all could be put right.

Let us undertake a more dispassionate consideration of whether there is a true or false conflict here. We need, perhaps, to separate two different issues because whenever there is an incidental question, as there is here in that succession may depend on legitimacy which in turn may depend on the validity of the marriage, the policies to be considered may differ

[220] Cf. *Masocco* v. *Schaaf* 234 App Div 181; 254 NYS 439 (1931).

[221] Ehrenzweig, *A Treatise on the Conflict of Laws* (1962), 352.

[222] [1964] *Duke LJ* 424, 425–6 (reviewing Ehrenzweig, above); and see Currie, *Selected Essays on the Conflict of Laws* (1963), 71–2.

[223] (1972) 72 *Col L Rev* 329, 365.

[224] Ibid., 366.

depending on the particular issue under review. If the issue is the validity of the marriage, the interest in the application of Italian law is obvious. A major factor is that of the separation of Church and State, emphasized by the fact that the rule requiring a civil ceremony was only changed as a result of the Lateran Treaty of 1929 between Italy and the Vatican. The argument that, though Italy had an interest in 1901 in the application of its rule, that interest had disappeared after 1929 cannot be supported. Although it was possible after 1929 (with the consent of the parties) to give civil effect to pre-1929 marriages where there was only a religious ceremony, this was not possible in *Vergnani* as the wife had died in 1912. The interest in the application of the law of Massachusetts to the formal validity of a marriage in 1901 in Italy between parties all of whose connections were with Italy except for the fact that one party intended to, and did, leave for Massachusetts after the ceremony is difficult to substantiate. So far as the marriage is concerned, the conflict seems false and the decision correct.

If the issue is classed as one as to legitimacy as such, the conflict again seems false. The child in question was conceived in Italy of parents domiciled and resident there and Italian nationals. His parents went through a ceremony of marriage there; he was born there and lived all his life there. He had no connection with any other state other than that he claimed property in Massachusetts. The interest of the latter state in applying its laws to determine legitimacy seems, at the most, minimal. Is the result likely to be different if the case is viewed as one of succession? Here the facts point more strongly towards an interest in the application of Massachusetts law, rather than of Italian law. The deceased was domiciled at death in Massachusetts, where his assets were to be found. Interestingly, under Italian law, an illegitimate child could succeed in the circumstances of this case, but not under the law of Massachusetts. It is very hard to understand why this right to succeed under Italian law should lead supporters of interest-analysis to conclude that the decision was wrong.[225] If this rule of Italian law indicates a true conflict, then Currie would have applied the law of Massachusetts as the law of the forum and upheld the decision, which we know he disliked.

So much for the vagaries of interest analysis. Would the decision be any different applying the Restatement Second? The marriage was invalid under the law of the place of celebration and so section 283(2) is inapplicable. We must seek the law of the country of the most significant

[225] Baade, (1972) 72 *Col L Rev* 329, 368. He also suggests that recognition of the marriage was merited because the husband was an immigrant into the USA, see 368 *et seq*. It is, however, one matter to decide whether to admit a couple into a country to stay on the basis that they are bound to each other by a religious ceremony; it may well be different to say that they are validly married for status purposes: remarriage, legitimacy, social security, taxation, and the like.

relationship to the parties, the marriage and the issue. At the time of the marriage ceremony, there seems little doubt that that country was Italy. The only criteria in section 6 which could point to the application of the law of Massachusetts to determine whether a civil ceremony was required might be 'the protection of justified expectations' and 'the relevant policies of the forum'. As to the former, there is no evidence that the parties did regard themselves as validly married[226] and as to the latter it is hard to identify any policy of Massachusetts which would be truly served by the application of its law.

This analysis of the Restatement Second, pointing to the correctness of *Vergnani*, might be criticized for failing correctly to identify the issue. If it is regarded as an issue of legitimacy rather than of marriage, then section 287(1) of the Restatement Second is relevant as providing the choice of law rule to govern legitimacy. It would apply the law of the state which has the most significant relationship to the child and the parent. It could only be Italy or Massachusetts. Both regard the child as illegitimate. If the issue is classed as one of succession to moveables (the husband left no immoveable property), the law to be applied, under section 261(1), to the question whether a person must be legitimate in order to succeed to moveables on intestacy, is the law of the deceased's last domicile on death. This would be Massachusetts. The question of legitimacy is referred by section 261(2) to section 287 and, as we have just seen, the child was illegitimate. So, once again, the decision was correct.

Divorce

Difference of approach to choice of law between common law and civil law systems

In the common law world, discussion of private international law issues affecting divorce has always centred on the two issues of jurisdiction to grant the relief and, more particularly, whether a foreign decree of divorce should be recognized. The question of choice of the applicable law to determine whether relief should be granted has merited little discussion in either the decisions or the literature. There were at one time obvious reasons for this. Divorce was regarded as a question of status. For that reason only the courts of the domicile could have jurisdiction to grant divorces and they applied their own law as the law of the country pre-eminently relevant to matters of status. When divorce jurisdiction was broadened to allow courts in countries other than the domicile to grant

[226] 32 NE 2d 272, 275.

divorces, there was little reconsideration of the choice of law rule. The law of the forum tended to be applied for 'the presence of foreign elements in any given case finds expression in the rule of jurisdiction, not choice of law'.[227]

The assumption throughout the common law world that choice of law in divorce creates no problems because the *lex fori* is in fact always applied does not now find a counterpart in civil law jurisdictions. However, in Savigny's time there was a happy coincidence between jurisdiction and choice of law in divorce, for he said:[228]

> Divorce is distinguished from the legal institutions relative to property, by the circumstance that the laws relating to it depend on the moral nature of marriage, and therefore have in themselves a strictly positive character. Hence the judge, in a case of divorce, must follow only the law of his own country without respect to the other relations of the spouses. This principle, however, will generally lead us back to the law of the domicile of the husband, because it is only there that a true jurisdiction for a divorce is established.

Once jurisdiction in divorce came to be based other than on the sole criterion of the law of the country governing status, a divorce choice of law rule had to be established. The basic rule in civil law jurisdictions is the application of the law of the nationality.[229] Undoubtedly, the force of nationality as a general choice of law connecting factor has weakened during this century and this is also true in the present context for, as Palsson points out: 'More frequently, the rule of the national law, while retained in principle, has become subject to various restrictions, exceptions and modifications, usually in favour of the *lex fori*'.[230] France, indeed, moved in favour of applying the law of the common domicile where the spouses were of different nationalities, even though one was French.[231] If, however, they lacked both common domicile and common nationality, recourse was then had to the *lex fori*.[232] Legislative change was introduced in 1975[233] to the effect that French law would be applied when both spouses were French nationals, when both were domiciled in

[227] Fleming, (1952) 1 *ICLQ* 381.

[228] *A Treatise on the Conflict of Laws*, Guthrie's Translation, 2nd edn. (1869), 298–9.

[229] Palsson, *International Encyclopedia of Comparative Law*, iii: ch. 16; *Marriage and Divorce in Comparative Conflict of Laws* (1974), 129 *et seq*; and see the Hague Convention to Regulate the Conflict of Laws and Jurisdiction in Regard to Divorce and Separation (1902), Arts. 1–4.

[230] Ibid., 130.

[231] Cass civ 17 April 1953 (Rivière), *Rev crit dr int pr* 1953, 412; Batiffol and Lagarde, *Droit international privé*, 6th edn. (1976), ii: 70–2; Carbonneau, (1978) 28 *Am J Comp L* 446, 449–52; Franceskakis (1975) *Rev crit dr int pr* 64, 553.

[232] Cass civ 15 May 1961 (Terwid).

[233] Law No. 75–618 of 11 July 1975, Art. 310 of the Code Civil; see Glendon, (1976) 24 *Am Jo Comp L* 199; Lasok, (1977) 51 *Tul L Rev* 259; Carbonneau, (1978) 28 *Am Jo Comp L* 446; Franceskakis (1975), *Rev crit dr int pr* 64, 553.

France (even if they had foreign nationality), and when the French court had jurisdiction because, for example, one spouse was a French national or the defendant spouse was domiciled in France, provided no foreign law considered itself competent. So, if the petitioner was habitually resident in England, the English courts would take jurisdiction and apply English law with the result that the French courts could not apply French law even though the petitioner was a French national. This provision has been criticized[234] for indicating only when French law is applicable and for giving no guidance as to the applicable law when the case is not one governed by French law. It does indicate, however, that the French courts will not always apply French law and that, when they do, the justification is usually because of common French nationality or domicile, rather than just because France is the forum. This brief consideration of the position in one civil law jurisdiction[235] indicates that it is not a self-evident truism that the *lex fori* must be regarded as the law applicable to divorce and it is with that in mind that we return to the Anglo-American common law position.

Impact of interest analysis on the common law approach

The arrival of interest analysis on the conflicts scene has led to little change in the American approach to choice of law in divorce. Although the automatic nature of jurisdiction-selecting rules has, in general, been rejected, consideration has rarely been given to the question whether the automatic application of the *lex fori* to divorce should be abandoned.[236] Cavers suggests that the 'troubled area' of family law and its problems of conflicting mores can be bypassed so far as choice of law is concerned because 'the principal questions here go to other branches of the subject: jurisdiction of courts and the recognition and enforcement of the judgments and decrees of other courts'.[237] Although at least one commentator has attempted to go further than this and consider the choice of law rule

[234] Batiffol and Lagarde, *Droit international privé*, 6th edn. (1976), II: 72–5; and see Franceskakis, (1975) *Rev crit dr int pr* 64, 553.

[235] There has been a clear movement in Belgium towards the application of the law of the forum; see the Act on the admissibility of divorce where at least one of the spouses is an alien, 27 June 1960; Rigaux, *Droit International Privé*, ii: *Droit positif belge* (1979), ss. 944 *et seq.*

[236] Reese, in his General Course of lectures at the Hague Academy of International Law [1976] II *Hague Recueil* 1, does not discuss divorce at all; Currie, in *Selected Essays on the Conflict of Laws* (1963), considers choice of law only in relation to financial support, see pp. 663 *et seq.* Swan in arguing for a new approach to marriage and divorce confines himself almost exclusively, so far as divorce is concerned, to divorce recognition, regarding application of some law other than the *lex fori* to determine the grounds of divorce as little more than a Utopian dream: (1974) 24 *U Tor LJ* 17, 48.

[237] *The Choice-of-Law Process* (1965), 117; and see [1970] III *Hague Recueil* 75, 245–6.

for divorce in the context of interest analysis,[238] there seems to be little general enthusiasm for venturing far beyond the application of the *lex fori*. The Restatement Second is similarly hesitant. It proposes, in section 285, the application of the law of the domiciliary state in which the action is brought. Put more crudely the rule is: where the proceedings are brought in the state of the domicile[239] apply that law, i.e., the *lex fori*. What if they are brought in some other jurisdiction envisaged by the Restatement, namely under section 72, the state with which either spouse has such a relationship 'as would make it reasonable for the state to dissolve the marriage'?[240] No direct answer is given. The inference from section 72 itself is that the *lex fori* would be applied, but the comment to section 285 is more cautious: 'It is uncertain whether it would be appropriate for the courts of a state where neither spouse is domiciled but which does have jurisdiction to grant a divorce to apply their own local law in determining whether a divorce should be granted.'[241]

Examples of leading cases in the common law world involving consideration, or even providing exemplification, of the question of choice of law in divorce are difficult to find. This is partly because the general rule in the USA is that divorce jurisdiction is based on domicile, with the result that courts apply their own law, but whether as *lex domicilii* or as *lex fori* is not normally investigated.[242] It is only when jurisdiction is based other than on domicile that the problem can arise and, though this is possible in England,[243] English law is applied without any examination of the choice of law issue.[244] It is a matter of debate in the USA whether it is constitutionally proper for jurisdiction to be taken other than on the basis of domicile and more particularly whether a divorce granted in such circumstances is entitled to recognition elsewhere in the USA. The Arkansas Supreme Court[245] has upheld the constitutionality of a state

[238] Seidelson, (1971) 21 *Buffalo L Rev* 315. His views are considered more fully below, see pp. 168–169.

[239] Under ss. 70, 71.

[240] One year's residence in the state is suggested as a sufficient connection; celebration of the marriage there is not; Comment (*b*) to s. 72.

[241] Comment (*d*) to s. 285.

[242] *Torlonia* v. *Torlonia* 108 Conn 292; 142 A 843 (1928) supports its application *qua lex domicilii*; and see *Whealton* v. *Whealton* 67 Cal 2d 656; 432 P 2d 979 (1967); *Alton* v. *Alton* 207 F 2d 667, 676–8 (1953). There are statutory provisions in a few states dealing with choice of law in divorce: Weintraub, *Commentary on the Conflict of Laws* (1971), 174; and see the Uniform Marriage and Divorce Act 1971, amended 1973, s. 302(*a*)(1).

[243] See Domicile and Matrimonial Proceedings Act 1973, s. 5.

[244] See *Zanelli* v. *Zanelli* (1948) 64 TLR 556. A similar approach is taken in Australia and New Zealand: Nygh, *Conflict of Laws in Australia*, 3rd edn. (1976), 312; and in Canada: Castel, *Canadian Conflict of Laws* (1977), 2: 115–16.

[245] *Wheat* v. *Wheat* 229 Ark 842; 318 SW 2d 793 (1958). Though it appears that the *lex fori* is applied: see *Walther* v. *Walther* 343 SW 2d 408 (1961). This conclusion is also supported by decisions concerned with the recognition of Arkansas divorces in other states: *Reeves* v. *Reeves* 209 So 2d 554 (1968); *Staples* v. *Staples* 232 So 2d 904 (1970).

law conferring divorce jurisdiction on the basis of three months' residence, but without determining the law to be applied to such a divorce petition.[246] There has, however, been some consideration given to this choice of law issue in a federal court decision in the USA and we shall take this case as our main divorce choice of law example.

Choice of law illustrated by Alton v. *Alton*

In *Alton* v. *Alton*,[247] both husband and wife lived in Connecticut. The wife visited the Virgin Islands and, after she had been there six weeks, petitioned for divorce. Her husband did not contest the proceedings and jurisdiction was based on a Virgin Islands statute requiring six weeks' residence to found jurisdiction.[248] The question arose before the federal courts as to whether the Virgin Islands court had had jurisdiction to grant a divorce decree. It was held by a majority in the United States Court of Appeals (Third Circuit) that there were constitutional objections to divorce jurisdiction being based other than on domicile, not just with regard to recognition of the decree in another jurisdiction, but also as to the jurisdiction of the court to grant it in the first place. In his dissenting judgment, Judge Hastie was prepared to uphold the validity and constitutionality of the Virgin Islands legislation; but he then went on to refer to the question of the law to be applied if jurisdiction was taken on residence alone. Without attempting to lay down general choice of law rules, he suggested[249] that, on the facts of the case before him, where both spouses were domiciled in Connecticut at the time of the divorce proceedings in the Virgin Islands, and where their estrangement had resulted from conduct in their matrimonial home state, the forum should apply the law of the state with the appropriate connection with the subject-matter, here Connecticut.

Here we have the dilemma over choice of law in divorce posed fairly sharply. Should the applicable law be determined by reference to the *lex fori*, the *lex domicilii* or the most closely related law? The approach in England, and those other Commonwealth countries where domicile as the sole criterion of jurisdiction has been abandoned, has been to apply the *lex fori* and thus to reject the approach of Judge Hastie. The Restatement Second in section 285 merely states the established rule that you apply the law of the domicile where that state has jurisdiction. It proffers no solution to our problem. Do we find any clearer guidance from the sup-

[246] A number of states have statutes conferring special divorce jurisdiction in the case of servicemen stationed, but not domiciled, in that state.

[247] 207 F 2d 667 (1953).

[248] The legislation was later held by the US Supreme Court to be *ultra vires* the Islands' legislature: *Granville-Smith* v. *Granville-Smith* 349 US 1 (1955).

[249] 207 F 2d 667, 684–5 (1953).

porters of interest analysis to the law to be applied were Judge Hastie to find himself representing the majority on the jurisdictional issue? Cavers says that this poses a choice of law problem 'with which I shall not attempt to wrestle'.[250] Baade[251] does attempt to pursue the problem a little further though primarily in the context of recognition, suggesting for example that a state should always recognise a foreign divorce granted to its domiciliaries on grounds available at home. Nevertheless, he appears willing to apply an interest-oriented choice of law test, whether the court took jurisdiction on the basis of domicile or residence, namely 'whether a rational construction of the local divorce statute in the light of its underlying purposes calls for its application to the case at hand'.[252] This seems to amount to a rebuttable presumption in favour of the *lex fori.*

The policies underlying substantive divorce law

It is suggested that analysis of the policies of different laws as to the grounds of divorce is unlikely to reveal much of value in helping to determine which should be applied in a case posing a choice of law problem. It has been said that the policies underlying a 'good' divorce law are

> (i) to buttress, rather than to undermine, the stability of marriage; and (ii) when, regrettably, a marriage has irretrievably broken down, to enable the empty legal shell to be destroyed with the maximum fairness, and the minimum bitterness, distress and humiliation.[253]

Two states may each have reformed their law in accordance with those policies—one may have an amalgam of fault and no-fault bases of divorce,[254] the other may rely solely on a period of separation.[255] The policies are identical; the result of their implementation dramatically different. The presence of adultery as a basis of divorce in one country and not in the other provides no guidance as to which law should be applied if the parties are domiciled in one country, but resident in the other where the divorce proceedings take place.

The policies underlying divorce choice of law rules

A more profitable exercise might be to examine the policies which should determine the appropriate divorce choice of law rule rather than those which may underlie the substantive law of divorce. So far as the common

[250] [1970] III *Hague Recueil* 75, 267. [251] (1972) 72 *Col L Rev* 329, 340–4.
[252] Ibid., 344.
[253] Report of the Law Commission on *Reform of the Grounds of Divorce: The Field of Choice* (1966) Cmnd 2123, para. 15.
[254] E.g., England: Matrimonial Causes Act 1973, s. 1.
[255] E.g., Australia: Family Law Act 1975, s. 48.

law rule of application of the *lex fori* is concerned, there is a clash of policies but, paradoxically, they lead to the same result. In support of the Anglo-Commonwealth approach, which avowedly supports the application of the *lex fori*, it can be said that it would be inconvenient and, in practice, undesirable to apply foreign law to divorce petitions, most of which are undefended. To do so would create delay and expense. Furthermore, 'to require English courts to dissolve marriages on exotic foreign grounds would be distasteful to the judges and unacceptable to public opinion'.[256] There is danger in these arguments. It is always easier (and cheaper) to apply the *lex fori*; but that argument is not permitted to prevail elsewhere in private international law. It cannot sensibly prevail where the interest of the parties is prospective, as it may be in marriage law, because they will not know what is to be the future forum in accordance with whose laws they must order their affairs. It ought not, in itself, to be conclusive where the parties' interest is, in a sense, retrospective, i.e., the determination of whether the marriage has in fact broken down, or whether one party has committed a matrimonial 'offence'. The issue must go before a court, though often only in a formal sense; so a judicial body is always available to resolve the choice of law issue. The 'exotic foreign grounds' argument is also suspect. If the courts take jurisdiction over 'exotic foreigners' then the pass has been sold and it is arguably no more bizarre to apply their personal law to the dissolution than to apply it to the creation of their marriage. Indeed, if jurisdictional grounds are widened well beyond domicile, but that connecting factor still reigns supreme over matters of personal status, it is arguable that the forum state has little interest in the application of its divorce laws to persons subject to the law of another country in matters of status. Is the application of exotic foreign grounds of divorce to foreign domiciliaries any less acceptable than the application of the forum's grounds to persons domiciled in a country where divorce cannot be obtained, just because one spouse has been resident in the forum for, say, a year, though not necessarily with any intention of remaining there after the divorce has been obtained?

There is undoubtedly a powerful argument in favour of the application of the *lex fori*, namely that divorce law is part of the *ius publicum* of the forum,[257] and that, therefore, its application is required as part of the forum's mandatory law. Cavers[258] rests the application of forum law in the USA on this basis.[259] The issue of divorce involves a decision as to

[256] Morris, *The Conflict of Laws*, 2nd edn (1980), 139.

[257] Wolff, *Private International Law*, 2nd edn. (1950), 373–4.

[258] [1970] III *Hague Recueil* 75, 245–6.

[259] Rather than on the coincidence between *lex fori* and *lex domicilii*, discussed below, p. 167. A further political justification has been provided by Leflar, *American Conflicts Law*, 3rd edn. (1977), 460, where he says that 'the rule [that forum law governs substantive

the desirability of the continuance of the marriage as a legal and social relationship within the society in which the court sits.[260] Indeed, he suggests that because the court is determining the continuance of a marital relationship within the context of a particular society, the link with that society, in order to justify the application of its laws, must be strong—stronger than mere presence, or even domicile alone—as is indicated by the fact that in many American states domicile for a specific minimum period, often quite substantial, is required to found jurisdiction.[261]

This argument in favour of the *lex fori* is at its most powerful when there are both narrow jurisdictional rules and narrow rules for the recognition of foreign decrees. The interest of the state, with which the parties have a strong connection, in having its law applied will be undermined if the parties can with jurisdictional ease acquire a divorce elsewhere, return to their home state and have that divorce recognized. In the main, in the USA the criteria for jurisdiction and recognition are narrow,[262] and so the social justification for the application of the *lex fori* is greater. When one turns to countries, such as several in the Commonwealth, where jurisdiction extends beyond domicile to include the habitual residence of either spouse[263] or the nationality of either[264] and where recognition is not confined to decrees of the domicile, but includes those of the courts of the country of residence or nationality,[265] it is much less obvious that the parties or the marriage have a close social connection with the divorce forum. If the court takes jurisdiction on a fairly tenuous jurisdictional basis, often related only to one spouse, it is not self-evident that the forum does provide the closest appropriate connection. Whilst it is true that 'the more restrictive the grounds of jurisdiction, the less serious are the objections that can be raised against the *lex fori* rule',[266] the

grounds for divorce] became practically necessary to maintenance of the American way of marital life. The rule furnished the safety valve that enabled states with limited grounds for divorce to retain laws that were apparently required by local political expediency but which were realistically impractical for many of their citizens. Without the forum rule such states would either have had to modernise their divorce laws or deny marital relief wholly to citizens who by currently accepted societal standards deserved relief.'

260 Indeed, the social link has been taken further so that a divorce may only be granted if the parties' conduct justified divorce both under the law of the domiciliary forum and under the law of the domicile at the time of the conduct in question: *Fitzgerald* v. *Fitzgerald* 66 NJ Super 277, 168 A 2d 851 (1961).

261 Cavers, [1970] III *Hague Recueil* 75, 246–7.

262 For cases where recognition extends beyond decrees of the domicile, properly so called, see Leflar, *American Conflicts Law*, 3rd edn. (1977), 457–9.

263 E.g., England: Domicile and Matrimonial Proceedings Act 1973, s. 5.

264 E.g., Australia: Family Law Act 1975, s. 59(3).

265 E.g., England: Recognition of Divorces and Legal Separations Act 1971, s. 3 (implementing the Hague Convention on the Recognition of Divorces and Legal Separations (1970)); Australia, Family Law Act 1975, s. 104; New Zealand, Matrimonial Proceedings Act 1963, s. 82.

266 Palsson, *International Encyclopedia of Comparative Law*, iii: ch. 16; *Marriage and Divorce in Comparative Conflict of Laws* (1974), 128.

recent extension of divorce jurisdiction in a number of countries has not led to any fundamental re-evaluation of the application of the law of the forum to divorce petitions.

A further difficulty with the *lex fori* choice of law rule in divorce is evident if our examination looks further than the interests of the forum state. It can be argued persuasively that there is a close link between a *lex fori* rule and the jurisdictional criteria of the forum for divorce proceedings. What happens, however, if the divorce proceedings are in some other state whose choice of law rule directs it to the law of the first state? An example might help. Let us assume that two Canadian citizens are habitually resident and domiciled in Ruritania. They petition the Ruritanian courts for divorce. Had proceedings been brought in a Canadian province, jurisdiction would have been declined[267] and, furthermore, Canadian divorce law would seem to be applied in Canada as the *lex fori*, i.e., there is a link between the jurisdictional and choice of law rules.[268] When the petition is brought in Ruritania, we shall assume that the Ruritanian courts will apply the law of the spouses' nationality, i.e., Canadian divorce law. It can be argued, however, that Canadian law is only to be applied in Canadian divorce proceedings. There is no rule of Canadian law appropriate to foreign proceedings and it has been argued that, in such a case, to apply Canadian law in the Ruritanian proceedings is to apply 'foreign law where it does not wish to be applied'.[269] A pragmatic answer might be that the introduction of rules of *renvoi* into the undeveloped field of divorce choice of law rules is a conclusion resolutely to be avoided. If, however, one accepts that *renvoi* has a part to play here, the Ruritanian court will have to answer a question as to the application of Canadian divorce law which could never arise for consideration in Canada.[270]

Finally, some might argue that the *lex fori* rule is unjust in that whether previous conduct by one spouse will justify divorce may depend on the forum to be relied on in the future for the divorce proceedings. For example, the spouses may be domiciled and resident in and nationals of State A, where the husband's conduct does not constitute such cruelty as will constitute grounds for divorce. If, however, the wife then acquires a residence in State B which takes divorce jurisdiction on the basis of residence and applies the *lex fori* she may succeed in her divorce petition if the husband's conduct amounts to cruelty under the law of State B even though it occurred at a time when neither spouse had any connection

[267] Divorce Act 1968, s. 5.
[268] Castel, *Canadian Conflict of Laws* (1977) ii: 115–16.
[269] Unger, (1967) 83 *LQR* 427, 434–5.
[270] See Wolff, *Private International Law*, 2nd edn. (1950), 377.

with State B.[271] The conduct of the husband had no effect at the time on the wife's right to divorce, but was retrospectively given this effect by the wife selecting a different forum. This is not, however, a convincing argument against the *lex fori* rule for, indeed, the same results can occur if there is a change of the personal law. Had the parties in the above example become domiciled in State B, the divorce would have been granted by applying the law of their then personal law, but the problem of retrospectivity remains.[272]

Turning to the arguments in favour of the application of the law of the domicile, or the law governing status as the law applicable to divorce proceedings, Weintraub finds these so powerful that they can only be satisfied by conferring exclusive jurisdiction on the courts of the domicile and applying that law:

> Transient personal jurisdiction is bad enough when invoked to render money judgments. It would be outrageous for a court with no other nexus with the marital status to undertake to end that status. Nor is this objection removed if the forum purports to apply the divorce law of the marital domicile. The same lack of interest in the marital status that makes it totally unreasonable for the forum to apply its own divorce law, creates a lack of confidence that the court will apply the divorce law of the marital domicile in such a manner as to avoid infringing upon the interest of the domicile in controlling the marital status of its citizens.[273]

On this analysis, the problem disappears, because the *lex fori* is invariably the *lex domicilii* and no choice between them needs to be made.

Weintraub's solution will satisfy few. It cannot be reconciled with the fact that many countries, whether from the civil or common law worlds, do assume jurisdiction on bases much broader than that of their primary criterion of marital status, whether it be domicile or nationality. A choice between the *lex fori* and the law governing marital status has to be made. What then are the arguments in favour of the application of the law of the domicile, or of the nationality, or whatever be the law to govern status?

The argument most often reiterated, but rarely substantiated in detail,[274] is that the dissolution of marriage affects the status of the parties and is not merely a procedural matter for the forum. The creation of the marital ties is regarded as a substantive issue to be governed by an appropriate choice of law rule. Nullity proceedings are not usually subjected to the marriage laws of the forum, nor in many jurisdictions is the

[271] This would seem to be the law in various common law jurisdictions: see North, *Private International Law of Matrimonial Causes* (1977), 150.

[272] See Wolff, *Private International Law*, 2nd edn. (1950), 375–6.

[273] Weintraub, *Commentary on the Conflict of Laws* (1971), 193–4.

[274] See, e.g., *Report of the Royal Commission on Marriage and Divorce* (1956), Cmd. 9678, paras. 836–9; Graveson, *Conflict of Laws*, 7th edn. (1974), 286–7.

essential validity of a marriage subject exclusively to the law of the place where it is celebrated. If choice of law rules are to be devised for the creation of marital obligations, why not similar rules for the dissolution of these marital bonds? It cannot seriously now be argued, as Story once did,[275] that divorce, unlike nullity, is so closely bound up with remedies as to merit a procedural classification and thereby justifies the application of the *lex fori*. Dissolution of marriage is no less substantive than its creation. The public policy of the forum may have a role to play, but not necessarily to the exclusion of other laws.

Paradoxically, one of the main attempts to analyse the arguments in favour of the application of the personal law to divorce has been made in the context of American 'interest analysis' with the objective of justifying broader jurisdictional rules. Seidelson has argued[276] that American courts could safely abandon their restrictive jurisdictional rules as to divorce if they were prepared to apply interest analysis to choice of law. The result of such analysis would, in his view, lead to the application of the law of the domicile, whatever country was the forum including even a 'disinterested third state'.[277] The virtue of such an approach, in his eyes, would be to deter forum-shopping and the establishment of 'divorce havens', with a correlative benefit of certainty in that the chances of recognition of divorce decrees from other jurisdictions applying such a choice of law rule would be greatly enhanced.

The interesting aspect of this approach is that it indicates that, whatever the forum, the country with the paramount interest in the application of its law is that of the domicile, i.e., the personal law. So this application of the modern rule-selecting approach reaches the same conclusion as that reached by those who adopt a jurisdiction-selecting approach and classify choice of law in divorce as a matter of substantive law. However, Seidelson's interest analysis suggests that a simple jurisdiction-selecting approach of applying the law of the domicile conceals a major problem in an age when sexual equality has meant that the common law world is in the process of abandoning the concept of the unity of domicile between husband and wife. If the spouses are domiciled in different countries, which domiciliary law is to be applied to their divorce petition?

> One could assert that each State has an exactly equal interest in the issue, since each State has the same legitimate interest in the marital status of its own domiciliary. Striking an even balance of interests between the 'competing' States is probably the most distracting and disturbing conclusion which a forum engaged in interest analysis can achieve. It bears the potential of reducing that sophisti-

[275] Story, *Conflict of Laws*, 8th edn. (1883), 254.
[276] (1971) 21 *Buffalo L Rev* 315. [277] See above, pp. 116–117.

cated method of resolving choice-of-law problems to a coin-flip. Happily, it can be avoided here neatly and legitimately.[278]

The author's means of avoidance is to conclude that the interests of the two domiciliary states are not evenly balanced, but that the scales come down in favour of the application of the law of the plaintiff's domicile both as to the grounds of divorce and as to any available defences. The reason for this conclusion is that it is only the law of the state of the plaintiff's domicile which intends to benefit him in the provision of the grounds of divorce. The defendant's domiciliary laws are not designed to be relied on by out-of-state plaintiffs.

Whilst it might be argued that this interest analysis solution is perhaps a little too neat, the problem it is intended to solve does illustrate a major difficulty with the application of the personal law to divorce, namely that of spouses who have different personal laws. The problem is well known also to those jurisdictions that apply the law of the nationality to govern divorce. It can take various forms: spouses of different nationalities, of dual nationality, or statelessness.[279] The problem admits of a variety of solutions: apply the law of the husband's nationality;[280] apply the law of the petitioner's nationality;[281] apply the law of the local nationality in the case of dual nationality;[282] or apply the law of the domicile in cases of statelessness. There is no doubt that the problems posed by spouses with different domiciles or nationalities can be resolved but, it may be argued, at a price—the price of complex rules and expensive litigation.

At the end of the day, the decision on choice of law rules in divorce must depend on a balance between principle, which undoubtedly points to the application of the personal law, and pragmatism which favours the *lex fori*. It is no surprise that the civil law supports the former and the common law the latter. What is worrying about the common law approach is that a rule which was historically justified by its jurisdictional link has been maintained with little real consideration of the implications of breaking that jurisdictional link.

[278] (1971) 21 *Buffalo L Rev* 315, 331–2.

[279] Palsson, *International Encyclopedia of Comparative Law*, iii: ch. 16; *Marriage and Divorce in Comparative Conflict of Laws* (1974), 131–8.

[280] E.g., Germany, EGBGB Art. 17. In Japan, under Art. 16 of the Law for the Application of Laws, divorce is governed by the law of the country of the husband's nationality at the time that the facts that constitute grounds for divorce occur, but the court cannot grant a divorce unless the facts also constitute grounds for divorce under Japanese law. An interesting illustration of the application of this rule is provided by a decision of the Tokyo Family Court, of 31 May 1976, reported in (1978) 22 *Japanese Annual of International Law* 165. English divorce law was applied to a petition brought by an English husband, even though he and his wife (who had acquired British nationality) were domiciled in Japan.

[281] E.g., Switzerland: BG 11 July (1968); though see now Art. 60 of the Swiss Draft Federal Law on Private International Law (1978).

[282] E.g., Germany, EGBGB Art. 17(3).

7

Choice in Choice of Law

INTRODUCTION

It is a truism that there are three fundamental questions which may arise in the course of examining a civil legal issue which has international aspects. First, if the issue were to involve litigation in this country, would our courts have jurisdiction to entertain the proceedings? Second, if the issue has already resulted in litigation in another jurisdiction will the decision of the foreign court be recognized and enforced in this country? Both these questions have an interesting, and narrowing, characteristic. They are concerned with matters which have reached the point of breakdown, i.e. of litigation and judicial decision-making. The third issue is really very different. It is concerned with the law to be applied to a civil legal issue whose circumstances involve factors connected with more than one jurisdiction. Of course, if the issue is litigated, the determination of the applicable law will be a necessary part of the process. There are, however, many circumstances, by far the majority, where the determination of the applicable law is made without any prospect of a legal dispute or litigation. Parties from different countries may be planning to get married and wish to know whether they are free to do so. A social security official may be trying to decide whether a woman was validly married abroad to the deceased so as to qualify for benefits as a widow. Companies negotiating an international sales contract need to clarify their mutual obligations in the light of the law to govern it. A middle-aged couple, with assets in several countries, are anxious to make a new will or to provide for their children by establishing a trust.

All of these circumstances raise choice of law issues and most of the examples just given involve a degree of concern over the legality or effectiveness of future conduct. One question that is posed thereby is whether, and to what extent, there is a freedom for the parties to choose the law to govern their transnational affairs. It has also to be considered whether any choice can be used to order future events or only to govern the situation when a dispute has arisen and litigation looms.

An expanded version of the 1992 Graveson Memorial Lecture, delivered on 19 March 1992 at King's College, London. The text of the lecture as delivered was published in (1992) 3 *King's College Law Journal* 29–48.

A Dutch author has recently suggested that

> the principle of party autonomy can be justified entirely by reference to the freedom of disposition the parties enjoy in the corresponding substantive (forum) law. This implies freedom of choice in all areas in which, in principle, the parties are deemed to be equal partners in a legal relationship or where they are allowed, by and large, to be their own master. Generally, these are the areas of substantive law where mandatory rules are scarce as in contracts, torts, matrimonial property or succession.[1]

This statement leads us to ask how far English private international law permits party autonomy in choice of law,[2] but it also conceals the fact that private international law rules may involve different kinds of choice. It is important to be clear, from the outset of any examination of these issues, that the nature of our rules of private international law is such that there can be two kinds of choice involved in the determination of the relevant rule to be applied to a particular case. The simplest way in which choice is exercised to determine the law to be applied, or whether a court is to have jurisdiction, is by the parties actually choosing by agreement the governing law, or selecting one or more countries before whose courts any litigation is to take place. One part, indeed a major part, of my concerns in this present discussion is to examine the types of case in which choice of that kind, whether express or implied, is to be permitted; whether the range of areas in which choice is acceptable ought to be extended; and what limits are, or might be, imposed on freedom of choice. It would be wrong, however, to exclude from consideration the element of choice which may be involved indirectly. One form that this may take is where it is not the applicable law which is chosen but rather the factors or elements which go to constitute the connecting factor which our rules of private international law have laid down for determining the applicable law. Another form is seen where the freedom to choose the jurisdiction in which to proceed carries with it a determination of the law to be applied. A further form is where choice is exercised through the rules relating to the pleading of foreign law. All these kinds of indirect choice merit some examination.

INDIRECT CHOICE

Indirect choice, both through choice of jurisdiction and of the elements within the appropriate connecting factor, may be exemplified by choice of law rules in the field of family law where no significant place has yet been

[1] De Boer, (1990) 54 *RabelsZ* 24, 37.

[2] Space does not permit consideration of another important aspect of choice, that in the jurisdictional context; see Dicey and Morris, *The Conflict of Laws*, 11th edn. (1987), 402–17.

found, either in the rules as formulated by the courts or in proposals for reform, for the idea of direct choice of the applicable law. Three or four different aspects of indirect choice may be illustrated by the choice of law rules relating to divorce and to marriage. These aspects involve both agreement between the spouses and unilateral choice by one of them.

Divorce

Turning first to divorce, this is an aspect of family law which has engendered very little examination of the choice of law issue.[3] It seems clearly to have been accepted that, if an English court has jurisdiction over a divorce petition, even though both parties are domiciled in another country,[4] then the substantive divorce law to be applied is that of the forum, i.e. English law. The same is also true of the law to be applied to important ancillary issues such as disputes over children or money. It may be argued that the almost unthinking application of the law of the forum does little to enhance the general choice of law process, but in the present context the selection of English law to be applied is made, in effect, by the decision of one of the spouses, the petitioner, to bring divorce proceedings in England. Two elements of this so-called 'choice' should be emphasized. The first is that it is unilateral, not requiring the agreement of the other spouse. The second is that it is not unlimited. English law will only be applied as the law of the forum if a jurisdictional link here can be established, through the fact that one of the parties is domiciled or habitually resident in England. Of course, if there is an alternative jurisdictional link established with another common law jurisdiction, which is also very likely to apply its own divorce law to any petition before its courts, a petitioner has the power to 'choose' the law to be applied by reason of the decision to petition there.[5]

Marriage

Marriage choice of law rules provide rather different examples of indirect choice. The most straightforward is that of the law to govern the formal validity of a marriage. There seems to be widespread acceptance that the

[3] But see North, [1980] I *Hague Recueil* 9, 77–88, above, pp. 158–169; [1990] I *Hague Recueil* 9, 112–14.

[4] E.g. by reason of the habitual residence in England of one of the spouses: Domicile and Matrimonial Proceedings Act 1973, s. 5(2)(b).

[5] Contrast Dutch law where, under the International Divorce Act 1981, a wider freedom of choice is permitted: De Boer, (1990) 54 *RabelsZ* 24, 38.

English (and general common law) choice of law rule here is that matters of formal validity are governed by the law of the place of celebration of the marriage. The selection of the country of celebration is one for the spouses jointly to make, given that they are both going to be present there for the marriage ceremony, at least if one disregards the rare instances of proxy marriages. Here, therefore, the choice by the parties of the place of celebration effectively constitutes a choice of the law to govern formalities.[6] Whilst, in many cases, that choice will be determined by social and domestic factors or even the desire for a package holiday including a wedding on a tropical island, it is not unknown for spouses to choose to marry in a particular country in order to take advantage of the legal rules there in force relating to the validity of a marriage.[7] Whilst, therefore, there is a real and fairly direct element of choice here involved, it has to be remembered that it is a limited choice. The law to be applied follows from the choice of the place of celebration. It is not possible, under present English choice of law rules (subject to an exception to be considered later), actually to choose a law different from that of the place of celebration to govern matters of formal validity.

When considering choice of law rules to govern essential validity, the position in relation to choice is somewhat more complicated, not least because there is no clear acceptance of what law actually governs matters of essential validity, or whether the same choice of law rule applies to all such matters. Leaving aside for the moment the varied suggestions that have been made, for example, to introduce separate choice of law rules for different aspects of essential validity or to introduce the concept of 'the proper law of the marriage',[8] there are two long-established contenders for acceptance as the connecting factor to decide the law to govern essential validity. The first, long associated with John Morris, is the dual domicile test, namely that one applies the law of each party's antenuptial domicile to determine their respective capacities to marry. The other test, associated with the name of Geoffrey Cheshire, is that one looks to see if the parties have, or had, an intended matrimonial home. If so, the law of the country of the intended matrimonial home is to govern matters of essential validity. If not, reference is to be made to the law of the husband's domicile at the time of the marriage. Much has been written about the respective merits of these two approaches and, though the weight of judicial authority tends to support the dual domicile approach, as the Law Commission has said 'there is no decision which prevents the

[6] The question of whether a choice has been freely made may raise issues as to the law governing consent to marry which would seem to be governed by the law applicable to issues of essential, rather than formal, validity.

[7] E.g. *Reed* v. *Reed* (1969) 6 DLR (3d) 617.

[8] See North, [1990] I *Hague Recueil* 9, 63–74.

Court of Appeal or the House of Lords from adopting either test.'[9] What is of interest in the present context is, however, the extent to which the two approaches reveal elements of 'choice' by the parties of the applicable law.

Not unlike the formal validity rule, the first branch of the Cheshire approach, 'the intended matrimonial home' test, provides a good instance of the parties making an indirect choice of the governing law, this time by choosing the country where they are to live. It is also to be classed as an agreed choice by both of them because, without that consensual element, there would be no matrimonial home. The choice is legally wide in that the matrimonial home could be anywhere. The constraints are social and economic. On the other hand, the choice is limited in that no law other than that of the intended matrimonial home can be selected. The connecting factor can be freely chosen but then the determination of the applicable law follows automatically. Support for the idea that the Cheshire approach embodies choice also comes, paradoxically, from the opposition that has been expressed to it on the ground that parties ought not to be given the freedom to select the law to govern matters of capacity.[10]

On the other hand, the Morris approach, the dual domicile test, involves a much more limited and more indirect element of choice by the parties. The determination of a person's domicile is governed by rules of law, which by way of aside, are both complex and in need of reform.[11] It is not possible expressly to choose a domicile. Expressions of such intent are to be given due consideration but they are not binding on a court and indeed have to be treated with some caution.

> It only too frequently happens that they cannot be taken at their face value. They may be interested statements designed to flatter or to deceive the hearer; they may represent nothing more than vain expectations unlikely to be fulfilled; and the very facility with which they can be made requires their sincerity to be manifested by some active step taken in furtherance of the expressed intention.[12]

This means that the way in which choice is exercised is simply by means of selecting those aspects of life, such as residence, citizenship, house purchase or even choice of a burial plot, which then cause a court to decide that the necessary intention and factual connection are present so as to lead to the conclusion that a domicile of choice has been acquired. Although it is undoubtedly the case that in some contexts, most notably taxation, such choices are consciously made in order to affect the conclusion as to the acquisition of a domicile, this seems to be far more

[9] Law Com. Working Paper No. 89 (1985), 60.

[10] E.g. *Muhammad* v. *Suna* 1956 SC 366, 370; and see Anton, *Private International Law*, 2nd edn. (1990), 429; North, [1990] I *Hague Recueil* 9, 65–6.

[11] See Law Com. No. 168 (1987).

[12] Cheshire and North, *Private International Law*, 12th edn. (1992), 149.

improbable in the context of the law to govern the essential validity of a marriage. Were the relevant connecting factor to be habitual residence, which is less hedged-about with technical rules, and which has, indeed, been proposed in Ireland as the major connecting factor for essential validity,[13] then it would be more likely that choice would in fact be exercised through selection of the connections which constitute habitual residence.

It has to be accepted that the element of choice of the applicable law involved in voluntary selection of those factors which lead to the conclusion of the acquisition of a domicile or habitual residence is both limited and indirect. On the other hand, there is considerably more reality of choice involved in the selection of the place of the intended matrimonial home, of the celebration of the marriage and, indeed, of the forum for a divorce petition. What is interesting is that this does not seem to have led on to any suggestion, either judicially or in law reform proposals, that the spouses should have a broader and more direct freedom to choose the law applicable to such matrimonial issues. The main reasons for this seem to be twofold. The first, adverted to already, is that issues of essential validity amount predominantly to issues of capacity and it is often stated that parties should not, by choosing the applicable law, be able to confer capacity on themselves. The second is that marriage is to be regarded as more of a status than a contract with the corollary that 'its incidents are determined not by the will of the parties but by the prescriptions of the law.'[14] Such a statement is however, in the international context, more impressive than convincing. It assumes that there is a readily identified, obviously correct 'law' to be applied, free from determination by the will of the parties. That that is a rash assumption in English private international law is revealed by the lack of certainty as to what law does in fact govern matters of essential validity. The issue has been discussed for well over a century and is still not finally resolved. It is also rash because, as has been seen, the parties may be indirect choice exercise a considerable influence on the determination of the substantive marriage law to be applied. Such indirect choice is seen at its most significant in the USA where the basic choice of law rule is that essential, as well as formal, validity is to be governed by the law of the place of celebration,[15] which place is, of course, chosen by the parties.

Whilst, nevertheless, choice in matrimonial matters is normally exercised at one remove, there is, however, one context in which the idea that the parties might directly express an intention as to the law to govern the validity of their marriage has prospered and this is the so-called 'common

[13] Irish Law Reform Commission Report (1985) LRC 19.

[14] Anton, *Private International Law*, 2nd edn. (1990), 418–19.

[15] See Scoles and Hay, *Conflict of Laws* (1982), 421 *et seq.*

law exception' to the rule that the law of the place of celebration of the marriage governs formal validity. It is accepted that in limited circumstances a marriage may be regarded as valid in England, even though local formalities have been ignored, provided that the English common law formalities of marriage have been satisfied. Under such rules it is necessary that the parties simply agree to take each other as husband and wife. There is debate whether the service must be conducted by an episcopally ordained clergyman.[16] The formal validity of foreign marriages has been upheld where, for example, as part of the colonial past it has been concluded that English common law was to be applied in parts of China[17] or in Singapore.[18] The common law exception has also been applied where there was held to be insuperable difficulty in complying with the local law. This may be exemplified by a marriage between two Lithuanians in Germany in 1945 when no German registry offices were functioning,[19] or a marriage in the home of the petitioner's parents in the Ukraine, in 1942, as the advancing German army occupied the town in question.[20] On the other hand, a marriage in Saigon, after its occupation at the end of the Vietnam War, has been held not to attract the common law exception as the civil authorities were functioning, even though the spouses intended at the time of the ceremony to become refugees, as in fact they soon did.[21]

A further, not dissimilar, type of case where the common law exception has been applied is where there have been marriages involving members of military forces in occupation of the country where the marriage took place, as occurred quite often in Europe at the end of the Second World War.[22] Although the concept of 'military forces' has been interpreted to include analogous persons 'such as members of an organised body of escaped prisoners of war',[23] it does not extend more generally to, for example, civilian members of a displaced persons' camp.[24] The interest of these decisions on the common law exception lies, in the present context, in the basis given for departing from the rule requiring compliance with the formalities of the place of celebration. In the earlier decisions,[25] a general idea emerged that the rule that formal validity is to be governed by the law of the place of celebration is based on the principle that the

[16] *R* v. *Millis* (1843–4) 10 Cl & Fin 534; *Preston* v. *Preston* [1963] P 411, 436.

[17] *Wolfenden* v. *Wolfenden* [1946] P 61.

[18] *Penhas* v. *Tan Soo Eng* [1953] AC 304.

[19] *Savenis* v. *Savenis* [1950] SASR 309.

[20] *Kuklycz* v. *Kuklycz* [1972] VR 50.

[21] *In the Marriage of X* (1983) 65 FLR 132.

[22] *Taczanowska* v. *Taczanowski* [1957] P 301; *Merker* v. *Merker* [1963] P 283; *Preston* v. *Preston* [1963] P 411.

[23] *Merker* v. *Merker*, above, 295.

[24] *Preston* v. *Preston*, above; cf. *Kochanski* v. *Kochanska* [1958] P 147.

[25] E.g. *Taczanowska* v. *Taczanowski* [1957] P 301, 325, 330, 332; *Kochanski* v. *Kochanska* [1958] P 147, 151.

parties, by marrying there, are deemed to submit to that law.[26] If, therefore, there are circumstances where it is patent that the parties do not submit, even if they could have done so, as in the case of occupying forces, then the presumption of submission is rebutted and some other choice of law rule, i.e. the common law exception, may be applied. This led courts to investigate whether parties had actually intended to submit to the local law,[27] opening up the prospect of extending the common law exception beyond the context of occupying forces and analogous bodies to a much broader range of circumstances where absence of submission could be shown. Indeed it was argued

> that it was open to any persons marrying abroad to elect whether they should be married by the local law or in some other way, and that if they did not subject themselves to the local law the English common law should be applied should the validity of the marriage be questioned in [the English] courts.[28]

Once it was seen, as in this argument, where a general principle of submission would lead, it was firmly rejected. If there were to be exceptions to the application of the law of the place of celebration they were to be specifically defined and the particular aspect of the common law marriage exception under review was confined, in effect, to occupying forces. The proper approach was clearly stated by Ormerod LJ:

> The canons of international comity demand that, on questions of form, one country should recognise the marriage laws of another, and in consequence it is now well established that persons choosing to marry in a foreign country shall be deemed to have submitted themselves to the marriage laws of that country. This rule does not apply in all circumstances, but it is not enough for the parties to say or to show by their actions that they do not intend to submit to those laws.[29]

Where then does this leave choice of the applicable law? Certainly, a wide concept of submission would have involved a rather bizarre form of choice. If there was no submission in the case of a foreign marriage, the parties' choice to reject the local law would have left applicable to the validity of their foreign marriage English rules of formal validity long since abandoned here. Nevertheless, the element of choice in the general rule remains. The parties can choose where to marry, but then, save in the most limited circumstances, they are taken in making that choice to have submitted themselves to the formal requirements of the local law. To do otherwise, it is said, would 'introduce anarchy in a field where order and comity are particularly required.'[30] What is interesting is that

[26] See *Ruding* v. *Smith* (1821) 2 Hag Con 371.
[27] E.g. *Lazarewicz* v. *Lazarewicz* [1962] P 171.
[28] *Merker* v. *Merker* [1963] P 283, 295.
[29] *Preston* v. *Preston* [1963] P 411, 427; and see at 435.
[30] *Merker* v. *Merker* [1963] P 283, 295.

the present rules combine both certainty and a wide-ranging indirect choice.

Choice through pleading

Another form of implied choice can be illustrated by the fact that the law reports provide many examples of cases where the foreign elements of a dispute have been ignored, with the result that English law alone has been applied. One striking feature of this situation is that such cases include landmark decisions on the development of English law. For example, the exposition of the doctrine of fundamental breach in the construction of exemption clauses stemmed from a dispute over a charter-party to carry coal from the east coast of the USA to Belgium, Holland or Germany.[31] It came before the English court by reason of questions of law stated by the arbitrators. Everyone seems simply to have assumed without discussion, or apparent reason, that English law was to be applied. Similarly, the development of remoteness of damage rules in contract is to be found in a dispute over the performance of a charter-party for the shipment of sugar from Constanza to Basra to which English law was applied apparently without debate.[32] This phenomenon is not confined to contract issues, for English law alone has been applied to a claim in tort by a Canadian for damages for injuries suffered in a water skiing accident off the beach in Monte Carlo,[33] and to a wife's claim for damages for nervous shock following a road accident in France in which she was injured and her husband killed.[34]

In the contractual examples just given, there was no prior choice by the parties of the law to govern the contract. However, even where there is such an express choice, there is ample evidence of English law being applied notwithstanding a contractual term to the contrary. For example, the development of choice of law rules to deal with problems arising from retention of title clauses has been hampered by the fact that, in a number of cases including that from which such 'Romalpa clauses' have taken their name,[35] effect has not been given to the express choice by the parties of a foreign governing law.

The examples just given stem from the common law rules relating to

[31] *Suisse Atlantique Société d'Armement Maritime SA* v. *NV Rotterdamsche Kolen Centrale* [1967] 1 AC 21.

[32] *C Czarnikow Ltd* v. *Koufos* [1969] 1 AC 350.

[33] *Winkworth* v. *Hubbard* [1960] 1 Lloyd's Rep 150.

[34] *Schneider* v. *Eisovitch* [1960] 2 QB 430.

[35] *Aluminium Industrie Vaassen BV* v. *Romalpa Aluminium Ltd.* [1976] 1 WLR 676; *Emerald Stainless Steel Ltd.* v. *South Side Distribution Ltd.* 1983 SLT 162; *Deutz Engines Ltd.* v. *Terex Ltd.* 1984 SLT 273.

the pleading and proof of foreign law.[36] Foreign law is to be proved as a matter of fact and it is entirely up to one or other of the parties to decide whether or not to plead evidence of foreign law. If neither does so, then the court assumes that the rules of the foreign legal system otherwise applicable are the same as English law, which law is then applied. There can, in fact, be at least three different types of situation involved. The first is where no attention is drawn to the foreign elements in the case, as for example in the two tort cases mentioned earlier. In these circumstances, the case proceeds as an entirely English case without there even being an assumption that foreign rules are the same as English rules; the case does not get as far as identifying which foreign rules might be applied were they to be proved. The second type of case is where it is apparent, for example from the terms of a contract which has been put in evidence, that the dispute is to be governed by foreign law but neither party chooses to plead it. The third type of case is really a variant on this but one where the parties' decision is express, rather than inferred from inactivity, namely where they agree, rightly or wrongly, that the foreign rules are the same as the English rules.[37]

The impact of the rules as to pleading foreign law has been described thus:

> The consequences of such *laissez faire* voluntarism are arresting and, to foreign eyes, surprising. It ensures that pleading foreign law is a private matter between the parties in dispute and, by effectively allowing litigants to transform a case into a domestic one, it makes the conflict of laws itself a voluntary body of law.[38]

What this means is that, through a procedural device, the parties can by agreement, which is more likely to stem from common inaction than from specific consensus, exercise a choice as to the law to govern their dispute. Admittedly the choice is limited in that failure to plead foreign law always leads to the application of the law of the English forum. The effect of the device is, however, not only to cause English law to be applied to an issue where the application of foreign law has not expressly been raised, but also to act in substance as a variation of a choice of law clause. If the parties agree that New York law is to govern their contract but neither pleads New York law in court, the effect is a consensual application of English law thus, in essence, varying the choice of law clause.[39]

[36] Cheshire and North, *Private International Law*, 12th edn. (1992), ch 7; and see Kahn-Freund, [1974] III *Hague Recueil* 139, 422–6.

[37] E.g. *E Pfeiffer Weinkellerei-Weineinkauf GmbH & Co.* v. *Arbuthnot Factors Ltd.* [1988] 1 WLR 150.

[38] Fentiman, (1992) 108 *LQR* 142, 149–50.

[39] See North, *Multum Non Multa, Festschrift für Kurt Lipstein* (1980), 205, 214, and above, p. 61.

It may be argued that there is a whole variety of reasons why foreign law is not, in fact, pleaded.[40] This is no doubt true. For example, it may be too complicated or expensive to determine the foreign rules of law;[41] there may be a lack of confidence that the process of proof using conflicting expert witnesses will in fact lead to a correct determination of the foreign law;[42] or it may indeed be the case that lawyers wish to avoid the 'uncertainties and ambiguities'[43] which are still to be found in the English choice of law process. Nevertheless, though the reasons for running to the security of the law of the forum may be mixed and may indeed differ as between the parties to the litigation, there seems little doubt that reliance on this pleading device can provide a valid example of freedom of choice, albeit one which is more often implicit than explicit.

DIRECT CHOICE

Contract

We tend today to regard the law of contract as providing the firmest example of the freedom of the parties directly to choose the legal system to govern their rights and obligations.[44] Forty or fifty years ago, that view was not regarded as self-evidently correct. Not least of the difficulties then perceived was that which arose from trying to determine what law would govern the validity of a contractual choice of law clause;[45] but there was a more fundamental difference of view. There were those who accorded wide, if not unlimited, freedom to the parties to choose the applicable law—the subjectivists; whilst the objectivists felt that one should seek to localize the contract, to find its natural seat, and in this quest the express intention of the parties was merely one factor to be considered, albeit a very significant one. This latter attitude found judicial expression as recently as 1983 in the statement by Lord Diplock that an express choice was 'one, but by no means the only, matter to be taken into consideration'[46] in identifying the applicable law. Nevertheless

[40] Fentiman, (1992) 108 *LQR* 142, 150–2; and see Schlesinger, (1973) 59 *Cornell L Rev* 1, 2–3.

[41] *Muduroglu Ltd.* v. *T C Ziraat Bankasi* [1986] QB 1225, 1246.

[42] It seems clear, for example, in *Sayers* v. *International Drilling Co. NV* [1971] 1 WLR 1176 that a crucial mistake was made as to the Dutch law relating to employment contracts; see De Boer, *Beyond Lex Loci Delicti* (1987), 185–6, and see above, pp. 90, 101.

[43] Fentiman, (1992) 108 *LQR* 142, 151.

[44] For an historical and comparative account of the development of autonomy in contract, see Yntema, (1952) 1 *Am Jo Comp L* 341.

[45] E.g. Cheshire, *International Contracts* (1948), 19; Morris, (1950) 3 *ILQ* 197; cf. Kahn-Freund, [1974] III *Hague Recueil* 139, 342–4.

[46] *The Hollandia* [1983] 1 AC 565, 576.

it became more broadly accepted that 'the proper law of the contract is the law which the parties intended to apply'.[47]

This issue of party autonomy has been put beyond doubt by the 1980 Rome Convention on the law applicable to contractual obligations, given the force of law in this country by the Contracts (Applicable Law) Act 1990.[48] Article 3(1) of the Convention is quite clear on this point, providing that:

> A contract shall be governed by the law chosen by the parties. The choice must be express or demonstrated with reasonable certainty by the terms of the contract or the circumstances of the case.

What is also worth noting is how unfettered this freedom is. At common law, there was debate as to the limits of the freedom of choice. We were told that the choice had to be 'bona fide and legal' and not contrary to public policy.[49] There was debate as to how far a law unconnected with the contract could be chosen; though it has been pointed out that commercial men are likely to have good reasons, which should be accepted, for such a choice.[50] Under the Convention, there are no real limits on the freedom of choice of the applicable law, as such. However, mandatory rules of the forum will continue to be applied,[51] and rules of the chosen law may be refused application as being contrary to the public policy of the forum.[52] These are likely to be relatively minor limitations in practice and the Convention marks a high point in the acceptance of party autonomy—an approach to contract choice of law which has been shown to have had wide acceptance 'in the private international law of all the Member States of the Community and of most other countries',[53] as well as being 'supported both by arbitration decisions and by international treaties designed to unify certain rules of conflict in relation to contracts.'[54]

Whilst there is no intention to examine closely the detailed rules on freedom of choice in contract, not least because such freedom is generally accepted, it may be of interest to point to reasons why such freedom is accepted here, because such reasons may well inform consideration of

[47] *Vita Food Products Inc.* v. *Unus Shipping Co. Ltd.* [1939] AC 277, 289–90.

[48] See Plender, *The European Contracts Convention* (1991), ch 5.

[49] *Vita Food* Case, above, at 290. [50] Mann, (1987) 36 *ICLQ* 437, 447.

[51] Art. 7(2). The UK has exercised the power of reservation, under Art. 22(1)(a), not to apply Art. 7(1); see Contracts (Applicable Law) Act 1990, s. 2(2), and see, above, pp. 26–27. It is also the case, under Art. 3(3), that choice of the law of one country when all the elements of the contract but for the choice are connected with the law of another country is not to prejudice the application of the mandatory rules of that second country.

[52] Art. 16.

[53] Giuliano and Lagarde Report on the Rome Convention, [1980] OJ C282/15, 31 October 1980; and see Yntema, (1952) 1 *Am Jo Comp L* 341, 345–53; Lando, (1987) 24 *Common Market L Rev* 159, 171–80.

[54] Ibid., OJ C282/16.

whether freedom of choice should be extended to choice of law rules in other contexts. One reason peculiar to contracts is that 'contracting parties can best select for themselves the law appropriate to the system of reciprocal obligations they intend to establish.'[55] If they voluntarily enter into a contract, then they should be allowed also to choose the applicable law. Other suggested reasons have a wider scope than that of contract. The parties may wish to secure the application of a system of law or indeed, through a jurisdiction clause, a forum which is 'neutral as between them'.[56] This interest could, in some circumstances, as we shall see, be relevant elsewhere in the law of obligations, in particular in the law of torts. Furthermore, issues raising matters of private international law can be redolent of uncertainty. Taking an example from the present context, the rules for the determination of the applicable law in contract used, at common law, to depend on finding the country of closest connection; that is still the case under the Rome Convention subject to the application of rebuttable presumptions, not the least of which is that of 'characteristic performance'.[57] Here lies uncertainty which to the businessman is both inconvenient and expensive. But such uncertainty is not the exclusive prerogative of contract choice of law rules. It can be found wherever the law has failed to develop clear choice of law rules, as is the case in the context of the essential validity of marriage, or where the rule is clear, but its application is not, as with any rule which is dependent on the present law of domicile as its operative connecting factor. Freedom of choice in contract can be justified as desirable because the parties need certainty in order to plan their future affairs. They are looking at their legal obligations prospectively rather than retrospectively—what Kahn-Freund has described as the 'prophylactic' function of choice of law rules.[58] This need to plan ahead is, as suggested earlier, not restricted to contracts. It can be seen most clearly also in relation to marriage, and to the making of wills and to the creation of trusts. It may have a role to play in the field of torts and in other aspects of property law.

It has been said in favour of freedom of choice in contract that 'To allow the parties to choose the localising elements, yet to restrict them in their choice of law, is inconsistent.'[59] This argument also has a force beyond contract. It could be taken to support freedom of choice virtually everywhere, in that parties often choose the elements which constitute a specific connecting factor, as has been shown earlier in relation to marriage. More specifically, it would support some freedom of choice where the general choice of law rule is based on the idea of closeness of connection as, for example, some have suggested for some types of marriage

[55] Anton, *Private International Law*, 2nd edn. (1990), 264. [56] Ibid.
[57] Art. 4(2), and see, above, pp. 40–41. [58] [1974] III *Hague Recueil* 147, 341, 344.
[59] Mann, (1950) 3 *ILQ* 60, 68.

issue,[60] or has variously been propounded in the field of tort in the form of the proper law of the tort,[61] as a flexible exception to the current double actionability[62] rules, or as the residual choice of law rule under the Law Commissions' proposals for reform.[63]

Choice of choice of law rules

Before turning, however, to look more directly at choice of law in tort, the wide freedom to choose the applicable law in contract leads on to a different, but related, issue. Though it is an issue theoretically of general application, it has arisen more recently in the context of contract choice of law rules and that is where it is most convenient to examine it. The broad question of whether parties are free to select the substantive law to be applied to a legal issue arising in the transnational context masks a logically anterior question. This is whether the parties have any freedom to choose the choice of law rules which are to be applied to determine the governing substantive law. What seems generally to have been accepted is that it is the law of the country of the forum, not the parties, which decides on the rules to be applied. Thus choice of law rules have been described as 'the rules voluntarily chosen by a given State for the decision of cases which have a foreign complexion.'[64] This has the effect that, when a court is considering the meaning and extent of a connecting factor such as domicile or habitual residence, it applies the rules laid down in forum law, as part of its rules of private international law, to resolve this issue. Reference is not generally made to rules relating to such issues under a foreign law. That is not an inviolable rule because English law can provide instances, in relation, for example, to the determination of a foreign domicile for divorce recognition purposes,[65] or for the purposes of the Civil Jurisdiction and Judgments Act 1982,[66] where reference is made to the foreign meaning of the concept of domicile. What has to be emphasized, however, is that this is done only because there is a rule (in the above examples, a statutory rule) of the forum which permits such reference to be made. The same can be said of the rule of English law that the determination whether a person is a foreign national is to be referred to the law of the foreign country concerned.

[60] See North, [1990] I *Hague Recueil* 9, 63–8.
[61] Morris, (1951) 64 *Harv L Rev* 881.
[62] *Boys* v. *Chaplin* [1971] AC 356.
[63] Law Com. No. 193 (1990), Draft Tort and Delict (Applicable Law) Bill, cl 2(3), (4).
[64] Baty, *Polarized Law* (1914), 148.
[65] Family Law Act 1986, s. 46(1)(b).
[66] S. 42(7), Sch. 1, Art. 52.

A broader example is provided by the doctrine of *renvoi* which allows, in a limited range of circumstances, for a reference to a foreign law by English choice of law rules to be construed as a reference to the whole of that foreign law, not just to its rules of substantive law but also to its rules of private international law. The result is that a case may be governed in England by the substantive law chosen by those foreign choice of law rules. This is not, however, a case of the parties deciding to apply the choice of law rules of a foreign state. Rather it is a case of those rules being allowed to be applied by the private international law rules of the forum, but only where the latter rules hold it to be appropriate to do so. Thus English private international law rules permit the doctrine of *renvoi* to operate in the context, for example, of testate[67] and intestate[68] succession but not of contract[69] or, probably, tort.[70]

From what has gone before, there seems little doubt of the correctness of the statement that the choice of law rules of a state 'are as much part of its own territorial law as those that regulate the conveyance of land in its own country.'[71] Why, then, is it even worth discussing whether the parties have any freedom to choose the applicable choice of law rules? The answer lies in a suggestion by Francis Mann that, at least in the field of contract, such a choice may be available.[72] This suggestion arose in the context of a further,[73] and sadly final, attack by him on the Contracts (Applicable Law) Act 1990 and the (1980) Rome Convention on the law applicable to contractual obligations to which it gives effect. Francis Mann and I have had very differing views as to the acceptability of the European Community-wide choice of law rules contained in the Rome Convention.[74] This is not the place, however, to examine that broad issue,[75] but rather his suggestion that, in his words, 'the unfortunate consequences which are likely to show up in the future'[76] might be avoided by contractual choice of law provisions. Terms suggested by him included

[67] E.g. *Re Annesley* [1926] Ch 692; *Re Ross* [1930] 1 Ch 377.

[68] E.g. *Re Johnson* [1903] 1 Ch 821; *Re O'Keefe* [1940] Ch 124.

[69] Contracts (Applicable Law) Act 1990, Sch. 1, Art. 15; and see *Amin Rasheed Shipping Corpn.* v. *Kuwait Insurance Co.* [1984] AC 50, 60–1.

[70] See *M'Elroy* v. *M'Allister* 1949 SC 110, 126.

[71] Cheshire and North, *Private International Law*, 12th edn. (1992), 39; and see Anton, *Private International Law*, 2nd edn. (1990), 2–3.

[72] (1991) 107 *LQR* 353.

[73] For an earlier one, see, e.g., (1983) 32 *ICLQ* 265, 266.

[74] See correspondence in *The Times*, 13 and 19 Dec. 1989.

[75] His comment, however, at (1991) 107 *LQR* 353, 355, that the 1990 Act was passed without consultation with lawyers and traders cannot be left to go unchallenged. Not only was there extensive consultation during the years of negotiation which led to the conclusion of the Rome Convention (see, e.g., the Law Commissions' Consultation paper of August 1974), there was also consultation by the Lord Chancellor's Department with judges and others on a range of issues before the Bill which became the 1990 Act was introduced.

[76] (1991) 107 *LQR* 353, 355.

choice by the parties of 'English law excluding the Act of 1990' or 'English law as in force on March 31, 1991', i.e. the day before the 1990 Act came into force. His justification for such an approach was that not all law is mandatory and that in contract the parties often have the freedom to exclude statutory provisions, such as those, for example, of the Sale of Goods Act 1979. Furthermore, as the Rome Convention expressly allows the parties freedom to choose the law to govern their contract,[77] it seems reasonable, it was said, for it not to preclude freedom to choose a system of choice of law independent of the Convention.

This suggestion raises a variety of problems. First, it has to be pointed out that the freedom to agree by contract not to apply implied terms in the Sale of Goods Act 1979 is a freedom which is different in kind from the freedom under consideration here. We are concerned with a freedom to agree by contract to determine the law to govern the validity of a contract otherwise than by reference to the choice of law rules laid down by the legislature of the forum for that purpose. There are two types of issue here, one of detail and the other of broad principle. The issue of detail is whether there is anything in the 1990 Act or in the Rome Convention to support the idea that the choice of law rules therein are voluntary, giving the parties freedom to decide whether or not they should operate. This issue has been examined by a more recent commentator who, through analysis of the provisions of the Convention, suggests that its choice of law rules are mandatory.[78] For example, the Convention gives states an express power[79] not to apply certain provisions,[80] and this carries a clear implication that there is no power in a state and, *a fortiori*, in parties to a particular contract to contract out of other provisions. Reliance is also placed on Article 15 of the Convention which excludes the operation of *renvoi* by stating that 'the application of the law of any country specified by this Convention means the application of the rules of law in force in that country other than its rules of private international law'. It is said, correctly in my view, that choice of the former English choice of law rules would infringe the provisions of Article 15 both because the choice was not of substantive contract law rules and because it was of rules which are no longer 'in force' in England. That does not, however, deal with the more fundamental argument that the parties may wish to choose the old common law choice of law rules, thus excluding the Convention rules, including Article 15 itself.

That takes us to the broader issue. There is no doubt that those who drafted the Rome Convention took the view that its choice of law provisions were mandatory, not optional. As is said in the Giuliano and Lagarde Report on the Convention, 'the chief aim of the Convention is

[77] See Art. 3. [78] Hogan, (1992) 108 *LQR* 12. [79] Art. 22(1).
[80] Arts. 7(1), 10(1)(e).

to introduce into the national laws of the EEC Member States a set of uniform rules on the law applicable to contractual obligations and on certain general points of private international law to the extent that these are linked with those obligations.'[81] It was made quite clear that those uniform rules are in substitution for existing national rules of private international law.[82] Furthermore, for such uniform rules to be other than mandatory would be inconsistent with one of the perceived objects of the Convention,[83] namely to act as an adjunct to the (1968) Brussels Convention on jurisdiction and enforcement of judgments in civil and commercial matters so as to ensure that, under the uniform jurisdictional rules, the same law is applied irrespective of the Contracting State in which the case is heard. No one has yet argued that the rules of the Brussels Convention as implemented by the Civil Jurisdiction and Judgments Act 1982 are optional!

It is suggested, therefore, that there is nothing in the new choice of law legislation on contracts which either does, or should, undermine the basic rule that it is for the forum, and not the parties, to determine what set of choice of law rules is to be applied. That is, of course, without prejudice to the question whether the forum's rules allow choice of the substantive law to be applied. Indeed the weakness in the Mann argument lies in the implied assumption that, even before the 1990 Act, parties could have chosen French rather than English choice of law rules to determine the law applicable to their contract. Of such freedom not only is there no evidence, but there is clear judicial authority that an English court had to apply English choice of law rules.[84] The broad freedom to choose the law applicable to contracts does not, therefore, extend to a freedom also to choose the choice of law rules applicable to contractual, or any other, issues.

Tort

As contractual obligations arise, in form at least, from the voluntary agreement of the parties, it is not surprising that, as we have seen, private international law rules extend that freedom to choice of the applicable substantive law. If, however, we turn to another major areas of the law of obligations, tort, is a similar freedom to be found? It is certainly the case that there is no reported judicial examination in England of whether the parties can choose the law to govern their liability in tort. Indeed, one

[81] [1980] OJ C282/8, 31 October 1980. [82] Ibid., C282/13.

[83] Ibid., C282/4–5; and see Plender, *The European Contracts Convention* (1991), 7.

[84] See, e.g. *Banco Atlantico SA* v. *The British Bank of the Middle East* [1990] 2 Lloyd's Rep 504, 506.

commentator in criticizing the idea of a 'proper law of the tort' seems to have assumed that such choice cannot be made because of differences in nature between contractual and tortious obligations:

as regards tort liability, the parties do not and in most cases cannot state before the tort is committed what law is to govern their liability, as they rarely even contemplate that a tort will be committed. They just commit or suffer one. Moreover, a court which is called upon to determine the proper law of a tort does so after it has occurred and in the light of what has already happened and where. The proper law of the contract is determined by the conduct of the parties before or at the time it is concluded, not when the breach takes place.[85]

That the exclusion of choice in the tort context is, however, not a universal view is clear. In Europe, for example, there is support in Germany[86] and the Netherlands[87] for some freedom to choose the law to govern tort liability. Moreover, the Swiss Law on Private International Law also confers an express but limited freedom of choice on the parties in tort cases;[88] it allows the parties, at any time after the tort was committed, to choose the application of the law of the forum,[89] i.e. Swiss law.[90] This is, of course, no wider a choice than parties to English litigation could make procedurally by declining to plead foreign law.[91] There is, however, American authority apparently upholding a wider freedom of choice. In *Camporese* v. *Port Authority of New York and New Jersey*[92] an action was brought in New York arising out of an accident in New Jersey. The plaintiff was injured when working on the construction of a building for the defendants. When sued by the plaintiff, the defendants sought contribution from the plaintiff's employers, a painting company. The case raised issues both as to the extent of the defendants' liability to the plaintiff and whether a contribution claim would lie where the injury sustained was covered by workmen's compensation.[93] To all these issues

[85] Collier, *Conflict of Laws* (1987), 183.

[86] See Kahn-Freund, [1974] III *Hague Recueil* 139, 341 n. 44.

[87] De Boer, *Beyond Lex Loci Delicti* (1987), 66–7, 101. It is interesting to note the discussion, on p. 67, n. 177, of the further Dutch proceedings in the leading case before the European Court of Justice on jurisdiction over tort claims under Art. 5(3) of the Brussels Convention on jurisdiction and enforcement of judgments: Case 21/76 *Bier BV* v. *Mines de Potasse d'Alsace SA* [1976] ECR 1735; [1978] QB 708, where a choice of Dutch law was upheld. See also De Boer, (1990) 54 *RabelsZ* 24, 38.

[88] Art. 132. For an English translation, see Symeonides, (1989) 37 *Am Jo Comp L* 187; and see Samuel, (1988) 37 *ICLQ* 681.

[89] An earlier draft of the Swiss Law allowed a choice also of the law of the parties' common habitual residence, see McCaffrey, (1980) 28 *Am Jo Comp L* 235, 280.

[90] The Dutch case referred to in n. 87 above also involved a choice of forum law.

[91] Discussed above, pp. 179–181.

[92] 415 NYS 2d 28 (1979), affd 426 NYS 2d 977 (1980).

[93] This situation is different from that where there is a contractual agreement governing the claim for contribution from an employer; see e.g. *Goodwin* v. *George Fischer Foundry Systems Inc.* 769 F 2d 708 (11th Cir 1985).

the New York court applied New Jersey law because 'the accident occurred in New Jersey and by agreement of the parties, the law of that state was applied to the substantive issues.'[94]

This willingness to give some reign to the parties' choice of the applicable law is also evidenced in the Law Commissions' work on the reform of the tort choice of law rules. In their substantial Working Paper,[95] published in 1984, two main Models for reform were proposed for consultation; one was essentially the application of the law of the place of the tort, subject to an exception in favour of the law of the country of closest connection; the other involved the application of the law of the country of closest connection subject to presumptions that that was the place of the tort. What is significant here is that both of those solutions were qualified by the parties' freedom to choose the applicable law. The Commissions provisionally proposed that 'it should be possible (before or after a tort or delict occurred) to agree by means of contract what law should govern the parties' mutual liability in tort or delict. Such agreement should be effective whether or not it results in the application of the law of the forum.'[96]

This proposal has been welcomed as 'long overdue';[97] though there is little doubt that, embodied in legislative form, it would need further elaboration in order to determine whether there were to be any limits on the freedom of choice in terms of the law which might be chosen, such as whether any other connection with the chosen law was required, and to determine the extent to which the public policy or mandatory rules of the forum, that is, English law, would continue to operate despite a choice by the parties.[98] There would be nothing new in all of that. After all it would amount simply to the application in the tort context of details which have been developed for choice of law in contract.[99] When we turn, however, to the Law Commissions' Report on Choice of Law in Tort and Delict[100] not only is there no provision in the draft Tort and Delict (Applicable Law) Bill allowing for freedom of choice, there is no discussion of the issue at all in the body of the Report. The matter has

[94] 415 NYS 2d 28, 29 (1979).

[95] Law Com. Working Paper No. 87 (1984). For comments thereon, see Fawcett, (1985) 48 *MLR* 439, and see above, pp. 82–83.

[96] Ibid., 265, and see para. 4.21.

[97] Castel, *Canadian Conflict of Laws*, 2nd edn. (1986), 621.

[98] One strange limitation that has been proposed is that freedom of choice should be allowed only if permitted by the law of the country or countries which would otherwise govern liability; see Kaye, *Private International Law of Tort and Product Liability* (1991), 63. To adopt such a limitation would defeat much of the purpose of permitting party autonomy in the field of tort law.

[99] Contracts (Applicable Law) Act 1990, Sch. 1, Arts. 3, 7, 16.

[100] Law Com. No. 193 (1990). For general discussion of the Report, see Kaye, *Private International Law of Tort and Product Liability* (1991), chs. 16–18; Carter, (1991) 107 *LQR* 405; North, (1991) 42 *NILQ* 183, 194–8, above, pp. 83–88.

disappeared without trace. Its exclusion from any legislation based on the draft Bill would effectively exclude it from English choice of law rules, because the draft Bill itself makes clear that the choice of law rules in tort are to be those laid down in the Bill. In any event, it seems highly improbable that courts would feel free to develop at common law a concept of party autonomy in tort alongside a regime of statutory choice of law rules.[101]

Whether the introduction of some freedom of choice were to be effected by legislation or by judicial development, there remains the question of whether it is desirable or realistic for the law to move in that direction. It is obviously the case that responsible people usually neither wish nor plan to commit torts against others. There is not the same degree of forward planning of relationships and obligations as exists in contract. That does not mean that there is no room for the operation of choice before a tort is committed. The possibility of being liable in tort is not necessarily far from people's minds. It is always, formally, present in terms of use of a motor vehicle through the need to take out at least third party insurance, coupled with the desirability of extending insurance cover through the Green Card scheme when taking the vehicle abroad. This was put graphically by Kahn-Freund over twenty years ago, when he said: '"When in Rome do as the Romans do" reads in our world "when in Rome see that your insurance policy covers the risks against which Romans insure."'[102] Obviously if I have a traffic accident in Rome in which an Italian is injured, there is little prospect that the victim and I will earlier have agreed what law is to govern his tort claim. The position may well be very different if the accident injures, instead, a passenger in my car who has travelled with me from England to Italy. Other striking examples can be provided by situations where the parties are in a contractual relationship but the plaintiff wishes to formulate a claim in tort, as where an employee injured abroad wishes to sue his employer[103] or a passenger injured on a foreign holiday coach trip wishes to sue the bus company. The contract of employment or of travel might well include a choice of law clause. It would not, it is suggested, be improper for that clause to extend from contractual to tortious liability or indeed for the contract to make separate choice of law provision for each.[104]

[101] See the discussion, above, pp. 184–187, of the idea that parties could choose not to apply the rules in the Contracts (Applicable Law) Act 1990.

[102] Kahn-Freund, [1968] II *Hague Recueil* 5, 44.

[103] E.g. *Coupland* v. *Arabian Gulf Oil Co.* [1983] 1 WLR 1136; *Johnson* v. *Coventry Churchill International Ltd.* [1992] 3 All ER 14; cf. *Matthews* v. *Kuwait Bechtel Corpn.* [1959] 2 QB 57.

[104] Though in the employment context, the freedom of choice might need to be restricted to the same extent as it is for contractual claims: Contracts (Applicable Law) Act 1990, Sch. 1, Art. 6; and see Morse, (1992) 41 *ICLQ* 1.

Once a tort has been committed, choice of the applicable law ceases to have a prophylactic or prospective planning role to play, but may well be at least as, if not more, significant. In such a case the plaintiff is now identified, as are the substantive tort laws which may have a claim to being applied. Arguments advanced earlier relating to expense, difficulties of proof of foreign law, and the uncertainties of the litigation process come into play. These are strengthened when the generally applicable tort choice of law rules are as unsatisfactory as are the present common law rules,[105] requiring as they do actionability by both the law of the forum and the place of the tort, coupled with an exception thereto of indeterminate range and scope.[106] Parties may well conclude that their dispute must be litigated but may, in some cases, be able to agree on the law to be applied. Subject to the broad public policy safeguards also available to a court when asked to apply foreign law, there seems no reason why the choice of the parties should be restricted, as in Switzerland or under the English pleading device, to the law of the forum. Indeed an obvious law on which to agree might be that of the place where the tort was committed. Certainly, the Law Commissions' reform proposals do not provide so clear an answer in all varied tort cases as to obviate the desirability of rules permitting choice being introduced in any implementing legislation. Such a course would be both prudent and practical.

Property

One of the earliest examples of freedom of choice of the applicable law is provided by the sixteenth century French private international law scholar, Dumoulin,[107] who accepted that the law to govern a marriage settlement should be that agreed by the spouses, with a presumption that that law is that of their matrimonial domicile.[108] Indeed it has been said of his conclusion that 'here was the germ of the doctrine of party autonomy in the law of contract.'[109] There is no doubt that the principle of autonomy continues to play a part in the private international law rules relating to property matters. What is less clear is why its influence is limited in the way in which it appears to be.

105 *Phillips* v. *Eyre* (1870) LR 6 QB 1; *Boys* v. *Chaplin* [1971] AC 356.

106 For criticisms, see North, [1990] I *Hague Recueil* 9, 206 *et seq*, and see above, pp. 75–77. For a recent example of the application of the exception, see *Johnson* v. *Coventry Churchill International Ltd.* [1992] 3 All ER 14.

107 See Westlake, *Private International Law*, 7th edn. (1925), 17.

108 Batiffol and Lagarde, *Droit International Privé*, 7th edn. (1983), II: 356 *et seq.*

109 Anton, *Private International Law*, 2nd edn. (1990), 19.

Marriage settlements

It is convenient to start our examination of freedom of choice in the context of property issues with that of marriage settlements, forming a bridge as it does with the rules on contracts generally.[110] There is no doubt that here the spouses have some freedom to select the law to govern their marriage contract.[111] This freedom has been expressed, however, in rather grudging terms, more as an exception than the rule. 'As a general rule the law of the matrimonial domicile is applicable to a contract in consideration of marriage. But this is not an absolute rule. It yields to an express stipulation that some other law shall apply.'[112] In fact it also yields to an implied choice of the governing law.[113]

There are potentially two kinds of limitation on this freedom of choice. The first concerns the type of issue in question. It seems clear that the proper law, including an expressly chosen law, should govern matters of essential validity and ought also to be applicable to formal validity.[114] A suggestion has been made[115] that freedom of choice should not extend to essential validity generally but only to matters of construction of the settlement. This idea, drawn by analogy from dicta in the context of testamentary settlements,[116] has little merit in determining the law to govern what is essentially a consensual relationship.[117] What is more doubtful is the issue of the law to govern capacity to enter a marriage settlement. Though the authorities are old and obscure,[118] the text writers seem clearly to accept that the proper law, rather than the domiciliary law, should govern this issue. However, it seems also widely to be accepted that, as with the rules applicable to contracts generally, there is no place here for choice of the applicable law by the parties. As was said in *Cooper* v. *Cooper*:[119]

[110] Choice of law relating to marriage settlements continues to be governed by common law rules because 'contractual obligations relating to . . . rights in property arising out of a matrimonial relationship' are excluded from the scope of the (1980) Rome Convention, see Contracts (Applicable Law) Act 1990, Sch. 1, Art. 2(b).

[111] E.g. *Trustees Executors and Agency Co. Ltd.* v. *Margottini* [1960] VR 417.

[112] *Re Fitzgerald* [1904] 1 Ch 573, 587.

[113] E.g. *Re Bankes* [1902] 2 Ch 333; *Re Fitzgerald* [1904] 1 Ch 573.

[114] Certainly *Van Grutten* v. *Digby* (1862) 31 Beav 561 supports the principle that a marriage settlement is formally valid if it satisfies the formal requirements of the law of the place of contracting or of the proper law, though in that case it had to be determined in the absence of choice.

[115] Anton, *Private International Law*, 1st edn. (1967), 451; cf. 2nd edn. (1990), 580.

[116] *Philipson-Stow* v. *Inland Revenue Commissioners* [1961] AC 727, 760.

[117] It is suggested below, pp. 195–199, that neither should this idea be supported in the context of wills.

[118] *Re Cooke's Trusts* (1887) 56 LJ Ch 637; *Cooper* v. *Cooper* (1883) 13 App Cas 88; *Viditz* v. *O'Hagan* [1899] 2 Ch 569, revsd [1900] 2 Ch 87.

[119] (1883) 13 App Cas 88, 108.

It is difficult to suppose that Mrs Cooper could confer capacity upon herself by contemplating a different country as the place where the contract was to be fulfilled, if that be the proper expression, or by contracting in view of an alteration of personal status which would bring with it a change of domicil.

The second type of limitation concerns the range of laws which may be chosen. In the absence of judicial guidance, authors are cautious, accepting freedom of choice 'at any rate if the transaction has a substantial connection with the selected law'.[120] Certainly in the leading decision exemplifying an express choice, a Scottish decision on appeal to the House of Lords, the spouses chose the same law as might well have been applied in the absence of choice.[121] However this caution is, it is suggested, unnecessary. There is no reason why the same freedom should not be afforded to the parties as in contracts generally. The common law limitations on freedom of choice have never been expressed in very clear terms, reference usually being made to the fact that the choice must be 'bona fide and legal'[122] which, it is suggested, provides sufficient protection, when combined with the requirement of the forum to apply its mandatory rules and public policy, to allow the parties otherwise to select the law of their choice.[123] Furthermore, it may well be, and indeed should be, that the common law rules here are influenced by the statutory developments introduced for contracts generally. Under the (1980) Rome Convention, implemented by the Contracts (Applicable Law) Act 1990, the parties are free, as has been seen earlier, to choose a wholly unconnected law subject only to the applicability of the public policy and mandatory rules of the forum.[124] There seems no reason why such freedom should not be applied to contractual issues which continue to fall within the common law rules. It also would seem proper to accept the operation of *depeçage* in relation to marriage settlements, i.e. that the parties should be free to choose different laws to govern different elements of the agreement.[125]

[120] Dicey and Morris, *The Conflict of Laws*, 11th edn. (1987), 1060. A similar view is adopted by Cheshire and North, *Private International Law*, 12th edn. (1992), 878; Anton, *Private International Law*, 2nd edn. (1990), 580.

[121] *Montgomery* v. *Zarifi* 1918 SC 128 (HL); and see *Re Hernando* (1884) 27 Ch D 284.

[122] *Vita Food Products Inc.* v. *Unus Shipping Co. Ltd* [1939] AC 277, 290.

[123] See North, [1990] I *Hague Recueil* 9, 166–7.

[124] Sch. 1, Arts. 7(2), 16. If the contract is wholly connected with one country apart from the choice of law clause, then the mandatory rules of that country also fall to be applied: Art. 3(3); see above, pp. 39, 44.

[125] Cf. 1990 Act, Sch. 1, Art. 3(1). There is certainly Scottish authority generally supporting *depeçage* in this context in the field of construction: *Hope Vere* v. *Hope Vere* (1906) 13 SLT 774, 776, affd (1907) 15 SLT 361 (HL).

Trusts

Support by analogy for a wide freedom of choice in the field of marriage settlements is provided not only by the new contract choice of law rules, but also by consideration of choice of law for trusts more generally, to which our attention must now turn. It seems to have been accepted at common law, in relation both to testamentary[126] and *inter vivos* trusts,[127] that the settlor might either expressly or impliedly choose the law to govern the validity of the trust. This would appear to have been the case whether the choice was of foreign law by an English domiciled testator or settlor, or of English law by a foreign domiciliary.[128] Such an approach is confirmed by the Recognition of Trusts Act 1987 which gives effect in this country to the (1986) Hague Convention on the law applicable to trusts and on their recognition. Under Article 6, a trust is to be governed by the law expressly or impliedly chosen. The chosen law is given wide effect in that it governs the validity of the trust (presumably both essential and formal), its construction, effects, and administration.[129] Furthermore, express approval is given to the idea that severable aspects of the trust may be governed by different laws.[130] One interesting facet of this general statutory freedom of choice is that it is subject to few limitations. There is no requirement (as hinted at at common law)[131] that the chosen law should be otherwise connected with the trust. A proposal, made during the negotiation of the Convention, to require some objective connection with the trust in question was rejected.[132] However, a choice will be disregarded if the concept of trust is unknown under the law chosen.[133] Notwithstanding the choice, English courts, as being those of the forum, may still disregard the choice of a law whose application would be contrary to public policy[134] and must[135] apply both English mandatory rules[136] and those of the law of a foreign country designated by our

[126] *Re Lord Cable* [1977] 1 WLR 7, 20; and see *Att-Gen.* v. *Campbell* (1872) LR 5 HL 524; *Re Healy's Will* 125 NYS 2d 486 (1953).

[127] Apart from the decisions on marriage settlements, see *Augustus* v. *Permanent Trustee Co. (Canberra) Ltd.* (1971) 124 CLR 245; and see *Harris Investments Ltd.* v. *Smith* [1934] DLR 748.

[128] Cf. *Canterbury Corpn.* v. *Wyburn and Melbourne Hospital* [1905] AC 89.

[129] Art. 8. [130] Art. 9.

[131] Dicey and Morris, *The Conflict of Laws*, 11th edn. (1987), 1074.

[132] Gaillard and Trautman, (1987) 35 *Am Jo Comp L* 307, 323; *Actes et Documents de la Quinzième Session*, (1985), II: 384.

[133] Art. 5. Other Contracting States may also refuse to recognize a trust which is most closely connected with a country where trusts are unknown but for the choice of the applicable law, the place of administration and the habitual residence of the trustee: Art. 13. The UK has chosen not to exercise this power in relation to foreign trusts.

[134] Art. 18. [135] Recognition of Trusts Act 1987, s. 1(3).

[136] Art. 16. The UK has exercised a power of reservation not to apply the mandatory rules of sufficiently closely connected third states under the second paragraph of this Article.

choice of law rules (being presumably other than those found in the Convention) in a range of listed matters, including for example matters of succession where provision is made for fixed shares in an estate for the benefit of a spouse or children.[137] These limitations are, however, not substantial and party autonomy is given very free rein.

The Trusts Convention only provides choice of law rules to govern the validity of a trust which has already been validly created. It makes clear in Article 4 that it is not concerned with the law to determine the validity of the instrument of creation, whether it be an *inter vivos* or a testamentary trust. If there is an *inter vivos* trust created by a contract then there is little doubt that the validity of the trust-creating contract is governed by the general rules applicable to contracts. There is, however, very little direct authority on whether parties may change the law to govern the validity of a voluntary settlement effected by deed; though the fact that the Australian courts have accorded full freedom to a settler to choose by deed the law to govern the trusts created thereunder provides some indirect support for freedom to determine the law to govern the validity of the instrument creating the trusts.[138] Further support is provided by the English decision in *Re Pilkington's Will Trusts*[139] where the court concluded that effect should be given to a deed, valid under Scots law but not English law, because the settlor intended Scots law to be applied.

It seems fair to conclude that the factors which have justified a wide freedom of choice in contract have similarly led to the conclusion that, both in the instrument creating an *inter vivos* trust and in relation to all trusts validly created, such freedom is also justified. One powerful argument here is that the dispositions of property which are being established are normally of a voluntary nature. Furthermore, the settlor, trustees, and beneficiaries are all likely to be anxious at the outset to know whether the instrument just created is valid and what legal regime is to govern its, possibly long, life.

Wills

This then leads on to the question whether similar freedom is to be permitted in the case of wills. If, as the Hague Trusts Convention permits, a testator may by will determine the law to govern the trusts created thereby, may he also by will determine the law to govern its, that is, the will's, validity? Orthodoxy suggests that there is one aspect of the law of wills where effect is certainly to be given to the intentions of the testator and that is in relation to construction of the will. Very often a testator

[137] Art. 15.
[138] *Augustus* v. *Permanent Trustee Co. (Canberra) Ltd.* (1971) 124 CLR 245, esp. 260.
[139] [1937] Ch 574.

gives no express indication of what law he intended to be applied to this matter, and the court presumes that he would have intended the law of his domicile at the time of making his will, rather than at death, to determine the meaning to be given to expressions in the will.[140] If, on the other hand, it is shown that the deceased had addressed his mind to the problem, as where a testatrix said that her will was to 'be considered in England the same as in France',[141] courts are prepared to give effect to such expressions of intention.[142]

This seems, however, to be the limit of freedom afforded to the testator, as was put quite starkly by Lord Denning some thirty years ago:

> The so-called exceptions to what I have referred—about the *construction* of a will—are not really exceptions at all: for in construing a will, so as to see what a testator meant, every civilised country looks to see what he intended—and for this purpose you may legitimately look at the law he had in mind—but you only do this as a guide to find his meaning. You do not do it so as to find out the law which regulates his dispositions. He has no choice about that. Apart from this one question of construction, the succession to movables is regulated by the law of his domicile: and the succession to immovables is regulated by the lex situs.[143]

This statement has been unquestioningly accepted as authoritative.[144] There is, it appears, no significant place for party autonomy in testate succession. Should this, however, be so? Like making a contract, making a will is a voluntary act. It is not necessary to do so in order to arrange for succession on death. The rules of intestate succession will fill any gap. The disposition of the estate made by the will is also a matter of choice—for example whether assets are left to grandchildren or to charity. Furthermore, the decision whether to establish trusts under the will is again one of choice and, as we have seen, the testator can choose the law to govern those trusts—but not, it appears, to govern the instrument creating them.

It is perfectly understandable that there should be some ways in which the freedom of a testator to dispose of his property as he wishes may be constrained. Obvious examples are the need to protect the financial position of relatives, and some legal systems require a proportion of the estate to be left to a widow or children, to give effect to rules on the remoteness of vesting or rules prohibiting gifts to charities, or to ensure that the law of the *situs* has ultimate control over land there. It is not, however, self-evident that such concerns should exclude, as opposed to limiting the effect of, freedom of choice.

[140] See *Philipson-Stow* v. *Inland Revenue Commissioners* [1961] AC 727, 761.
[141] *Re Price* [1900] 1 Ch 442.
[142] E.g. *Bradford* v. *Young* (1885) 29 Ch D 617, 623, 625.
[143] *Philipson-Stow* v. *Inland Revenue Commissioners* [1961] AC 727, 761–2.
[144] Dicey and Morris, *The Conflict of Laws*, 11th edn. (1987), 1023.

There is, of course, some limited indirect choice open to a testator in that the essential validity of a will of moveables is governed by the law of his domicile on death. However, the testator may have made his will having in mind the law of his domicile at the time of making it, only for his beneficiaries to find the testator's wishes frustrated by a conclusion that his domicile had changed before death. It is, of course, an answer to say that if the testator changed his domicile he should change his will, but that is requiring him to do indirectly what free choice would have allowed him to do directly. Furthermore, the complexities of the law of domicile are such that he may not know whether or not it has changed.

It is worth asking, in the light of the fact that party autonomy has not yet been accepted in the English choice of law rules relating to wills, whether the current choice of law rules, i.e. the application of the law of the *situs* to immoveables and of the testator's domicile on death to moveables, are without blemish, criticism or exception. It would appear that the case for the application of the law of the *situs* to testate succession to immoveables is greatly weakened by the strength of the criticism of the application of that law to intestate succession to immoveables.[145] It is said that 'in modern law it is a quite unnecessary complication to have different conflict rules for intestate succession to movables and immovables.'[146] Such an argument ought to be just as strong when, as often happens, a testator disposes in the one will of both forms of property. The case in such circumstances for applying the law of the testator's last domicile to such a will is not, it is suggested, because there is some intrinsic merit in the domiciliary law governing testate succession to immoveables. Indeed it probably has to be accepted that some ultimate residual regard will need to be had to the rules of the *situs* relating to the formal transfer of property. The law of the domicile is recommended, rather, for application primarily to ensure that one law applies to succession to both forms of property. Once, however, there is a breach in the rule that the law of the *situs* applies to immoveables, that opens up the question whether it is acceptable that the applicable law be other than that of the domicile—provided the same law applies to succession to both moveables and immoveables.

It seems in fact to have been accepted that the law of the domicile is not invariably to be applied to all issues of essential validity concerning testate succession to moveables. If bequests infringe the rule against perpetuities of the law of the domicile but not of the country where the property is situated and to be administered, then courts in the USA[147]

[145] E.g. *Re Collens* [1986] Ch 505, 512–13.

[146] Dicey and Morris, *The Conflict of Laws*, 11th edn. (1987), 1007.

[147] E.g. *Chamberlain* v. *Chamberlain* (1870) 43 NY 424; *Re Chappell's Estate* 124 Wash 128; 213 P 684 (1923).

and in Australia[148] have been prepared to uphold validity under the law of the country of administration. This has been justified on the ground that it is no concern of the law of the domicile, even if that be England, to impose its rules on remoteness of vesting so as to prevent a foreign beneficiary from enjoying foreign assets in a foreign country. Conversely, of course, English courts may regard it as only right to apply the rule against perpetuities to a trust of English assets notwithstanding the foreign domicile of the testator.[149] This could be justified either on the basis that England is the forum, or the place of administration.

What these examples reveal is that the orthodox rule that testate succession to moveables is governed by the law of the testator's last domicile, or by the law of the *situs* of the property in the case of immoveables, is not without exception or criticism. The domicile rule is, to a degree, convenient—as convenient as any rule which relies on the complex law of domicile. It is hard, however, to claim for it a degree of exclusivity such as might be the case if the issue of succession could be classed as one of status. Such a classification might justify its exclusive application to the issue of capacity to make a will, but not generally to essential validity. As reference is made to the law of the domicile on death, rather than when the will was made, the applicable law is not necessarily even the law which the testator had in contemplation when he made his will. It is suggested that it would not be unreasonable to extend to the voluntary act of making a will some freedom specifically to determine the law to govern its validity. The present rules have longevity in their favour, having been first established some two hundred years ago, but the policy reasons for applying the law of the domicile (or that of the *situs*) to matters of essential validity of wills do not seem to be so strong as to exclude the case for choice.[150]

Indeed the voluntary nature of a will and the desirability of determining its incidents and effects when it is made provide strong arguments for party autonomy. As pointed out earlier, if the testator can choose the law to govern the essential validity of the trusts he creates by his will, is it not reasonable that he should have some freedom to choose the law to govern the validity of the legal instrument which creates those trusts?[151] It

[148] *Re Mitchner* [1922] St R Qd 252.

[149] See Dicey and Morris, *The Conflict of Laws* 11th edn. (1987), 1019.

[150] The position of formal validity is somewhat different as the relevant choice of laws are statutory, being laid down in the Wills Act 1963 and, moreover, they implement the 1961 Hague Convention on the Formal Validity of Wills.

[151] It is also reasonable to suggest that freedom of choice has effect elsewhere in the law of property. For example, in the case of assignment, reference is made either to the contract of assignment or to that under which the original debt arose: Contracts (Applicable Law) Act 1990, Sch. 1, Art. 12. Freedom of choice will apply to both those contracts. A case can also be made for party autonomy when dealing with the transfer of tangible moveables, leaving only a residual role for the law of the *situs*.

should not be overlooked that the case for freedom of choice, albeit of a somewhat limited kind, has been accepted in the (1988) Hague Convention on the law applicable to succession to the estates of deceased persons. Whilst this has not, as yet, proved to be a particularly successful Hague Convention,[152] and is one which I believe to be seriously flawed in a number of respects,[153] it has the interesting feature of allowing the deceased to choose the law to govern succession to his estate, whether testate or intestate. Indeed this freedom of choice has been described as a 'main characteristic' of the Convention.[154] Choice takes two forms. The deceased may, under Article 5(1), choose the law of his nationality or habitual residence, either at the time of choice or of death, to govern succession to his whole estate. This cautious approach, limiting the range of choices, was thought desirable because party autonomy in succession matters was a new proposition for virtually all states.[155] Freedom of choice is, however, extended in that the deceased may choose other laws, such as the law of the *situs*, to govern succession to particular assets, though subject to the mandatory rules of the otherwise applicable law.[156] Whilst this two-pronged approach makes for an unnecessarily complex structure of rules, and whilst it may be argued that the general freedom of choice conferred by the Convention is unduly limited, nevertheless the party autonomy provisions of the Convention undoubtedly provide a helpful model on which reform of our succession choice of law rules might build.

CONCLUSIONS

The choice of law process involves, as I have endeavoured to show, a range of ways in which the parties may influence the law to govern the transnational legal issue with which they may be faced. This influence is less obvious where it is exercised through indirect choice of connecting factors, through choice of the forum, or through choice of English law by reason of pleading no other. Whilst, however, it may be less obvious than direct choice of the applicable law, it is not a negligible influence. Direct choice of the applicable law, so long regarded as a characteristic of contract but not of other areas of law, is undoubtedly growing in acceptability. It is now established in the law of trusts and of marriage settlements,

[152] It has been signed by only two states and ratified by none.

[153] North, [1990] I *Hague Recueil* 9, 278–82.

[154] Waters, Explanatory Report on the Convention, *Actes et Documents de la Seizième Session*, (1990), II: 526, 535.

[155] Switzerland was an exception; see Lagarde, (1989) 78 *Rev crit dr int privé* 249, 260, and see the Swiss Statute on Private International Law, 1987, Arts. 90–91.

[156] Art. 6.

and forms part of the law reform debate on choice of law in tort and in succession.

This is, I suggest, a significant and welcome development. Ease of travel and communication mean that the lives of far more people are touched by transnational problems than ever was the case a few decades ago. Wisely, the majority wish to avoid the difficulties which may arise and which private international law rules are designed to resolve. They certainly wish to avoid the cost and anxiety of the litigation process. Choice of law rules should be designed to fulfil this prophylactic role. This is why choice in choice of law is so important.

8

The Draft UK/US Judgments Convention: A British Viewpoint

INTRODUCTION

THIS essay provides a case study of the attempts to negotiate a convention between the United Kingdom and the USA on the recognition of judgments in civil and commercial matters. In the absence of such a convention, the rules for the recognition of such judgments are to be found at common law.[1] Furthermore, if there is no such convention in existence, United States defendants to litigation elsewhere in the European Community could be at a particular disadvantage. This is because of the impact of the Brussels Convention on jurisdiction and the enforcement of judgments in civil and commercial matters (1968), given effect in the United Kingdom by the Civil Jurisdiction and Judgments Act 1982. Although that Convention lays down jurisdiction and recognition rules for cases involving defendants domiciled in a Contracting State within the Community, it also provides for the virtually automatic recognition of judgments given by courts in Contracting States against defendants domiciled elsewhere. This is so even though the basis on which the court assumed jurisdiction might be regarded as exorbitant.[2] So, in principle, a judgment of a French court in favour of a plaintiff who is a French national and against a New York domiciled defendant would be enforceable in London against the defendant's English assets,[3] irrespective of the exorbitant nature of the French jurisdictional rule based on the plaintiff's French nationality.

Protection for the position of a defendant domiciled outside any of the Contracting States to the Brussels Convention is provided by Article 59 which allows Contracting States to enter into conventions with third countries on the recognition and enforcement of judgments. Such conventions would allow a Contracting State to decline to recognise a judgment given in another Contracting State and, on exorbitant jurisdictional

Reprinted by special permission of Northwestern University School of Law, *Northwestern Journal of International Law and Business*, 1: 1, 219–39 (1979).

[1] Cheshire and North, *Private International Law*, 12th edn. (1992), 348–92.

[2] 1982 Act, Sch. 1, Art. 3, and see below, p. 207.

[3] See below, p. 207.

grounds,[4] against a defendant domiciled or habitually resident in the third state. So, in the example given above, such a convention between the USA and the United Kingdom would lead to the non-recognition of the French judgment. The negotiation of just such a draft convention is discussed below. That discussion takes the matter to the position in the negotiations in late 1978. It highlights, *inter alia*, the difficulties that existed in achieving agreement on a convention which did not provide some limit on the level of damages for which a judgment might be enforced and which included judgments in anti-trust matters.

These difficulties led to the negotiation of further amendments to the draft convention in September 1978, and another version was published in the United Kingdom in March 1979 for consultation purposes.[5] This achieved no wider consensus in the United Kingdom than had the earlier versions and in 1980 the whole project was abandoned, with the Lord Chancellor making the following statement:

> A substantial proportion of the bodies which commented on the Consultative Paper felt that a Convention might be harmful in view of the very high damages awarded by American juries, especially in personal injury and product liability cases; and that it would not be possible to devise any means of mitigating the enforcement of such judgments which would not be excessively difficult to operate in practice. Taking these and other views into consideration, Her Majesty's Government have decided not to pursue negotiations on a draft Convention, and have so informed the United States authorities.[6]

The conclusion that should not be drawn from that outcome is that the negotiation of conventions between the United Kingdom and non-European Community states which enable the latter to take advantage of the benefits conferred by Article 59 of the Brussels Convention cannot be achieved. It is rather that the draft convention with the USA attempted to achieve too much in that it aimed to produce a statutory code of recognition rules and procedures. In so doing, it seemed to go further than the existing common law recognition rules, of which many critics were surprisingly ignorant, and raised the spectre of wide-ranging judgments of United States courts becoming enforceable in England, for the first time, against English defendants.

There have now been two recognition conventions successfully negotiated between the United Kingdom and other common law jurisdictions, conferring on the latter the protections permitted by Article 59, and one of these Conventions might provide a model for any resumed negotia-

[4] As listed in Art. 3.

[5] Lord Chancellor's Department, *Proposed Convention Between the United Kingdom and the United States for the Reciprocal Recognition and Enforcement of Judgments in Civil Matters*, Third Consultative Paper, March 1979.

[6] *Hansard*, HL Debs, 410: 1864, 26 June 1980.

tions with the USA, were there to be the political will so to proceed. The first of these two Conventions was formally concluded between the United Kingdom and Canada in 1984[7] and came into force on 1 January 1987. It has a dual purpose. First it enables the United Kingdom to extend the Foreign Judgments (Reciprocal Enforcement) Act 1933 to the Canadian Provinces.[8] It does this by setting out extensively, as in the draft UK/US convention, the scope of the Convention, the procedures for registration and enforcement, the acceptable bases of jurisdiction in the original court and the grounds for refusal of registration. Secondly, it provides for Canada the benefits of the protection permitted by Article 59 of the Brussels Convention.[9]

The second Convention was agreed in August 1990 between the United Kingdom and Australia[10] though it has not yet been brought into force. It is case in different and much shorter form than the United Kingdom/Canada Convention. It does not purport to change the main existing bases of recognition. So, for example, judgments given in the Australian States will continue to be recognized in the United Kingdom under the provisions of the Administration of Justice Act 1920, whilst judgments of United Kingdom courts will still be recognized in those States under their equivalent of the Foreign Judgments (Reciprocal Enforcement) Act 1933.[11] No obvious attempt has been made to eradicate this absence of true reciprocity.[12] Essentially the Convention provides that a judgment obtained in one country shall be recognized and enforced in the other on terms no less favourable than those applicable under existing recognition legislation or provided by the common law rules of the recognizing court on recognition and enforcement.[13] The Convention then goes on to provide[14] for Australia the benefits of the protection permitted by Article 59 of the Brussels Convention.

Whilst the Canadian Convention is unlikely to provide a useful model for future negotiations between the United Kingdom and the USA (because it is cast in much the same form as the abortive draft convention), it might be asked whether there is scope in developing the approach of the Australian Convention. That convention does not create new recognition rules. It merely confirms existing ones. Would it, therefore, be adequate to confer Article 59 protection on the USA for a UK/US

[7] (1984) Cmnd. 9337. See also SI 1986 No. 2027. For Canadian analysis of the negotiations which led to the conclusion of the Convention, see the *Proceedings of the Sixty Fourth Annual Meeting of the Uniform Law Conference of Canada* (1982), 64–75.

[8] It has, in fact, now been extended to all Canadian Provinces and Territories (apart from Quebec): SI 1992 No. 1731.

[9] See Art. IX of the UK/Canada Convention.

[10] (1991) Cm. 1394.

[11] See Art. 2(1)(a)(i) of the UK/Australia Convention.

[12] Dicey and Morris, *The Conflict of Laws*, 11th edn. (1987), 481.

[13] Art. 2(1) of the UK/Australia Convention.

[14] Art. 3.

convention simply to embody agreement that a judgment of a court in one country shall be recognized and enforced in the other on terms no less favourable than are provided by the common law rules of recognition and enforcement in the recognizing state?[15] What Article 59 requires is, first, 'a convention on recognition and enforcement of judgments' between a Contracting State and a third State. That would appear to be satisfied by a convention confirming the common law rules, and there is nothing to cast doubt on that in the Jenard and Schlosser Reports on the Brussels Convention.[16] It is then permitted, by Article 59, for the parties to agree not to recognize judgments given in other Contracting States which are founded on any of the exorbitant jurisdictional rules listed in Article 3 if the defendant is domiciled or habitually resident in the third state. No difficulty of compatibility with the common law recognition rules is likely to be envisaged here because such exorbitant judgments would not be recognized thereunder in any event. If within the letter, is such a simple convention also within the spirit of Article 59? The Schlosser Report states that 'it is intended that the Contracting States should remain free to conclude conventions with third States excluding the recognition and enforcement of judgments based on exorbitant jurisdictions.'[17] There can be little double that a 'common law rules' convention as outlined above would do just that. It would also achieve it without the possibility of justified anxiety as to the greater likelihood of US judgments becoming newly enforceable in the UK. Whether there is a political desire to venture down this route remains to be seen.

* * *

[15] Cf. Art. 2(1)(b) of the UK/Australia Convention.

[16] [1979] OJ C59/61–2, 142–3.

[17] Ibid., C59/142.

THE BACKGROUND

On 22 January 1972, the Treaty of Accession to the European Economic Community[1] was signed in Brussels on behalf of the six original Member States[2] and of the three new Member States.[3] Undoubtedly that was a momentous occasion for the nine States involved, especially for the three new members of the European Economic Community (EEC). Certainly, it was to have profound political, economic, and legal effects within the United Kingdom. For example, lawyers and legislators in the United Kingdom have had to come to terms with major inroads into the sovereignty of Parliament resulting from the treaty obligations requiring the United Kingdom to give effect to EEC legislation. Judges are faced with the problems of applying, and interpreting, an increasing amount of so-called English law of foreign origin.[4] This not only involves legislation in the form of directives, regulations, and conventions, but also binding decisions of the European Court of Justice in Luxembourg.[5] This process has been described by Lord Denning MR in a characteristically memorable way:

> The first and fundamental point is that the Treaty concerns only those matters which have a European element, that is to say, matters which affect people or property in the nine countries of the common market besides ourselves. The Treaty does not touch any of the matters which concern solely England and the people in it. These are still governed by English law. They are not affected by the Treaty. But when we come to matters with a European element, the Treaty is like an incoming tide. It flows into the estuaries and up the rivers. It cannot be held back, [sic] Parliament has decreed that the Treaty is henceforward to be part of our law. It is equal in force to any statute.[6]

The American reader may wonder at the significance to him of the tide of EEC law flowing up the Thames.[7] Nevertheless, part of the flotsam to be found floating on this tide is the draft UK/US convention for the reciprocal recognition and enforcement of judgments in civil matters.[8] This flotsam is certain to flow across the Atlantic and then up the Mississippi, or up the St. Lawrence seaway to the Great Lakes. The genesis of this draft convention is to be found, as implied above, in the Act of Accession

[1] [1972] OJ L73.

[2] The original Member States are Belgium, Federal Republic of Germany, France, Italy, Luxembourg, and the Netherlands.

[3] The United Kingdom, Denmark, and Ireland.

[4] Dagtoglou, (1978) 37 *CLJ* 76.

[5] See Dagtoglou, n. 4 above.

[6] *Bulmer Ltd.* v. *Bollinger SA* [1974] AC 401, 418.

[7] See Nadelmann, (1977) 41 *Law and Contemporary Problems* 54, 58–62.

[8] Draft convention providing for the reciprocal recognition and enforcement of judgments in civil matters, Cmnd. No. 6771 (1977) (hereafter cited as UK/US draft convention).

by the new Member States to the original EEC Treaties which was annexed to the 1972 Treaty of Accession.[9] Under Article 3(2) of the Act of Accession, the new Member States undertook to accede to the conventions provided for in Article 220 of the EEC Treaty, i.e., the Treaty of Rome.[10] One of these is the Convention on jurisdiction and enforcement of judgments in civil and commercial matters.[11] This Convention came into force among the six original Member States of the EEC in 1973. However, the new Member States were given until October 1978 to finalize their accession to it.[12] In order to better understand how this accord on jurisdiction and recognition of foreign judgments affects the United States and led to the draft UK/US Convention,[13] a brief account of it is necessary.

The 1968 Convention provides rules as to jurisdiction in civil and commercial matters and the basic rule[14] is that a person domiciled in an EEC State[15] shall be sued in the courts of that State. To that basic rule there are a considerable number of exceptions, such as a provision[16] that a person domiciled in an EEC State may also be sued in another Member State in a tort action if that is the place of the harm. There are also additional grounds of jurisdiction in insurance matters,[17] consumer contract claims,[18] and in certain cases a choice of forum is permitted.[19] Exceptionally exclusive grounds of jurisdiction are laid down irrespective of domicile in such matters as claims concerning rights *in rem* in immoveable property or the validity of patents, trademarks and the like.[20] The essential pattern, however, of the jurisdictional rules of the Convention is that they apply only to defendants domiciled in an EEC State. The corollary of this is that the Member States are free to provide whatever differing jurisdictional rules they like in cases falling outside the provisions of the Convention. So, for example, French courts may continue to assume jurisdiction on the basis that the plaintiff is a French national[21] provided the defendant is not domiciled elsewhere in the EEC.

[9] N. 1 above.

[10] Treaty Instituting the European Economic Community, done March 25 1957, 298 UNTS 11.

[11] The Convention on the jurisdiction of courts and the recognition and enforcement of judgments in civil and commercial matters (1968), [1972] OJ L299. (hereafter cited as Convention on jurisdiction of courts).

[12] The Convention on the accession of the new Member States to the 1968 Convention was signed in Luxembourg in October 1978, [1978] OJ L304.

[13] For a detailed analysis of the Convention, see Droz, *Compétence Judiciare et Effets des Jugements dans le Marché Commun: Etude de la Convention de Bruxelles du 27 Septembre 1968* (1972).

[14] Convention on jurisdiction of courts, n. 11 above, Art. 2.

[15] It is generally for each Member State to define domicile for itself: ibid., Arts. 52–3.

[16] Ibid., Art. 5(3).

[17] Ibid., Arts. 7–12A.

[18] Ibid., Arts. 13–15.

[19] Ibid., Art. 17.

[20] Ibid., Art. 16.

[21] C Civ, Arts. 14–15.

When one turns to the recognition provisions of the Convention,[22] the general scheme is that all judgments of a Member State shall be recognized elsewhere in the EEC, whether or not jurisdiction in the original State was assumed on the basis of the jurisdictional provisions of the Convention. Thus, a judgment in a Member State against a person domiciled in a country outside the EEC must, in principle, be recognized elsewhere in the EEC no matter how exorbitant the original grounds of jurisdiction. Let us return to, and develop, the French example just given.

An action is brought in France by a French national against a United States company with assets in the United States and the United Kingdom. The company has no connection with France or assets there, and the action is based on a breach of contract elsewhere. Judgment in that action would not be recognized at common law in England because the French court would not be regarded as having an internationally valid basis of jurisdiction over the defendant.[23] Nor would the judgment be recognized in England under a bilateral recognition convention concluded between the United Kingdom and France[24] within the terms of the Foreign Judgments (Reciprocal Enforcement) Act of 1933.[25] It would also seem to be unlikely that such a judgment would be recognized in the United States.[26] Furthermore, the English courts would not have taken jurisdiction over a claim by the French plaintiff against the American corporate defendant if the defendant was not doing business in the United Kingdom and there was no English connection other than having assets there. However, once the EEC Convention comes into force in the United Kingdom, all is changed. Although the English courts will continue to have no jurisdiction over such a case, they will be required to recognize and enforce the French judgment in England notwithstanding its internationally exorbitant nature. In that way, the English assets of the defendant company become available to the French plaintiff, and the tide of EEC law can be seen to have crossed the Atlantic.

THE NEED FOR A UK/US CONVENTION

The international repercussions of the EEC Convention have caused concern in, for example, the United States[27] and Australia,[28] but they were

[22] Convention on jurisdiction of courts, n. 11 above, Arts. 26, 30.
[23] Cheshire, *Private International Law* 9th edn. (1974), 632–47.
[24] Ibid., 667–72.
[25] Cheshire, *Private International Law*, n. 23 above, 667–72.
[26] Restatement (2d) of Conflict of Laws 1, para. 92, Comment (e) (1971).
[27] See, e.g., Nadelmann, n. 7 above, 58–62.
[28] Pryles and Trindade, (1974) 48 *Aus LJ* 185, 192–5.

not unforeseen by the drafters of the EEC Convention. The difficulty is intended to be met by Article 59:[29]

> This Convention shall not prevent a Contracting State from assuming, in a convention on the recognition and enforcement of judgments, an obligation towards a third State not to recognise judgments given in other Contracting States against defendants domiciled or habitually resident in the third State where, in cases provided for in Article 4, the judgment could only be founded on a ground of jurisdiction specified in the second paragraph of Article 3.[30]

What this means in practice is that, if the United States and the United Kingdom conclude a bilateral convention within the terms of Article 59, the United Kingdom would deny recognition to the French judgment in the earlier example. Here, therefore, are the origins of the draft UK/US Judgments Convention with which this essay is primarily concerned.[31] It is undoubtedly true that a bilateral convention on recognition and enforcement of judgments such as one following the pattern of the Foreign Judgments (Reciprocal Enforcement) Act of 1933,[32] has much, from a United Kingdom standpoint, to commend it in its own right. Indeed, there has been recent English judicial encouragement for some form of bilateral convention.[33] Nevertheless the major impetus for the present negotiations between the United States and the United Kingdom is the need for such a convention in order to shelter American defendants behind the protection afforded by Article 59 of the EEC Convention.

Negotiations on the UK/US Judgments Convention were carried on simultaneously with the United Kingdom's negotiations on accession to the EEC Convention. The bilateral negotiations resulted in a draft convention being initialled by officials from the United Kingdom and the United States in October 1976.[34] This draft did not bind the two States, and it was published in the United Kingdom in April 1977[35] to enable consideration to be given to it by all interested parties. Very considerable interest, and at times anxiety, has been shown in the draft convention on both sides of the Atlantic. Indeed, the opposition in the United Kingdom to the draft convention from various interested groups, especially the insurance industry, led to the announcement by the Attorney General in Parliament in June 1978 that 'further negotiations on it are probable.'[36]

[29] UK/US draft convention, n. 8 above.

[30] Ibid. The cases provided for in Art. 4 are those in which the defendant is domiciled outside a Member State. The grounds of jurisdiction listed in Art. 3 are the main 'exorbitant' grounds of jurisdiction in the Member States, including Arts. 14 and 15 of the French Civil Code used in the earlier example.

[31] See *Business Week* 21 February 1977, 50.

[32] Cheshire, *Private International Law*, n. 23 above.

[33] *Perry* v. *Zissis* [1977] 1 Lloyd's Rep 607, 614, 617.

[34] UK/US draft convention, n. 8 above. [35] Ibid.

[36] *Hansard*, HC Official Report, 952: 321 (1978).

Probability became reality in September 1978 when further negotiations took place.

THE DRAFT CONVENTION

It is not intended here to provide a detailed analysis of the provisions of the draft convention in its present published form. That has been done already by commentators in both the United States[37] and the United Kingdom.[38] My purpose is to examine some of the problems that the draft convention has been thought to pose when viewed through British eyes; but, to that end, it is necessary to describe in outline at least the salient features of the convention.

Its Provisions in Outline

The draft convention does not affect the grounds on which courts in the two countries may take jurisdiction. Its purpose is to lay down the circumstances in which the courts in one country will recognize and enforce judgments given in the other. The convention applies to all judgments given in civil and commercial matters but there are two sets of exclusions. The first gives an indication of that which falls outside 'civil and commercial matters,'[39] so that matters of family law,[40] status and capacity,[41] maintenance claims,[42] and matters of succession[43] are excluded, as are bankruptcy and winding-up matters,[44] questions of social security,[45] and the judicial administration of estates.[46] The second category[47] of exclusions relates to particular categories or aspects of judgments in civil and commercial matters which are not to be enforceable. These include not only interlocutory matters[48] and judgments for the disclosure of evidence,[49] but also judgments 'to the extent that they are for punitive or multiple damages',[50] and claims for taxes, customs duties, and the like.[51]

Even if a judgment falls within the draft convention, it may be denied recognition on a number of grounds,[52] some well-known at common law,

[37] Hays and Walker, (1976) 11 *Tex Int LJ* 421 (commenting on an earlier draft); Smit, (1977) 17 *Va J Int L* 443.

[38] Mathers, (1977) 127 *New LJ* 777, 819; North, (1978) 128 *New LJ* 315.

[39] UK/US draft convention, n. 8 above, Art. 2(3).

[40] Ibid., Art. 2(3)(b).

[41] Ibid., Art. 2(3)(a).

[42] Ibid., Art. 2(3)(c).

[43] Ibid., Art. 2(3)(d).

[44] Ibid., Art. 2(3)(e).

[45] Ibid., Art. 2(3)(f).

[46] Ibid., Art. 2(3)(g).

[47] Ibid., Art. 2(2). This category of judgments is excluded except for purposes of Art. 18, discussed below, p. 212.

[48] Ibid., Art. 2(2)(c).

[49] Ibid., Art. 2(2)(d).

[50] Ibid., Art. 2(2)(b).

[51] Ibid., Art. 2(2)(a).

[52] Ibid., Arts. 7–8.

such as the judgment being contrary to public policy[53] or having been obtained by fraud or without due notice having been given to the defendant.[54] There are a number of other grounds of non-recognition such as where the judgment is inconsistent with one in, or required to be recognized in, 'the court addressed'[55] (the court where recognition is sought), where the respondent enjoys immunity in the court addressed,[56] where the judgment to be enforced is for a sum of money which exceeds a statutory limit under the law of the court addressed which applies under that court's rules of private international law,[57] or where the court addressed would have applied its own law to the case and the judgment would disregard mandatory provisions of that law.[58] Some further limitations on recognition may be seen in that a judgment will be denied recognition unless it has 'binding effect' in the 'territory of origin,'[59] i.e., in the law district where originally granted. Further, recognition may be deferred if the judgment is subject to review in the court of origin and if the court addressed is satisfied that review has been or will be sought.[60] Nor is recognition required if, by reason of the subject matter or by the terms of a trust instrument, exclusive jurisdiction lies, under the law of the court addressed, in a court other than that of the territory of origin,[61] or if the original proceedings were brought in violation of an agreement by the parties to submit to another court.[62]

Once these hurdles are surmounted, the foreign judgment will be recognized if it satisfies one of a number of varied jurisdictional criteria.[63] In many ways these are the heart of the draft convention. Some of the grounds are similar to those which, in the United Kingdom at least, exist under the common law rules on recognition of foreign judgments, while others are more novel. Some of the grounds are general; others relate to particular types of claims.

The general grounds are as follows: where the person against whom the judgment is sought to be enforced was the plaintiff in the foreign proceedings;[64] where the habitual residence or principal place of business or place of incorporation of the defendant is within the jurisdiction of the foreign court;[65] where the defendant had a branch within the jurisdiction and the proceedings relate to business done through that branch;[66] where there exists an agreement in writing to submit to the jurisdiction;[67] and where an agent has been appointed to receive service within the jurisdiction in relation to proceedings concerning business conducted within the jurisdiction.[68]

[53] UK/US draft convention, n. 8 above, Art. 7(a).
[54] Ibid., Art. 7(b).
[55] Ibid., Art. 7(c)(i).
[56] Ibid., Art. 7(d).
[57] Ibid., Art. 8(c).
[58] Ibid., Art. 8(d).
[59] Ibid., Art. 4(1)(b).
[60] Ibid., Art. 5(1).
[61] Ibid., Art. 6(a), (c).
[62] Ibid., Art. 6(b).
[63] Ibid., Arts. 10–11.
[64] Ibid., Art. 10(a).
[65] Ibid., Art. 10(b).
[66] Ibid., Art. 10(c).
[67] Ibid., Art. 10(d).
[68] Ibid., Art. 10(e).

So far as the special grounds of jurisdiction are concerned, they may be summarized as follows: where the action is to determine rights of ownership or possession over moveable or immoveable property, the fact that the property was situated in the jurisdiction;[69] where the action concerns a trust, the fact that the trust's principal place of administration was within that territory or that the trust instrument provided that the court should have jurisdiction;[70] where, in a contractual claim, the parties reside or have their place of business within the jurisdiction and the contractual obligation was to be performed there;[71] where, in the case of a contract to supply goods or services, the contract was preceded by advertising in, or directed to, the territory of origin and the parties contemplated that the goods were to be used or the services performed in that jurisdiction;[72] where, in an action for damages for personal injury or damage to property, the acts occasioning the injury substantially occurred and the damage was suffered in the Contracting State (the United States or the United Kingdom) and either the injury or the damage occurred in the territory or origin (the individual American state or part of the United Kingdom whose judgment is in issue).[73]

So far as all these grounds of jurisdiction are concerned, the court addressed shall not be bound by any conclusions reached by the court of origin,[74] i.e., conclusions of law reached from findings of fact, such as where the defendant was habitually resident. However, the court addressed shall be bound by findings of fact made in the court of origin unless the respondent establishes they were incorrect, and if the defendant appeared in the court of origin and failed to challenge the jurisdiction, he cannot contest such findings in the court addressed.[75]

The provisions of the draft convention do not prevent the recognition of a judgment under the general law of the state addressed.[76] For instance, a court in the United Kingdom could recognize a United States judgment given in jurisdictional circumstances falling outside the convention if that was permitted at common law, e.g., submission to the jurisdiction. But, of course, such grounds of recognition could be abolished either at the time of implementation of the convention or at any time thereafter.

If a judgment satisfies all of the jurisdictional and other criteria for recognition, the procedures for recognition and enforcement are as laid down in Articles 14–16 of the convention. Simply put, the convention requires the production of a copy of the foreign judgment,[77] documentary evidence as to the notice given to the defendant[78] and the grounds on

[69] Ibid., Art. 10(h).
[70] Ibid., Art. 10(i).
[71] Ibid., Art. 10(g).
[72] Ibid., Art. 10(f).
[73] Ibid., Art. 10(j).
[74] Ibid., Art. 12.
[75] Ibid.
[76] Ibid., Art. 3, discussed further below, pp. 216–217.
[77] Ibid., Art. 15(2)(a).
[78] Ibid., Art. 15(2)(b).

which jurisdiction was assumed,[79] and a statement of the grounds relied upon to establish jurisdiction under the convention.[80] No special procedure is required for recognition. For enforcement the following procedures are to be followed. An American judgment will be registered in the United Kingdom by application to a court of competent jurisdiction,[81] i.e., in the appropriate part of the United Kingdom. Enforcement in the United States of a judgment from a United Kingdom court will involve application being made to the appropriate court exercising judgment in the territory where enforcement is sought, and enforcement is to be by the simplest and most rapid method provided in that jurisdiction for the enforcement of non-local judgments.[82]

The final provision of the draft convention to which reference ought to be made in this brief survey of its contents is Article 18 under the head of 'recognition and enforcement of third state judgments.' This relates to one of the justifications, from the United States point of view, for having such a convention. Subject to other treaty obligations, a judgment of a third state given against a national, domiciliary, or resident of one Contracting State, i.e., the United States or the United Kingdom, shall be denied recognition and enforcement by the other Contracting State if it would not have been recognized or enforced had it been given against a person similarly connected with the state addressed.[83] It is this provision which ties in with Article 59 of the EEC Convention[84] so that, in the earlier example,[85] a judgment by a French court, assuming jurisdiction on the basis of the plaintiff's French nationality, against a company domiciled in some part of the United States will be denied recognition in England under Article 18 of the draft convention because such judgment would be denied recognition had the defendant company been domiciled in some part of the United Kingdom.

Reactions to the Draft Convention

What sort of reception has this draft convention received? The fact that there is a need for it at all, in terms of the EEC Convention, has been the subject of sharp criticism in the United States. The EEC Convention has been castigated as discriminating against the United States with the corollary that 'this discrimination is indefensible on any ground.'[86] Indeed, it has been said of the effect of the original EEC Convention that:

[79] UK/US draft convention, n. 8 above, Art. 2(c).
[80] Ibid., Art. 16(2).
[81] Ibid., Art. 16(2).
[82] Ibid., Art. 16(1).
[83] Ibid., Art. 18(1)(a).
[84] Discussed above pp. 207–208.
[85] Above, pp. 206–207.
[86] Smit, n. 37 above, 468.

The Six of the Common Market—or persons for them—found it proper to challenge the rest of the world. No legal issue exists; the complaint is considered justified by commentators. The challenge should be taken up. The Six could be invited to agree on submission of the matter to the International Court of Justice. The test would be 'due process of law', a concept which has general standing.[87]

On the other hand, the draft UK/US convention has been welcomed in the United States on the wider ground that it will 'assure much needed uniformity in the recognition and enforcement of English judgments in the United States.'[88] But even this welcome for the draft convention has not been wholly uncritical. A general criticism is that the convention is too detailed and that it would have been better to have had a less specific convention—one that did not provide detailed solutions to problems which have not yet arisen, with general principles which would leave room for future development.[89] American commentators have also made detailed criticisms of the provisions of the draft convention, such as whether the exclusion of various types of judgment from the convention can be justified.[90]

While some commentators in the United Kingdom have guardedly welcomed the draft convention,[91] the general reaction has been hostile. Indeed, it has been described as 'an act of sheer folly.'[92] The hostility has come both from lawyers[93] and from commercial men.[94] Their criticisms have been both general and particular but have been made from a standpoint very different from that of the American criticism. The main attack has been on the ground that the convention is one which the United States is anxious to conclude because of the impact of the EEC Convention but that it is one which has few, if any, advantages for the United Kingdom and, indeed, contains major trading disadvantages. Hence come such comments as:

The commercial and economic effects on those manufacturers who export to the United States cannot be over-estimated and it seems likely that this could lead to many manufacturers withdrawing altogether from the American market. Thus the effect of this Convention will be very advantageous indeed to the U.S.A. and one cannot see anything but a great disadvantage for this country and its overseas trade. One has only to look at the comparative size of the population and the

[87] Nadelmann, n. 7 above, 61.

[88] Hay and Walker, n. 37 above, 449.

[89] Smit, n. 37 above, 445–6, 468.

[90] Ibid., 448–53. See also Hay and Walker, n. 37 above, 425–6.

[91] E.g. North, n. 38 above; Clark, *The Post Magazine & Ins. Monitor*, 25 May 1978, 1364–5.

[92] Payne, *J Chartered Ins Inst* April 1978, 57, 59.

[93] E.g., Memorandum submitted by a Joint Working Party of the Senate of the Inns of Court and the Bar and The Law Society to the Lord Chancellor's Office (June 1978) (hereafter cited as Joint Working Party Memorandum); (1978) 25 *Guardian Gazette* 202.

[94] Payne, *Policy* July 1977, 566, 576; Robertson, *Pol'y Holder Ins J* 26 May 1978, 972.

vast difference in the respective legal systems to wonder why it is necessary to put this legislation into effect. In most relevant cases this will result in what amounts to an abrogation of our legal system in favour of one containing so many features that are totally abhorrent to us.[95]

Similar strongly worded opposition to the draft Convention has come from lawyers:

We know of no-one who has been able to identify any *substantial* advantage that will accrue to the U.K. from the proposed Convention. It is a Treaty which confers benefits of a major nature on the U.S. without any corresponding benefit to the U.K. . . . . If there is to be a Treaty . . . it is imperative first that it eliminates certain important difficulties with which U.K. manufacturers and suppliers are at present faced and second that any extension of common law procedures should only be considered where no disadvantages to the U.K. will flow from it.[96]

Furthermore, the criticisms of the draft convention have not been limited to those which have appeared in the general press and in legal and other professional journals. It is clear that representations have been made to the United Kingdom government by a wide range of firms and trade associations, and there have been discussions between the United Kingdom government and representatives of the insurance industry and others.[97]

ASSESSMENT OF THE CRITICISMS OF THE DRAFT CONVENTION

All of this constitutes a picture of great anxiety and concern over the draft convention in the United Kingdom. Indeed, there is powerful opposition to the implementation of the draft convention in its published form, hence the need for further negotiations. Some of the criticism is over-stated and fails to set the draft convention against the background of the present law, while other criticisms point to real difficulties that the convention might pose for British exporters in the field of products liability.

One thing that has to be made clear from the outset, and which is forgotten at times in the United Kingdom criticism, is that judgments from courts in the United States are recognized in the United Kingdom under the common law rules for the recognition of foreign judgments.[98] The impact of the draft convention has to be assessed on the basis of how many more United States judgments will be recognized in the United Kingdom. Here there are factors to be weighed on both sides of the scales.

[95] Payne, n. 94 above, 566, 572.
[96] Joint Working Party Memorandum, n. 93 above.
[97] *Hansard*, HC Official Report, 952: 321 (1978).
[98] North, n. 23 above, 629–78.

Judgments are recognized in the United Kingdom already, but only if separate proceedings are taken on the judgment against the judgment debtor in the courts in the United Kingdom.[99] Under the convention, recognition and enforcement will be by the apparently easier process of registration. What is questionable is whether the fact that an action at common law has to be taken on the judgment is a serious deterrent in cases where large sums of money are in issue, especially when the judgment creditor may apply for summary judgment[100] on the ground that the debtor has no defence.[101] Nevertheless, enforcement may in theory be easier under the draft convention, and the very existence of such a convention could encourage enforcement.

Various types of judgments in civil and commercial matters are excluded from the draft convention.[102] Several of these merely mirror exceptions which are generally accepted at common law, such as judgments for taxes. One important exception in the convention concerns the exclusion of judgments 'to the extent that they are for punitive or multiple damages.'[103] In the United Kingdom, foreign judgments which are of a penal nature are not enforced,[104] but it has been suggested that this non-enforceability does not apply to foreign judgments for exemplary damages which may well be recognized in the United Kingdom.[105] That suggests that the draft convention provides an exception to recognition not found at common law and one which is of major significance given the anxieties expressed in the United Kingdom over recognition of United States products liability judgments which often contain a large element of exemplary damages.[106] The exclusion of judgments for multiple damages is most obviously aimed at treble damage awards in the United States in anti-trust cases.[107] While this is welcomed in the United Kingdom, there is a wider concern over judgments in anti-trust cases. The English courts have had to consider, at the highest level, the implications in England of American anti-trust proceedings against United Kingdom multinational companies,[108] and the prospect of anti-trust actions in the United States

[99] Ibid., 632. [100] RSC, O 14.

[101] *Grant* v. *Easton* (1883) 13 QBD 302. See also Dicey and Morris, *The Conflict of Laws*, 9th edn. (1973), 988–9.

[102] Above, p. 209. [103] UK/US draft convention, n. 8 above, Art. 2(2)(b).

[104] *Huntington* v. *Attrill* [1883] AC 150. See also Foreign Judgments (Reciprocal Enforcement) Act 1933, s. 1.

[105] *SA Consortium General Textiles* v. *Sun and Sand Agencies Ltd.* [1978] QB 279, 299–300.

[106] Cf. Smit, n. 37 above, 499, who opposes the inclusion of this exception in the draft convention.

[107] See also *Desforge* v. *West St Paul* 231 Minn 205; 42 NW 2d 633 (1950) (trespass to land).

[108] *Re Westinghouse Uranium Contract* [1978] AC 547. It should be pointed out that judgments for disclosure of evidence are not enforceable under the draft convention: Art. 2(2)(d).

against British companies has led to the criticism that the exception for multiple damages is too narrow. It has been argued, therefore, that all judgments in anti-trust matters should be excluded from the convention—an argument which is not unaffected by the passing by Congress of the Antitrust Improvement Act of 1976.[109]

While detailed criticism has been made of a number of the provisions of the draft convention,[110] the other major areas of difficulty are the questions of the survival of common law rules of recognition[111] and the convention's own jurisdictional rules.[112] Article 3 states that the convention shall not prevent the recognition in the court addressed of a judgment of a court of the territory of origin if that judgment would otherwise be recognized under the law of the court addressed. So, if an English court would recognize a New York judgment under common law rules not included in the convention, as where the defendant is regarded as having submitted to the jurisdiction of the New York court, that judgment would still be recognized in England by reason of Article 3 provided that English common law remained unchanged.

There is considerable conflict of opinion as to the effect of Article 3 on recognition in the United Kingdom which hinges on the words at the end of the last paragraph. As has been said, English courts will recognize foreign judgments if the defendant submitted or agreed to submit to the jurisdiction of the foreign court.[113] Furthermore, a much-criticized[114] decision of the Court of Appeal[115] has made it clear that an appearance made solely for the purpose of inviting the court to exercise its discretion not to exert jurisdiction that it has under its own local law constitutes submission. The court left open whether an appearance solely to protest against the jurisdiction of the court amounts to submission thereto, but it had no doubt that a conditional appearance with an application to set aside an order for service out of the jurisdiction does constitute voluntary submission.[116] If the principle of submission continued to apply to the

[109] 15 USC, paras. 1311–14 (1976).

[110] See e.g., Joint Working Party Memorandum, n. 93 above, where it is suggested that further consideration be given to such matters as the definition of interlocutory judgments in Art. 2(2)(c), the drafting of Art. 5(2), and whether provision should be made in Art. 7 for effect to be given to a set-off or counterclaim, and that the convention should not be applied to non-money judgments, such as reinstatement of plant, contribution by way of services, or a judgment requiring divestment of assets. It may well be, however, that this last point is adequately covered by the discretion in Art. 15(1) to refuse enforcement of an order for forms of relief other than the payment of money.

[111] UK/US draft convention, n. 8 above, Art. 3.

[112] Ibid., Art. 10.

[113] Dicey and Morris, *The Conflict of Laws*, 9th edn. (1973), 996–1000.

[114] See e.g., Collins, (1976) 92 *LQR* 268, 280–7; Solomons, (1976) 25 *ICLQ* 665; cf. Collier, (1975) 34 *CLJ* 219.

[115] *Henry* v. *Geoprosco International Ltd.* [1976] QB 726. (But see now the Civil Jurisdiction and Judgments Act 1982, s. 33).

[116] Ibid., 748.

recognition of American judgments in the United Kingdom after the draft convention was implemented, it is true that the jurisdictional bases for the recognition of foreign judgments in the United Kingdom would have been widened.

If, on the other hand, recognition of American judgments was restricted, in cases falling within the draft convention, to the recognition rules there provided, a major difficulty now faced by United Kingdom defendants would be overcome. As I have indicated elsewhere,[117] an English exporter with assets in say, New York, is faced with a dilemma if the proceedings, to which he believes he has a good defence, are brought against him in New York under jurisdictional circumstances falling outside the rules of the draft convention. He must choose between defending the proceedings in New York, which will amount in English eyes to submission, or letting the proceedings go by default, in which case a default judgment will be met out of his New York assets. The resolution of this dilemma lies in Article 3. If the United Kingdom implements the convention and leaves the common law rules untouched, the dilemma remains. If, however, the United Kingdom implements the convention and, at the same time, disapplies the common law rule based on submission to cases covered by the convention—and Article 3 would permit this—the dilemma disappears and a major source of criticism of the recognition rules also disappears. Some paragraphs of Article 10 of the draft convention would then amount to an addition to the bases of recognition, while abolition of submission as a basis would constitute a major subtraction. It must be noted that this is not an inevitable result of the convention as drafted, but rather a possible consequence of the way in which it might be implemented in the United Kingdom.[118]

Let us now turn to Article 10 of the draft convention which contains the main list of jurisdictional connecting factors in the court of origin which will justify recognition in the court addressed. It is at these bases, and the way in which they are likely to operate in relation to United Kingdom recognition of American products liability claims, that the full blast of English criticism has been directed. These jurisdictional bases, and the criticisms of them, need to be examined against the background of the existing law as to recognition. Two questions need to be asked: first, how far will the grounds of jurisdiction in the convention make recognition easier in the United Kingdom than it is now, and second, is the scope of the rule contained in the draft convention clear and unambiguous?

The general grounds of jurisdiction in Article 10 follow very much the pattern of the English common law recognition rules. There can be very

[117] North, n. 38 above, 316.
[118] See Joint Working Party Memorandum, n. 93 above, para. 14.

little objection to recognizing a foreign judgment where the person against whom recognition is sought brought the original proceedings.[119] This adds nothing to the common law, being a case of submission *par excellence*. Recognition based on the habitual residence of the defendant in the territory of origin at the time of the original proceedings[120] is like, but narrower than, the common law rule of recognition based on residence, or even mere presence, in the foreign jurisdiction. Such a narrowing of the common law rules is similarly to be found in the case of a defendant who is not a natural person, for then the appropriate connecting factor is that he had a principal place of business in the territory of origin or, if unincorporated, had his headquarters there. The common law rule merely requires the corporate defendant to carry on business in the foreign country at a definite and reasonably permanent place.[121] So far as definition is concerned, habitual residence is increasingly well-known as an international connecting factor and may be defined by an exchange of notes between the United Kingdom and the United States,[122] and it is equally suggested that the identification of a 'place of business' should cause little difficulty. Article 10 goes on to provide that the court of origin had jurisdiction if the defendant had 'a branch or other establishment' in the territory of origin and the proceedings were in respect of a transaction or occurrence arising from business done through that establishment. This is, again, similar to an existing jurisdictional rule: namely, that found in section 4(2)(a)(v) of the Foreign Judgments (Reciprocal Enforcement) Act of 1933.[123] While that statute does not apply to the recognition in the United Kingdom of United States judgments, it is a reasonable jurisdictional ground and one which has caused no difficulty in practice. The use of the phrase 'branch or other establishment' is novel, but it is a novelty which stems from the EEC Convention[124] and one to which the United Kingdom courts at least will have to become accustomed.

An agreement in writing or an oral agreement confirmed in writing to submit to the jurisdiction of the court[125] is a narrower ground than the common law one of submission. There is, however, a possibility that the requirement of writing, or written confirmation, may cause difficulty as it has in the interpretation of the EEC Convention by the European Court,[126] and one would hope for an amendment of this heading of juris-

[119] UK/US draft convention, n. 8 above, Art. 10(a).
[120] Ibid., Art. 10(b).
[121] *Littauer Glove Corp.* v. *F W Millington Ltd.* (1928) 44 TLR 746.
[122] UK/US draft convention, n. 8 above, Art. 22.
[123] See Dicey and Morris, n. 10 above, 1002.
[124] UK/US draft convention, n. 8 above, Art. 5(5). [125] Ibid., Art. 10(d).
[126] *Colzani* v. *Rüwa* Case 24/76 [1976] ECR 1831; *Galeries Segoura* v. *Bonakdarian* Case 25/76 [1976] ECR 1851.

diction along the same lines as the amendment now made to the EEC Convention.[127]

The final ground of jurisdiction is that of the appointment of, or legal duty to appoint, an agent to receive service within the territory of origin in relation to proceedings concerning business conducted there.[128] This is the general ground that has attracted most criticism in the United Kingdom, though it should not be forgotten that Article 10 has not escaped criticism in the United States, but that criticism has been for being too narrow, rather than too broad, in its effects.[129] The criticism of this general ground is directed primarily at jurisdiction being founded, internationally, on a legal duty to appoint an agent. British exporters to the United States often find themselves under a legal duty, by state law, to appoint agents to receive service, and there is a fear in the United Kingdom that the convention would encourage this practice. On the other hand, actual appointment of an agent to receive process, whether because of a legal duty to do so or otherwise, would appear to be an obvious and reasonable case of voluntary submission such as to justify assumption of jurisdiction.

It is, however, the special 'grounds of jurisdiction' where criticism has been the strongest and, in particular, those which could relate to products liability claims.[130] The first of these is Article 10(f):

> [I]n the case of a contract to supply goods or services the conclusion of the contract was preceded by an invitation to treat made by advertisement or otherwise either in or specifically directed to the territory of origin and the use of the goods or the performance of the services was in the contemplation of the parties to the contract to occur in whole or in substantial part in that territory.[131]

There is a provision in the EEC Convention[132] which covers much of the same ground but which is far more limited in scope in that it only applies to certain classes of consumer contract. The criticism of Article 10(f) that has been voiced is that it is too wide in scope. It is not in terms restricted to contractual claims. If it were, it would indeed be likely to arouse the anxieties of United Kingdom exporting producers and their insurers.[133] While it can be argued that it is not even necessary that there be a contract between plaintiff and defendant in order to bring a case within this

[127] See Convention on Jurisdiction of Courts, n. 11 above, Art. 17(1), as amended by the 1978 Accession Convention, [1978] OJ L304.

[128] UK/US draft convention, n. 8 above, Art. 10(e).

[129] Smit, n. 37 above, 559–62.

[130] There has been little opposition to Art. 10(h), jurisdiction over immoveables and tangible moveables based on the *situs* of the property, and Art. 10(i), jurisdiction over trusts based on the trust's principal place of administration.

[131] UK/US draft convention, n. 8 above.

[132] Convention on jurisdiction of courts, n. 11 above, Art. 13.

[133] North, n. 38 above, 316–17.

heading, so long as there is a contract with someone, there does seem to be justification for a jurisdiction at least founded on the substance of Article 10(f). A major step in any renegotiation would be to restrict it to contractual claims. Arguably, it might also be restricted to actions by consumers. Then if the plaintiff takes all the steps necessary for the conclusion of the contract in his own state in response to an invitation to negotiate made there, by advertising or otherwise, it is legitimate for the courts of that state to assume jurisdiction over his contractual claim. It is suggested that this is a legitimate ground in terms of consumer protection and not one which ought unreasonably to worry United Kingdom exporters.

Article 10(g) is, in terms, restricted to contractual claims, and it applies to those cases where the parties resided, or had a place of business, in the territory of origin at the time the contract was concluded and the obligation in issue was to be wholly or mainly performed there. This does not amount to much in the way of extension of the common law jurisdictional rule based on residence. It is different in that the relevant date for the residence is the date of contract and not of the proceedings, but it is qualified by the other significant requirements of the residence of both parties in the territory of origin and the need for the obligation to be performed there. The latter criterion may be novel in terms of the common law, but, again, it is one with which United Kingdom lawyers at least will become familiar in the EEC Convention.[134]

The one remaining ground of jurisdiction and the one most relevant to the fear of products liability judgments being enforceable in the United Kingdom is Article 10(j) which provides for jurisdiction where

> in the case of an action to recover damages for physical injuries to the person or for damage to tangible property, the acts or omissions that occasioned the injury or damage substantially occurred, and the injury or damage was suffered, in the Contracting State in which the court of origin was exercising jurisdiction, and either those acts or omissions substantially occurred or that injury or damage was suffered in the territory of origin.[135]

The effect of this can best be illustrated by one example from a United Kingdom viewpoint. An English company exports machinery to the United States to be assembled there. The company's employees in New York put the machinery together in a negligent manner, and when the machinery is used in Illinois, the plaintiff is injured there. A judgment of an Illinois court would fall for recognition in England by reason of Article 10(j). This is because the act or omission causing the injury occurred and the injury was suffered in the Contracting State, i.e., the

[134] Convention on jurisdiction of courts, n. 11 above, Art. 5(1).
[135] UK/US draft convention, n. 8 above.

United States, and the injury was suffered in Illinois, the territory of origin.

At common law, there is no specific ground of recognition based on the commission of a tort, or of any element thereof, within the jurisdiction. However, Article 10(j) is only of significance in those cases where the defendant does not have a sufficient business nexus with the territory of origin so as to satisfy the general heads of jurisdiction of Article 10. At first sight, the likelihood of Article 10(j) resulting in English exporters being exposed to an increased number of United States products liability claims enforced in England is slight, for the act or omission on which the action is based must have substantially occurred in the United States. If a product is defective, this is usually attributable to its manufacture, and that will have taken place in England. No doubt cases of misconduct in the United States could occur, as in the example given earlier of the export of machinery to be assembled abroad, but even then only if the improper assembly in the United States is by the exporter.

One particular situation has, however, given rise to a good deal of alarm and that relates to inadequate warnings. If goods are exported from England to the United States and they fail to display what, in the United States, is regarded as an adequate warning (for example, as to their proper use) it is certainly arguable that the failure to warn occurs in the United States.[136] The anxiety of English manufacturers and their insurers[137] is exacerbated by the judicial attitude of some courts in the United States, as to the wide range of circumstances where there has been a failure to warn of the dangers of a product.[138]

A further possible danger seen in the United Kingdom[139] is that American courts may interpret the phrase 'the acts or omissions that occasioned the injury or damage' as including a sale or resale in the United States of goods manufactured in England, i.e., putting the object into the stream of commerce. This is a fear which ignores Article 12 of the draft convention, for the court addressed, i.e., the English court in such a case, is not bound by any conclusions reached by the court of origin relevant to the application of Article 10. While the English court is usually bound by findings of fact, a finding as to where an act or omission substantially occurred is a conclusion of law rather than a finding of fact.

[136] *Distillers Co. (Biochemicals)* v. *Thompson* [1971] AC 458.

[137] See Payne, n. 92 above, 57.

[138] Owles, (1978) 128 *New LJ* 1014.

[139] Joint Working Party Memorandum, n. 93 above, para. 50.

CONCLUSIONS

There is no doubt that opposition in the United Kingdom to the present draft of the UK/US convention is well organized, articulate, and, so far as it has led to further negotiations, effective. Whether it is wholly justified is another matter. It is clear that, in some respects, the convention will have the effect that American judgments will be more readily recognized in the United Kingdom; in other respects, and perhaps to a lesser degree, they will cease to be recognized. The additional burden on United Kingdom defendants of American judgments not being recognized here cannot be said to justify the weight of opposition there has been to this draft convention. There are other reasons for it. The draft convention seems to have concentrated the minds of manufacturers and insurers on the possibility of United States judgments being enforced here in products liability cases in a way that the present common law rules never have. This is not really surprising because the possibility of change invites comment and discussion. However, many of the criticisms of the draft convention which have been put forward seem just as relevant to the present common law rules on recognition, e.g., the high level of damage awards, including exemplary damages. If, under the present law, English manufacturers were regularly subjected to actions in the English courts for the enforcement against them of American judgments, then any extension of that situation would obviously cause anxiety, but there is no evidence that this is what does happen or that the anxieties voiced over the convention's rules have been voiced over similar common law rules.

A further reason for anxiety seems to be that a variety of bodies have recommended either in the United Kingdom context,[140] or in a wider European context,[141] that some form of strict products liability should be introduced. There is a fear on the part of manufacturers that this will lead to a 'claims explosion' in the United Kingdom, even though the legal background of American products liability is very different.[142] The possibility of the introduction of strict products liability in the United Kingdom is a very live issue at the moment, and this has focused attention on the development of products liability law in the United States,

[140] Report of the Law Commissions on Liability for Defective Products, Law Com. No. 82, (1977); Report of the Commission on Civil Liability and Compensation for Personal Injury, Cmd. No. 7054–I, 255–74 (1978).

[141] Council of Europe Convention on Products Liability in Regard to Personal Injury and Death (1977); proposal for a Council Directive relating to the Approximation of the Laws, Regulations and Administrative Provisions of the Member States Concerning Liability for Defective Products, Bull. Eur. Comm. (Supp 1976). (See now the final Directive No. 85/374 EC implemented in the UK by Part I of the Consumer Protection Act 1987.)

[142] North, n. 38 above, 318.

and thus on the possibility of such American judgments being enforced in the United Kingdom.

Not everyone is opposed to the draft convention, for it has been said that 'the interests of both insurers and the public would best be served by ratification of the Convention and subsequent implementation.'[143] Furthermore, the opposition to it is concentrated in the field of products liability. This opposition ignores the advantages that may come to English plaintiffs who may wish to enforce judgments in the United States, especially in the majority of states which have not adopted the Uniform Money Judgments Recognition Act.[144] It ignores the wide international justification for mutual recognition of judgments in all commercial fields, not just products liability. Indeed, it was this which prompted Roskill LJ to comment:

> There is, therefore, no provision between our two countries for reciprocal enforcement. Some of us, I hope it is not out of place to say, have long regretted this, and this case is perhaps a good illustration . . . of how the difficulties which have arisen could have been avoided if [the Foreign Judgments (Reciprocal Enforcement) Act] applied between this country and the United States.[145]

Nevertheless, there seems little doubt that, without significant amendment, at least in so far as products liability claims and the level of damages for which such judgments may be enforced are concerned, there will be continued vigorous opposition in the United Kingdom to the implementation of this draft convention.

[143] Clark, n. 91 above, 1364. [144] Hay and Walker, n. 37 above, 449.
[145] *Perry* v. *Zissis* [1977] 1 Lloyd's Rep 607, 614, 617.

9

Hague Conventions and the Reform of English Conflict of Laws

INTRODUCTION

By mid-1980, the United Kingdom had ratified seven conventions concluded by the Hague Conference on Private International Law, and signed one other.[1] There has been no change in the United Kingdom position in relation to the conventions existing at that date,[2] but there have been five further conventions concluded since then, two of which the United Kingdom has ratified and implemented.[3] On a wider plane, there has been continuing progress in broadening the scope of the work of the Hague Conference. Membership of the Conference has expanded over the past decade or so from twenty-nine members in 1980 to thirty-seven today. Furthermore, another twenty-eight States have acceded to one or more Hague Conventions.

Some consideration is given below[4] to the extent to which the work of the Hague Conference can have a sterilizing effect on the law reform

Reprinted with the permission of the Dalhousie Law Journal from (1981) 6 *Dalhousie LJ* 417–48. This is a slightly expanded version of the Sixth Horace E. Read Memorial Lecture delivered at the Dalhousie Law School on 29 September 1980.

[1] At that time Canada, whose activities within the Hague Conference are discussed below, pp. 233–236, had not signed, ratified or acceded to any. The current Canadian position is that it has signed the (1984) Convention on the law applicable to trusts and on their recognition, acceded to the (1965) Convention on the service abroad of judicial and extrajudicial documents in civil or commercial matters, and ratified the (1980) Convention on the civil aspects of international child abduction.

[2] It might, however, be noted that the (1965) convention on jurisdiction, applicable law and recognition of decrees relating to adoptions, below, pp. 239–240, is now embodied in the Adoption Act 1976, whilst the (1970) Convention on the recognition of divorces and judicial separations, below, pp. 238–239, is now given effect by the Family Law Act 1986, Part II.

[3] The (1980) Convention on the civil aspects of international child abduction (discussed below, pp. 249–250), implemented in the Child Abduction and Custody Act 1985, Part I, and the (1984) Convention on the law applicable to trusts and on their recognition, implemented in the Recognition of Trusts Act 1987. Both these statutes are interesting in that they exemplify a more modern trend in the implementation of private international law conventions of scheduling the conventions to the main Acts, rather than as in the past the substance of the convention being embodied in English legislative form, see below pp. 231. Other major examples of this more recent trend are the Civil Jurisdiction and Judgments Act 1982 and the Contracts (Applicable Law) Act 1990.

[4] Pp. 238–243.

process. The particular example is taken of the way in which negotiation of the (1976) Convention on celebration and recognition of the validity of marriages and later consideration of its merits impeded the process of reform of choice of law rules in marriage and on the recognition of foreign nullity decrees. That Convention has proved to be far from successful[5] and only three countries have ratified it, though one of those is Australia where it is given effect by the Marriage Amendment Act 1985. In the United Kingdom, it was firmly rejected by the Law Commissions as a basis for law reform, given that the Government had indicated that it did not propose to sign or ratify the Convention.[6] It was, however, not until 1984 that the Law Commissions were able to make recommendations on reform of the rules relating to the recognition of foreign nullity decrees,[7] and only in 1987 that their final report on choice of law in marriage was published.[8] The sterilization effect of the Hague Marriage Convention on the latter topic was, in the event, very limited because the Commissions chose to make few proposals for change;[9] but substantial reform of the nullity recognition rules was held up for well over a decade.

The suggestion is made below[10] that conventions designed to improve the international administration of justice, i.e. conventions which are primarily of a procedural or administrative nature, have proved to be amongst the most successful of the Hague Conventions. This is certainly borne out by one of the two more recent conventions which the United Kingdom has implemented, namely the (1980) Convention on the civil aspects of international child abduction.[11] It has, to date, been ratified or acceded to by twenty-four States, and signed by three more. There is no doubt that in the United Kingdom the Convention and its implementing legislation (Part I of the Child Custody and Abduction Act 1985) is increasingly being relied on[12] to seek the return both to and from the United Kingdom of children who have been wrongfully removed from or to other countries which are parties to the Convention. A great strength of the Convention is its provision of effective international procedures for

[5] See further North, [1980] I *Hague Recueil* 9, 92–8; [1990] I *Hague Recueil* 9, 74–81.

[6] Law Com. Working Paper No. 89 (1985), para. 1.3 and App. A, and see Law Com. No. 137 (1984), para. 1.3.

[7] Law Com. No. 137 (1984), implemented by the Family Law Act 1985, Part II.

[8] Law Com. No. 165 (1987).

[9] Ibid., paras. 2.11–2.15. Such proposals as they did make were given effect by the Foreign Marriage (Amendment) Act 1988.

[10] See pp. 245–247.

[11] It is referred to briefly below, pp. 249–250, in its draft form. Another of the more recent and 'procedural' conventions is the (1980) Convention on international access to justice, but this has not attracted support from the UK or any other common law jurisdiction. For Canadian criticism of this Convention, see the *Proceedings of the Sixty-Fourth Annual Meeting of the Uniform Law Conference of Canada* (1982), 423–4.

[12] See Cheshire and North, *Private International Law*, 12th edn. (1992), 733–7.

a child to be found and returned, though their true effectiveness does depend on the vigour with which they are implemented and pursued in each country which is a party to the Convention. It is noteworthy that, so far as the United Kingdom is concerned, matters can be dealt with very effectively, as is illustrated by one decision where less than three months elapsed between a request by the Australian authorities for the return of a child brought to England and the decision of the House of Lords on the litigation and appeals which ensued.[13]

The Child Abduction Convention in its draft form is also considered below[14] in the context of an examination of the situation where various international agencies and national law reform bodies have become involved in the same issue at the same time—a good indication, of course, of such issue's current social importance. This multiplicity of activity in the field of child custody and abduction issues is well illustrated by the fact that in the United Kingdom there are now three sets of relevant statutory provisions. As a result of the work of the Law Commissions,[15] there is a uniform set of jurisdictional rules for courts hearing custody matters[16] in the United Kingdom, coupled with an effective and virtually automatic system for the recognition of the orders of such courts throughout the United Kingdom.[17] Secondly, the Hague Child Abduction Convention is given effect by Part I of the Child Custody and Abduction Act 1985, whilst, thirdly, Part II of that Act gives effect to the (1980) Council of Europe Convention on recognition and enforcement of decisions concerning custody of children and on the restoration of custody of children.[18] As indicated below,[19] there are significant differences between the two Conventions, both as to their scope and as to the bases for refusing the return of a child. Nevertheless, some twelve countries, including the United Kingdom, are parties to both Conventions—perhaps on the principle that you cannot have too much of a good thing. There seems, however, to be a growing view[20] that, if a case falls within both, the person seeking the return of the child is better advised to rely on the Hague Convention.[21]

Another example given below[22] of possibly conflicting activities in the

[13] *Re J (A Minor) (Abduction: Custody Rights)* [1990] 2 AC 562.

[14] See pp. 249–250. [15] Law Com. No. 138 (1985).

[16] The term 'custody order' is no longer used in English domestic legislation, see Children Act 1989, s. 8.

[17] Family Law Act 1986, Part I, amended for England and Wales by the Children Act 1989; see Cheshire and North, *Private International Law*, 12th edn. (1992), 721–33.

[18] The European Convention is considered below, pp. 249–250. [19] See p. 250.

[20] Cheshire and North, *Private International Law*, 740.

[21] The Institute of International Law is currently giving active consideration to the question as to how wider international agreement and co-operation in child abduction matters might be achieved, using the Hague Convention as the model for its deliberations.

[22] See pp. 251–252.

same field is that of obligations, with a potential for conflict between work in the European Community and the Hague Conference. It was in 1980 that the then Member States of the European Community concluded in Rome the Convention on the law applicable to contractual obligations, which came into force in 1991 and was given effect in the United Kingdom by the Contracts (Applicable Law) Act 1990.[23] There seems little doubt that the existence of this choice of law convention has inhibited acceptance by European Community Member States of Hague Conventions in related fields. For example, since 1980, there have been no further ratifications by such States of the 1955 Hague Convention on the law applicable to international sale of goods. Of course that may substantially be due to the conclusion in 1986 of a further Hague Convention on the law applicable to contracts for the international sale of goods. However, to date, no European Community Member State has ratified this later Convention and, of such States, only the Netherlands has signed it. There seems still to be no prospect that the United Kingdom will sign or ratify either Hague Sales Convention.[24] It is also suggested below[25] that European Community activity in the field of choice of law for non-contractual obligations would be likely to inhibit United Kingdom acceptance of the Hague Traffic Accidents Convention of 1971 and the Products Liability Convention of 1973. In fact, no progress at all has been made within the European Community on the drafting of a non-contractual obligations convention, and none seems likely.[26] This has not, however, made the two Hague Conventions in this field appear any more acceptable in the United Kingdom, and the Law Commissions have, in effect, recommended that effect should not be given to them.[27]

One final recent convention to which reference might be made is the (1984) Convention on the law applicable to trusts and on their recognition, implemented in the United Kingdom by the Recognition of Trusts Act 1987.[28] As its title implies the Convention, having defined the types of trust which fall within its scope,[29] makes provision for the determination of the law to govern the trust, both where the settlor has made a choice of the governing law[30] and in the absence of such choice.[31] It then goes on to provide that a trust created in accordance with the choice of law rules laid down in the Convention shall be recognized as a trust and

[23] The Rome Convention is more fully discussed, above, pp. 23–50.

[24] For a critical analysis of the Convention, see McLachlan, (1986) 102 *LQR* 591; but contrast Pellichet, [1987] I *Hague Recueil* 9.

[25] See p. 252. [26] See above, pp. 83–88.

[27] Law Com. Working Paper No. 87 (1984), paras. 5.5, 5.11–5.12; Law Com. No. 193 (1990), para. 3.22.

[28] On which see Cheshire and North, *Private International Law*, 12th edn. (1992), 880–91.

[29] Arts. 2, 3 and 20; and see Recognition of Trusts Act 1987, s. 1(2).

[30] Art. 6. [31] Art. 7.

to stipulate what are the implications and effects of recognition.[32] United Kingdom response to the conclusion of this Convention in 1984 was speedy and interesting. It was remarkably speedy in that the whole process of consultation, drafting and legislative implementation took only two-and-a-half years from the date when the Convention was concluded at The Hague. For law reform that has to be regarded as rapid implementation. Such speed of response is interesting for two reasons. First, it illustrates the fact that implementation is far more likely where the convention rules are not significantly controversial and where the existing English rules of private international law are unclear, unformed and uncertain, as was the case with the choice of law rules for trusts. Second, the United Kingdom, as with other common law countries where the trust is a familiar concept, had a real self-interest in seeing widespread implementation of the Trusts Convention, especially in civil law countries which would, as a consequence and perhaps for the first time, recognize trusts. If the common law countries did not readily implement the Convention, the chances of civil law countries doing so was likely to be diminished. It is not without significance that, out of the eight countries which have ratified or signed the Convention to date, four are common law jurisdictions.[33]

* * *

[32] Arts. 11–14.

[33] The most recent Hague Convention is that prepared in 1988 on the law applicable to succession to the estates of deceased persons. Whilst it undoubtedly contains features which constitute an improvement on the current choice of law rules for testate and intestate succession, I have suggested elsewhere that it is seriously flawed as a law reform measure, and that the need for international harmonization in this field does not appear to have been demonstrated; see North, [1990] I *Hague Recueil* 9, 280–2, and see above, p. 199. The Lord Chancellor's Department issued a Consultation Paper in 1990 inviting views on whether the UK should sign and ratify the Convention. So far it has done neither. In fact only two countries have signed it and none has ratified.

INTRODUCTION

OVER twenty years ago, Horace Read said: 'The first half of this century has seen the emergence of legislation as the chief instrument of change and innovation in the law'.[1] True though this comment was in 1959, it has received added force in the common law world[2] by the 'explosion of law reform'[3] which has taken place since the mid-sixties. The creation of permanent statutory law reform agencies has tilted the balance even further towards legislation as the instrument of legal change. This is for two reasons. Despite the occasional judicial attempt to jump the legislative gun,[4] the means of implementing proposals from law reform commissions is by means of legislation, and this is assisted by the practice of many such bodies of appending draft Bills to their final reports. The fact that such agencies exist seems in recent years, in England at least, to have caused the judges in a number of instances to argue that major change in the law is not for them, but for the legislature. For instance, Lord Simon of Glaisdale dissented in the landmark decision of the House of Lords in *Miliangos* v. *George Frank (Textiles) Ltd.*,[5] which decided that English courts could in future give judgment in foreign currencies, not just in sterling, the foreign currency to be converted into sterling as at the date when the court authorizes enforcement of the judgment. In Lord Simon's view:

> I do not think that this is a law reform which should or can be properly imposed by judges; it is, on the contrary, essentially a decision which demands a far wider range of review than is available to courts following our traditional and valuable adversary system—the sort of review compassed by an interdepartmental committee.[6]

This echoes the forceful approach of Lord Kilbrandon in a criminal appeal to the House of Lords the previous year where he said:

[1] Read, (1959) 13 *U Tor LJ* 81. [2] Especially in the Commonwealth.

[3] Gower, (1973) 23 *U Tor LJ* 257.

[4] *Levison* v. *Patent Carpet Cleaning Co. Ltd.* [1978] QB 69 where Lord Denning MR, at p. 79, said:

> In such circumstances as here the Law Commission in 1975 recommended that a term which exempts the stronger party from his ordinary common law liability should not be given effect except when it is reasonable . . . and there is a bill now before Parliament which gives effect to the test of reasonableness. This is a gratifying piece of law reform: but I do not think we need wait for that bill to be passed into law. You never know what may happen to a bill.

See now the Unfair Contract Terms Act 1977.

[5] [1976] AC 443.

[6] Ibid., 480. A broadly based Working Party has, in fact, assisted the Law Commission with further work in the field of foreign money liabilities; see Law Commission Fourteenth Annual Report 1978–9 (1980), Law Com. No. 97 (1980), para. 2.43 and App. 2.

If there is one lesson which has been learned since the setting up of the Law Commission it is this, that law reform by lawyers for lawyers (unless in exceptionally technical matters) is not socially acceptable. An alteration in a fundamental doctrine of our law . . . could not properly be given effect to save after the widest reference to interests, both social and intellectual, far transcending those available in the judicial committee of your Lordships' House.[7]

More recently, the House of Lords[8] has refused to alter the rule that the English courts will not take jurisdiction over actions concerning title to foreign land.[9] Lord Wilberforce took the view that the nature of the rule does not favour revision (assuming such to be logically desirable) by judicial decision, but rather by legislation.[10]

It may not noted that two of these House of Lords decisions in which anxiety has been expressed about judicial law-making concern issues in the conflict of laws. Here there is a further dimension to the question of law reform—the desire to achieve reform and harmonization through widespread international agreement. Not only does such reform come about by legislation but by legislation implementing an internationally agreed convention. United Kingdom legislative practice with conflict of laws conventions has been to turn the Convention rules into our traditional statutory form, rather than to have a short Act with the Convention given effect to in a Schedule, as tends often to be done in uniform substantive law conventions.[11]

There are a number of international law reform bodies which over the years have concerned themselves with matters of the conflict of laws. Some of these have been regional, such as the developments in Latin America in the Montevideo Treaties of 1889 and 1940 and the Bustamante Code of 1928, the five Scandinavian Conventions concluded between 1931 and 1934, the draft Benelux uniform laws of 1951 and 1968, the work of the Council of Europe and, most recently, the activities of the EEC in the field of harmonization of private international law.[12] Other activity has been on a wider international basis and some problems affecting the conflict of laws have been dealt with by the Unidroit Institute in Rome, by the United Nations in the United Nations Commission on International Trade Law (UNCITRAL) and, again more recently, by the Commonwealth Secretariat, particularly in the field of

[7] *DPP* v. *Lynch* [1975] AC 653, 700.

[8] *Hesperides Hotels* v. *Aegean Turkish Holidays Ltd.* [1979] AC 509.

[9] *British South Africa Co.* v. *Companhia de Moçambique* [1893] AC 602.

[10] [1979] AC 509, 537.

[11] E.g. transport conventions, see Carriage of Goods by Sea Act 1971; Carriage of Passengers by Road Act 1974; and see the Uniform Laws on International Sales Act 1967.

[12] See the Convention on jurisdiction and the enforcement of judgments in civil and commercial matters (1968) and its amending Convention of 1978; and most recently the Convention on the law applicable to contractual obligations (1980).

recognition of foreign judgments and child custody disputes. Undoubtedly, however, the most significant international body in the field of reform and harmonization of the conflict of laws has been the Hague Conference on Private International Law.

THE HAGUE CONFERENCE ON PRIVATE INTERNATIONAL LAW

The idea of an international conference for the codification of private international law had been actively fostered in the late nineteenth century by the Italian scholar (and Foreign Minister) Mancini.[13] This idea came to fruition some five years after his death, with the first meeting of the Hague Conference on Private International Law in 1893, under the chairmanship of the Dutch scholar, Asser, who presided over the next three conferences as well.[14] The early work of the Conference between 1893 and 1904 resulted in the conclusion of conventions on marriage, divorce, guardianship, the effects of marriage on the spouses' property rights, judicial pronouncements of legal incapacity, and civil procedure. There was then a gap in the work of the Conference until sessions in 1925 and 1928, but none of the Conventions agreed at these two later sessions were ever brought into force. The early work of the Conference had two particular interconnected characteristics. It was dominated by the principle of nationality as a connecting factor, and was essentially a regional conference, being restricted to European states. Indeed the early Conventions have been scathingly criticized by Kahn-Freund as an expression of 'Continental European parochialism which mistook Europe for the world'.[15]

There was no meeting of the Conference after 1928 until its renaissance in 1951 when the Member States laid down, in a separate Treaty, a new statute for the Conference. They also established the Permanent Bureau as a small full time secretariat which operates under the guidance of the Netherlands Standing Government Committee, described by a former Secretary-General as 'the very heart of the Hague Conference'.[16] Since 1951 there have been regular sessions of the conference, usually every four years, which have resulted in the conclusion of nearly thirty conventions. The membership of the Conference has grown and diversified. No longer is it exclusively a Western European, civil law based regional body. The membership of twenty-nine countries includes not only all the countries of Western Europe, both common and civil law jurisdictions,

[13] For full accounts of the history of the Hague Conference, see Offerhaus, (1959) 16 *Annuaire Suisse de droit international* 27; van Hoogstraten, (1963) 12 *ICLQ* 148; Nadelmann, (1965) 30 *Law and Contemporary Problems* 291; Vitta, [1969] I *Hague Recueil* 113, 133–52; Nadelmann, (1972) 19 *Netherlands Int Law Rev* 107.

[14] 1894, 1900, 1904.

[15] [1974] III *Hague Recueil* 139, 190.

[16] Van Hoogstraten, (1963) 12 *ICLQ* 148, 152.

but also Canada and the United States, three South American states (Argentina, Suriname, and Venezuela) as well as Australia, Czechoslovakia, Egypt, Israel, Japan and Yugoslavia. With this truly international membership has come the need, and willingness, to bridge the often substantial legal differences between the Member States, seen most forcibly in the abandonment of nationality as the exclusive connecting factor.[17] Indeed the movement away from Mancini's principle of nationality has been the price to be paid for a movement towards his other guiding principle of universality.[18]

CANADA AND THE HAGUE CONFERENCE

Canada joined the Hague Conference on October 7, 1968, but the record of Canadian acceptance of Hague Conventions cannot be described as impressive. Canada has never signed, ratified or acceded to any Hague Convention, whether concluded before or after Canada joined the deliberations of the Hague Conference. That apparently gloomy picture can be lightened a little. Formal accession by Canada to any convention concluded before 1968 poses very real difficulties because none of those earlier conventions contains a federal-state clause in a form appropriate to Canada's federal system.[19] Nevertheless, these earlier Hague Conventions have not been wholly ignored in Canada. The main arena for their consideration has been the annual meetings of the Conference of Commissioners of Uniformity of Legislation in Canada. This body, in whose work Horace Read played a prominent and distinguished part for many years, produced the Uniform Wills Act in 1929 and Part II of this Act dealt with the Conflict of Laws. Despite the fact that this Part was revised in 1953,[20] further consideration was given in 1959 to the possibility of amending these uniform provisions,[21] a project which was shelved the following year when it became apparent that the Hague Conference would consider the question of the formal validity of wills.[22] In 1961 the Hague Conference concluded a Convention on the conflict of laws

[17] See de Winter, [1969] III *Hague Recueil* 349.

[18] Vitta, [1969] I *Hague Recueil* 113, 150.

[19] Proceedings of the Fifty-fifth Annual Meeting of the Conference of Commissioners on Uniformity of Legislation in Canada (1973), 124.

[20] Proceedings of the Thirty-fifth Annual Meeting of the Conference of Commissioners on Uniformity of Legislation in Canada (1953), 51. These revised provisions were substantially enacted in Ontario (1954), Newfoundland (1955), New Brunswick (1959), Alberta (1960), and British Columbia (1960).

[21] Proceedings of the Forty-first Annual Meeting of the Conference of Commissioners on Uniformity of Legislation in Canada (1959), 132–6.

[22] Proceedings of the Forty-second Annual Meeting of the Conference of Commissioners on Uniformity of Legislation in Canada (1960), 90.

relating to the form of testamentary dispositions and this Convention was implemented in the United Kingdom by the Wills Act 1963. In 1966 the uniformity commissioners substantially adopted[23] that legislation as an amendment to that part of the Uniform Wills Act dealing with the conflict of laws relating to formal validity. However, only three Provinces[24] have adopted these reformed choice of law rules and the fact that the attempt to implement the 1961 Hague Convention in Canada has been relatively unsuccessful has been the source of some criticism.[25] One reason is, perhaps, that the English model of the Wills Act 1963 fits very uneasily into the present general structure of the Uniform Wills Act.[26] Nevertheless, this work on the law of wills does provide a legal landmark as the first attempt to translate into Canadian law the substance of a Hague Convention.[27]

The conflict rules in the Uniform Wills Act are not the only example of such activity and we must turn again to the work of the Uniformity Commissioners, this time in the field of tort law. At the Eleventh Session of the Hague Conference on Private International Law (1968) a convention was adopted on the law applicable to traffic accidents, and a report on this convention was considered by the Uniformity Commissioners in 1970.[28] They recommended the adoption of a Uniform Conflict of Laws (Traffic Accidents) Act modelled on the Hague Convention.[29] Although this Uniform Act has, so far, only formed the basis for legislation in the Yukon Territory,[30] it marks a further step (albeit small) in the acceptance in Canada of Hague Conventions.

Although no further legislative steps appear to have been taken to implement other Hague Conventions in Canada, it should not be assumed that Canada has abandoned interest in the work of the Hague Conference. Far from it. Not only has Canada been most effectively represented at all the Sessions of the Hague Conference since 1968, close liaison has been established between the Department of Justice and the Uniformity Commissioners so far as advice in the preparation for the various meetings and in considering the conventions which emerge are

[23] Proceedings of the Forty-eighth Annual Meeting of the Conference of Commissioners on Uniformity of Legislation in Canada (1966), 23–4, 131–40.

[24] Manitoba, Act to amend the Wills Act 1975, ss. 37–44; Newfoundland, Wills (Amendment) Act 1976, s. 1; and Ontario, Succession Law Reform Act 1977, ss. 34–41. See also the Law Reform Commission of British Columbia, Working Paper No. 28: The Making and Revocation of Wills (1980), ch. VII.

[25] Casswell, (1977) 15 *Osgoode Hall L Rev* 165.

[26] Castel, *Canadian Conflict of Laws* (1977), ii: 460–1.

[27] It is significant that the attempt was by the use of a model law, rather than direct Canadian accession to the Convention under Art. 16, and see below, pp. 255–256.

[28] Proceedings of the Fifty-second Annual Meeting of the Conference of Commissioners on Uniformity of Legislation in Canada (1970), 38, 215–62.

[29] Ibid., 40, 263–70.

[30] Conflict of Laws (Traffic Accidents) Ordinance, OY 1972 (First Session) c. 3.

concerned, and to this end a Special Committee on International Conventions on Private International Law was set up in 1971.[31] This Committee works closely with the Department of Justice's Advisory Group on Private International Law and Unification of Law.

So far as implementation is concerned, the work of these bodies over the past few years seems to have led them to the following conclusions. Direct implementation of Hague Conventions concluded before Canada joined the Hague Conference will be impossible because of the absence from those earlier conventions of a satisfactory federal-state clause. In virtually all the conventions concluded from 1968 onwards, that problem has been overcome and so the main issue has been to establish priority of treatment of these various conventions and to decide what legislative action, federal or provincial, would be necessary to implement them. Over the years priority seems to have been given to examining the Conventions on the recognition of divorces and legal separations (1970),[32] the international administration of estates of deceased persons (1973),[33] the service abroad of judicial and extra-judicial documents in civil and commercial matters (1965), and on the taking of evidence abroad in civil or commercial matters (1970). These last two Conventions do not have federal-state clauses but it is thought that, in different ways, this problem could be overcome.[34] Certainly, detailed consideration has been given to the ways in which they could be implemented in the Provinces.[35]

There are undoubted problems for a federal state, such as Canada, in ratifying and implementing international conventions in the field of private law. They have been explained by others far more competent in federal constitutional law than I.[36] Although the mixture of legal systems in the United Kingdom creates some complexities in this field, they have not

[31] See e.g., Proceedings of the Fifty-fifth Annual Meeting of the Conference of Commissioners on Uniformity of Legislation in Canada (1973), 125.

[32] Though this may have to await revision of the Divorce Act 1968, see Proceedings of the Fifty-Fifth Annual Meeting of the Conference of Commissioners on Uniformity of Legislation in Canada (1973), 125. (See now the Divorce Act 1985).

[33] This is being examined by the Ontario Law Reform Commission; see their Thirteenth Annual Report 1979, 12. The Ontario Law Reform Commission has also examined the Hague Convention on the Law Applicable to Products Liability (1972) but has concluded that the approach of the Convention should not be adopted for the reform of the Ontario choice of law rules relating to products liability, see Report on Products Liability (1979), 116–17.

[34] See Proceedings of the Sixtieth Annual Meeting of the Conference of Commissioners on Uniformity of Legislation in Canada (1978), 167, 170.

[35] See Proceedings of the Sixty-First Annual Meeting of the Conference of Commissioners on Uniformity of Legislation in Canada (1979), 232–304.

[36] See Castel, (1967) 45 *Can Bar Rev* 1, 23–31; Proceedings of the Fifty-Second Annual Meeting of the Conference of Commissioners on Uniformity of Legislation in Canada (1970), 157–76, 206–14; Proceedings of the Fifth-Eighth Annual Meeting of the Conference of Commissioners on Uniformity of Legislation in Canada (1975), 120–3; Fischer, (1974) 20 *McGill LJ* 44, 73–6; Glenn, (1977) 55 *Can Bar Rev* 586, 594–5, 604–5.

been very great and have not prevented the United Kingdom from ratifying and implementing a number of Hague Conventions. Assuming that the particular constitutional difficulties in Canada can be overcome, are there lessons that Canada may learn from the British experience of Hague Conventions as a means of reforming the conflict of laws? It is to this question that I want to devote the rest of this essay.

THE UNITED KINGDOM AND THE HAGUE CONFERENCE

The history of United Kingdom participation in the work of the Hague Conference is much longer than that of Canada.[37] The British Government declined an invitation in 1892 from the Dutch Government to join the Conference at its inception; but in 1925, the United Kingdom, though not a member, sent a delegation to the Session of the Hague Conference held that year, but they did not stay for the whole session and did not sign the Final Act. Their stamina had improved by the time of the Sixth Session in 1928 when they not only sent in written observations, but also attended and indeed signed the Final Act. As we have seen, there was then a gap of over twenty years in the activities of the Hague Conference, until it was resuscitated with the Seventh Session in 1951, the year in which the Statute under which it operates was laid down. From that Session onwards, a British delegation has always attended the proceedings. It was not, however, until 15 July 1955 that the United Kingdom formally joined the Hague Conference. Between 1951 and 1980 there have been seven sessions of the Hague Conference and these have produced some twenty-six Conventions of which all but nine are in force. However, the United Kingdom has not acceded to any of the four concluded before it formally joined the Hague Conference and, of the others, has ratified (and implemented) only seven and signed one other. This might be compared with the records of such countries as France which has ratified 15 and signed 2 others, the Netherlands which has ratified 12 and signed 6, and Portugal which has ratified 10 and signed 6. In defence of the United Kingdom's failure to sign, though not to ratify, is the fact that there is a difference in approach between foreign ministries to the question of signature of international conventions. Some countries take the view that it is desirable to sign as soon as possible as a gesture of international goodwill even though the prospects of ultimate ratification may not be great; others only sign when there is a real prospect of ratification and implementation. This latter tends to be the

[37] The earlier history has been well catalogued by van Hoogstraten, (1963) 12 *ICLQ* 148.

British approach[38] and the implementation of the one Hague Convention that the United Kingdom has signed but not ratified (that on the international administration of the estates of deceased persons (1973)) has been under consideration for some considerable time.[39]

This is not the place to examine in detail the merits and demerits of all the post-war Hague Conventions and I intend to concentrate primarily on those which the United Kingdom has ratified. However, that leaves nearly 20 Conventions in which the United Kingdom has shown no interest in their implementation. But before undue criticism is levelled at those in the United Kingdom concerned with the conflict of laws for this lack of interest, it should be pointed out that there are two groups of conventions which have not yet entered into force. The first group is five conventions concluded up to 1965[40] which can only muster six ratifications between them and none of which has been signed or ratified by the United Kingdom. The second group of conventions are those resulting from the work of the Thirteenth Session in 1976,[41] none of which has yet received the necessary number of ratifications to bring it into force.[42] The really successful conventions, which the United Kingdom has not ratified, stem from the earlier period of post-war activity of the Hague Conference, namely those on civil procedure (1954),[43] on the law applicable to maintenance obligations towards children (1956)[44] and on the recognition and enforcement of decisions relating to such obligations (1958).[45]

[38] See *Hansard*, HC Deb, 816: 1555 (1971); HL Deb 360: 40.

[39] See e.g. the Eighth Annual Report of the Law Commission, 1972–3, Law Com. No. 58, para. 64, and the Fourteenth Annual Report of the Law Commission, 1978–9, Law Com. No. 97, para. 2.47.

[40] Convention sur la loi applicable au transfert de la propriété en cas de vente à caractere international d'objets mobiliers corporels (1958); Convention sur la competence du for contractuel en cas de ventre à caractère international d'objets mobiliers corporels (1958); Convention pour régler les conflits entre la loi nationale et la loi du domicile (1955); Convention concernant la reconnaissance de la personalité juridique des sociétés, associations et fondations étrangères (1956); Convention on the choice of court (1965).

[41] Convention on the law applicable to matrimonial property regimes; Convention on celebration and recognition of the validity of marriages; Convention on the law applicable to agency.

[42] The one other convention not in force has been signed by the UK, the Convention on the international administration of the estates of deceased persons (1972). There is also one other Convention and a Protocol thereto (Convention on the recognition and enforcement of judgments in civil and commercial matters (1971), and the supplementary protocol to this Convention (1971)) which is of little consequence because, though in force, only two countries (the Netherlands and Cyprus) have ratified it.

[43] Convention relative à la procedure civile (1954), ratified or acceded to by 20 Members States and by 7 others.

[44] Convention sur la loi applicable aux obligations alimentaires envers les enfants (1956), ratified by 12 Member States.

[45] Convention concernant la reconnaissance et l'exécution des decisions en matière d'obligations alimentaires envers les enfants (1958), ratified or acceded to by 16 Member States.

It will become clear that the United Kingdom's experience of Hague Conventions is mixed. If success is measured in terms of implementation, then some types of convention have been more successful than others. Furthermore the chances of ratification and implementation are greatly enhanced if certain factors are present. So let us turn to consider the impact of Hague Conventions on reform of the conflict of laws in the United Kingdom and to examine what seem to be the characteristics of successful, and unsuccessful, conventions.

IMPETUS OR STERILIZATION?

A strong argument in favour of the work of the Hague Conference in the context of law reform is the impetus that it provides. It may well be that attempts by interested parties have failed to convince either the government or the legislature of the need for reform of some particular conflict of laws rules. If the Hague Conference produces a convention, it may then become that much easier, not only to point out that others have seen the need for change, but also to suggest that a legislative vehicle, or at least its chassis, is available in the form of the convention. An example of such fortuitous timing of a Hague convention can be provided in the field of family law. In 1968, the Eleventh Session of the Hague Conference produced a Convention on the recognition of divorces and legal separations. This was finally concluded in 1970 and early in that year the Law Commission and Scottish Law Commission were asked to advise on the legislation necessary to permit the United Kingdom Government to ratify the Convention which, on 19 May 1970, it announced its intention of doing.[46] By November 1970, the two Commissions had reported[47] with a draft Bill appended to their report; the Recognition of Divorces and Legal Separations Act 1971 received Royal Assent on 27 July 1971 and came into force on 1 January 1972. Very speedy work, motivated you might think by international pressure on the United Kingdom. Not a bit of it. The Divorce Convention requires three ratifications to bring it into force,[48] but, at the time when the Law Commissions were asked to examine the Divorce Convention, no state had ratified it and only the United Kingdom had signed it. It did not come into force until 24 August 1975.[49] Indeed it was said during the debates on the Bill, 'We are leading the world in legislating to give effect

[46] The UK signed the Convention on 1 June 1970 and ratified it on 21 May 1974.

[47] Law Com. No. 34; Scot. Law Com. No. 16 (1970).

[48] Art. 27.

[49] The three ratifications then were Denmark, Sweden and the UK. Since then it has also been ratified by Finland, Norway, Switzerland and Czechoslovakia.

to the intent of the Convention.'[50] The reason for all the interest is to be found in the House of Lords' decision on recognition of foreign divorces in *Indyka* v. *Indyka*.[51] Although it liberalized the jurisdictional bases on which courts would recognize foreign divorce decrees by providing that all that was required was that one spouse should have had a 'real and substantial connection' with the country where the divorce was obtained, the decision brought a great deal of uncertainty in its wake for which it attracted substantial criticism.[52] During its passage through Parliament, the Bill implementing the Divorce Convention was continually referred to as a major measure of law reform. Mention was also made in Parliament of the work of the Hague Conference and in fairly dramatic terms, such as that the problem of divorce recognition made 'international agreement imperative'.[53] However, this was pretty specious reasoning because, although the recognition rules of the Divorce Convention are based on reciprocity, the clear view was expressed in Parliament that the Bill should not be limited to the recognition of divorces obtained in countries which were parties to the Divorce Convention, for, indeed, at that time there were no other parties.[54]

The Divorce Convention coincided with a pressing domestic need for reform of the divorce recognition rules. The Convention, combined with the report and draft legislation of the two Law Commissions, provided the necessary impetus for legislative time to be made available to cure what was generally regarded as a defect in the law.

Another example of an impetus for domestic law reform being provided by a Hague Convention is seen in the field of adoption. The Adoption Act 1968 was passed in the United Kingdom to implement the Hague Convention on jurisdiction, applicable law and recognition of decrees relating to adoption (1965). The 1968 Act was drafted in an appallingly complex manner, so much so that some years ago I expressed the view 'that it is hoped that it may never be brought into force'.[55] Parts of the 1968 Act dealing with jurisdiction were repealed and replaced by simpler provisions[56] before the Convention was eventually ratified and

[50] *Hansard* HC Deb, 821: 165–6. The Solicitor-General said: 'We are blazing the trail for other countries by passing these provisions into our domestic law'; ibid., 168.

[51] [1969] 1 AC 33. Judgment was actually given in May 1967. The decision has been widely applied in Canada, see Castel, *Canadian Conflict of Laws* (1977), ii: 327.

[52] See e.g. North, (1968) 31 *MLR* 257, 283, and see Lipstein, [1967] *CLJ* 182; *Hansard*, HL Deb, 315: 185; *Hansard*, HC Deb, 816: 549.

[53] *Hansard*, HL Deb, 315: 485; and see HC Deb, 816: 1548.

[54] *Hansard*, HL Deb, 315: 492; HC Deb, 816: 1554, 1555.

[55] Cheshire, *Private International Law*, 9th edn. (1974), 467; a Canadian commentator was similarly critical, regarding the probable value of the Convention as 'very small in relation to the technicality and awkwardness which courts would encounter in making adoptions under the Convention'; Blom, (1973) 22 *ICLQ* 109, 153.

[56] Children Act 1975, s. 24. (See now the Adoption Act 1976, ss. 14, 15, 17.)

brought into force in 1978. The Convention itself has had little direct effect on the English rules as to jurisdiction and recognition of foreign adoptions because it only applies as between States parties to it and they number only two (Austria and Switzerland) in addition to the United Kingdom. However, not only did the legislation implementing the Convention rules also provide some amendment to the jurisdictional rules for non-Convention cases, it made far-reaching changes in the English recognition rules. The 1968 Act gave the Secretary of State power to designate foreign adoptions as 'overseas adoptions', whose recognition in England is to all intents and purposes automatic, and such adoptions are to be given the same incidents and effects as if they were English adoptions. This procedure has been applied to adoptions in a large number of Commonwealth countries (including Canada), the USA, South Africa, and all Western European countries.[57] Recognition of Austrian and Swiss adoptions is, in this context, insignificant but the decision to implement the Adoption Convention led to legislation of much greater significance.

Unfortunately, the work of the Hague Conference can also have a completely opposite effect on the reform of the conflict laws. Far from being an impetus, it can prove to be a source of unfortunate and, in the event, totally unproductive delay. It can have a sterilizing effect. This aspect can be illustrated by a later Hague Convention, still in the field of family law, namely the Convention on celebration and recognition of the validity of marriages, one of the fruits of the 1976 Session. To appreciate the impact, or rather lack thereof, of this Convention on law reform, I need to take you back a few years in the work of the English Law Commission. From the earliest days, family law, including its conflict rules, loomed large in the work of the Commission. As we have seen, recognition of foreign divorces and legal separations was the subject of legislation in 1971;[58] the next year saw the courts being given wide jurisdiction over polygamous marriages.[59] In 1973, new jurisdictional rules for all matrimonial causes were laid down[60] and a Working Paper was published on the question of the jurisdiction and scope of declarations as to status.[61] Two major topics in the family law area of conflict of laws remained—recognition of foreign nullity decrees and choice of law in marriage. Work had proceeded on these topics in both Commissions for two or three years and two draft Working Papers were produced for internal discussion. However, in 1973, it became known that the agenda for the 1976 Session of the Hague Conference was to include the topic of

[57] SI 1973, No. 19. [58] Recognition of Divorces and Legal Separations Act 1971.

[59] Matrimonial Proceedings (Polygamous Marriages) Act 1972; see now the Matrimonial Causes Act 1973, s. 47.

[60] Domicile and Matrimonial Proceedings Act 1973.

[61] Working Paper No. 48 (1973).

'the conflict of laws in respect of marriage . . . to include, as the case may be, questions relating to the recognition abroad of decisions in respect of the existence or validity of marriages.' In the light of this, the two Commissions suspended their work in this field, convinced that 'satisfactory reform can only be achieved with international agreement'.[62] It is undoubtedly true that the problem of limping marriages can best be cured by international agreement—provided satisfactory international agreement can be reached.

What then happened in the 1976 Session of the Hague Conference to the two problems on which United Kingdom law reformers had suspended work three years earlier? Despite the submission by the United Kingdom of a whole draft Part of a Convention to cover the topic,[63] recognition of foreign nullity decrees was excluded from the work of the Conference. To deal with this topic was thought to create more problems than could be solved[64]—what some might regard as a counsel of despair. While it is true that nullity recognition raises fewer problems than divorce, there is, in England, a steady trickle of such cases[65] and, indeed, the common law rules to be applied to them are left in some doubt since both the English nullity jurisdictional rules and the divorce recognition rules had been changed.[66]

Was there any greater success in 1976 in providing a comprehensive set of choice of law rules for marriage? A Convention certainly emerged from the deliberations of the 1976 Session, but this Convention on celebration and recognition of the validity of marriage did not meet with immediate acclaim. While four States have signed it,[67] as yet none have ratified. Appraisal of the Convention by commentators has not been over-enthusiastic[68] and indeed somewhat critical.[69] While the Convention may be an effective measure of harmonization, it is far less appropriate as a measure of law reform. If the latter characteristic is lacking, the chances for the implementation of a substantive choice of law convention[70] are not great. A brief examination of the Convention may reveal why it is

[62] Law Commission Eighth Annual Report 1972–3, Law Com. No. 58, para. 49.

[63] It was modelled on the 1970 Divorce Recognition Convention.

[64] See *Actes et Documents de la Treizième session de la Conférence de La Haye de droit international privé*, III: 122–3, 292.

[65] E.g. *Law* v. *Gustin* [1976] Fam 155; *Perrini* v. *Perrini* [1979] Fam 84.

[66] See Dicey and Morris, *The Conflict of Laws*, 10th edn. (1980), 380–4; North, *Private International Law of Matrimonial Causes* (1977), ch. 12; Cheshire and North, *Private International Law*, 10th edn. (1979), 406–16, and see Smith, (1980) 96 *LQR* 380. (See now the Family Law Act 1986, Part II, and Law Com. No. 165 (1987)).

[67] Australia, Egypt, Luxembourg, Portugal, but see above, p. 226.

[68] See Batiffol, (1977) 66 *Rev crit dr int pr* 451, 467–82; Glenn, (1977) 55 *Can Bar Rev* 586, 588–95; Lalive, (1978) 34 *Annuaire Suisse de droit international* 31.

[69] E.g. Reese, (1977) 25 *Am Jo Comp L* 393, 394; (1979) 20 *Virginia J of Int Law* 25, 35–6.

[70] The difference between substantive and procedural conventions is discussed further, below, pp. 245–247.

not an effective law reform measure. The Convention falls into two main parts, Chapter I, which is optional, deals with the rules for the celebration of marriage in a Contracting State. The basic rule for formal requirements is that they are to be governed by the law of the place of celebration. In the case of essential validity, the Convention provides that a marriage must be celebrated in a Contracting State if the prospective spouses satisfy the substantive requirements of the internal law of that state and one of them habitually resides there or is a national thereof; or if the spouses satisfy the substantive requirements of the law applicable under the choice of law rules, whatever they may be, of the State of celebration. Not only does this Chapter provide a substantial inroad into the rule that a state will normally require all the requirements of its marriage law, formal and essential, to be complied with before a marriage can be celebrated there, but it also falls far short of providing a complete code of choice of law rules for marriage in that state.

The same criticism can be made of Chapter II, which is not optional, and which deals with the recognition of the validity of a marriage celebrated in another Contracting State. Its basic rule is that a marriage which is validly entered into under the law of the state of celebration shall be regarded as valid in all other Contracting States. Again this falls far short of a choice of law code for foreign marriages. Both chapters leave a large number of issues still dependent on the unharmonized and unreformed choice of law rules of the individual states. For example, Chapter I preserves, without defining, the choice of law rules of the state of celebration[71] and Chapter II only applies to the recognition of marriages which are valid under the law of the state of celebration. Recognition of marriages invalid under that law, but essentially valid under, say, the law of the domicile, is left to the unamended choice of law rules of the individual states.

It seems to me very doubtful whether such a Convention alone would be regarded as meeting the need for reform of the choice of law rules relating to marriage. If the incomplete rules in the Convention were regarded as meritorious, then of course they could be included as part of a legislative law reform package; thereby achieving the twin aims of desired reform and at least some international harmonization. If the Convention rules are, however, regarded as providing little improvement in the present choice of law rules and certainly not providing a model for more broadly based reform (as I believe to be the case here), then the Convention is in many ways counter-productive.

What then has the Marriage Convention achieved so far as reform of English law is concerned? The answer must be—very little. Work was sus-

[71] Art. 3(2).

pended for about seven years on the two issues of choice of law in marriage and the recognition of foreign nullity decrees. There are no Convention rules on the latter topic and those on the former are not very satisfactory in themselves and certainly do not provide a complete choice of law code for marriage. The Law Commissions later returned to one of these topics[72] (foreign nullity decrees) as the subject of law reform within the United Kingdom. Satisfactory international law reform and harmonization of these sensitive topics has proved elusive. The Hague Conventions early this century on marriage and divorce[73] were not very successful and it may be that these areas of family law impinge so directly on the social and cultural structure of individual states that the compromises necessary for international agreement really satisfy no one.[74] I am not intending to suggest that international uniformity is not a desirable goal, quite the contrary. But it is often difficult to achieve, and unsuccessful attempts mean the postponement of other law reform activities in that field.

INTERNATIONAL AGREEMENT AS A NECESSARY MEDIUM FOR NATIONAL LAW REFORM

Not only may the impetus for national reform come from international activity, as we have seen,[75] it may indeed only be possible to achieve national reform through the medium of international agreement.[76] Two examples may be given where the need for reform of national law seemed only to be realizable through a Hague Convention. The first example, that of the formal validity of wills, led to successful law reform; the second example is the less happy one of attempts to reform the law of domicile.

The Hague Convention on the conflict of laws relating to the form of testamentary dispositions was concluded in 1961 and provides, like divorce, another example of a happily timed Convention. It dealt with an area of law which was in need of reform both in England and in other

[72] See Law Commission, Fourteenth Annual Report 1978–9, Law Com. No. 97 (1980), para. 2.46. (See now the Family Law Act 1986, Part II and Law Com. No. 165 (1987)).

[73] Convention pour régler les conflits de lois en matière de mariage (1902); Convention pour régler les conflits de lois et de jurisdictions en matière de divorce et de separation de corps (1902). For the reasons for their lack of success, see de Winter, [1969] III *Hague Recueil* 347, 376–83; Wolff, *Private International Law*, 2nd edn. (1950), 50, 313; Palsson, *Marriage and Divorce in Comparative Conflict of Laws* (1974), 29–30.

[74] The dangers of compromise are discussed below, pp. 252–254.

[75] Discussed above, pp. 238–240.

[76] It has been said by Graveson, (1968) 16 *Am Jo Comp L* 4, 7, that:

> It may appear that the only way to achieve an internal reform of law is through the international unification of the particular branch of law, so that the local law is reformed and assimilated to an international pattern achieved through some convention, and the political weakness of local or national opinion is fortified by the international opinion which lies behind an acceptable international project.

common law jurisdictions. It provided the impetus for the English Wills Act 1963 and, as we have seen,[77] some Canadian Provinces soon followed suit, as did a number of Australian States.[78]

So far as the United Kingdom was concerned, the need for reform of the conflict of laws relating to wills was clear. Until the 1963 Act the formal validity of a will had depended on Lord Kingsdown's Act of 1861. This Act had improved on the rigid common law position that the formal validity of a will of moveables was governed by the testator's domicile on death by also permitting validation of the wills of British subjects under the law of the country where the will was made, or, if the will was made outside the United Kingdom, under the law of the domicile at the time of making the will. This set of criteria for formal validity had long been criticized,[79] especially as it was confined to the wills of British subjects and drew an unhappy distinction between wills made in the United Kingdom and elsewhere. However, nothing was done. The electoral appeal of the reform of the conflict rules relating to wills was not great! Then, in 1956 at the Eighth Hague Conference the United Kingdom took the initiative in instigating the consideration of the formal validity of wills by the Hague Conference at its Ninth Session in 1960.[80] Furthermore, in 1958, the Lord Chancellor's Private International Law Committee reported[81] that the law was undoubtedly in need of reform and should be changed along lines very similar to those which emerged in the Hague Convention agreed at the 1960 Session, namely that all wills, whether or not of British subjects, whether relating to moveables or immoveables, and whether made in the United Kingdom or elsewhere, should be formally valid if valid under any one of the following laws: that of the place where it was made, of the testator's domicile at the time of making, or of death, or of the testator's nationality at the time the will was made, or at death. Additionally, a will of immoveables would be formally valid under the *lex situs*. All of these grounds were accepted in the Hague Convention, but reference to the testator's habitual residence at the time of making the will or at death was also added.

This Convention achieved the twin objectives of providing much needed reform at home and also widespread international agreement. By 1980 fifteen countries had ratified it; furthermore another seven countries not parties to the Hague Conference had acceded to it; and, as we have seen, it has been relied on for the reform of the law in countries which have not become parties to the Convention. Like divorce, the need for reform existed already; the Hague Conference agreed with the United Kingdom's general approach. International agreement meant that legisla-

[77] See above, pp. 233–234.
[78] Nygh, *Conflict of Laws*, 3rd edn. (1976), 480–1.
[79] E.g. Morris, (1946) 62 *LQR* 170, 173–6.
[80] See Graveson, (1961) 10 *ICLQ* 18, 21–2.
[81] Fourth Report, Cmd 491 (1958).

tive interest, and thus time, was provided. Indeed, the Bill which became the Wills Act 1963 passed through both Houses of Parliament virtually without debate.[82]

The Wills Convention provides a striking example, by its substantial implementation in parts of Canada and Australia, of reform through the medium of a Convention agreed by a body to which neither Canada nor Australia at that time belonged.[83] Reform of the law of domicile provides a less happy illustration of the impact that international agreement may have on national law reform.[84] Criticism of the English rules as to domicile can be found throughout the first half of this century;[85] but no steps were taken to reform the law until a draft Convention was agreed by the Hague Conference in 1951 'pour régler les conflits entre la loi nationale et la loi du domicile'. In December 1952 the Lord Chancellor invited the newly created Private International Law Committee to consider whether amendment of the law of domicile was desirable and whether the United Kingdom should accede to the draft Hague Convention. The Committee answered both questions in the affirmative.[86] Attempts were made to implement the Committee's proposals but the draft Bills provoked powerful opposition; they were abandoned and the matter was referred back to the Private International Law Committee which repeated its support for the original reform proposals but acknowledged that substantial opposition to the proposals had been generated and that whether any further law reform action should be taken was a matter of policy on which the Committee made no recommendation.[87] No further action was taken and ten years' law reform activity petered out, a sad end to the story.[88] However, had it not been for the work of the Hague Conference, the question of reform of domicile might never have been taken up at all: 'Britain's desire to modify the complex English concept of domicile derived from her aspiration to become a party to the convention.'[89]

SUBSTANCE OR PROCEDURE?

Conventions which make procedural improvements in the international administration of justice, improvements which require reciprocal

[82] *Hansard*, HL 251: 513–14, 1265–6, 1458, 1459; HC 679: 886–95.

[83] And see Vitta, [1969] I *Hague Recueil* 113, 184–6.

[84] Ibid., 183–4.

[85] E.g. Foster, (1935) 16 *BYBIL* 84, 84–88; Morris, *Cases on Private International Law*, 1st edn. (1939), 22; Wolff, *Private International Law*, 1st edn. (1945), 122–4; Cheshire, (1945) 61 *LQR* 352, 363–4; Cheshire, *Private International Law*, 4th edn. (1952), 182–4.

[86] First Report of the Private International Law Committee (1954), Cmd. 9068.

[87] Seventh Report of the Private International Law Committee (1963), Cmnd 1955; and see Mann, (1959) 8 *ICLQ* 457; (1963) 12 *ICLQ* 1326.

[88] Van Hoogstraten, (1963) 12 *ICLQ* 148, 159.

[89] Vitta, [1969] I *Hague Recueil* 113, 184. (See now Law Com. No. 168 (1987)).

international agreement, have proved to be some of the most successful Hague Conventions in terms of ratifications and three such conventions have been ratified by the United Kingdom.[90]

They are the Convention abolishing the requirement of legalisation for foreign public documents (1961),[91] the Convention on the service abroad of judicial and extra-judicial documents in civil or commercial matters (1965) [92] and the Convention on the taking of evidence abroad in civil or commercial matters (1970).[93] The first of these, which abolished the need for any diplomatic or consular legalisation of foreign public documents, was a procedural simplification which came into effect in England in 1965 without the need for any legislative measures.[94] The second of these Conventions provides a simplified process for the service of documents, both judicial and extra-judicial, from one Contracting State to another. The United Kingdom brought this Convention into force in 1969 by means of amendment to the Rules of the Supreme Court[95]—no primary legislation was necessary. The third of these essentially procedural Conventions is that on the taking of evidence abroad which came into force in the United Kingdom in 1976 with the passage of the Evidence (Proceedings in Other Jurisdictions) Act 1975. Not only does the 1975 Act implement the Convention, it lays down a complete code for the taking of evidence in any part of the United Kingdom on behalf of courts elsewhere in the United Kingdom or abroad. So its scope is much wider than that of the Convention. Provisions on the taking of evidence abroad existed in a number of bilateral conventions which the United Kingdom had concluded with other states: so there was no great novelty in the 1969 Convention. Even though its provisions were less liberal than those of some of the bilateral conventions, ratification of it could lead to the United Kingdom having reciprocal arrangements on this topic with a wider range of countries.[96]

The passage through Parliament of the Bill which later became the 1975 Act was without incident and almost without debate.[97] It was pointed out that English law as regards the taking of evidence for foreign proceedings

[90] The UK is not a party to one of the most successful of all, the 1954 Convention on civil procedure, which in 1980 had been ratified by 20 Member States and acceded to by another 7 non-Member States.

[91] Ratified by 15 Member States and acceded to by 13 non-Member States.

[92] Ratified by 16 Member States and acceded to by 3 non-Member States.

[93] Ratified by 12 Member States and acceded to by 1 non-Member State.

[94] See *The Supreme Court Practice* 1979, i: 38/10/3. English law has no conception of the legalisation of documents and the Convention has had the effect of reducing the requirement elsewhere—a development welcomed by English lawyers: see Wortley, (1958) 32 *Tul L Rev* 541, 545; and see Amram, (1974) 60 *American Bar Association Journal* 310.

[95] See now RSC O 11, r 5. Other similar bilateral conventions have been implemented under RSC O 11, r 6.

[96] Edwards, (1969) 18 *ICLQ* 619, 646.

[97] *Hansard*, HC 884: 2208–10; HL 360: 34–42.

was in need of reform and modernization and so the Hague Convention provided the impetus for legislation to reform and codify the law on this topic and to widen the scope of international co-operation by implementing the Convention.[98] This provides another example of the relative ease with which international procedural law reform can be implemented and of the significant contribution that the Hague Conference has made to this aspect of private international law. It ought, however, to be mentioned that the 1975 Act has since proved to be more contentious than perhaps Parliament realised at the time. The House of Lords[99] has since refused to permit the procedures of the Act to be used to enable testimony to be taken in England for the purposes of antitrust proceedings in the United States, where there was a danger of the witnesses to be questioned incriminating themselves so far as possible later American proceedings were concerned, and where to allow the evidence to be given would be regarded as prejudicial to the sovereignty of the United Kingdom.[100]

Procedural conventions may owe their success to a number of factors. Reform of the machinery for dealing with cross-border legal issues requires uniform international procedures and harmonization to a much greater extent than does reform of substantive choice of law rules. It may be possible to implement procedural reforms without primary legislation, thereby avoiding the pitfalls of the legislative timetable. Finally, civil servants who have to operate the procedural machinery may subconsciously be more receptive to reforms which ease the burdens of their lives than to those which deal with matters of substance, and it may be that the consent of their political masters to procedural changes is obtained with greater ease.

TOO MANY COOKS?

There is one other Hague Convention of a substantially procedural kind which the United Kingdom has ratified and implemented, namely the Convention on the recognition and enforcement of decisions relating to maintenance obligations (1973).[101] Under this Convention, decisions given in one Contracting State in respect of a wide range of maintenance obligations must be recognized and enforced in the other Contracting States provided certain jurisdictional criteria are satisfied, the most significant being the habitual residence or nationality of either the maintenance

[98] *Hansard*, HC 884: 2210; and see HL 360: 40.

[99] *Re Westinghouse Electric Corporation Uranium Contract* [1978] AC 547.

[100] Ibid., 615–17, 630–2, 639–40, 650–1.

[101] It was ratified by the UK on 1 March 1980 and was implemented by the Reciprocal Enforcement of Maintenance Orders (Hague Convention Countries) Order 1979; SI 1979 No 1317.

debtor or creditor, or the defendant's submission to the jurisdiction.[102] Subject to certain grounds of non-recognition, such as that the decision was obtained by fraud or is manifestly contrary to the public policy of the State where enforcement is sought,[103] the foreign order is in principle to be enforced as if it were an order of the state addressed.

This Convention provides not only a further example of the greater ease with which procedural reforms may be implemented but also a good illustration of a problem which is ever increasing in the area of international law reform generally, that of 'too many cooks'. There may be widespread acceptance that 'something must be done' about a particular problem, with the result that there is pressure to include the problem on the agenda of a number of law reform bodies, and perhaps on the agenda for bilateral intergovernment discussions. The result is a series of schemes for improvement, all of which may have considerable merit but differing scope. There may then be pressures of different kinds for the acceptance of some or all of these schemes. Those who have conducted successful bilateral reciprocal negotiations with another state wish to see the concluded agreement implemented; active participation by one's national delegation in more broadly based international discussions which lead to an acceptable convention also generates a force for implementation. If all the schemes are based on reciprocity and each scheme covers a relatively small number of countries, indeed perhaps only two countries, improvement of the law is achieved by piecemeal implementation. There is a price for such improvement in terms of the coherent structure of the law and in terms of the complexity which practising lawyers must master, often at the financial expense of their clients.

This problem may be illustrated by the state of English law on recognition of foreign maintenance orders after the bringing into force of the Hague Maintenance Obligations Convention of 1973. Maintenance orders made in Scotland and Northern Ireland can be registered and enforced in England under the Maintenance Orders Act 1950;[104] orders made in a large number of Commonwealth countries may be registered and enforced in England under the Maintenance Orders (Facilities for Enforcement) Act 1920; recognition of orders made in other Commonwealth and a range of non-Commonwealth countries falls under Part I of the Maintenance Orders (Reciprocal Enforcement) Act 1972. Part II of that Act implements the United Nations Convention on the Recovery Abroad of Maintenance (1956) and provides a different set of procedures for enforcement of the orders of countries which are parties to that Convention. Some countries fall within more than one regime,[105] but

[102] Art 7. [103] Art 5. [104] S. 16.

[105] E.g. Barbados, France, Norway, Sweden and Switzerland fall under both Parts I and II of the 1972 Act.

it is assumed that the most efficacious one will be used. That is not an end to this complexity because there is provision under section 40 of the 1972 Act for special reciprocal arrangements to be made with individual countries and for these arrangements to be brought into force by statutory instrument. This provision now covers recognition of maintenance orders from the Republic of Ireland, a majority of states of the United States and the states which are parties to the 1973 Hague Convention. The implementation of that Convention was made relatively easy by the existence of the appropriate machinery for delegated legislation; though section 40 provides a very wide reaching power to rewrite a large proportion of the 1972 Act. The statutory instrument implementing the Hague Convention amounts to a statement that so far as recognition of the orders from Contracting States are concerned, the first twenty-four sections of the 1972 Act shall be either amended or disapplied and, indeed, the delegated legislation contains a completely redrafted Part I of the 1972 Act.

The result is that a solicitor wishing to advise on the recognition of a foreign maintenance order has to decide whether it falls within the regimes provided by two multilateral international conventions, a whole series of bilateral reciprocal agreements, inter-UK legislation or the common law.[106] It cannot be said that the addition of the six countries parties to the 1973 Hague Convention creates this complexity, but recognition of maintenance orders does provide a striking example of the results of piecemeal reform stemming from different international agreements. A variety of schemes may in some cases be inevitable because of the differing reciprocal needs of different countries; but from the point of view of simplicity and certainty, the fewer the separate schemes the better.

A further example of the complexity that may stem from a variety of concurrent initiatives all dealing with the same serious problem is provided by an item on the agenda for the 1980 Session of the Hague Conference—child kidnapping and the recognition of foreign custody orders. Seen from a United Kingdom point of view, this topic is the subject of at least four separate initiatives. The Law Commission and Scottish Law Commission published a working paper in 1976[107] dealing with both jurisdiction over and recognition of custody orders within the United Kingdom and agreement has been reached on the major policy issues for the preparation of a final report. The Council of Europe concluded a Convention on the recognition and enforcement of decisions

[106] For a fuller account of the present position, see Law Com. Working Paper No. 77 (1980); Financial Relief after Foreign Divorce, Appendix. (Added complexity now stems from recognition of maintenance orders under the Civil Jurisdiction and Judgments Acts 1982 and 1991).

[107] Law Com. Working Paper No. 68: Scottish Law Commission Memorandum No. 23 (1976).

concerning custody and on restoration of custody of children which was signed by the United Kingdom in May 1980. A draft convention on the civil aspects of international child abduction has been prepared by a Special Commission of the Hague Conference which is to be submitted to the main session of the conference in October 1980 and active interest has been expressed by the Commonwealth Secretariat[108] and a number of member states of the Commonwealth, including Canada, in the preparation of a scheme to deal at least with child kidnapping. There has even been some initiative within the EEC to provide at least special administrative machinery for dealing with the recognition and enforcement of custody orders of the courts of the Member States of the EEC. Everyone agrees that there is a pressing social problem to be resolved—as international travel becomes relatively cheaper the problem gets greater. Agreement on the solutions is, however, much more difficult.

There are significant differences between the two major initiatives: the Council of Europe Convention and the draft Hague Convention. The former deals primarily with the recognition and enforcement of all child custody orders and is subject to no mandatory time limit. The Hague Convention deals only with cases of improper removal, i.e. child kidnapping, and proceedings must be initiated within six months of the improper removal. To that extent its scope is narrower than that of the Council of Europe Convention; but in one important respect its scope is broader, for it applies to all cases of improper removal, whether or not there has been a prior court order. A further difference between the two conventions is that, under the draft Hague Convention, the power of the court to refuse to return a child who has been improperly removed is exercisable on different and more restricted grounds than those applicable under the Council of Europe Convention.

While concurrent initiatives create complexity, it is not a complete answer to say that only one body should deal with the topic or that a state which is a member of more than one of these international bodies should wait and see what they all produce and then choose one of them. There are two reasons for treating such solutions with caution. The first is that of the membership of the bodies. The Hague Conference has twenty-nine members; the Council of Europe a slightly small number. Some countries are members of both bodies; others are not. Maximum international agreement can only be achieved by implementing both Conventions, provided they are not incompatible. Furthermore, there are often strong political pressures against adopting a wait and see attitude. Foreign ministries may well take a different view of the merits of a convention from that taken by lawyers. If a convention does no harm and

[108] See Eekelaar, *The International Abduction of Children by a Parent or Guardian*, (1980), a paper prepared for the Commonwealth Secretariat.

some good, why wait for the possibility of a better one if international goodwill may be realized by signing and indeed ratifying the present one? There is also a more direct political pressure in a subject as emotive as custody disputes. Members of Parliament are often able to produce instances where one of their constituents is at the moment unable to recover a child but would have been able to do so if a particular convention was in force. It is not an unreasonable reaction of a government to act quickly to stop the problem recurring—but the result may once again be piecemeal and complicated international law reform.

The agenda for the 1980 Session of the Hague Conference provides another example of a difficulty created by several bodies operating in the same field. This time the clash is between the work of the Hague Conference and that of the EEC in the field of contractual choice of law rules. After about ten years of negotiations the nine Member States of the EEC have agreed on a Convention on the law applicable to contractual obligations which was concluded in Rome on 19 June 1980. It provides a new set of choice law rules in contract for all cases, whether or not connected with the EEC, coming before the courts of the Member States. This EEC initiative in the reform and harmonization of the conflict of laws has been attacked[109] as tending to supplant the work of the Hague Conference with its more broadly based membership and indeed the fact that work was progressing in the EEC context seems to have been a major factor contributing to the decision of the Hague Conference in 1976 not to take up the suggestion of working on a contract choice of law convention.[110] Criticism of this clash of interests has been forceful.

> The Common Market has apparently chosen to pre-empt for itself codification of the rules of conflict of laws, thus blocking the Hague Conference from doing the job for which it was created. This is a heavy responsibility. Having the Conference operate at the Market's pleasure, to pick up crumbs here and there is not likely to appeal to the other member States.[111]

The problem is not, however, limited to future work of the Conference but extends to the existing Conventions. The EEC contract convention lays down choice of law rules applicable to all international contracts: but is also preserves other international conventions to which Member States are parties.[112] The most significant of these is the 1955 Hague Convention on the law applicable to international sale of goods. Sale of goods is probably the most important international contract and four Member States of the EEC[113] are parties to the 1955 Convention. As this

[109] Nadelmann, (1977) 1 *Law and Contemporary Problems* 2: 54, 64–71. (For analysis of the Convention, see above, pp. 23–50.)

[110] Ibid., 65–9. [111] Ibid., 71. [112] Art. 21.

[113] Belgium, Denmark, France and Italy.

Convention prevails over the EEC Convention, the harmonization objective of the latter is defeated if about half the Member States of the EEC apply the choice of law rules of the 1955 Convention to the most important international contract. The result has been a desire on the part of those EEC States not parties to the 1955 Hague Convention that the others should denounce it. Indeed, even if all the Member States of the EEC became parties to the Hague Convention, a significant element of harmonization would be lacking because different choice of law rules would apply to sale of goods contracts and to other contracts; this would lead to great complexity, especially with regard to those transactions which combine sale of goods with other obligations. There is, however, a desire at the Hague Conference to attract wider acceptance of internationally agreed choice of law rules for sale of goods which is manifested by the inclusion on the agenda for the 1980 Session of a draft convention, adopted in 1979 by a Special Commission, on the law applicable to certain consumer sales.

This competition between law reform proposals in the field of obligations[114] is likely, in my opinion, to have the result that the United Kingdom will not now sign the 1955 Hague Sales Convention,[115] or whatever revision of it or whatever consumer sales convention emerge from the 1980 Session of the Hague Conference. Similar conflict is to be seen between the Hague Conference and the EEC in the field of tort law. The United Kingdom has signed neither the Hague Traffic Accidents Convention of 1971 nor the Products Liability Convention of 1973 and is, in my view, most unlikely to do so at least while negotiations on a choice of law convention on non-contractual obligations may proceed in the EEC.

THE DANGERS OF COMPROMISE

Reform of the law on a national basis has a major advantage over reform through an international agency—the need for compromise is much reduced. It is not, however, entirely eliminated. Legislative acceptability may require some compromises to be made. Where the state includes more than one legal system, as in both the United Kingdom and Canada, there may be conflicting views necessitating skilled reconciliation. However, international bodies with a membership representing fundamen-

[114] There is the possibility of even wider conflict as the Eleventh Session of UNCITRAL, meeting in 1978, decided to include unification of conflict rules for international sales on its programme of future work, though with no particular priority until it was seen whether the Hague Conference revised the 1955 Convention.

[115] For criticism of the Convention, see Jacobson, (1954) 3 *ICLQ* 659.

tally different legal and political systems can usually only reach agreement by means of substantial compromise—certainly if there is to be any real hope of widespread acceptance of the agreement or convention which emerges. Sometimes this process of compromise is wholly beneficial in that it provides international respectability for the abandonment of criticized national rules which might not otherwise be achieved. A striking illustration of this is the ever increasing use by the Hague Conference of habitual residence as a connecting factor to bridge the gap between the common law world's reliance on domicile and the civil law system's dependence on nationality. Indeed this has led in the United Kingdom to much wider acceptance of habitual residence as a connecting factor, even outside the Hague Conventions in which it originated. Domicile has not been abandoned but has become an alternative connecting factor to habitual residence in, for example, the rules as to the jurisdiction of the courts over matrimonial causes.[116]

Compromise can, on the other hand, lead to unsatisfactory solutions which satisfy no one, a 'lowest common denominator' approach to law reform. This can take two forms. The first is the use of reservations. Agreement may only be reached in negotiations by making some provision optional, by giving a state the power to declare that it will not apply the rule. A striking example of this is Part I of the 1976 Hague Marriage Convention whose rules as to the celebration of marriages in the forum state are optional.[117] A random glance at the last eight Hague Conventions shows that all but two contain powers of reservation. The wider the powers and their exercise, the less international uniformity that is achieved, though such uniformity is itself the mainspring of reform on the international, rather than the national, plane.

There is a real danger that governments, legislators and law reformers may say: 'If that is the best international uniformity you can get, we would rather have domestic law reform without the uniformity'. One must remember, before criticizing that reaction too severely, that implementation of a Hague Convention is no guarantee of widespread uniformity. Statistically, the twenty-six Conventions concluded in the post-war period up to 1980 average about six ratifications per Convention. Indeed some international uniformity may be achieved even via unilateral reform in that other similar-minded jurisdictions in, for example, the common law world might choose to adopt some or all of the changes made in another jurisdiction. The greater the co-operation between different law reform agencies, the more likely this is to happen.

The other form in which compromise may be seen is in the formulation of very complex rules. The particular problem which worries one state or

[116] Domicile and Matrimonial Proceedings Act 1973.

[117] See Art. 16.

group of states and which cannot be accommodated in the general rule is made the subject of an exception, and then the exceptions grow. Similarly, compromise between certainty and the desire to have a different outcome depending on the various law/fact patterns involved leads to complexity. Both of these approaches are illustrated by the two Hague Conventions in the field of tort law. The Traffic Accidents Convention (1971) has, in Article 3, a general choice of law rule that the internal law of the State where the accident occurred is to be applied. Ensuing articles provide a long list of exceptions to this rule depending on the origins of the vehicle and of the parties.[118] The Products Liability Convention (1973) does not even start with a simple basic rule but applies the law of the State of the place of injury only if that State is also either the plaintiff's habitual residence, the defendant's principal place of business or the place where the plaintiff acquired the product.[119] Again, further exceptions then follow. These rules amount to an attempt to identify the most likely factual circumstances to arise and the law that would be applicable under a flexible general proper law approach and then to cast those solutions in the form of specific rules. A structure of complex rules is inevitable. They are likely to look even more complex when transposed into the statutory form necessary in the United Kingdom for their implementation and I suspect that this is one, at least, of the reasons why the United Kingdom has neither signed nor ratified either of these Conventions. As Cavers has suggested, 'the proper law of the tort is an artifact that courts are better qualified to fashion than conventions'.[120]

CONCLUSIONS

In the Preface to the first edition of his *Private International Law*, Geoffrey Cheshire gave as one of the fascinations of the subject that 'it has been only lightly touched by the paralysing hand of the Parliamentary draftsman'. What was true in 1935 is, as we have seen, much less true today, paradoxically because we live in an age of institutional law reform. The fact that the product of the work of such bodies, whether national or international, is ultimately legislation means that the new rules of law are cast in the statutory concrete of Acts of Parliament. However, rules designed to serve the interests and legal systems of a wide variety of states are most likely to be successful when they avoid the

[118] For Canadian criticism of the complexity of this Convention, see Castel and Crepeau, (1971) 18 *Am Jo Comp L* 17, 23–5. Other defects are indicated by Newman, (1969) 18 *ICLQ* 643.

[119] Art., 4.

[120] Cavers, (1977) 26 *ICLQ* 703, 728. For forceful criticism of the complexity of the Products Liability Convention, see Tebbens, *International Product Liability* (1979), 333–60.

complexity of much modern legislation: when they lay down general rules, not overcluttered with detailed exceptions. Changing patterns in society and in commerce suggest that flexibility is a virtue—especially as amendment of internationally agreed conventions can only be achieved by the slow process of further international negotiation.

The United Kingdom's experience of the Hague Conventions has been that complicated conventions stand less chance of implementation than simple ones; that conventions designed to simplify the international administration of justice have proved more acceptable than those concerned with substantive conflict of laws rules; that conventions which fulfil an existing need for reform are more likely to be implemented than those whose main objective is seen to be change in the interests of international harmonization; and, finally, that the increase in the number of bodies concerned with law reform in the international context has led inevitably to a lessening of the impact of the work of the Hague Conference and to increased complexity in the law when the rules of Hague Conventions have to be dovetailed in with the reforms proposed by other bodies.

One problem that the United Kingdom does not face is that posed by a federal constitutional system. Many areas of the conflict of laws in Canada fall within provincial rather than federal legislative jurisdiction. On a number of occasions Canadian authors[121] have suggested that the most practicable means of giving effect in Canada to Hague Conventions is by model laws rather than by formal ratification and implementation.[122] The disadvantage with such an approach is that, while some Hague Conventions, though cast in the form of treaties, are in essence sets of uniform rules, others apply in terms only to relations with the other Contracting States. This disadvantage is not always insuperable if a country is prepared to abandon the element of reciprocity involved. For example the Divorce Recognition Convention of 1970 only applies to the recognition in one Contracting State of divorces and legal separations obtained in another Contracting State. Nevertheless, the United Kingdom legislation implementing that Convention[123] applies to all foreign divorces

[121] E.g. Kos-Rabcewicz-Zubkowski, (1966) 26 *R du B* 229; Castel, (1967) 45 *Can Bar Rev* 1, 10–19; Proceedings of the Fifty-Second Annual Meeting of the Conference of Commissioners on Uniformity of Legislation in Canada (1970), 157–214; Lederman, in *Canadian Perspectives on International Law and Organisation*, ed. MacDonald, Morris, Johnston (1974), 137, 147–50.

[122] For discussion of the attempts to persuade the Hague Conference to produce model laws rather than international treaties, and of the merits of the two approaches, see Nadelmann and Reese, (1958) 7 *Am Jo Comp L* 239; Nadelmann, in *International Trade Arbitration*, ed. Domke (1958), 167; Amram, (1960) 54 *Proceedings of Am Soc of Int Law* 62; Droz, [1961] *Rev int de droit comparé* 507; Nadelmann, (1968) 16 *Am Jo Comp L* 28.

[123] Recognition of Divorces and Legal Separations Act 1971. (See now the Family Law Act 1986, Part II).

and legal separations no matter where obtained and including grounds of recognition[124] wider than those in the Convention.[125] Where, however, reciprocal machinery is required model laws provide no answer.[126]

Horace Read was more enthusiastic about model laws, as might befit a long-serving member of the Conference of Commissioners on Uniformity of Legislation in Canada, and it is perhaps appropriate to conclude this essay with his view, expressed in 1969, on the way in which Canada could best gain the advantages of members of the Hague Conference. He said:

> 'In this country the advantages of membership in the Hague Conference could be better gained, not by formal adherence to the conventions but by active participation in its work and use of its conventions as models for uniform acts. In this way, perhaps with an occasional slight departure from uniformity, greater flexibility and adaptability to conditions peculiar to this country could be ensured'.[127]

[124] Recognition of Divorces and Legal Separations Act 1971, s. 6.

[125] The UK took advantage of Art. 17 of the Convention which permits a Contracting State to have rules more favourable to recognition than those in the Convention.

[126] E.g. under the Convention concerning the International Administration of the Estates of Deceased Persons (1973).

[127] *The Ansul* (Dalhousie University Law School) January 1969.

Index